THE BEST OF LAKEWOOD PUBLICATIONS'
STRATEGIES & TECHNIQUES FOR MANAGERS & TRAINERS

BASIC TRAINING: THE LANGUAGE OF CORPORATE EDUCATION

An abridged encyclopedia from
TRAINING *Magazine*

Third Edition

Compiled By DAVE ZIELINSKI
from articles that have been published in

TRAINING

The Magazine Covering the Human Side of Business

◆ Lakewood Publications

The Complete New Training Library:

Book 1 *Basic Training: The Language of Corporate Education*
Book 2 *Adult Learning in Your Classroom*
Book 3 *The Best of Creative Training Techniques*
Book 4 *Designing Training for Results*
Book 5 *The Training Mix: Choosing and Using Media and Methods*
Book 6 *Managing Training in the Organization, Book I*
Book 7 *Managing Training in the Organization, Book II*
Book 8 *Delivering Training: Mastery in the Classroom*
Book 9 *Evaluating Training's Impact*
Book 10 *Using Technology-Delivered Learning*
Book 11 *The Effective Performance Consultant*
Book 12 *Making Training Pay Off On the Job*

Bulk reprints of individual articles may be quoted and purchased through:

Reprint Services
315 Fifth Avenue N.W.
St. Paul, MN 55112
(800) 707-7798 or (612) 633-0578

LAKEWOOD BOOKS
50 South Ninth Street
Minneapolis, MN 55402
(800) 707-7769 or (612) 333-0471
Fax: (612) 333-6526
Web Page Address: http://www.lakewoodpub.com

Editorial Director: Linda Klemstein
Editor: Dave Zielinski
Production Editor: Susan Abbott
Production Manager: Pat Grawert
Cover Design: Julie Tilka
Proofreader: Patty Pryor-Nolan

Lakewood Publications, Inc. is a subsidiary of VNU/USA. Lakewood Publications, Inc. publishes *TRAINING Magazine, Presentations* magazine, *Training Directors' Forum Newsletter, Creative Training Techniques Newsletter, The Lakewood Report On Technology for Learning Newsletter, Potentials In Marketing* magazine, and other business periodicals, books, research, and conferences.

ISBN 0-943210-51-8

10 9 8 7 6 5 4 3 2 1

THE NEW TRAINING LIBRARY

Contemporary training and performance improvement ideas, strategies
and techniques for managers and HRD professionals

Welcome to *The New Training Library*. Before you read on, there are a few things you should know about this series of books and how it came into existence.

Each book in *The New Training Library* contains articles originally published in *TRAINING Magazine*, *The Training Directors' Forum Newsletter*, *Creative Training Techniques Newsletter*, or *The Lakewood Report On Technology for Learning Newsletter*, all Lakewood publications that explore contemporary human resources development issues, trends and ideas from different angles and perspectives. While there is some overlap among the books in the series, each of them stands on its own.

Our editors selected articles to illuminate a particular theme or subject area — from the dynamics of adult occupational learning, to designing cost-effective training programs, to powerful performance consulting, to measuring training's ROI. And more.

The pervasive style of the selected articles is that of magazine and newsletter journalism, opinion and commentary. In this accessible, nonacademic style, the authors address the real and immediate challenges you face as practicing HRD professionals or as managers and motivators of people.

The edited articles are contained between the covers of the books in *The New Training Library*. Not, to repeat, as the definitive texts or final words on any one subject area, but as books that serve a different and (depending who you are) maybe even more useful purpose.

As the training profession evolves, it demands a solid understanding of the original ideas, theories and systems that shape its development. Today's training professionals also must be prepared to absorb, assimilate and put into perspective an astonishing amount of new information. Like doctors, lawyers, bankers or other professionals, HRD professionals can never stop learning. Not if they want to be effective. Certainly not if they want to get ahead.

The publications that form the core of *The New Training Library* have become among the most widely read and influential in the field because their editors have never forgotten that fundamental need. In addition to featuring the best writers, theorists and practitioners in HRD, each publication also meets the HRD professional's need to understand the newest techniques, strategies and approaches to tough workplace challenges within the context of the established body of HRD knowledge.

Thus, each publication I've discussed here is carefully balanced to appeal to relative novices in HRD as well as to seasoned professionals. And so are the books in *The New Training Library*, which represents a comprehensive and systematic collection of current ideas and practical responses to meeting workplace challenges (in many cases, articulated by those who first formulated them) within the context of HRD's most enduring, time-tested fundamentals. In other words, these books manage to be both timeless and relevant to the challenges you now face in the rapidly evolving American workplace.

Plus, the books in *The New Training Library* are designed so you can find useful information fast. And with that information, you probably can meet a challenge, solve a problem or defuse a crisis right away. It's a fact that HRD changes constantly, especially today. But I think you'll find, due to the care with which the contents of these books were selected and to the editorial strengths of the publications in which this material first appeared, *The New Training Library* series will be as useful many years from now as it is today.

Philip Jones
Editorial Director
Lakewood Publications

TABLE OF CONTENTS

ACCELERATED LEARNING
Madness With a Method 1
By Ron Zemke
• In Search of the Theory
• Notes From Accelerated-Learning Converts

ACTION LEARNING
Taming Real Problems in Real Time 7
By Paul Froiland
• Action Learning in Action

ADULT LEARNING THEORY
What Do We Know for Sure? 13
By Ron Zemke and Susan Zemke
• Self-Directed Learning: Adults Who Do It Their Way
• A Hierarchy of Value

ASSESSMENT CENTERS
A Method with Proven Mettle 19
By Chris Lee

BEHAVIOR MODELING
The 'Monkey See, Monkey Do' Principle 21
By Ron Zemke

BEHAVIORAL OBJECTIVES
Writing Behavioral Objectives 25
By Ron Zemke

The Whens, Whys and Hows of Behavioral Objectives .27
By James M. Lewis

BENCHMARKING
The Limits of Benchmarking 31
By Marc Hequet

BRAINSTORMING
Guidelines for Generating Ideas 35
By Will Lorey

CASE METHOD TRAINING
Making Case Studies Come Alive 37
By Phillip H. Owenby

CD-ROM
The Rise of CD-ROM 41
By Mark Fritz

CERTIFICATION
Certifiable! Certification Fever Hits the Computer Industry 45
By Bob Filipczak
• The Fever Spreads

Certification for Trainers: Thumbs Up 49
By Chris Lee

COMPETENCIES
Making Competencies Pay Off 53
By Timm J. Esque and Thomas F. Gilbert
• Competencies vs. Accomplishments / Thomas Gilbert

Competency-Based Training vs.
Criterion-Referenced Instruction: What's The Difference? 57
By Ron Zemke

COMPUTER-BASED TRAINING (CBT)
Engaged: The Nature of Computer Interactivity 61
By Bob Filipczak
• More Interactivity: The Short Course
• With a Lot of Help from My Friends
• This Is Just a Rehearsal

CORPORATE CULTURE
Raiders of the Corporate Culture 67
By Chris Lee
• Case In Point / Chris Lee

CREATIVITY TRAINING
Creativity Training Gets Creative 73
By Marc Hequet

CUSTOMIZED TRAINING
How to Customize Off-The-Shelf Training 77
By Bob Filipczak
• Massaging the Media

DISTANCE LEARNING
Putting the Learning into Distance Learning 81
By Bob Filipczak
• Distributed Resources

ELECTRONIC PERFORMANCE SUPPORT SYSTEMS
Should Every Worker Have a Line in the Information Stream? 85
By Marc Hequet

EMPOWERMENT
If Empowerment is So Good, Why Does It Hurt? 89
By Lawrence Holpp
• The Premature Team / Lawrence Holpp

EVALUATION
Prove It! Does Your Training Make a Difference? 93
By Beverly Geber
• The 4 Levels of Evaluation
• How Arthur Andersen Calculated ROI
• Rx for Good Performance

ROI of Soft-Skills Training 99
By Judith Pine and Judith C. Tingley

EXPERIENTIAL TRAINING
Making Outdoor Experiential Training Work 103
By Glenn Martin Tarullo

FEEDBACK
How to Get the Most Out of 360-Degree Feedback 107
By Gary Yukl and Richard Lepsinger

FRONT-END ANALYSIS
An Interview with Joe Harless 111

HAWTHORNE EFFECT
The Hawthorne Effect: Orwell or Buscaglia? 115
By Beverly Geber

INSTRUCTIONAL SYSTEMS DESIGN (ISD) METHOD
ISD: Technology for Everyone 117
By Tom W. Goad

INTRANETS
Training on Intranets? The Hope and the Hype 119
By Bob Filipczak
• 'Chunking CBT' for Intranet Delivery
• Intranets As Performance Support Tools
• More Resources

ISO 9000
What You Should Know About ISO 9000 125
By Suzan L. Jackson

JOB AIDS
Performance Aids: How to Make the Most of Them 129
By Joel Rakow

JOHARI WINDOW
Improve Communications With the Johari Window 131
By Will Lorey

LEARNING STYLES
Different Strokes: Learning Styles in the Classroom **133**
By Bob Filipczak
- How to Read This Article
- Learning Styles Escape Classroom! City in Panic! Details at 11

MBTI
Second Thoughts About the Myers-Briggs Type Indicator **137**
By Ron Zemke

MENTORING
The Democratic Version of Mentoring **141**
By Erik Gunn
- Mentoring Do's and Don'ts / Erik Gunn

MIND MAPPING
Brainstorming on Paper **145**
By Chris Lee

MULTIMEDIA-BASED TRAINING
On the Trail of Better Multimedia **147**
By Bob Filipczak
- Where to Find Authoring Products

NEEDS ANALYSIS
Concept in Search of Content **151**
By Ron Zemke

NEUROLINGUISTIC PROGRAMMING
A Second Look at NLP **153**
By Marilyn Darling
- A Mini Glossary / Marilyn Darling

ORGANIZATION DEVELOPMENT
Training and OD: Separated at Birth? **157**
By Allison Rossett

OUTSOURCING
Can You Outsource Your Brain? **161**
By Marc Hequet

PARETO PRINCIPLE
Why Things Aren't Fair **165**
By Ron Zemke

PARTICIPATORY LEARNING
Getting Them to Open Up **167**
By Dugan Laird and Forrest Belcher

PEER TRAINING
Frick Teaches Frack **171**
By Bob Filipczak

PERFORMANCE TECHNOLOGY
Blueprint For the Learning Organization? 175
By Jack Gordon

PRODUCTIVITY
What Exactly Are We Talking About? 181
By Chris Lee

PYGMALION EFFECT
Self-Fulfilling Prophecy: Better Management by Magic 183
By Len Sandler

ROLE-PLAYS
How to Turn Bystanders into Role-Players 187
By Dugan Laird and Ruth Sizemore House

SELF-DIRECTED WORKTEAMS
5 Ways to Sink Self-Managed Teams 189
By Lawrence Holpp

SIMULATIONS
10 Secrets of Successful Simulations 193
By R. Garry Shirts

SMALL-BITE TRAINING
No Time to Train 197
By Chris Lee and Ron Zemke

SOCRATIC METHOD
Socratic is More Emphatic 203
By Paul J. Micali

SOFT-SKILLS TRAINING
The Myth of Soft-Skills Training 205
By James C. Georges
• It's All About Buy-In

SYSTEMS APPROACH
The Systems View of Human Performance 209
By Geary A. Rummler and Alan P. Brache

THEORY X / THEORY Y
Theory X or Theory Y? 215
By Beverly Geber

TRANSFER OF TRAINING
How to Make Training 'Stick' 217
By Jack Gordon

VALIDITY
Validity and Reliability 219
By Dale Feuer

VIDEOCONFERENCING
   A Trainer's Guide to Videoconferencing 221
   By Michael Emery and Margaret Schubert
   • Basics
   • Tips For the Trainer . . .
   • Using Visual Aids

WOO-WOO
   The Woo-Woo Factor 227
   By Jack Gordon

ACCELERATED LEARNING

Madness with a Method

BY RON ZEMKE

The 1970s were a boom time for new — and sometimes wacky-sounding — training ideas. Some have stood the test of time and become downright respectable: training by computer, the systems approach, the videocassette, andragogy, learner-centered instruction and distance learning come quickly to mind. Others, like transactional analysis, 16 mm film and behavior modification, have gone the way of long sideburns, sitar music, and purple dress shirts.

One of the more curious survivors of that era is an approach commonly referred to as accelerated learning. Though accelerated learning, as it is practiced today, embraces a veritable delicatessen of nontraditional learning designs and techniques, its '70s roots lie in an unorthodox approach to learning a foreign language. The technique, developed by Bulgarian psychiatrist Georgi Lozanov, was originally called suggestopedia or suggestology. The results of Lozanov's system were impressive: It enhanced the activity in the brain's right hemisphere, thereby dramatically increasing the amount of material that could be covered in a given time; boosted learning efficiency; and increased information retention significantly over time.

According to the mythos of accelerated learning, it all started with Lozanov's sleep-learning experiments. He found that students who had material for the next day's foreign-language lesson played many times over a loudspeaker system while they slept performed much better than students without this sleep-learning experience. When some of the students' loudspeakers were accidentally turned off, however, they still performed as well as students who actually had the sleep-learning experience. That is, students who had no sleep-learning experience but thought they had, performed as if they had had the experience. This and other experiments led Lozanov to develop his suggestopedic method, first for foreign-language skills and then for subjects such as mathematics and the sciences.

The classic Lozanov method in a nutshell: Baroque music plays as the students enter the room and sit in comfortable Barcaloungerlike chairs. In the first session the instructor seeks to lower trainee learning barriers by explaining how things will work and reassuring them that the tasks will be easy, relaxing and enjoyable (in other words, not like school). Let's say Bulgarian students are learning to speak English. Everybody gets a printed text of the lesson in the form of an English dialogue with Bulgarian translation. The teacher reads the English dialogue while everybody follows along in the text. Then a student reads one part of the lesson and the teacher another. Different students continue to read different parts of the lesson. The idea here is repetition without boredom.

Then comes the "active concert" part of the process. The music is still baroque, but livelier. With students breathing deeply (originally, they counted their breaths) and following along in the text, the teacher reads through the English dialogue three times in different tones — normal, soft, loud. Once a week or so, the active concert is followed by a passive concert. Here, the students lean back in their chairs, eyes closed. The teacher reads aloud through a week's worth of lessons, but the students are told to pay no attention — just to listen to the music.

Lozanov stressed that the passive concert did not involve hypnosis. The students were not in a trance and remained aware of their surroundings. The instruction was not subliminal, but superliminal: You know it's there, but you're not paying conscious attention to it.

New Permutations

Accelerated learning, done the original Lozanov way, scarcely exists today, save in a few isolated pockets of practice mostly associated with language learning. But a modified version of the method can be sighted in school classrooms and training facilities in the United States, Canada, Australia and the United Kingdom. Accelerated learning has become much more of a multimedia, multimethod hodgepodge of instructional games, metaphorical activities, highly physical learner participation and background music.

David Meier, director of the Center for Accelerated Learning in Lake Geneva, WI, described today's practice in a recent article in the center's newsletter. It has evolved into "a variety of wholistic learning techniques that can be incorporated into new or existing development programs," Meier writes. "Accelerated-learning methods seek to involve participants in the learning process and overcome negative views toward learning itself or toward their own ability to learn."

Meier goes on to explain that accelerated learning emphasizes collaborative activities and mutual exchange among trainees. It relies on action exercises and devices such as metaphors, themes, mnemonics, props, music and color to create an enjoyable setting "conducive to learning and increasing both the relevancy and retention of knowledge."

Does it sound as if an accelerated-learning-based training program could be a wild affair? You're right; many, if not most, are just that. A sampler:

• At Wisconsin Electric's Point Beach Nuclear Power Plant in Two Rivers, WI, a deadly dull refresher course about the plant's electrical-distribution system was transformed into a giant game. The game is constructed on the floor of the training room by the workshop participants, who then role-play electric current as it runs through the system, and as transmission is disrupted.

• At the American Express operations center in Fort Lauderdale, FL, courses in credit operations, customer

IN SEARCH OF THE THEORY

Suggestopedia, the generally agreed-upon foundation of today's accelerated-learning movement, is fairly easy to follow — once the latter-day mysticism and needless obfuscation are stripped away.

Georgi Lozanov, the Bulgarian psychiatrist who coined the term and created the basic practices, believes that in every learning situation mind, body and emotion play important roles. They can either assist or hinder learning. Lozanov defined three primary barriers that make this most natural of human functions seem difficult:

- *Moral-ethical barrier.* Cultural and social patterns and beliefs that make the new knowledge unacceptable to the learner.
- *Rational-logical barrier.* Information perceived as illogical and unacceptable to the learners' ways of viewing the world.
- *Intuitive-emotional barrier.* Information or simply the instructor's way of presenting that triggers a negative response in the learner.

Lozanov also hypothesized three ways to overcome or circumvent these barriers:

- *Psychologically.* Organize the material in ways that are acceptable emotionally and intellectually to the learner.
- *Didactically.* Present the same material through multiple information channels (audio, visual, somatic, emotional) to increase the probability of acceptance and retention.
- *Artistically.* Use pleasing visual displays and certain sorts of musical accompaniment to help lower or limit the impact of a barrier.

And, since all good things apparently come in threes, Lozanov also penned three core principles that drive the practices:

- The most effective learning takes place when the conscious and subconscious mind are unified.
- People learn best when they are relaxed and enjoying themselves.
- The "suggestive" part of the method works by tapping mental reserves that are present in everyone but hiding behind the barriers.

Sun Microsystems' Kathleen Barclay, who has been exploring the suggestology and accelerated-learning literature as part of her doctoral thesis, believes that few avowed advocates actually know the details of the Lozanov method. Nonetheless, she suggests that a unified, seven-ingredient model is at work in all successful accelerated-learning programs. It owes much to Lozanov and his suggestopedic method and theory.

Briefly, the seven ingredients are:

- *Trainee "state" management.* Draw on curiosity, anticipation, suspense, confidence building, delight and exploration to ready trainees for learning.
- *Total immersion environment.* Create training "themes," appealing to all the senses, and use music, stories and suggestive decor to immerse the trainee in the subject matter.
- *Mind-set management.* Address trainees' learning barriers and mental reservations about the training at the outset of the experience.
- *Planned format variety.* Use memory "keys" such as music, humor, rhyme, color and so forth to make the learning amenable to a variety of learning styles and intelligences.
- *Participant-centered activities.* Involve learners in decision-making about course direction, methods, schedules and so on.
- *Use suggestion.* Manage success and failure cues in the physical environment by subtly — semiconsciously — suggesting positive outcomes and dispelling fear of failure.
- *Emotional engagement.* Add affective elements to the instruction, such as calls to action and celebration, to cement learning at a visceral level.

Whether accelerated learning as it is practiced today is a theory in search of validation or simply a compendium of good ideas is debatable. But either way, there is something here to examine carefully and take seriously.

— *Ron Zemke*

---

service, payment and billing services, and quality enhancement went through the accelerated-learning regenerator and came out highly transformed. In one course, employees are sent on a scavenger hunt to learn travel industry terminology. In another, employees play a game based on the TV game show "Jeopardy" to reinforce credit card law. In a third course, trainees simulate or act out the way an expert system interacts with a database to resynthesize information.

- At American Family Insurance Co. in Madison, WI, insurance adjusters who handle personal injury cases learn the ins and outs of traumatic injuries of the extremities by role-playing the component parts of joints. They understand how suscep-tible these joints are to damage after experiencing the dynamic functioning of bone cartilage, muscles, tendons, ligaments and bursa.

- At Arizona Public Service, a utility in Phoenix, customer service reps review technical terms by playing a restaurant game. Trainees acting as "diners" are presented a menu of terms. "Waiters" must match the term "ordered" from the menu with definitions written on paper plates in a mock kitchen area, and then serve them up to the diners. Everyone takes a turn at "dining" and "waiting."

Kindergarten Teachers Run Amok?

It would be easy to dismiss all this as an epidemic-size attack of a mutant kindergarten-teacher virus were it not for the stunning results practitioners claim and, in many instances, document.

Ellen Leibl, the casualty claims trainer who created and teaches American Family's traumatic injuries course, claims her new program borders on the miraculous. She tried numerous methods to teach this content, she says, but trainees struggled with it. "Even when I showed them pictures and models, it was difficult for trainees to remember the functioning and relationship between the components. After I started doing the program the new way, they routinely comment how easy the material is to learn. I'm doing a long-term follow-up, and it looks as if hardly anyone forgets the material anymore," she says.

Richard Coco, manager of instruction and evaluation for operations training at American Express, did a follow-up study of the training conducted at the Fort Lauderdale facility. He found that trainees who went through the accelerated-learning courses produced higher quality work back on the job and were able to handle more customer contacts in less time than control group trainees.

Almost as impressive as the learning and performance outcomes claimed for these courses is the variety of subject matter being taught using the accelerated-learning approach. At Florida Community College in Jacksonville, general accounting, Lotus 1-2-3 and FoxPro database courses have been rewritten to include accelerated-learning design considerations. The principles also figure prominently in a medical claims processing course at The Travelers Insurance Co., an electronics program at Kodak Corp., and a course on payroll processing for accountants at Commonwealth Edison.

Trainees' reactions to accelerated-learning programs are equally interesting. Bunny Howard, head of the office systems technology department of Florida Community College, marvels at the motivation of trainees. "We have no attendance problems," she says. "My last Lotus class had 22 students. Normally for a night class over 15 weeks, you have a number of absences. I had one absence the entire semester — one gentleman's mother had a heart attack. The attrition rate is the same — I don't have anyone dropping out."

The fun-and-games approach has also had an impact on learning. "My students finish a workload in four class blocks that used to take 10 or 11. And over the last three years I've only had a couple of students that didn't end up with a grade of 'A,'" reports Howard, who originally thought the accelerated-learning approach would be motivational, but would lead to less content mastery.

Arlan Tietel, a training manager at 3M Co. in St. Paul, MN, became an accelerated-learning advocate after attending a proprietary seminar called "The Accounting Game." The seminar, conducted by Quantum Educational Discoveries of Boulder, CO, targets people who have little or no accounting experience. Participants learn basic accounting principles by working together to manage an imaginary lemonade stand. But that description doesn't come close to explaining the rock music, plastic ray guns, whistles and propeller beanies in the program. Nor does it do justice to the pandemonium that accompanies — and enhances — the learning.

Tietel says the seminar impressed him. After one day of this enjoyable and energizing craziness, he could confidently read and generate a financial statement. Even more impressive: A month after he took the course he sat down with one of the company's controllers and was able to carry on a

---

"When I first went to an accelerated-learning course I thought to myself, 'Goodness. What's new here? I used many of these techniques when I was a Cub Scout den mother.'"

---

cogent conversation on financial issues. "So much so that he couldn't believe I didn't have an accounting background," laughs Tietel.

Tietel got an extra bonus out of the program: He could apply most of the zaniness he experienced to his own training assignments. "I was still doing sales training, so I just integrated some of the techniques and they worked great," he says. "And no one seemed the least put off by them, either."

What's On The Grill?

If you are excited by reported outcomes like these, but not so sure you can see what's behind the sizzle, you're not alone. It isn't always clear what's on the grill — even to some of the advocates.

Susan Clancy-Kelly is a free-lance multimedia developer and Internet instructor in Wiltshire, England, who has used accelerated-learning techniques in her programs for several years. She concedes that the underpinnings holding accelerated learning together as a unified body of knowledge can be, shall we say, obtuse. "The theoretical part is a bit woolly," she says. "When I first went to an accelerated-learning course I thought to myself, 'Goodness. What's new here? I used to use many of these techniques when I was a Cub Scout den mother. It's simply a different age group.' It took a bit to see the method in the madness."

Just the same, Clancy-Kelly believes that an underlying philosophy is important to accelerated learning. "It's not simply an entertaining toolbox without a philosophy," she insists. "I tell my clients that the programs I develop are accelerated-learning based, and that that means several things. The philosophy is that you must appeal to all the senses of the learners — sight, touch, sound, thought — to fully engage them in the learning process and help them rapidly internalize the material. I also warn them that I work to make the process fun and that some of the tools are a bit unusual compared to most stand-up, lecture-based training."

Kathleen Barclay, field training manager for Sun Microsystems Computer Co. in Mountain View, CA, understands quite well the wooliness issue surrounding accelerated learning. "I make a distinction between suggestology and accelerated learning," she says. "One is a methodology and the other is methods — independent techniques that are used with or without an understanding of the methodology and theory."

Barclay, who uses accelerated-learning designs in her training and is researching suggestology and accelerated learning for a doctoral thesis, suggests that the need for speed in the business world has led to both easy acceptance and a lack of understanding about accelerated learning on the theoretical level. "There is a lot of pressure on education groups to perform faster and better in companies that compete on a global scale," she says. "So any approach or set of techniques that promises to aid that are easily accepted right now — and management couldn't care less about the underpinnings as long as the training is quick and works."

Yet Barclay is concerned that trainers who simply throw a toolbox of techniques at their "hurry up and train someone" assignments will be without resource if the programs they've mounted fail to perform to expectations. "For instance," she says, "you can't necessarily go from a culture that expects training to be an

NOTES FROM ACCELERATED-LEARNING CONVERTS

My interest in accelerated learning was renewed after an 18-year hiatus thanks to a series of enthusiastic Internet messages. Recently, Joan Vanden Hazel, an instructional designer in KPMG, Canada's National Professional Development office in Toronto, posted the following on the Penn State University education department's training and development bulletin board, TRDEV-L:

"A colleague of mine is interested in possibly attending a workshop on accelerated learning and asked that I query this list to see if anyone has attended such a seminar and what they thought of it. Specifically:

"Was the workshop effective — did it meet its proclaimed goals?

"Did you have practical knowledge and skills to bring back to the workplace?

"What kind of change were you able to implement as a result of this workshop?

"Who would you recommend attend this workshop?"

Vanden Hazel's query was met with a flurry of enthusiastic responses, and triggered a string of discourse that continued for several weeks. This internetting tribe of often skeptical, "don't let 'em feed you that crap" electro-pen pals seemed exceptionally enthusiastic about the whole thing. The following responses are representative:

• "I am fairly new to the training area and inherited numerous technical modules and workshops built around lecture — i.e., I talk, you listen and take notes, ask questions and take quizzes. Accelerated learning taps into the group's knowledge and experience and through different techniques and activities the learning becomes self-directed. I am completely sold on the concept, although some of the old-time trainers in my unit scoff at the idea of having fun while you learn."

• "Speaking for my training group as a whole, there was plenty to bring back. Many were skeptical of using this type of training technique, but once they tried it, they were converts."

• "[I was able to shorten] many of my courses. The most shining example is that on 48 hours' notice, I designed, developed and delivered a two-hour workshop on a new product for the sales force that is still being talked about as the best training session in the history of the company. I used coaching, fun, self-instruction, music, color and competition to facilitate the learning. I was given a bonus for the effectiveness of the training."

• "I was able to remove almost entirely all of the lecture portions of my workshops, and they have become enjoyable places to be, both for the participants and myself."

• "Anyone who is currently making training presentations can certainly benefit from [an] accelerated-learning [workshop]. Also, it can be very useful to have key managerial types attend. They get quite an eye-opener, and you will get much better support for your 'classes where you play with all the toys.'"

To Vanden Hazel's surprise, all of the feedback was positive. She notes one concern, however: "Most of the feedback from trainers described their improved training and delivery skills. Very few people reflected on the improved or accelerated learning of the participants in a course they have delivered subsequent to having taken accelerated learning."

So if nothing else, accelerated learning can make a dramatic impact on the trainers who see it in action and adopt it in their day-to-day efforts.

— Ron Zemke

---

instructor going through 200 foils to one that accepts team learning, with fun and games and no lecture, in one fell swoop. And without a grounding in the theory, it could be difficult to pick a place to start." Still, she isn't sure that the "methods" approach is all negative. "You really have to ask: Isn't it better to have people using the methods they see in others' work and at least accomplishing some improvement, even if they don't know how these things go together and why?"

Is There A 'There' There?

Talk with a sample of accelerated-learning practitioners, and you'll quickly conclude the techniques they use seem to work. But getting a grip on the theoretical foundations is more elusive. You often feel as though there is, in fact, no such thing as an accelerated-learning theory (see box page 62).

Bobbi DePorter, president of the International Alliance for Learning (IAL, formerly the Society for Accelerated Learning and Training), an Oceanside, CA-based association dedicated to the advancement of accelerated learning, attributes this feeling to the dynamic nature of the field. "In the beginning we were very strict. We brought in carpenters to build chairs at the exact angle of Lozanov's chairs, bought the same music, copied his approach exactly," says DePorter, who studied with Lozanov in the '70s. But accelerated learning, she contends, encompasses more than suggestology. "In all our conferences there is a large contingent of neurolinguistic programming. There's educational kinesiology and brain research. All of these things came after suggestology. They influence learning practices and are now part of what we think of as accelerative learning."

According to a promotional brochure from IAL that purports to answer the question, "What is Accelerative Learning?" it is simply "a rich potpourri of innovative ideas and experiences." Among the many elements of teaching and learning that comprise the accelerated-learning potpourri are:

• *The human brain.* It can be helped to perceive more effectively, to process, assimilate and integrate new information with existing knowledge.

The adult learner's brain is subject to the same needs as that of a child. Learning should be "childlike, but not childish." Learning should be fun because it is a natural and intrinsically rewarding activity.

• *The learning environment.* Factors that may facilitate or detract from the learning process include lighting, temperature, acoustics, seating arrangement, color and decor. Visual aids also enhance learning.

• *Music.* Music facilitates learning by creating emotional engagement and memorability. Music cues can provide a kind of acoustic separation

---

for group activities and can influence pace, tone and energy level.

- *Imagination.* Imaginative games and activities enrich verbal and written information with physical movement, color, depth and positive emotions for learners of all ages.

- *Suggestion.* A trainer's attitude, body language, choice of words, and expectations about the participants continuously communicate. Subtle suggestions exert a powerful effect on trainees' attitudes and learning. Other trainees, co-workers, bosses, and the overall classroom environment are also influential.

- *A positive mental state.* Creating a positive mental state, facilitated by a rich variety of learning tasks, music, movement and exercise, keeps energy levels up and attention focused.

- *The arts.* Music, poetry, pictures and literature are used to cultivate self-understanding, emotional involvement, and the ability to apply knowledge to real life.

- *Individual intelligence.* The theory of "multiple intelligences," which is reflected in individual learning styles, is widely accepted in accelerated-learning circles. Students' learning skills are said to vary as much as their fingerprints. Thus, a wide array of learning experiences must be provided to permit all learners to be successful.

- *Emotional state.* Emotions exert a powerful influence on learning. Teaching and learning processes must be "brain compatible." That's why it's so important to create a low-stress, fun-filled learning environment.

Research in the neurosciences has demonstrated that midbrain or limbic-system brain structures are the seat of our emotions and of many hormones that govern our physiological state. Stress and fear induce chemical changes in the brain that can incapacitate its ability to perceive, process and

remember new information, or to recall previous learning. Information tagged with intense emotions tends to be retained the longest. Thus, accelerated learning emphasizes the need to create positive emotional impact.

It would be easy to dismiss all this as an epidemic-size attack of a mutant kindergarten-teacher virus were it not for the stunning results practitioners claim and, in many instances, document.

- *Self-esteem.* Self-esteem, self-confidence and personal expectations can greatly affect the motivation and achievement of learners. Attitudes toward one's learning ability are acquired and confirmed in the home and at school, and affect the outcome of one's entire life.

- *Learning objectives.* Learning outcomes must be clearly defined for all stakeholders. Learners must comprehend the relevance of their learning to their lives.

- *Adaptability.* Measurements of student progress provide data for the continuous improvement of teaching and learning processes. The idea is to do more of what works well — and less of what does not work — to improve the quality, efficiency and results of education.

- *Cooperation.* Cooperative activities allow students with all levels of ability to benefit as mentors and learners, develop interpersonal skills, and more fully develop their creative

talents.

The fact that accelerated learning encompasses this grab bag of characteristics is fine with DePorter. "Accelerative learning has gotten to be a very loose term. However anybody is describing affective, effective learning that makes a difference, that is positive — accelerative learning encompasses it. What Dr. Lozanov taught is still at the core; the principles of rapport, music, environment are all there. All the rest has spiraled out from that core."

Meier, of the Center for Accelerated Learning, isn't so sure that the nod to Lozanov is even very important: "I think Lozanov provided romance and momentum for the act of questioning present notions of the day about learning and education. Until the '70s, education and training were under the tutelage of a post-Gutenberg, rationalistic, digital approach to learning, life, science — everything. The lecture method was a creation of the Dark Ages." In earlier ages, he notes, learning was much more wholistic. "Tribal people all the way up to Homer used rhythm, rhyme, music and chanting to teach. Homer was a rap artist, really. Descartes — pedal-to-the-metal, rational Descartes — disembodied intellect from the whole person. What accelerated learning does, what Lozanov did, is reintroduce the somatic element and make learning a whole-person endeavor again."

Is accelerated learning an emerging theory of wholistic learning with assumptions, propositions and reliable proof of performance? Or is it simply an assemblage of common sense, good teaching practices and instructional prejudices? That remains to be seen. Look past it as fluffy and airy-fairy, if you will. But do so at your own risk.

ACTION LEARNING

Taming Real Problems in Real Time

BY PAUL FROILAND

There's a problem at the Grinchling Co., maker of amazing Grinchling Chocolate Bars, which have taken the American candy market by storm. Phenomenal demand for the new chocolate bar has persuaded the company to hire scores of workers at its domestic plants and to begin construction of new plants in Stuttgart, Germany, and Manila, the Philippines. But the managers who will be in charge of the international plants are command-and-control types with no training in managing workers of other cultures.

Mr. Grinchling, the company president, brings in Nosweat Consultants to run a two-week training program for the future international managers, featuring such films as "Ich bin ein Stuttgarter" and "Say Hello to Manila." The managers get a great deal of generic information about managing Germans and Filipinos. Six months later, the foreign plants are ready to begin production, and the managers have forgotten all the sure-fire tips they learned in training. They institute their old, familiar command-and-control methods at the new plants. Workers at Grinchling Schokolade in Stuttgart rebel and go on strike. The workers in Manila call in sick in hordes, and production falls severely.

What went wrong?

It may be an overdrawn case of *When Training Doesn't Work*, but it is quite the opposite of what happens when action learning works. Action learning, say its proponents, is as old as the medieval craft-guild system: You learn by doing. A real work challenge is the centerpiece of an action-learning experience. Teams or work groups take an actual problem to the training program, work on solving it, commit to an action plan, and are accountable for carrying out the plan.

Of course, real-life applications of the method are not always so clear-cut. Action-learning programs often encompass a variety of other elements. Some practitioners, for example, consider personal development an essential component of action learning. Participants may attend outdoor experiential courses where they climb ropes or rappel down cliffs. Or they may be placed in situations that require them to confront viewpoints unfamiliar — and sometimes opposed — to their own. Some action-learning courses involve high stakes for participants — executives may have to bet their annual bonus on their solution to a problem, for example — while others involve little or low risk.

In contrast, Grinchling managers attended classroom training that depicted hypothetical instances of cross-cultural interaction. The training was not framed in terms of a real problem or challenge, such as how can I make the Stuttgart plant run profitably and smoothly within 60 days? The managers were not held accountable for putting into practice what they learned in training. So they tackled their foreign assignments by conducting business as usual. And they nearly ruined the company.

Noel Tichy, of the University of Michigan's business school in Ann Arbor, is one of the foremost proponents of action learning. Michigan, in fact, uses action learning in its MBA program so that students "get their hands dirty," learning the curriculum by taking on real-life work challenges at area businesses. Tichy also has used action learning to help such companies as General Electric and Ameritech overturn and rebuild their corporate cultures.

"The problem with management is that we treat it as a quasi-scientific thing," Tichy says. "Management is a clinical practice. You don't train heart surgeons by having them read Harvard cases. Management development has to get much closer to the real world. How do you train people in the crafts? That's all we're talking about. The basic principles apply all the way to the shop floor."

John Murphy, formerly corporate director of executive education and quality education at GTE Corp. in Stanford, CT, implemented an action-learning approach to problem solving during the '80s that the company continues to use today. Now president of Executive Edge Inc., a Fairfield, CT, consulting firm, Murphy defines action learning as the opposite of the classroom-training model, which assumes that training or "development" is a discrete activity that precedes the real work it is intended to shape; that is, first people receive training, then they go out and achieve business results. That, he says, is backwards; rather, "You put [people] in a legitimate work situation [intending] the achievement of results for which they have accountability. Then, in collaboration with them, you provide them with the just-in-time learning that everyone needs in order not to make a disaster out of the responsibility they have."

How It Works

A typical action-learning project involves groups of between six and 30 employees (sometimes including vendors and customers). There are a few variations on how the groups are composed. Some groups include a single "stakeholder" for the work problem that is being dealt with; the rest of the participants come from different businesses within large corporations or different functions within smaller ones. These nonstakeholders are included to provide the group with fresh perspectives on the problem at hand. Sometimes all the participants have a stake in solving the problem — in other words, they all work in the same department or division of the company. Or, in a multistakeholder group, participants from a variety of divisions focus on their own particular issues, taking turns examining each others' problems.

ACTION LEARNING IN ACTION

Michael Gilliam, a vice president and general manager of the Global Business Center of Cigna International Property and Casualty Corp. in Philadelphia, spent four intensive weeks in an action-learning group.

"The problem that we were charged with was analyzing the strategies of one of our [property-casualty insurance] business units over the last three years," Gilliam says. The group was not supposed to come up with a new business strategy, just make recommendations as to whether the existing strategies needed minor adjustments, whether they were wrong altogether, or whether they were being implemented incorrectly. The group was required to produce a paper with its recommendations at the end of the four weeks.

Gilliam's group consisted of 11 cross-disciplinary upper- and middle-management members from various divisions of Cigna — Cigna International, Cigna's domestic division, benefits, investment and several others. No two people came from the same division, and there were no vendors or clients included in the group. Group members abandoned their jobs for the duration of the process and met off-site.

"The first week was a mixture of academics, [consultation with] some professors from Harvard and Wharton, plus a briefing from the division staff that had the business problem," Gilliam says. "We absorbed a lot of data about the business problem as well as data on strategy, and [applying] academics to strategy.

"The second week we split into four teams and traveled the country. We conducted about 100 interviews with employees, distributors and customers on a one-to-one basis.

"The third week we assimilated the data," Gilliam continues, "and the fourth week we formed the recommendations and wrote a 40-plus-page paper." At the end of the fourth week, the group presented its recommendation to the president and entire executive staff of the troubled division. The executives were given a few hours to read the paper and then come back and put questions to the action-learning group.

The results? "The [division] executives were very complimentary, open and receptive to our recommendations," says Gilliam. The recommendations are currently being implemented.

Gilliam is extremely high on the action-learning process as he experienced it. "I think participating in this is the best thing I've ever done both from a work and educational standpoint — and the most exhausting thing I've ever done from a physical and mental standpoint," he says. "Generally, we were working in excess of 15 hours a day over the last two weeks. And we were self-managed, so it was our own excitement and adrenalin that was pushing our 15-hour days." Gilliam says he would highly recommend the process to anyone — "if they have the stamina."

One of the most important things that Gilliam believes came from this was "learning the dynamics of teamwork and what can be accomplished with a group of highly skilled people who are truly focused for an extended period. That's hard to duplicate in the classroom or any sort of corporate environment," he says.

"You're basically living with 11 people for four weeks," he continues. "People are burned from a mental standpoint, and they have to learn how to cope and get along. It's exciting to watch the dynamics of that happen."

One example of a multistakeholder action-learning group is the ongoing "Gap Group" process, used for leadership development at AT&T in Morristown, NJ. The name came from each group's goal of identifying and surmounting the gaps in performance or output that a division faces. High-potential managers each bring in a business problem confronting their division and work in small groups with six or seven peers from other divisions. The process lasts seven days; one day is dedicated to each manager's business problem.

The stakeholder for each problem presents the issue for two hours. The group then wrestles with the problem and tests the "definition" that the stakeholder has presented. Participants propose alternative ways to look at the problem, as well as possible solutions. The group receives guidance either from a group-process expert, usually a consultant, or from subject-matter experts, often business-school professors. When the group settles on a possible solution, the stakeholder makes out an action plan for his problem. He is accountable for producing the results the action plan calls for within the time period he designates. The group may meet informally after that to check progress, or just stay in touch by telephone. The manager of the leadership program will also call participants at intervals to remind them they are accountable for solving the problem.

Gap Groups are composed of as diverse a membership as possible. "We tried it once the other way," says Joe Galarneau, executive education director at AT&T. "We tried having people who were all from sales, for example, and they would always say, 'I've tried that; I've tried that' to every suggestion that was raised."

Group members at AT&T also make action plans for personal behavioral changes that they wish to make based on insights gained during the Gap Group process, but there is no mechanism that makes them accountable for these.

Probably no two companies use action learning the same way. One key difference is between those who use "accountability" strictly in the honor-system sense vs. those who use accountability combined with risk. In the second type of application, you stand to lose money or at least face if you don't carry out your action plan.

At AT&T, an example of the first type of company, the members of an action-learning group are held "accountable" for producing the result their action plan specifies. Should they fail to produce it, however, it is up to them to find out why. They are trusted to do this and don't face any particular risk.

In the second type of group, there is accountability *and* risk. Tichy describes it best: "The key in action learning is you have to create performance anxiety [with] the illusion of pretty high risk," he says. "So [your group] did a crummy report; you're not going to lose your job, but you're going to be professionally embarrassed. And that's usually enough inducement to pull the all-nighters. And when you put people under that kind of pressure, you can see what kind of team members they are and how effective [they are]."

Another example of risk may be the loss of a bonus for executives if they fail to take appropriate action and produce results. Yet another type of risk: getting kicked off the action team for failing to do what you said you would on the problem.

GE Medical Systems in Milwaukee uses the action-learning model that Tichy introduced throughout the corporation. Teams are composed of about two-thirds stakeholders and one-third high-potential people whom the company wants to develop, according to John Christman, training manager. Team members who will become facilitators for GE's famous Work-Out sessions are trained in the action-learning process. (The Work-Out sessions themselves could be considered a form of action learning: Teams of knowledgeable stakeholders are chartered to develop action plans for solutions to resolve business issues or improve processes. They are then empowered to enact these solutions.) Work-Out facilitators are not allowed into the action-learning course unless they have a problem, an owner of the problem, and a date already scheduled to begin meeting on the problem.

Corning Inc. in Corning, NY, offers an elective course in action learning to teach work teams how to apply the method. Corning owns a large plant in State College, PA, that manufactures glass for TV picture tubes. Employees wishing to get into an action-learning training group there must come from a work team that is trying to solve a real business problem, such as how to improve employee-to-employee relations. "They bring their own real problem with them," says former director of education and training J. Edwin O'Brien, "and as they're learning the process, they're applying it to a back-home operation. The team has the responsibility to solve the problem."

Corning also uses action learning for diversity training at its State College plant. Action-learning groups at State College are gender- and race-balanced, and deal with what often

become highly volatile issues of sexual and racial harassment — who can touch whom where, for example, and whether it doesn't really matter because they both know it's kidding. (It's *not* kidding and not welcome, according to women in two of the groups that O'Brien observed.) The action that has resulted from the groups is a monitoring system for employee complaints about other employees or supervisors. The system is used to determine whether there is a racial or gender component to complaints, an issue that had not been considered before the action-learning project was started.

Other companies try to create action-learning groups that represent

---

"Management is a clinical practice. You don't train heart surgeons by having them read Harvard cases."

---

as diverse a spectrum of employees as possible, and some even include willing clients. Cigna International Property and Casualty Corp., the Philadelphia insurance company, puts people in action-learning groups that work 40 hours a week for four to five weeks. Each group is assigned a single problem that faces just one of Cigna's divisions. Usually only one or two people in the group will be from that division; every other division president will also send one or two people.

Cigna's most recent group was charged with evaluating the entire business strategy of one segment of the company, according to Marilyn Gardner, vice president for corporate training in Philadelphia. The property-casualty business that was under examination was losing money, and the group was supposed to determine whether the business's current strategy was viable.

The first week the group immersed itself in the particulars of the business in question. After that, group members went out into the field and interviewed customers, competitors, employees and intermediaries who helped sell that business, to determine the soundness of the current strategy. Following that, the group gathered

again and listened to the advice of an expert from Harvard Business School and another from the Wharton School of Business. The group concluded its charge with a recommendation for a new business strategy, and the business is now acting on that strategy. (See accompanying story for a participant's view of that group.)

Going Global

Some organizations use action learning for larger issues, such as refocusing a company along global lines.

Whirlpool Corp., in Benton Harbor, MI, held its first-ever worldwide leadership conference in 1990 in Switzerland, bringing in 140 top executives, according to Tom Helton, corporate director of organization and leadership development. The issue they faced: global integration after Whirlpool's acquisition of N.V. Philips, a European subsidiary that had plants in Germany, Italy, France and England.

During the conference the 140 participants brainstormed and generated a list of 300 projects that they saw as advancing the integration of the now international company. The CEO and executive committee picked 15 of these projects, which they labeled Whirlpool 1 company challenges. Each project had American and European co-chairpersons, and project leaders divided all 140 members among their teams. The 15 projects were chartered at the meeting — with deliverables required — and the teams were sent off to work.

One of the 15 projects included the articulation and detailing of the process by which the company created products. Other projects included the global-management reporting system that has since been instituted at the company, and the development of a quality initiative. According to Helton, results from the more successful of the projects are "still reverberating through the company."

If the Training Fits . . .

Many companies use action learning at the executive level. John Lawrie, president of Applied Psychology Inc. in Crawfordsville, IN, thinks that there is a natural fit between executives, who are doers, and action learning, which is learning by doing.

"At [executive] levels you get a natural selection of people who know how to fix things, because things always get screwed up," Lawrie says.

"Now if you put people who have been rewarded for this action style into an academic setting, what happens is that [the learning] falls through the cracks. If the trainee is a 'Do it! Jump on it!' type, then that's what we should do instead of talking about it."

Many agree with Lawrie's view that action learning is the natural province of executives. Michael Gilliam, vice president and general manager of the Global Business Center for Cigna, believes action learning is best done with managers "on a fairly high level," although he thinks any group of people can benefit from it.

Larry Ward, manager of executive development for the Dow Chemical Co. in Midland, MI, conducted a needs analysis of Dow's top 300 executives across the world to find what they perceived their development needs to be. "The feedback was so generic that I couldn't figure out where the heck you could go with it," he says. "I got things back like 'dealing with ambiguity.' " As a result, Dow called in a consultant, who sat down with the top 17 executives and asked them what key issues Dow needed to deal with in order to survive the next 10 years. Action-learning groups were formed around such issues as Dow's commitment to the eco-system, reconsidering the company's internal systems, and clarifying its strategic intent.

The reason that executives and managers seem to thrive best with action learning, according to Victoria Marsick, an associate professor of adult education at Teachers College at Columbia University in New York, is that the types of projects undertaken are usually seen as "more intensely meaningful" to managers and executives, and they are more willing than lower-level employees to take on accountability for the results. "At lower levels," Marsick says, "the project is often handed over to them from some senior manager, and they don't see the intrinsic worth of it."

Consultant Murphy agrees with Marsick. "The top three levels of management, like it or not, are the greatest force for change and accountability in a company," he says.

On the other hand, it *is* possible to use action learning successfully at lower levels. Consultant Lawrie says that for that to happen, one of the ingredients of the action plan must be getting the buy-in of the boss. "One of

the critical pieces in [line workers'] environment is their boss," he says. "Part of the plan has to include how the group is going to present its notions to the boss. Which ones is he likely to go for? Which is he likely to turn down? Why?"

Patricia Stacey, a consultant with Action Learning Associates in Ann Arbor, MI, also sees possibilities for line workers using the process. In fact, she says, "The problem is that people at the top get these wonderful, grandiose ideas, but have no clue about what's going on at the bottom. If you get the right people in the room who know what the process is, they can fix it."

"The key in action learning is to create performance anxiety with the illusion of pretty high risk."

She suggests that for action learning to work at the line level, workers must make a commitment to their supervisor that, once the problem is mapped out, they will fix it and save either a target dollar amount or target percentage of cycle time. Then they have to return at the end of the allotted time and demonstrate that they've done it. "Otherwise," she says, "a [rule] of action learning says that if you can't do the job, you have no business being there. People have to be willing to take that risk and make it happen."

Does a lot of this sound like tenets of the total-quality movement? In fact, many of the techniques that quality-improvement teams routinely use to solve problems or improve processes borrow from action-learning methods.

At Whirlpool, line managers run action-learning groups composed of front-line workers. "We have close to 100 percent of our line managers actually conducting the [action] training," says Helton. The role of training and HR people has become largely one of training line managers to be trainers, he says. One incentive for line workers to participate is that they've all become stakeholders in the company since employee stock options were granted a few years ago. Whirlpool

was trading at $37 a share when the options were granted; it's trading in the $60 range now. Employees see the results in their pockets when they tackle and solve company problems.

One problem that Whirlpool employees handled using action learning was recovering overpaid duty on compressors that the company was importing from a Brazilian affiliate. Members of the procurement group formed a team that took on the issue of what processes they would need to implement the company's strategies for inventory control and cost reduction. The team found a process that recovers the duty, saving the company hundreds of thousands of dollars a year.

'Whoopee in the Woods'

Although personal-growth training may be extrinsic to a strict definition of action learning, many companies insist that it is one of the keys to making action learning work. The idea is that group members are encouraged to consider other points of view. For this reason many organizations regard a consultant or group facilitator as essential. If the action-learning group were run by someone who already works at the sponsoring company, that someone likely would have a similar perspective to those in the group.

In the pursuit of personal growth and better group dynamics, action-learning groups often are sent to outdoor "ropes" and rock-climbing courses to enhance team trust and harmony. Proponents insist that team-building exercises improve the efforts of a team working on a business problem. Likewise, they contend, individual contributions are enhanced when team members are forced to examine things from new perspectives. According to Marsick, the notion that action learning ought to be merged with personal-development activities began in Sweden, which, along with other European countries, has a much longer history with the process than America does.

"The [Swedish] model typically adds to the project [opportunities] for people to look at things in new ways," Marsick says. "They deliberately try to startle people out of the way they look at things. They may take the group of managers to interview a group of theater people about their ideas of leadership. They are forced to meet with hippies and other fringe groups that Swedish managers wouldn't normally interact with. When you put people in situations that are very different from what they are ordinarily in, it's often uncomfortable for them, and it forces them into new ways of thinking."

In the United States, the startling experiences usually come in the guise of Outward Bound types of courses, which offer team-based challenges and are designed to help group members learn more about each other while they develop a team commitment. "The Outward Bound things contribute a lot to the personal learning," says Marsick, "and they create conditions for a team to work together more effectively. That would jump[-start] the efficacy of the team as a learning group."

At Ameritech, a "Baby Bell" company in Hoffman Estates, IL, action-learning groups not only go through Outward Bound exercises, they also visit soup kitchens. "People learn best when they're out of their comfort zone," says Bob Knowling, vice president and head of the Ameritech Institute.

Ropes and rocks courses are not essential, says Michigan's Tichy, "but they are a useful social technology for kick starting team development." He often uses such activities with action-learning groups, he says, but only in conjunction with real team issues. "This kind of 'whoopee in the woods' stuff is no different than the sensitivity-training fad in the '60s. You've got to link it to real stuff fast."

Marvin Weisbord, a consultant in Plainfield, NJ, is co-director of a non-profit organization called SearchNet, which uses action learning to help people program community-planning conferences. According to Weisbord, outdoor courses are just one way of adding to action learning. "You can do it with swings and sliding boards, with hopscotch and jump ropes," he says. "You can do it with coat hangers, stamp collections, rock 'n' roll. All these programs are tied to is getting yourself into a situation in which you are vulnerable and you don't know the answer and the outcome is not assured and bulling your way through." He also cautions, however, that all these exercises have to be tied to the learning task in some way.

Others are less sold on incorporating an experiential element. Whirlpool's Helton says that when his company first experimented with what it thought was action learning, employees went through outdoor courses in conjunction with classroom learning. They always gave the outdoor courses rave reviews. "The problem is, however," Helton says, "when that kind of thing is looked at from a business perspective, the senior leadership here was asking, 'How is that helping me move the company to achieve the goals we've set?' And that's a tough one to answer."

Whirlpool eventually abandoned the outdoors courses and set up an action-learning system that integrated three-level teams: the manager of a unit, his or her direct subordinates, and their direct subordinates. "What you get then," says Helton, "is everybody in the room who's needed to make a change." The teams then undertake a real business problem, have customized workshops, go out to work individually on their projects, then reconvene for more training.

"People at the top get these wonderful, grandiose ideas, but have no clue about what's going on at the bottom."

Consultant Murphy is the most outspoken in his disdain for tying outdoor courses and the like to action-learning projects. If the whole point of action learning is to work on real business problems, he argues, what in the world is anyone but a lumberjack or a forest ranger doing out in the woods? "I think ropes courses and rock climbing are a crock," he says. "The company is full of [metaphorical] fields and ropes and rocks: Why isn't *that* the experience in the experiential learning? Nothing builds a team better than the excitement of having met an incredibly difficult goal. If you have to go to a rock pile to get that, you're just not linking the business reality to the training opportunity. To me, taking your employees to a ropes course is saying that you don't know how to do that with your own company."

Insecure Executives

Advocates and users of action learning are glowing in their assessments of its possibilities. But some organizations would consider it anathema. "If you don't have the appropriate leadership," says Tichy, "it isn't going to work. I did a massive action-learning process at Honeywell Systems in the early '80s, but they didn't execute. They didn't have the leadership . . . . In fact, it can probably make your leaders look worse. Companies that have insecure people will find this absolutely threatening. Those are the guys that come in with their body/mind guards and their written scripts, and they do their one-way speech and they're whisked away in a limo. [Action learning] is mix it up, get out there and scrimmage."

Other organizations, Tichy says, *think* they're doing action learning but don't give it enough time, don't choose significant projects, and don't take real risks. "It's kind of a traditional 'We'll pitch it to the CEO,' " he says. "Life goes on. I go back to my division and the program falls apart." You have to put people at sufficient risk and track their projects, he says, and you have to tie it into the company's measurement and reward systems.

Consultant Lawrie describes another situation in which action learning would be unlikely to succeed: "[When] you have a very authoritarian boss with people who have been with him over the years. They're so conditioned to be told what to do, and he's so conditioned to [telling them] and being rewarded for it, that it would be a mistake to try action learning."

Ready for Takeoff?

Will action learning be the next big movement in training? Perhaps and perhaps not. Joe Raelin, who teaches at Boston College's Carroll School of Management, came upon the European version of action learning while on sabbatical in Lancaster, England. There, he found two major MBA programs similar to Tichy's at Michigan, in which students learned by studying real-life problems at companies.

Back in the United States, however, Raelin says he doesn't see any widespread rush to embrace it. Although he considers himself somewhat of a promoter of the process, he says he's been having a hard time launching it in this country. He suspects two reasons for the resistance: "First, it may well be that this country's corporate directors are not willing to have someone poke around in critical problems in their organizations; it's a resistance to culture change.

"Second, action learning is not a product or an outcome; it's a process. And we tend to be outcome-oriented rather than process-oriented," he says.

Tichy, on the other hand, is absolutely bullish on the prospects of action learning. "No question that it's taking off," he says, "It's related not to action learning having been refined or further developed; it's the firing of [CEO John] Akers [by IBM] and [Bob] Stempel [by General Motors], it's the taking out of Paul Lego at Westinghouse and James Robinson [at American Express], and all of a sudden transformation becomes a serious game. Then you ask yourself, 'How the hell am I going to change the culture?' Doing some old way of training isn't going to work. The marketplace is forcing them to change and they're realizing they have to break free of the old stuff."

Or, as John Murphy puts it: "I don't want awareness training; I want to know how to do this damned thing."

That's the essence of action learning.

Notes:

ADULT LEARNING THEORY

What Do We Know for Sure?

BY RON ZEMKE
AND SUSAN ZEMKE

Learning refers to relatively permanent changes in an individual which are related to past experience and the opportunity to learn, including practice, rather than to physiological changes such as fatigue, adaptation, drug-effects, motivation, maturation or senescence.

— Handbook of
General Psychology

Learning: knowledge or skill acquired by instruction or study.

— Webster's
New Collegiate Dictionary

Learning is but an adjunct of ourselves.

— Shakespeare

However you care to define it, learning is as natural to human beings as breathing, eating, sleeping, playing or procreating. And as far as anyone can tell, we maintain that natural capacity as long as any of the others. For the last century and a half or so, educators and psychologists have tried to develop ways to deliver instruction, practice and experience that enhance this innate capacity to learn.

For the last 20 to 75 years, depending on who's doing the counting, an evolving school of thought has defined adult learners (as opposed to children, adolescents, college sophomores and lab rats) as a unique subgroup in need of specialized study, theory and educational practices.

Adult-learning theory emerged from the academic backwaters in 1973 with the publication of Malcolm Knowles' highly readable book, *The Adult Learner: A Neglected Species.* Knowles, then a Boston University professor, scored an instant hit with adult educators and trainers. In *The Adult Learner* he dusted off the word

"andragogy," a term popular in German education circles in the early 1800s, and used it to label his attempt to create a unified theory of adult learning. Knowles' contentions were based on four assumptions:

• As they mature, adults tend to prefer self-direction.

• Adults' experiences are a rich resource for learning. Adults learn more effectively through experiential techniques such as discussion or problem-solving than they do through, say, passive listening.

• Adults are aware of specific learning needs generated by real-life events such as marriage, divorce, taking a new job, losing a job and so on.

• Adults are competency-based learners, meaning that they want to learn a skill or acquire knowledge that they can apply pragmatically to their immediate circumstances.

The concept of andragogy generated a flurry of debate and study. Today, andragogy is considered something less than the all-encompassing explanation of adult learning that Knowles had hoped it would be. Knowles himself later acknowledged that pedagogy and andragogy probably represent the ends of a spectrum that ranges from teacher-directed to student-directed learning. Both approaches, he and others now suggest, are appropriate with children and adults, depending on the situation.

Sharan B. Merriam, a professor of adult education at the University of Georgia, summarizes the current state of adult-learning theory this way:

"It is doubtful that a phenomenon as complex as adult learning will ever be explained by a single theory, model or set of principles. Instead, we have a case of the proverbial elephant being described differently depending on who is talking and on which part of the animal is examined. In the first

half of this century, psychologists took the lead in explaining learning behavior; from the 1960s onward, adult educators began formulating their own ideas about adult learning and, in particular, about how it might differ from learning in childhood. Both of these approaches are still operative. Where we are headed, it seems, is toward a multifaceted understanding of adult learning, reflecting the inherent richness and complexity of the phenomenon."

Fourteen years ago, in the June 1981 issue of TRAINING, we published a review of adult-learning theory and research titled "30 Things We Know for Sure About Adult Learning." We recently revisited the information pile from which we culled that article. We then added more than 300 new references to the stack and asked ourselves, "Has anything changed?"

As far as solid, reliable information goes, most of what the literature has to tell us today is what it told us then. But while we haven't seen the equivalent of the dramatic changes wrought by Knowles and the andragogy movement in the early 1970s, some important differences in nuance and understanding have occurred that add to our knowledge of the training craft.

As in our previous synthesis, we have divided what we garnered from our scan into three basic categories:

1. Things we know about adult learners and their motivation.

2. Things we know about designing curricula for adults.

3. Things we know about working with adults in the classroom.

The same caution applies now as did then: These categories are neither definitive nor exclusive. They overlap more than a little. But they help us understand the implications that current theory and research hold for our day-to-day work in training and development.

Motivation To Learn

Adults can be ordered into a classroom and prodded into seats, but they can't be forced to learn. On the other hand, adults who see a need or have a desire to know something new are quite resourceful. Witness the legions of gainfully employed people enrolled in continuing education programs at community colleges, vo-techs and universities around the world, not to mention the success of proprietary self-development seminars, sports-skills camps, and independent study groups in virtually every industrial and postindustrial country.

When the conditions are right, adults seek out and demand learning experiences. Much of what we know about adult motivation to learn describes those conditions and comes from the work of Allen Tough, Carol Aslanian, Henry Brickell and others engaged in the study of self-directed learning. The key to using adults' "natural" motivation to learn is tapping into their most teachable moments: those points in their lives

SELF-DIRECTED LEARNING: ADULTS WHO DO IT THEIR WAY

The developing area of self-directed learning offers plenty of evidence that adults are perfectly capable of acquiring skills, knowledge and self-insight on their own. They don't necessarily need any experts to design or manage the learning process for them. And when they perceive a need to learn something, they don't stand around waiting for such experts to appear.

In the 1970s, Toronto researcher Allen Tough, a faculty member at the Ontario Institute for Studies in Education, found that typical adults spend 500 or more hours a year engaged in five "learning projects" of their own design. That finding greatly surprised most adult-learning experts, and subsequent research disputes Tough's numbers (one highly regarded study put the figures closer to three learning projects and 150 hours a year). Whatever the "true" numbers may be, adults' status as self-directed learners is well established.

A significant amount of research focuses on the way adults organize their self-directed learning projects. Some researchers contend the process is linear and orderly; some suggest it is more a haphazard, trial-and-error affair. Whatever the case, Malcolm Knowles, Tough and others have worked out a useful heuristic for making the most of a self-directed learning effort.

Step "zero": You become aware that there is indeed something you need to learn. Let's say you buy a new graphics software package and don't have the foggiest idea how to use it.

Step 1: You identify what you want to learn. Do you want to become a high-tech Van Gogh with that new software or just learn to plop prepackaged cartoons into reports?

Step 2: You diagnose the skill or knowledge you need to achieve the end you have in mind. Think of it as a do-it-yourself needs assessment: You load the graphics program, fiddle with the menus, and see what you can make it do without opening the manual. (You know you do.)

Step 3: You develop a plan of inquiry and a list of resources. Translation: Browse the manual, call two people who already use the program, and check the local bookstore for a "Graphics for Dummies" guide.

Step 4: You begin proactive learning. You start to read the manual, you try the program, you fit some graphics into an old report. And when you get stumped, you call people on your list to help you get unstuck.

Step 5: You evaluate whether you have met your learning objectives. The next time you have a report due, you try using the package for real.

Step 6: You re-diagnose your learning needs and repeat the process.

Knowles adds one important caveat to his enthusiasm for self-directed learning: Self-direction is only effective when the learner has some basic level of experience with the content. "Pedagogical methods are appropriate in those cases in which the adult is indeed a dependent learner," he told TRAINING. "For example, the person may have no experience with a personal computer. The andragogical teacher will have to provide didactic instruction up to the point where the learner has acquired enough information and skill to be able to direct his or her own learning."

According to Tough's research, self-directed learners tend to be eclectic in their choices of media and method. While adults prefer self-direction 7-to-1 over group-learning experiences led by a professional educator, they will attend lectures and short seminars if these seem the shortest route to the desired destination.

Apparently, the self-directed learner is very efficiency-minded. Tough suggests that the typical adult asks, "What is the cheapest, easiest, fastest way for me to learn to do that?" and then proceeds along this self-determined route. An obvious implication for corporate trainers: Trainees must have a hand in shaping the curriculum of a program.

Tough's research further suggests that an adult's typical learning project is hardly a solitary affair. He finds that the average self-directed learner enlists 10.6 other people in a given project. Adults engaged in regular self-directed learning projects develop learning networks to help themselves acquire the skills and knowledge they need. In return, they act as learning resources for others.

More evidence of the collaborative tendencies of adult learners comes from a five-year study conducted during the mid-1980s by Honeywell Corp. in Minneapolis. The company found that on-the-job experiences, relationships with others, and formal training accounted for 50 percent, 30 percent and 20 percent, respectively, of a manager's ability to manage effectively on new assignments. In other words, managers learned more about succeeding in a new position through trial and error and by getting a little help from their friends than from formal training.

People familiar with successful self-directed work teams suggest that acquiring and using learning resources is an important part of a team's discipline. The idea of a group of like-minded adults coming together (unfacilitated) to meet mutual learning goals has a long history. In 1727 Benjamin Franklin created a group he called the "Junto." It was composed of fellow entrepreneurs who shared the belief that "individuals associated can do more for society, and themselves, than they can in isolation." Franklin's Junto was, in turn, founded on an earlier form, the Friendly Societies, developed in England by writer Daniel DeFoe.

In the 1990s, encouraged by the recent "learning organization" rhetoric, several corporations have experimented with the idea of making space and resources available for groups of employees to design and conduct their own ongoing learning without the intervention of a trainer or manager.

when they believe they need to learn something new or different.

For example, several longitudinal studies in corporations have demonstrated that newly promoted supervisors and managers should be trained as quickly as possible. The longer such training is delayed, the less impact it appears to have on job performance.

In short, there is a window of opportunity during which adults are most receptive to learning — and a time after which they cannot be enticed with a chateaubriand or a baseball bat.

The idea of a window of opportunity applies not only to people's motivation to learn, but also to their ability to retain what they *do* learn. If trainees begin to acquire a new skill but then have no opportunity to practice it, the skill will quickly fade. Information-technology trainers have been reporting that training on a new software package or upgraded hardware configuration loses its effectiveness unless the equipment or software is installed and ready to use. The longer the group has to wait for the new system, the less impact the training has on effective use. This is a reconfirmation of an old lesson: Use it or lose it.

• *Adult learning is problem-centered.* People do learn for the sake of learning: Hobbyists go to model-train conventions and take archery classes, retirees take golf and tennis lessons, and lots of people join book clubs. None of that is job- or "problem-" related. But more often than not, adults seek out learning experiences to cope with life-changing events. Marriage, divorce, a new job, a promotion, being fired, retirement, death of a loved one — these sorts of occurrences often create a perceived need to learn.

The more life-changing events adults face, the more likely they are to seek out related learning experiences. In fact, learning may be a coping response to significant life changes for many people: some knit, some drink, some go to school. People who are highly educated are more likely to seek out learning opportunities as opposed to other coping options.

The impulse to go learn something in response to a life-changing event is to some extent generic: The subject that the person suddenly desires to learn about won't always pertain directly to the change that sparked the desire. Witness the divorcee who

signs up for a course in art history. Predictably, however, adults usually will seek out and respond best to learning experiences that they perceive as directly addressing the changes that face them. If a change is primarily work-related, a learner will be more motivated if the learning event is primarily work-related.

Adults are generally willing to engage in learning experiences before, after or even during the life-changing event. Once convinced that the change is a certainty, they will engage in any learning that promises to help them through the transition, including seminars on coping with change.

• *Adult learners can also be motivated by appealing to personal growth or gain.*

Adults can be ordered into a classroom and prodded into seats, but they can't be forced to learn.

Though immediate utility is most often the motivation behind adults' learning efforts, it's not the only motivation. For instance, some evidence suggests that adults more readily engage in job-skills training if they see it as relevant to the rest of their lives as well. Adult learners also can be motivated by the promise of increasing or maintaining their sense of self-esteem or pleasure. Developing a new skill or expanding current knowledge can do both, depending on the individual's perceptions.

A newer subfield of adult learning sometimes referred to as "feminist pedagogy" suggests that emancipation from domination is a strong motivator. While most of the research in this area is related to feminist issues, the idea may have wider scope. You could argue that line employees who are enthusiastic about team training and participation techniques are motivated, in part, because they anticipate being liberated from management dominance in the workplace.

• *Motivation to learn can be increased.* While it may be true that "the best motivation is self-motivation," some evidence suggests that adult learners who are with you in body but not in spirit can be led into

participating and learning. If you can stimulate curiosity about the subject matter, demonstrate early on that the learning will be immediately useful, and ensure low risk for learners, you can convert some of the uncaring. Sometimes simply exploring learners' positive and negative expectations can clear the air and increase participation.

Curriculum Design

Knowles cautions that adults confronted with a classroom and 30 chairs facing forward know exactly how to act: like bored 12-year-olds. Twelve to 18 years of pedagogic conditioning can do that to you. But the warning is important for designers of adult-learning experiences. If you think that those 30 forward-facing chairs represent the optimum learning environment, don't be surprised if you end up with bored compliance. The most dramatic alternative is self-directed curriculum design (see sidebar), but adult-learning theory offers clues for corporate curriculum design as well.

• *The learning experience should be problem-centered.* Working adults are likely to be less enthralled by survey courses than are full-time, professional students. Adults tend to prefer single-concept, single-theory courses that focus on applying the concept to relevant problems. This tendency increases with age. The learning experience should acknowledge and be relevant to the learner's personal goals for the program.

• *Preprogram assessment is important.* It is almost unconscionable to design a program that doesn't take into account the entry-level knowledge and understanding of participants. To begin a team-building experience or diversity seminar without assessing where individuals stand on critical issues, without ferreting out information on the state of relationships in the company, or without clearly defining management's goals for the training borders on malpractice.

• *The learning design should promote information integration.* To remember and use new information, adults need to be able to integrate it with what they already know. Information that conflicts sharply with what they already hold to be true, and thus forces them to re-evaluate the old material, is integrated more slowly. Information that has little conceptual overlap with what they already know also is acquired more slowly. Fast-paced, complex or unusual learning exercises will interfere with the learning of concepts or data they are intended to teach if the new information is too "foreign" to participants.

Adults tend to want a structure to help them keep track of details and facts in relation to one another. One school of thought suggests that adults have "personal maps of reality" in their heads that they use to organize information and experiences. Instruction should help the learner place new information on that "map."

Information conveyed through storytelling is more than entertaining; evidence suggests that it is more easily integrated with existing knowledge. Well "storied" information has a sort of learning adhesive that makes it stick to previous learning and experience.

To help learners organize and integrate information, present one idea at a time. Summarize frequently to facilitate retention and recall. And pace the training so that learners can master one element before moving on to the next.

• *Exercises and cases should have fidelity.* Adults are not enthusiastic about far-fetched cases and artificial exercises. They prefer activities that are realistic and involving, that stimulate thinking, and that have some (but not too much) challenge. Adults evaluate exercises and games quickly and decide whether they are entertaining, useful or just plain silly.

The term "praxis," a Greek word meaning "exercise or practice of an art, science or skill," has begun to appear in the adult-learning literature to describe exercises and activities. The concept acknowledges that while adults prefer "active" to "passive" learning (meaning that they like exercises, cases, games and simulations), the activity must contain a reflective element if learning (or change) is to occur. The literature enthusiastically endorses interactive computer simulations and games as high-fidelity learning experiences, though it holds little data that evaluate these methods.

• *Feedback and recognition should be planned.* Learners need to know what they are trying to accomplish and how they are doing. The program design should include time to explore participants' goals and expectations, to acknowledge those that will not be met, and to discuss both participants' and trainers' responsibilities during the training.

Adults tend to take errors personally and to let them affect their self-esteem. Therefore, they're liable to stick to tried-and-true solutions and take few risks. Adults will even misinterpret feedback that corrects errors as positive confirmation. If you plan to ask participants to give each other feedback, demonstrate beforehand how to give effective feedback.

Most adults aren't used to sitting passively for long stretches. Without activity, they turn into mushrooms before your eyes.

• *Curriculum design should, where possible, account for learning-style differences.* If we've learned anything from all the attention paid to the Myers-Briggs Type Instrument, DISC and Neurolinguistic Programming in the last decade, it is that adults do have learning-style differences and your design should accommodate them. (For more on adjusting to learning-style differences, see "Different Strokes: Learning Styles in the Classroom," page 133.)

Do not, by the way, assume that all instruction must take place in a classroom/seminar/workshop. While most adults learn well when they have an opportunity to share their life experiences and actively contribute to the learning effort, plenty of people also learn well from nonhuman media. Tough and others have found that adults planning self-directed learning projects routinely include books, television, computer-based training, and other solitary media.

Regardless of media and learning style, most adults prefer straightforward how-to content. As many as 80 percent of the polled adults in one study cited the need to learn applications and how-to information as their primary motivation for involving themselves in a learning project, self-directed or otherwise.

• *Design should accommodate adults' continued growth and changing values.* While not as hot a topic in the literature as it once was, the idea that adults go through developmental stages just

as young children and adolescents do is still with us. Not only do adults' needs and interests continually change, so do their values. A seminar group composed of new college recruits and one composed of 50-year-olds can be quite different. The trainer must take into account the life stages and values of the participants. In an orientation course for new employees, for instance, recent college grads might require not just indoctrination into the company's culture but some background information about the business world in general. With the 50-year-olds, the trainer may more safely assume that they have such background knowledge.

Equally important to curriculum designers is whether concepts are in concert or conflict with the organizational and personal values learners accept as valid. A company attempting to move from, say, a low-profile, reactive market strategy to an aggressive, high-visibility stance will likely encounter significant resistance from employees schooled in the "old way." Changing an organization's values dramatically requires more than new brochures and a few buckets of paint. Changing people's long-held values takes careful, planned intervention. New or radically different ideas must be explained repeatedly and in different ways before they will be understood and accepted.

• *Designing in transfer strategies.* More often than we care to admit, the training was a smash hit with the participants, but the performance problem didn't go away. And more often than not, the fault lies in a training design that stops at the classroom door. Adults engage in workplace-learning activities for a productive end. The training is supposed to "transfer" to the real work environment; something is supposed to change back on the job. Failure to design transfer activities into the training breaks the implicit contract between trainer and trainee.

Transfer strategies include pre- and post-training activities, as well as discussions during training that focus on using the new knowledge or skills back on the job. Proven pretraining strategies such as self-assessments, discussions with supervisors that define expectations, and prework such as reading or data-gathering set the stage for effective transfer of training. Successful post-instruction strategies include application discussions with supervisors, refresher training, and support group meetings for graduates of the training.

In The Classroom

Prior to the Knowles era of adult-learning theory, most of the research in adult education focused on teacher behavior. So it is ironic that we still know so little about effective classroom facilitation techniques. Yes, tomes have been written on the subject, but most of what is presented as "proven" is simply a compost of tricks, tips and theory passed on from master performers to their acolytes.

The problem with that approach to accumulating wisdom is that it usually takes an objective observer to distill the essence of how to become a master performer. As communications guru Marshall McLuhan put it, "We don't know who discovered water, but we can be pretty sure it wasn't a fish."

Still, it is possible to piece together the common threads that run through all this advice, and suggest some useful guidelines.

• *Create a safe and comfortable environment.* If you've ever walked into a dark hotel meeting room the morning after a late-night party and wondered how in the heck you are going to turn this into a learning environment, you know the importance of staging. Both the physical and psychological environment must be managed. Light, sound, heat, cold, supplies and amenities must be conducive to thought, focus and serious discourse. Participants need a mix of known and unknown, active and passive, serious and whimsical to keep them involved at an optimum level.

• *Facilitation is more effective than lecture.* Straight lecture is effective when trainees have zero grounding in the subject matter; when rules and regulations have to be passed along; and when matters of finance, fact or law are the subject of the training. But facilitation tends to work better to engage learners in setting objectives, to tap into learners' experience and opinions to create parts of the content,

and to help participants reach consensus.

What constitutes good facilitation? While there are myriad views, most agree that a good facilitator:

– Establishes goals and clarifies expectations (both the facilitator's and the participants').

Helping adults learn requires patience, flexibility, humor — and a strong belief that what you're doing matters.

– Gives up the need to hold forth and be in control.
– Uses questioning techniques to provoke thinking, stimulate recall, challenge beliefs, confront opinions, draw implications and promote conclusions.
– Understands that adults have something real to lose in a classroom. Their egos are on the line when they are asked to risk trying a new behavior in front of peers.
– Balances the many factors that make up a learning event: presentation of new material, debate, discussion, and sharing of relevant trainee experiences. And does all this within the allotted time.
– Develops a learning environment that draws on participants' experiences, protects minority opinion, keeps disagreements civil, makes connections among various opinions and ideas, and reminds the group of the variety of possible solutions to the problem.
– Uses descriptive feedback and reinforces participants for their contributions and accomplishments.

• *Actively promotes understanding and retention.* In some ways this is as simple as recognizing that most adults aren't used to sitting passively for long stretches. Without activity, they turn into mushrooms before your eyes. But there is more to it than that. Despite (and frequently because of) the presence of an instructor/authority figure, many participants are reluctant to share ideas, feelings, confusion and annoyance with the group. Techniques such as breaking participants into small groups increase the chance that the reticent will contribute and collaborate.

The opportunity to exercise new skills in the relative safety of the training room is critical. Frequently participants are hesitant to try out new and untested skills in front of others. Using small praxis teams that practice, reflect and try again can overcome the reluctance to risk.

Helping adults acquire new skills and knowledge is an exhilarating, irritating, challenging and frustrating way to make a living. It takes patience, forbearance, flexibility, humor, and a strong belief that what you're doing matters. If we keep trying and prodding and testing and trying again, we might yet turn this art form into a science of sorts.

For Further Reading

Brookfield, S.D. *Understanding and Facilitating Adult Learning.* San Francisco: Jossey-Bass, 1986.

Cross, K.P. *Adults as Learners: Increasing Participation and Facilitating Learning.* San Francisco: Jossey-Bass, 1981.

Knowles, M.S. *The Modern Practice of Adult Education: From Pedagogy to Andragogy.* (2nd ed.) New York: Cambridge Books, 1980.

Knowles, M.S. *The Adult Learner: A Neglected Species.* (3rd ed.) Houston: Gulf Publishing Co., 1984.

Merriam, S.B. "An Update on Adult Learning Theory," *New Directions for Adult and Continuing Education,* No. 57, Spring 1993. San Francisco: Jossey-Bass.

ASSESSMENT CENTERS

A Method with Proven Mettle

BY CHRIS LEE

Douglas Bray lays out a succinct rationale for the technology: "It's easier to increase skill in someone already skilled than in a klutz."

Bray should know. Recently retired as the director of basic human resources research at AT&T, currently chairman of the board of Pittsburgh, PA-based Development Dimensions International (DDI), he is generally acknowledged as the father of the assessment center. During his nearly 30 years at AT&T, Bray conceived and led the pioneering Management Progress Study (MPS), an eight-year project initially undertaken in 1956 that followed the growth and development of 400 AT&T managers. Its purpose was to pinpoint the cognitive, motivational and attitudinal characteristics that have an impact on managerial careers.

In order to do so, Bray and his colleagues at AT&T put the men (all were men) through a three-and-a-half day assessment center. A wide range of techniques were used, including paper-and-pencil tests, an in-basket exercise, projective tests, clinical interviews, and participation in group problem-solving and leaderless group discussion. Each year for the following eight years, data was collected on the men to determine their career progress. When the results were released, the assessment center method proved its mettle: 82% of the college men and 75% of the noncollege men who were promoted into middle management were correctly identified by the assessment center staff; the assessors also were right about 94% of both college and noncollege men who were not promoted.

Bray's MPS is a unique piece of industrial research in that the data remains "uncontaminated": The assessment results have never been given to either the individuals assessed or company officials. Yet the results so impressed AT&T's management that operational (i.e., "working") assessment centers spread rapidly throughout the system; centers have been established nationwide and thousands of managers have gone through them.

Roots

Although AT&T's assessment center project is perhaps the best-known and remains the model for industrial applications, the methodology actually is rooted in military selection programs. The pre-World War II German military used the multiple assessment approach, which remains a key concept of current assessment centers, to select officers. In *Assessment Centers and Managerial Performance* (Academic Press, Inc., New York, 1982), George C. Thornton III and William C. Byham write: "The German military psychologists launched the multiple assessment of leadership capabilities. Many features of current management assessment center programs can be traced to this source, including multiple assessors, complex situational tests and a desire to measure characteristics more complex than atomistic traits."

According to Thornton and Byham's historical account of the development of the assessment center, the British and American militaries also contributed to the technology during the World War II era. The British developed a better definition of leadership, used group-testing techniques such as leaderless discussion groups, conducted the first validation studies and provided the first evidence of predictive validity. The American Office of Strategic Services (OSS) used assessment centers, under the guidance of Harvard psychologist Henry Murray, to select candidates for positions ranging from secretary to cloak-and-dagger specialist. The OSS contributed elaborate situational exercises and better observation procedures to the evolving methodology, say Thornton and Byham.

Today the assessment center method is used by thousands of organizations in the United States and abroad to evaluate employees' supervisory and managerial potential, their developmental needs or both. William Byham, president of DDI, puts the present count of assessment centers in U.S. organizations at 2,000 — up from just 20 in 1970 — and adds to that total several hundred more operating in Japan, South Africa and Australia.

Seventy-five percent of assessment centers in this country are used to evaluate three types of positions, Byham says. "The greatest use is for first-level foremen in industrial settings, followed by sales managers (to avoid the old problem of turning your best salesperson into a mediocre sales manager) and supervisors in clerical situations."

Standards

Different organizations use assessment centers quite differently, of course, and many pick and choose techniques, depending upon the application they have in mind. But to be considered a true assessment center, according to the Standards and Ethical Considerations for Assessment Center Operations, prepared by a task force of interested parties and published in the February 1980 issue of *The Personnel Administrator*, a center must have several characteristics.

- Multiple assessment techniques, including at least one job-related simulation exercise — group problem-solving, in-basket exercise, interview simulation, etc.
- Multiple assessors, who receive training before participating in a center.
- Judgments based on pooled information from these multiple assessors and techniques.
- A separation in time between the behavioral observation and overall evaluation.
- Dimensions of performance that

have been identified by a job analysis.

• Exercises designed to provide information on these dimensions.

A traditional assessment center normally operates as follows: A group of six to 12 candidates are sequestered with three or more assessors (who may be line managers, members of the personnel staff or psychologists) who have been trained to observe and evaluate behavior. Managers who act as assessors are usually two or more levels above the participant in the organization, but do not supervise the participant. They observe the participants' behavior in management games, leaderless group discussions, role-playing exercises and other activities. Some organizations also combine simulation techniques with background interviews and tests.

The idea, as Byham says, is to "use behavior to predict behavior. It is organized around dimensions that are related to job success — leading, delegating, planning and so on."

Next, the assessors must integrate the data they have gathered through their observations. After the simulations, they meet and report their ratings for each participant on each exercise. They make independent judgments on overall ratings before meeting with one another to reach a consensus or prediction of management success.

Assessment Designs International, a Winter Park, FL consulting firm, has come up with its own relatively succinct definition of an assessment center: "A process in which individuals have the opportunity to participate in a series of situations which resemble what they might be called on to do in an actual job. They are observed in situational or simulation exercises, that is, work samples, while assessors who are well trained in observation and documentation methodology evaluate their performance in a fair and impartial manner."

One of the key points in the process, says Steve Cohen, executive vice president of ADI, is training line managers as assessors. "It's critical," he says. "It takes time, but one of the benefits is that they learn about evaluation and documentation."

Assessor training, Bray agrees, is one of the method's greatest strengths. But it also is perhaps its greatest weakness. "When you have real-life managers making decisions, the organiza-

tion pays attention. With outsiders or personnel types acting as assessors, management tends to be less believing. The downside is training them to do it."

Assessor training, he says, normally lasts from two to five days; he considers five days of training optimal. "The major problem with assessment centers is staffing. The organization has to make a commitment to free up the people for training as well as going through the [assessment/evaluation] process."

Assessment centers should reinforce people's strengths, rather than give away their weaknesses.

The payoff

Although the demanding nature of assessment centers makes them an expensive proposition for organizations, many obviously consider them worth the investment. At Montgomery Ward and Co., Inc. in Chicago, Patrick D. Jimerson, director of corporate training and development, has been using assessment centers for several years to determine the developmental needs of buyers and store managers — at an up-front cost of $100,000. "The most immediate return on your investment is not what you do [with the participants]," he says. "That may not pay off for a year or more. But the assessors learn what they need to be doing back on the job to be more effective. They start to practice the behavior they see as high performance."

Most organizations use assessment centers for selection, development or some combination of the two. According to ADI's Cohen, the trend has been away from using the method strictly for selection, partly because of the expense involved. "Since the mid-'70s, [organizations] have been gravitating toward using them for development." He estimates the breakdown among ADI's clients to be 50% for selection purposes, 20% for development purposes and 30% for a combination of both.

Bray considers the move toward using the assessment center method for development "a lot of cultural noise. People like 'development' better than 'selection,' " he says. "There's a lot of talk about using it for development or trying to use it for both. Some people use assessment centers for selection and then try to use them for development after people have gone through the process. There's nothing wrong with that but, in a sense, the company is not getting its money's worth."

Jimerson feels that assessment centers are best positioned as developmental tools. "If people feel that it is something that reinforces their strengths, rather than gives away their weaknesses, they won't feel as though they've been thrown to the wolves." One way to do this, he says, is to involve the managers and employees who are going to be assessed in the process of building an assessment center, i.e., analyzing jobs and coming up with objective dimensions for those jobs.

This way, too, he adds, people will be more likely to accept the results. "If I'm going to run, say, a computer center for three days and I *know* I did badly on part of the simulation, I can support a decision [to hire someone else] if I can see how I ranked according to objective criteria."

Bray takes a philosophical view of participant reactions. "People adjust to everything in life. If you've got 10 employees and one is going to get promoted, nine are not," he says. "It's better to get the news clearly and objectively than by slow water torture — anticipating a promotion every six months and not getting it. That's more demoralizing."

Cohen agrees that participants ordinarily accept their evaluations. "We get very high participant reactions. They may not like the results, but they can't argue with the process. The assessment center is the most effective single tool to evaluate potential and the most legally valid."

Jimerson feels that people like to be measured against a norm or standard that is at least quasi-objective. "I say 'quasi-objective' because until we have something magic, like [Star Trek's] Dr. McCoy's tricorder, that measures performance *objectively*, the assessment center method is a good tool."

BEHAVIOR MODELING

The 'Monkey See, Monkey Do' Principle

BY RON ZEMKE

Monkey A sees Monkey B dig up a red root and eat it. Monkey B smacks his lips, jumps about excitedly, begins digging again. Monkey A "gets the picture," does some digging of his own, finds a red root, eats it, likes it, and digs for more. Simple as it may seem, this scenario captures the essentials of an emerging approach to the development of training. This new approach, based on the principles of social-learning theory, is known as behavior modeling.

Behavior Modeling and Social-learning Theory

Few trainers have more than a vague familiarity with behavior modeling and its parent, social-learning theory. Part of that unfamiliarity has to do with origins. Social-learning theory is a byproduct of investigations by Albert Bandura, James Aronfreed, and others into the development of moral behavior in children. The specific question they investigated was: "If people tend to behave in ways that lead to satisfaction in any situation, why do they often appear to forego rewards in order to behave in ways that are socially acceptable, even in private?" The learning model they evolved to answer this question — social-learning theory — emphasizes two simple mechanisms: *conditioning* and the *observation of models*.

Conditioning, a la Bandura, is essentially Skinner's reinforcement-of-behavior concept but with a strong emphasis on interpersonal attention, approval and affection as powerful reinforcers. As children, we learn to repeat behavior that gains parental approval, and we learn to avoid actions that bring withdrawal of affection and/or punishment and disapproval. The approval and disapproval of others remain powerful rewards and punishments throughout our lives.

The social-learning approach recognizes the importance of internal events, such as thoughts and memories, on the control of our behavior but insists that all behavior is at least indirectly controlled by external cues. As we become adults, we learn to reward and punish ourselves "internally" in imitation of previously encountered "external" reward and punishment. Once we've been burned by a hot stove, chances are slim that we'll touch one again, regardless of "social" pressures.

Modeling or observational learning is the way we learn from others' experiences. It takes place in two steps: acquisition and performance. In the first step, we see others act, and we *acquire* a mental picture of the act and its consequences. After the mental image is acquired, we *perform* or try out the act ourselves. This is, of course, where conditioning principles come into play. If we find the consequences of imitating the model rewarding, we're likely to act that way again.

Obviously, you and I don't imitate and try out every behavior we see others engaged in. In fact, adults seem to apply quite a few restrictions to whom and what they will parrot. We are most likely to try out a new behavior if we see someone prestigious, powerful and competent doing it. (How many of us, for instance, dusted off our old tennis racket and ambled onto the court because a significant role model — some personal idol or strong influence — encouraged us through example?)

But our expectations and experiences with reward and punishment in similar situations also mediate the chances that we'll try the modeled behavior. A five-foot-five, 35-year-old male watching Bill Walton play a magnificent game of basketball may not be encouraged by the example to play a little one-on-one. But a five-foot-five, 15-year-old female might be.

A growing number of trainers are learning that the social-learning-theory approach leads to a radically different framework for designing training, one that is particularly useful to those who train others to do complex motor-skill tasks and those who train others in interpersonal communication tasks. The use of modeling in the technical-training context has long been recognized. Anyone who has tried to write or even read repair instructions for anything more complex than a rubber band appreciates modeling and learning by imitation. In technical training, the score has always been: talk about it = 0; see diagrams of it = 10; watch someone do it = 1,000.

The big news now is that interpersonal skills, such as those needed to sell or conduct effective performance reviews, can be effectively taught and learned using modeling and social reinforcement. Trainers at IBM, General Electric, AT&T, Levitz Furniture, and others are finding that supervisory, sales, and customer-relations skills are learned faster and more effectively when taught from a modeling base.

Bandura suggests that the social-learning theory is a successful training design tool because it mirrors critical features of the real world in the training experience. In fact, Dr. Bandura bluntly downgrades the efficiency of learning from textbooks and lectures, and from word descriptions of things learnable from direct example.

The marked discrepancy between textbook and social reality is largely attributable to the fact that certain critical conditions present in natural situations are rarely, if ever, reproduced in laboratory studies of learning. In laboratory investigations, experimenters arrange comparatively benign environments in which errors do not create fatal consequences for the organism. By contrast, natural environments are loaded with potentially lethal consequences for those unfortunate enough to perform hazardous errors. For this reason, it would be exceedingly injudicious to rely on differential reinforcement of trial-and-error performances in teaching children to swim, adolescents to drive automobiles, medical students to conduct surgical operations, or adults to develop complex occupational and social competencies.

There are several reasons why modeling influences are heavily favored in promoting everyday learning. Under circumstances in which mistakes are costly or dangerous, skillful performances can be established without needless errors by providing competent models who demonstrate the required activities. Some complex behaviors can be produced solely through the influence of models. If children had no opportunity to hear speech, it would be virtually impossible to teach them the linguistic skills that constitute a language. When desired forms of behavior can be conveyed only by social cues, modeling is an indispensable aspect of learning. Even in instances where it is possible to establish new response patterns through other means, the process of acquisition can be considerably shortened by providing appropriate models.*

Dr. William C. Byham, president of Development Dimensions International, a Pittsburgh, PA-based training company that uses behavior modeling in its program designs, suggests, "Modeling is the way we've all learned from day one. Our whole developmental history is one of modeling the behavior of others. Look, I talk to a lot of successful managers and quiz them about their success. To a person, they claim that the most important experience in their career was working for an exceptional manager at some time — usually early — in their career. They seem to be saying they had a manager who was a good model and mentor. Unfortunately, that's an experience most of us won't have. And that's why I'm so high on giving people good models to learn from instead of textbooks and lectures."

In short, then, social-learning theory and research strongly suggest that, when conditions are right, a trainee can learn rapidly and effectively from exposure to a model performing the desired behavior.

---

*Albert Bandura, *Psychological Modeling* (New York: Lieber-Atherton, Inc., 1971).

Applying Modeling and Social Learning to Training

The first interpersonal-skills training using behavior-modeling techniques in industry was conducted in 1970 at General Electric by Mel Sorcher. The objective of this first course was to reduce the turnover of hard-core employees by helping them adapt to and cope with a job in industry. Both hard-core employees and their first-line supervisors were trained in taking and giving constructive criticism, asking for and giving help, and establishing mutual trust and respect. The actual training was light on human-relations theory and attitude messages and long on visual examples — films of people doing good interpersonal relating — and role play. Basically, the training was exceptionally successful.

Simply exposing trainees to film and video images of people doing things isn't "modeling."

Six months after the original training, 72% of the 39 hard-core employees who had been trained and who worked for supervisors who had been trained remained on the job. Only 28% of the 25 hard-core employees who had not been trained and who worked for untrained supervisors did not leave. More important, Goldstein and Sorcher synthesized the important elements of the modeling-training approach, and it has been used widely in the development of interpersonal skills ever since.

Question: So what's the big deal? Don't we, more or less, use modeling in all our training? Most of us show movies — that sounds like modeling — and most of us give live demonstrations. That, too, sounds like modeling. And lots of us use practice and role playing, and that sounds like social reinforcement. So why all the hubbul?

For starters, simply exposing trainees to film and video images of people doing things isn't modeling. A recent stopwatch study of 15 commercial training films revealed that, out of 420 minutes of film, the largest block of time (235 minutes or 56%) was

devoted to explaining the skills. Twenty-two percent or 92 minutes were titles and transitions, 13% or 55 minutes showed people doing the skill *incorrectly*, and only 9% or 38 minutes showed people doing the skill correctly or modeling the behavior. That is an average of 2.6 minutes of correct-skill demonstration per film. Producers of training films would not be surprised at these numbers since they conceptualize their job as dramatizing and communicating an idea rather than providing a source of skill models.

The moral is that simply putting your message on film doesn't qualify the product as a source of behavior modeling experience. Even showing trainees a film or videotape composed solely of examples of people doing the behavior or demonstrating the skill correctly isn't a learning shoo-in. By analogy, you and I can go to a tennis tournament, watch Connors and Evert play perfect tennis and not learn anything new about the game. *Unless* we attend with the conscious intent of "going to school" on Connors' footwork or Evert's backhand, we won't come away with any new backhand or footwork models.

In training based on modeling and social learning, care is given to facilitating three processes in the trainees:

• Attention — making sure the trainees attend to the pertinent aspects of the behavior being modeled;

• Retention — helping the trainees remember the original observation points in the form;

• Reinforcement and motivation — using practice and positive reinforcement to translate observational learning into skilled performance.

Development Dimensions' Byham suggests that these three processes are promoted by adhering to a specific sequence of events in the training:

1. *Overview.* The instructor discusses the objective and importance of the skill module.

2. *Critical steps.* The instructor describes the specific behavior or critical steps of the activity to be learned.

3. *Positive model.* A film or videotape shows an individual effectively utilizing the skill.

4. *Critique of the film.* The instructor and participants discuss the things done correctly in the film, with particular emphasis on how the model utilized the critical steps.

5. *Skill practice.* Trainees practice the skills in pairs, with one trainee act-

ing the supervisor, salesperson or whatever and the second acting the employee, buyer and so forth. At least one other trainee observes the practice, using a prepared guide.

6. *Skill practice feedback.* After the practice session, the trainee receives feedback from observers and the instructor that emphasizes things done correctly. Where the behavior could have been more effective, alternative positive behaviors are suggested.

7. *Transfer.* Participants write out, practice, and receive feedback on situations they will face back on the job.

Byham also passes along the following tips and tricks for those who contemplate building a program around modeling concepts.

• Do a good needs analysis. Solving the wrong problem is *still* the trainer's number-one pitfall.

• Determine the specific situations where the new behavior is expected to manifest itself.

• Determine the minimum critical steps of the activity or skill to be mastered; don't complicate matters by listing too many critical steps.

• Spend up to 50% of the training time on the trainees' on-job problems. (Development Dimensions courses typically devote 10 minutes to viewing the filmed model in a three-hour training sequence.)

• Keep the feedback sessions positive. The goal is to create a series of success experiences for the trainees.

• Develop the training group into a mutual support group.

• Don't expect a one-shot training program to yield a big behavior change. Work on one skill at a time over a period of weeks. Give trainees time and space to try out the new behaviors and come back for consultation with the rest of the group and the instructor.

Research on the effectiveness of behavior modeling in clinical and school settings is persuasive. Most assertiveness training is done through modeling, and has an impressive composite track record. But how effective is the approach in our world, the normal adult learning context? There is an equally impressive accumulation of studies that say the approach is effective in business and industry.

We have already mentioned Sorcher's work and the book based on his and Goldstein's successes. Robert F. Burnaska, also of GE, reports that a course developed to improve the interpersonal skills of the managers of professional employees was equally successful. A one-month follow-up comparison of 62 trained and 62 untrained middle managers showed that trained managers were better at *performance problem discussion, work assignment discussion,* and *giving recognition to an average employee* than were the untrained managers. In addition, a five-month follow-up found trained managers even better than they were at the one-month follow-up.

At AT&T, Joseph L. Moses and Richard J. Ritchie developed a behavior-modeling-oriented supervisory-relationships training program following the Goldstein and Sorcher model and evaluated the results, using an assessment-center approach. A team of specially trained individuals observed and evaluated 90 trained and 93 untrained first-level supervisors performing a variety of simulation exercises. Two months after the program, both groups were given cases of excessive absence, an alleged discrimination complaint, and a case of suspected theft. In all simulated sit-

uations, the trained group utilized "appropriate skills" and handled the situations significantly better than did the untrained group.

Preston E. Smith of IBM office products division reports that modeling training of *meeting effectiveness skills, discussing opinions survey results,* and *customer complaint handling* has paid off handsomely for his organization. Trained managers were rated higher on employee opinion surveys after training than before. In addition, customer-satisfaction ratings and sales-quota results were higher for branches managed by trained managers.

Lest we seem about to leap too quickly onto the behavior-modeling bandwagon, let's review three facts about the technique. First, the behavior-modeling approach comes from a learning model — social-learning theory — that has an impressive set of credentials. Second, a number of trainers are finding that the application of modeling principles is further reducing their dependence on the "spray and pray" approach to training. Third, good, solid evaluations are verifying the effectiveness.

But, as the folks at "Ma Bell" remind us, "The system is the solution." And no new training program or technique can overcome bad products, poor market positioning, or a management team that fights change. With this in mind, we should avoid setting expectations for behavior modeling that it can't fulfill. But we also should be glad we have an innovation, a new tool, that helps us perform better professionally. Who knows what will happen if we begin to model the professionalism we profess?

BEHAVIORAL OBJECTIVES

Writing Behavioral Objectives

BY RON ZEMKE

In 1962 Robert F. Mager wrote a brief little book titled *Preparing Objectives for Programmed Instruction.* It was based on his research into the common characteristics of that new and daring training tool, programmed instruction. What he found was devastatingly simple. The best programs made a point of telling both trainee and trainer:

• what the learner should be able to *do* at the end of training,

• under what conditions,

• and to what degree of success.

He called these statements of desired learning outcomes "behavioral objectives." He renamed them "performance objectives" in a later edition of the book, which was also rechristened as *Preparing Instructional Objectives.*

As simple as "good" objectives look, they can be mighty slippery to construct. It's easy to write mush-mouthed objectives that really don't describe something measurable. For instance, "The student will acquire a developing awareness of the place of the earth in the scope of the universe" is pretty mushy. It's also easy to slide into the error of specifying behaviors instead of outcomes; of confusing ends and means. "The trainee will be able to utilize a 42Q6 weld tester to determine the acceptability of student welds" looks like an instructional objective, but is really just a partial specification of a task or sub-objective. It is not a statement of a desired learning goal or performance outcome.

But objectives do more than just tell us what to measure and how. They are the anvil upon which we shape and hone media and method selections, test learning sequences, exercises and ideas. If you can't write measurable objectives to guide the instructional development process, you haven't finished analyzing the tasks you want learned.

Results-focused instructional objectives do one other thing: They make distinct some key differences between training, education and development.

Key to the difference is the specificity of what the learning is for and the immediacy of the pay-back to the organization. Development is a long-term investment. It is a set of activities aimed at giving an employee a series of experiences that enhance, in a more or less general way, the long-term value of the individual to the organization. "Education" implies a shorter-term investment, but it is still quite general. Call education a set of activities aimed at developing the overall competence of the person as a person, and concerned with behavior off the job as well as on the job.

Training, on the other hand, is charged with preparing people to do specific jobs to necessary standards, changing the unskilled to skilled, the unknowing to knowledgeable, the ineffective to effective. Trainers help their trainees exchange old skills for new. Trainers make the highly technical highly learnable. Trainers help people crack the very specific codes of doing a very specific job in order to make a very specific living.

This conceptualization of training makes it a very "accountable" function. While many educators can and often do claim exemption from requirements that they produce measurable results on grounds that the real outcome of their work is not immediately amenable to measurement, the trainer must welcome and relish the measurement process. Measurement against objectives tells the trainer if the learning lasts beyond the training experience. And measurements of the ultimate results — changes in actual job performance — tell the trainer whether or not the whole process was on target.

BEHAVIORAL OBJECTIVES

The Whens, Whys and Hows of Behavioral Objectives

BY JAMES M. LEWIS

Behavioral objectives mostly live on action verbs. Only action verbs which specifically mention the overt behavior of the respondent at the end of instruction in concrete, measurable terms contain high nutritive value for learning. Other verbs are junk food. Thus, *turn, twist* and *kick* are good action verbs; *think, feel* and *reflect* are not. There are verbs in the English language rich in meaning, richer in action. Just as they carry a message to a reader, they can also function effectively in an instructional and training environment.

But what of behavioral objectives themselves? What can they be expected to do and not do? When are they appropriate or inappropriate? What alternatives are available, and when should they be considered? Here's an action verb review of what various researchers have discovered about effective use of behavioral objectives which may help you in planning, designing, delivering and evaluating training.

What To Expect From Behavioral Objectives

★ **REJECT** all high hopes that behavioral objectives alone will improve performance in cognitive or psychomotor areas. There is not enough evidence to justify those claims. In fact, of 84 studies, 40 find behavioral objectives have a significant effect on achievement, but 44 studies do not. Similarly, of six studies which have dealt with psychomotor areas, two note a significant treatment effect of objectives while the other four do not.

☆ **ANTICIPATE** strong support for behavioral objectives from trainees in the affective area. Eleven of 17 studies reviewed suggest a significant improvement in student attitudes toward behavioral objectives.

★ **DISREGARD** claims that specific behavioral objectives facilitate greater performance than general objectives. Of 13 studies reviewed, only three report specific objectives lead to significant learner achievement; 10 studies report no significant effect from specific compared to general objectives.

> ☆ **EFFECTIVE**
> ★ **INEFFECTIVE**

☆ **ACCEPT** the limitations of behavioral objectives. Empirical studies seem to indicate that behavioral objectives do not increase incidental learning (not related to objectives) and retention. Of nine studies which have attempted to measure this impact, only three have found a significant effect. Again, of 13 studies measuring the effect of behavioral objectives on retention, four cite a significant increase, but nine do not.

In addition, some evidence in the literature suggests behavioral objectives are *not* helpful in certain cognitive skills and operations. First, Merrill (1970) and Yelon and Schmidt (1972) report behavioral objectives do not increase reasoning ability. Second, Hartley and Davies (1976) indicate behavioral objectives are not useful in learning tasks calling for knowledge and comprehension. Third, Olsen

(1971) says behavioral objectives do not influence generalization of principles and concepts. Fourth, while Hartley and Davies observe that behavioral objectives are useful in higher level learning tasks calling for analysis, synthesis and evaluation, Zeman (1978) does not find behavioral objectives significantly useful in those same cognitive operations.

☆ **OVERCOME** certain myths associated with behavioral objectives. For example, do behavioral objectives in exact sciences yield better results than in humanities? It is easy to construct objectives in exact sciences. They do not, however, show a greater effect in sciences than in humanities. In fact, better results have been observed in courses such as English poetry, reading and education than in biology, economics, math and physics. A second myth is that, in an individualized setting, older learners — college and above — will derive more benefit than younger students from behavioral objectives. The literature indicates academic age is immaterial.

☆ **WELCOME** the additional advantages of behavioral objectives. Koch (1972) finds that using behavioral objectives improves the confidence of learners in their subject matter. Merrill and Towle (1972) report behavioral objectives reduce anxiety.

★ **REFRAIN** from hoping that by using behavioral objectives you will perform well in every aspect of training. While there is evidence to suggest behavioral objectives lead to better lesson plans, there is no evidence to suggest that objectives will automatically improve personal poise and personality, the sequencing and presentation of instructional units, or the application of basic principles of learning.

Using Behavioral Objectives In Instructional Planning

☆ **INVESTIGATE** pre-existing subject knowledge, since it can he critical in learning with behavioral objectives. Obreiter (1978) says behavioral objectives are more influential with students who have previous subject matter experience than those without it. Varano (1977) reports IQ and previous knowledge of subject matter both influence achievement and retention with behavioral objectives.

☆ **FIND OUT** what learners consider important in a text. Research indicates that judged importance of a text element determines whether objectives will facilitate learning or not. According to Duell (1974) and Melton (1978), if a learner judges an element to be important, it will be learned whether or not it is related to an objective. Objectives in those circumstances may be unnecessary, but provide them if learners consider elements of a text unimportant.

☆ **ADOPT** behavioral objectives techniques if relevant information — needed by the objectives — is given to the students. Seven studies out of nine show that students informed of behavioral objectives (with relevant information) progress through an instructional unit in less time than those not informed of objectives.

☆ **EMPLOY** behavioral objectives in an individualized learning situation. Ritter (1975) says self-paced learners complete courses faster than their instructor-paced counterparts when both use behavioral objectives.

★ **RESIST** the temptation to see grade point averages or aptitude measures as significant factors in performance while using behavioral objectives. Taylor (1976) indicates grade point averages do not influence such performance, while Baker (1976) says learner aptitudes are ineffective for predicting cognitive achievement with behavioral objectives.

★ **STOP** worrying that high academic qualifications or extensive teaching experience are needed to write behavioral objectives. Studies do not indicate that those with higher credentials or broader experience know more about behavioral objectives or express a more positive attitude toward them.

★ **FORGET** about instructors' personality types while accepting and interpreting the meaning of behavioral objectives. Smith (1970) and Hogen (1977) find no relation-ship between personality types and preference and interpretation of behavioral objectives in actual practice.

☆ **PARTICIPATE** in the decision-making process to use behavioral objectives. If there are staff meetings where behavioral objectives are discussed, your active participation may help you win approval to use them. Stahl (1972) maintains the greater an individual's participation in such a process, the greater the chances of using behavioral objectives.

Using Behavioral Objectives In Instructional Design

☆ **DETERMINE** reader comprehension ability. If reading ability is high, behavioral objectives may be less effective — students who can comprehend better perform better anyway. Rashkoff (1976) says entry-level high reading comprehension is more effective when learning with behavioral objectives than low-level comprehension, but Petty (1974) reports learners in the upper quartile who are given behavioral objectives do not perform better than those in the same quartile not given objectives. In fact, Keyser (1976) shows that individuals with higher reading ability learn more when *no* behavioral objectives are involved.

☆ **WATCH** the difficulty level of the objectives and the text material. According to Brown (1970), the difficulty level of the objectives influences performance. Keyser (1976) demonstrates that performance objectives are more effective with difficult text than with easy material.

☆ **INVESTIGATE** characteristics which may make objectives redundant in a text. For instance, Duchastel (1979) finds the structure of the text can be as effective as behavioral objectives. Structure, by itself, can orient learning; if the text

is well structured, behavioral objectives do not add much effect.

☆ **FURNISH** operational definitions of verbs used in objectives. Zeigler (1974) says definitions plus information on the utilization and importance of the objectives appear to aid achievement.

★ **REFRAIN** from giving details — terminal behaviors, conditions of occurrences, criterion of minimal performance — for each behavioral objective. Janeczko (1971) and Lovett (1971) demonstrate that increasing the knowledge of behavioral objectives does not increase achievement.

★ **AVOID** listing highly specific behavioral objectives instead of general objectives, especially at the beginning of a text. Thinly chopped behavioral objectives are not a written guarantee for performance. General objectives can do the job equally well. In fact, among the 13 studies reviewed, only three note a significant treatment effect from giving specific objectives.

★ **ELIMINATE** giving only partial presentations of objectives prior to instruction. According to Bastress (1971) and Shields (1973), partial presentation of objectives is less effective than a full presentation at the beginning of instruction.

☆ **PROVIDE** an adequate number of behavioral objectives based on the density of the text. Providing too many objectives for a simple task or too few for many tasks should be avoided. There appears to be a relationship between the number of specific objectives to be listed and the density of relevant information in the text. Rothkopf and Kaplan (1972, 1974) report an increase in the density of instructional objectives decreases the probability that an instructional task will be learned. They add that the probability of achieving any given objective decreases as the number of objective-relevant sentences in a text and the number of specific objectives increases.

☆ **DISTRIBUTE** behavioral objectives among the text segments instead of presenting all objectives prior to the text. Games, Johnson and Klare (1967), Kaplan (1974), and Yelon and Schmidt (1972) all point out that such a practice results in greater learning.

☆ **USE** other techniques, such as pretests, directions, questions and advance organizers to support or to provide variety in instructional text. Empirical studies show that, compared with these preinstructional techniques, behavioral objectives are not significantly more effective. Papay (1971), Song (1975), Stalians (1978) and Varano (1977) agree on this point.

☆ **OFFER** specific behavioral objectives at the end of a unit rather than at the beginning. Frase (1968), Keyser (1976) and Rothkopf (1966) say post-behavioral objectives are more effective than pre-behavioral objectives. In addition, such a use of objectives increases incidental learning — learning not related to the objectives.

Using Behavioral Objectives As You Train

☆ **USE** behavioral objectives as guides to your training. Use them in your lesson plans. They may help you concentrate on the relevant elements of the unit and thus facilitate learning. In addition, when you use behavioral objectives you will be cognizant of the expected learner behavior: the relationship between objectives and the concept or skill to be learned.

☆ **INSIST** on learners reading behavioral objectives. According to Engel (1968), assuring that learners read behavioral objectives is a critical factor in objectives-related learning.

☆ **WORK** on the reading ability of students — the ability to focus on items of information required by objectives. Jones (1974) and Stalians (1978) indicate that ability to concentrate on items of information required by objectives influences achievement with behavioral objectives.

☆ **COMMUNICATE** specific objectives to subjects. Such verbal contact with learners may facilitate more objectives-related (intentional) learning. Studies done by Dalis (1970), Rothkopf and Kaplan (1972), and Wingard (1976) show such a practice pays rich dividends.

☆ **PRESENT** objectives during instruction. Kaplan (1974, 1976) finds that exposing objectives during instruction improves objectives-related learning, as well as increasing overt response. And repeat objectives two or three times during instruction. Such a drill may help learners master relevant items. Yelon and Schmidt (1972) show that presenting objectives twice during instruction improves their effect.

★ **AVOID** training people how to use behavioral objectives. Brown (1970), Lawrence (1972), Morse and Tillman (1972), and Sink (1973) find that learners trained in the use of behavioral objectives do not perform significantly better than those not trained. Secondly, avoid asking learners' opinions about whether the objectives are related to the course or not.

☆ **RECOGNIZE** learner personality characteristics while using behavioral objectives. According to Kueter (1970), objectives are less effective with submissive, self-controlled, considerate and conscientious students. Kelly (1972) observes that personality variables (introvert vs. extrovert, stable vs. unstable) influence performance with behavioral objectives.

☆ **USE** other techniques, such as questions and feedback, to support or provide variety. Compared with behavioral objectives, such techniques are proven to be equally effective, if not better. Basset (1973) and Viel (1975) find that providing feedback is as effective as providing objectives. Papay (1971) indicates objectives are less effective than questions.

☆ **TRAIN** learners to take sample test items rather than letting them read a list of behavioral objectives. Such training may reduce test anxiety among learners and may even aid recall of relevant elements. Derr (1978) says students learning through sample test items will be more effective on cognitive posttests than those learning through behavioral objectives.

The Limits of Benchmarking

BY MARC HEQUET

How can you possibly go wrong modeling yourself after the best? Well, you can. The practice of benchmarking had scarcely taken its place in the pantheon of sacred quality techniques when heresy flared: Measuring yourself against world-class companies doesn't always help.

Benchmarkers are still pondering that ominous news from the "Best Practices Report," an international study of 580 service and manufacturing businesses published last October by Ernst & Young and the American Quality Foundation.

Among the study's findings: Benchmarking against world-class performers is demonstrably helpful only to top-performing companies, defined in the study as those with a return on assets (ROA) higher than 6.9 percent. Medium performers show "no compelling positive impact." Low performers, with an ROA below 2 percent, actually show negative results from benchmarking their marketing and sales systems.

How can this be? The study suggests that low performers don't have the quality infrastructure ready to support the organizationwide change necessary to emulate the best. Instead, low-performing companies should focus on nurturing cross-functional teams; training and empowering workers, especially those who deal directly with customers; and on getting better at what they already do.

What, no benchmarking? "Benchmarking is commonly understood as imitating the best," says Josh Hammond, president of the American Quality Foundation (AQF). "Another definition is seeing who does a process better and imitating them. Our report says you should benchmark within your reach."

Some quality managers say they knew that all along. "You don't take plays out of the San Francisco 49ers' playbook if you are a high school team that hasn't learned how to block and tackle," says AQF director Dana Cound, vice president and quality manager with GenCorp, an automotive supplier in Akron, OH. "You focus on fundamentals. You focus on plays you can execute. That's consistent with my experience and observations in the workplace."

Other benchmarking advocates, however, are unconvinced. "I'm puzzled," muses Linda DeBerry, managing director of human resource development with Federal Express, a top performer in customer satisfaction. "Benchmarking means continuing improvement toward world-class practices, trying to identify gaps in your process and then ramping those up. Why wouldn't it be helpful to do that?"

Also unpersuaded by the findings is John Early, research and development vice president with the Juran Institute Inc. of Wilton, CT, a quality consulting firm. "If you're going to go to the trouble to benchmark," says Early, "do it against people who do it well."

The Boom

Benchmarking compares how your company does something to how others do it. Compare widely enough and you'll find who does what best. Measure the activity carefully enough and you'll know how far you have to go to beat the best. And, not least important, ask the right questions of benchmarking partners and you'll get a pretty fair idea of *how* to beat the best.

The modern benchmarking boom dates to 1979, when Xerox Corp. found that competitor Canon's new midsize photocopier sold for what it cost Xerox to *make* such a machine. Unnerved, the American company scurried to adopt a series of Japanese techniques that helped it reduce unit production costs.

In 1980, engineers at then-beleaguered Ford Motor Co. trucked in 50 midsize autos from competitors around the world and dismantled them part by part. Ford found 400 "best-in-class" features in those cars, and designed 80 percent of them into the well-received Taurus and Sable models introduced in 1985.

Since then, business has gone bonkers for benchmarking. A key contributing factor is the Malcolm Baldrige National Quality Award, first offered in 1988, which features benchmarking in its criteria. Relatively few companies actually enter the Baldrige competition — only 90 in 1992. But the U.S. Department of Commerce has distributed 650,000 copies of benchmarking-loaded Baldrige criteria since 1988. Companies use the criteria as a foundation for their quality efforts.

The International Benchmarking Clearinghouse, founded in February 1992 by the American Productivity and Quality Center in Houston, had 128 member organizations by late 1992 and was growing by about 10 more per month. The clearinghouse provides networking services for benchmarkers, giving companies a way to contact other companies that want to benchmark. It also offers information services, with a library and eight specialists who can track down top performers in various categories as specific as, say, reduced corporate travel costs. And it provides training, publications and benchmarking services — for example, it helps companies study their own business processes in preparation for benchmarking against others.

Early on, the Benchmarking Clearinghouse received 300 calls a week from people wanting information. It has mailed out 100,000 pieces of information, and says its ad in *Fortune* magazine in September drew the greatest response ever for a *Fortune* ad, more than 900 requests for information.

The benchmarking boom has prompted unprecedented levels of information sharing among once tight-lipped companies, including competitors. Particularly when they are in the chase for the Baldrige, companies have gone the distance from coy to candid. "They've opened the kimono far wider than anyone thought they would," quips Marion Steeples, president of Resources for Quality Inc. in Denver and a Baldrige examiner since 1988.

World-class performers are swamped with requests for benchmarking. L.L. Bean, the Freeport, ME-based cataloger admired for its customer satisfaction levels, logistics and distribution systems, gets 10 benchmarking-related inquiries a day, although it hosted only 35 visits in 1991. Federal Express' DeBerry says one aerospace company benchmarker got huffy when she wouldn't provide him with two days of her time. "I said I wanted him to limit his focus," sighs DeBerry. "Instead of two days of my time, he sent me eight pages of questions."

Trouble Is . . .

Surely those benchmarking hordes can't be misinformed. Why shouldn't the tactic be uniformly beneficial?

A key reason is that benchmarking is only one element in the quality picture. If you're out there comparing yourself against the best but haven't prepared the ground back home to make serious changes, benchmarking is probably a waste of time.

What does an organization need to do before it launches into a benchmarking frenzy?

• Swallowing your pride is a good first step. "Top management has got to acknowledge that they're not the best, at least not in everything they want to be," says Early of the Juran Institute. "Top management has to be prepared to learn from others and prepared to make changes and to learn about supporting people as they make those changes — and not shoot the messenger when someone comes back and says, 'Our stuff stinks.'"

• A company working up to benchmarking must also be ready for major transformations. Benchmarking may uncover needs for changes in reporting relationships, for revamping compensation, for corporate reorganization, even for peeling away whole management layers.

• To rise to performance goals uncovered in comparisons with other companies, an organization must be prepared to train its workers in how to work smarter to meet those challenges. Otherwise, the result could be a corporate headache. "An increase in motivation but no increase in means

to achieve — that's called butting your head against the wall," says Carla O'Dell, director of the International Benchmarking Clearinghouse.

• Get cross-functional. Suppose benchmarking uncovers a top performer that ships orders the same day they are received. Simply plastering that promise atop your own otherwise unchanged shipping operation is a recipe for disaster. Can the warehouse support such a promise? How about transportation? Finance?

• Then there's the grunt work. Benchmarking is an arduous process that often involves precise measurement and comparison of narrowly

---

"An increase in motivation but no increase in means to achieve — that's called butting your head against the wall."

---

defined activities. It means learning intimate details about your own organization, its functions, its processes, its end results. Last year a manufacturer came to benchmark with Federal Express but wouldn't share information FedEx asked for, violating one of the givens of benchmarking etiquette. Eventually, Federal Express figured out why: The visitors didn't know the answers about their own company.

Information gathered about your own organization can be so instructive that you may decide to put off benchmarking against other companies until you have made some changes. A previously undetected bottleneck in materials flow, for example, may stick out like a sore thumb. Once you've taken care of it, you can get back to benchmarking.

• Manage the scope. Your initial idea of what to study probably will be too ambitious. "Saying you want to benchmark the distribution process is like saying you want to benchmark world hunger," says O'Dell. "It will take you forever. But if you want to benchmark order entry because that looks like where some big gains are for you, that is a little more handleable." Figure out what specific pieces of information you want to compare company-to-company.

• Then go to a good business

library, or a good consultant, and find companies that are skilled at doing what you want to do.

Boo-Boos

Benchmarking boo-boos are great fun — as long as they happen to someone else.

Take the example of the left hand not having a clue what the right hand is up to. One team from a computer peripherals company eagerly went a-benchmarking — and found to its embarrassment that three other teams from its own company were doing a site visit at the same benchmarking partner, on the same day, all unbeknownst to one another. "It annoyed the heck out of the target company," says O'Dell.

An example of benchmarking too broadly: A company sought to have its customer service organization answer the phone in so many rings. It benchmarked around, found out who answered calls fastest, and set three rings as a target for its own customer service people. Result: Failure. Why? The benchmarkers analyzed only the top measures. Yes, the best performers in the target company answered the phone in three rings, and the average call took 30 seconds to handle. But the benchmarkers didn't look below the surface. They didn't break out calls by time of day, by how many workers were answering, by how much time each worker spent answering phones vs. working on other tasks. The moral: A little knowledge is dangerous. Go deeply into detail when you're getting a grip on somebody else's process.

And then there's the oh-why-bother syndrome. Benchmarkers from an electronics business brought back the news that others in the industry developed new products in half the time it took their own company. Outcome: Instead of buckling down to telescope cycle time, the laggard company decided to drop its slow-cycling lines — which, says O'Dell, turned out to be a lousy business decision.

Training

Benchmarking only works in an enlightened environment. That's where training comes in. First benchmarkers must be trained in matters such as process analysis, conducting effective interviews and constructing good questionnaires. Then every affected person in the organization must be given the quality training vital to putting benchmark-derived changes in place.

Match your undertrained workers against those in a world-class company, and your attempts to imitate the paragon's processes are almost bound to look clownish. But educate your workers first — about the meaning of benchmarking, about its role in a total quality workplace — and they are likely to compare more favorably.

This kind of training is a long-term proposition. "It's not usually a Friday morning exercise," says consultant Early. "If you're benchmarking how to open and sort mail, it can be a fairly short exercise. But if you're benchmarking product development, it's long and complicated. Often with people on the best benchmarking teams, while [benchmarking is] not their full-time job, it's a big piece of their job."

Count on several weeks to several months for each benchmarking cycle, with training-as-you-go. "The training isn't rocket science," says Early, "but it's different than most people are used to doing."

And when one cycle is complete, count on starting another, and another, in perpetuity. Benchmarkers are aiming at a moving target.

Learning From the Second-Best?

Should medium- and low-performing companies forget entirely about benchmarking, as the Ernst & Young-AQF study seems to suggest? Not necessarily.

But if you don't benchmark with the best, whom do you use as a target? Do you call up a few companies and say, "Look, we really stink, but you're only mediocre. Can we talk?"

OK, don't do that. Greg Lea, director of market-driven quality for the application business systems line at IBM's Rochester, MN, location, a 1990 Baldrige winner, says he agrees with the study's finding that low-performing companies tend to get overwhelmed when they try to benchmark against the best. He does not conclude, however, that low performers ought to give up benchmarking entirely.

IBM Rochester hosts companies that view, for example, its sophisticated customer satisfaction management process and go away stunned, not knowing where to start.

What does IBM tell them? "Start small," says Lea. "Take some one subprocess that we do and implement

that. Start with a customer survey or an 800 number."

And, he says, companies that are low performers overall may still be excellent in some areas, and could benchmark against world-class performers in those areas. It's not unusual, says Lea, for a company to be very good at something and not realize it.

In a sense, in fact, benchmarking actually may be easier for low-performing companies than for world-class ones. High performers must go far afield to find somebody from whom they can still learn something. A low performer may not even need to go outside its own plant.

Internal benchmarking can be very useful for companies of any caliber. DeBerry says Federal Express has benchmarked its process for tracking training enrollments against its own internal billing process.

Formal, precisely measured benchmarking has its uses. But less formal, less metric benchmarking can work as well. An example of a benchmarked

---

"Look, we really stink, but you're only mediocre. Can we talk?"

---

idea that spread throughout automotive supplier GenCorp: Let plant floor workers, not engineers, write job instructions. Engineers often have trouble communicating in the parlance of the plant floor. GenCorp finds that the workers write better instructions because they write in plain language.

AT&T Universal Card Services (UCS), a 1992 Baldrige winner, benchmarked in three phases — and some don't exactly resemble classic benchmarking. First, the company hired managers from the credit-card industry who already possessed considerable expertise. "They brought with them quite a bit of knowledge, and we put our business together [by drawing upon that expertise]," says Rob Davis, vice president and chief quality officer. "We decided that kind of benchmarking, if you will, was enough to take us through two years."

AT&T UCS also did more formal benchmarking, entering a few carefully chosen partnerships to study particular needs, including heightening

awareness of corporate values. This is an area that doesn't particularly lend itself to metrics. UCS went to Walt Disney Co. to learn how that world-class performer instilled its corporate culture in employees. Among the lessons: Disney begins building in corporate culture from the time prospective workers interview. Among the translated practices back at UCS: "When somebody comes to work, before we tell them about insurance and other benefits, we tell them about what's important to the business [in terms of] our philosophy and our values," says Davis.

Indeed, getting beyond the measurements can be an important step for a benchmarker. Says Davis: "I know how quickly I deliver a piece of plastic to a new customer and I know how quickly a competitor does that. That's a hard fact. The tougher piece is process. What I'm really after is something to help me deliver that result."

But beware of idea stealing. Pilfering a process and patching it onto your organization is a tactic likely to blow up in your face.

This is due to the paramount need for a clear understanding of the process in question. Consider three practices you discover at a target company, only one of which has a direct bearing on the bottom line. So you transplant only that single practice to your company, right? But what if Practice A supports Practice B, which supports Practice C? Disregarding A and B will bring about the collapse of C, and there goes your bottom line.

When people go benchmarking and see cascade training — in which supervisors train their direct reports from the top of the company down — the visitors might think that's a great idea. But unless they have achieved a cultural transformation at their own company, unless their own company has come to value training and change, no doubt some die-hard middle managers will put up an umbrella in the cascade, and sections of the company will never get the training. Either that, or the message may become so garbled that it's useless by the time it gets to the plant floor.

When you see what looks like a good idea to copy, listen to all the relevant information. At one AT&T UCS benchmarking partner, workers first said they loved their four-day workweek. But they also loved the family atmosphere, a park close to the office, job security and other factors. An overeager benchmarker who listened only to the part about the four-day workweek and tried to impose that without supporting factors might have set off an employee rebellion.

Another consideration: Benchmarking can be a complex relationship. One partner — or both — may have a hidden agenda. The quality vice president for a medical products manufacturer once visited a world-class company to study its processes for employee involvement and empowerment. He soon realized that the world-class performer was looking for more than a benchmarking partner — it wanted to sell to the medical products manufacturer and its corporate parent. Was the quality VP miffed? Not at all. "I think it's an excellent business strategy," he says admiringly.

So, study or no study, get out there and benchmark. But don't do it for its own sake. Benchmark what's strategically important to your company. If your strategy is to go to electronic billing eventually, don't benchmark your paper billing process to find out how to make it more efficient, says IBM's Lea.

And be patient. "Not every benchmarking act will be successful," Lea says. "You will go to find something at a company touted as having a good process and when you get there find nothing of value. That happens a lot. You won't bat 1.000, but at least if you focus on the processes that are important to you, you're not wasting a lot of effort."

What's the most important lesson to draw from the E&Y-AQF study? "Companies have to start [from] where they are instead of where they want to be," summarizes GenCorp's Cound. "Benchmarking can pay off like gangbusters — I don't want to demean it. But it's not for everybody, not for every stage of growth and maturity."

Notes:

BRAINSTORMING

Guidelines for Generating Ideas

BY WILL LOREY

In the scramble to get everyone aboard the quality circle (QC) bandwagon, *brainstorming* is being recommended as a QC technique to use right now.

One of its appeals is simplicity. All that a brainstorming session requires is a group of people who have an active interest in the topic, and a stimulating leader. Brainstorming can be likened to a "bull session" in a relaxing atmosphere — but a bull session designed to generate ideas and inspire creativity. Frequently the end result of brainstorming is ideas that are truly ingenious, and one final idea that is implemented with everyone's commitment.

As used within organizations, brainstorming starts when a group of employees with similar work experience are asked if they would like to meet on company time for up to two hours to discuss some work-related issues. A conference room removed from the immediate work area is desirable, with the chairs arranged in a large semicircle or U-shape.

Depending on the size of the group, one or two people should take notes. In starting the session, the facilitator normally will:

1. Announce the time available for this meeting, and when and where the next meeting will be held.

2. State the problem area to be discussed in basic terms and ask the group to consider only one or two focal points.

3. Encourage each participant to set aside their logical, analytical and reasoning mind and to free up their spontaneous self.

4. Insist that no evaluative remarks, either those of a critical or humorous nature, be made about any ideas, and inform the group that no idea will be explored in-depth until later in the session.

5. Encourage ideas that build upon another idea since they frequently are most helpful.

6. Open the floor to ideas from any group member. The more ideas the better.

After about 30 to 40 minutes, the facilitator can stop the session for a short break. Upon its return, the group can either separate the ideas contributed into two categories such as "immediately useful" and "potentially useful," or it may list ideas in order of usefulness, dropping those that are impractical. It is at this stage that ideas can be "massaged" for possible implementation. But a note of caution. Care has to be taken not to forget that many "weird" ideas may have value for later use. We can utilize all ideas, those thought possible *or* impossible, by listing the ideas both downward and across flip-pad sheets thus creating an Idea Matrix. By looking at each idea in various combinations, you can probably produce still more ideas.

For a group new to brainstorming, many experts recommend a *trial* session using fun exercises like the following to loosen up the flow of ideas:

You are single, living alone. Just before you have to go to an important evening party, a small fire breaks out in your closet. While the damage is not extensive, all of your clothes are destroyed. The stores are closed, your neighbors gone. What would you do to be able to attend the party?

Another brainstorming technique, similar to that already discussed, uses the round-robin method. Between 10 and 15 employees, all from the same department, meet in a conference room or similar area removed from the work area. The facilitator makes sure employees know each other and then sets out some simple guidelines:

We will be here for about two hours.

There will be no interruptions.

Each of your bosses agreed not to call you out except in a real emergency.

I will act as monitor only to keep the group on track and to record your ideas on the chalkboard (flip pads).

At the outset no one should discuss or comment on anyone else's idea. If you do, I will have to stop you. Building on another suggestion or idea, however, is encouraged.

In about one hour we will take a short break and then come back and discuss each idea.

Starting with one member, the facilitator working around the group in round-robin fashion, asks for one idea on how *productivity* might be *measured* in the department. Starting with how to measure work has a twofold value in that it gets each member to start thinking about how standards of performance can be set, and it leads them to think of ways to improve/increase the work that they do.

At the end of this first session, the facilitator reviews all the ideas generated and combines similar ideas on one or two flip-pad sheets. Then the group members are asked individually to write down priority numbers for each idea now posted. After collecting that data, the facilitator develops a final ranking from the number of points assigned to each individual measurement. Now the facilitator can move on to generating new ideas on how to improve productivity or wait until another meeting.

In concluding this first attempt at brainstorming the facilitator must thank everyone for their ideas and their interest and stress that while all the ideas cannot be utilized, those that support department objectives will be evaluated for *immediate use.*

Still another variation is the Gordon Technique. In this method, the group attacks the underlying *concept* of the problem rather than the problem itself, and ideas are explored at length and examined from many perspectives — social, economic, financial and mechanical. For example, if an innovative sales approach is needed for a new product, the facilitator would introduce the subject of market shape.

Depending on how a session is

conducted, brainstorming can be extremely effective — or a complete waste of time. Even *Webster's New Collegiate Dictionary* (Springfield, MA, G.C. Merriam Co., 1974) is of two minds about brainstorming and lists it as (a) a sudden bright idea or (b) a harebrained idea. But perhaps Thomas Paine had the final thought when he stated: "The sublime and the ridiculous are often so nearly related, that it is difficult to class them separately. One step above the sublime makes the ridiculous, and one step above the ridiculous makes the sublime again." Brainstorming will produce ideas; it is our job to determine which are ridiculous and which are sublime.

Notes:

Making Case Studies Come Alive

BY PHILLIP H. OWENBY

The trouble with training is it's too serious. Too seriously presented, that is. And oftentimes "serious" means "boring." Ask some of the people who attended your company's last training program, and you'll discover an unfortunate truth: Many training programs that deal strictly with technical, job-related subjects *are* boring.

That need not be the case. Yes, training is a serious business — companies shouldn't waste their money and time if it isn't. But "serious" describes the purpose and the results of training, not necessarily the means trainers use to reach those ends.

You can grab and hold the attention of learners, even in a class on something as straightforward and pedestrian as statistical process control. And you don't have to use colorful visual aids, computer-based learning modules or other high-tech solutions to do it. Often, all you need to spice up training is a good case study.

What Makes A Good Case Study?

You probably think of a case study as a training activity that involves reading and analyzing a job-related situation to arrive at a course-sanctioned solution. So far, so good. Every trainer knows that involvement, problem solving and learning-by-doing are effective learning methods, and that case studies are a good way to give learners those experiences.

But not always.

It's true that *good* case studies do these things, but many case studies used in training don't qualify as good. That is, they aren't very interesting or stimulating.

You can write better case studies by following some of the principles used by successful writers. Consider Isaac Asimov. In addition to the science fiction stories that made him famous, he has written a raft of nonfiction books on scientific and technical subjects. Why is he so successful? Because he writes in a style that attracts and sustains the interest of even the technologically illiterate.

In his nonfiction books, Asimov often uses true stories to explain scientific developments — stories about real people and how they discovered the wonders he writes about. His stories also explain how scientific and technological advances affect the lives of people now and how they are likely to affect people in the future.

Asimov describes his subjects precisely and accurately, but his style is conversational. He knows how to explain technical subjects to people. The approach that works for him — human interest, clarity and simplicity — can also work for you when you write job-related case studies.

You may be thinking, "I'm no Isaac Asimov. I'm an engineer who does training. How can I write good case studies?" It's not as hard as you might think. It's really just a matter of remembering what makes a tale — any tale — interesting to your audience.

Here are seven tips for writing good case studies that will involve learners and increase their interest in the course material.

1 Write your case study in the form of a story. This point is crucial. Stories have universal appeal because they offer readers vicarious adventures. Everybody appreciates a story, whether it's in the form of a fairy tale, comic book, television serial, blockbuster movie or supermarket tabloid. One reason gossip is a popular pastime, in fact, is because it offers a chance to tell stories about others.

A good case study, one that grabs and holds trainees' attention, will have a storytelling, gossipy quality to it.

2 Name the characters in your case studies. And don't settle automatically for John Smith or Mary Jones. Be a little adventurous: Use names like Melvin, Quintin, Katrina and Veronica.

Better yet, give characters humorous names. Preston Ready or Iva Problem are names that pun certain character traits in case studies. They lend an element of humor and help lead trainees to the conclusions you want them to reach. The 17th century Englishman John Bunyan, author of *Pilgrim's Progress*, knew this principle well. He used puns when he named his characters Christian, Sloth and Mr. Worldly-Wise.

Giving your characters names helps bring them to life. And bringing the characters to life makes case studies come alive to learners.

3 Put words in the mouths of characters. Good storytellers add dialogue to their stories. Remember the dialogue from childhood stories?

"Who's been sleeping in my bed?" asked Poppa Bear in *Goldilocks and the Three Bears*.

"Fee fie fo fum; I smell the blood of an Englishman," said the giant in *Jack and the Beanstalk*. "Be he alive or be he dead, I'll grind his bones to bake my bread!"

You don't need to be fancy or literary when you create dialogue, but you do need to avoid sounding false, corny or "Hollywood." Strive for authenticity. Make your characters sound the way people in your company talk in everyday life.

4 Use realistic details. Describe details specifically, accurately and familiarly to make your case study sound authentic.

Don't describe things in general terms. For example, don't call it a "tool," a "radiation detector" or a "computer storage medium." Call it a "⅞-inch socket wrench," a "100 mr dosimeter" or an "800K floppy disk."

Take pains to include only information you know is correct. Do not, for example, refer to ignition points in a modern automobile. Take the trouble to find out exactly what acronyms mean. For example, in the nuclear industry, BWR refers to boiling water reactor, not big wide receiver.

Research and use the nicknames, slang terms and shoptalk expressions common to situations like the one in the case study. If you know that manufacturing workers in your company ask permission to use nonconforming material by saying, "Can we MXR it?" (material exception request), then don't have the workers in your case study say, "Can we use this nonconforming material?" You'll risk losing credibility with trainees. (Caution: For the benefit of trainees who are new to the company, use notes in your case study to explain what these expressions mean.)

5 Be descriptive. Help learners enter the world of your case study by appealing to both eyes and ears.

"Terry flipped the switch to the slurry pump. Instantly, he saw a bright blue-white flash and smelled burning oil. A second later he heard a noise that sounded like sheet metal being torn."

This kind of vivid, detailed description puts the learner into the situation far better than, "The pump made a loud abnormal-sounding noise." It also gives more real information to trainees.

6 Make the flow easy to follow. Since the case study is a story about a job-related problem, learners will follow it better if you present it in roughly chronological order. That is, present the events and information pretty much as they would occur in real life. Although using flashbacks to explain developments is a common device in fiction writing, it can be confusing in a case study.

7 Be both complete and mysterious. Put all the information into the case study that is necessary for your trainees to answer the questions you will ask them. Trainees must be able to find the pertinent facts within the body of the case study, either directly or by inferring them from accompanying references or aids.

Nothing is more irritating to trainees than feeling they have been set up. A case study has at least as much moral weight as a sporting con-

test, and in sports there are certain rules, standards of fairness and chances to win. Remember how much you hated trick questions in the tests you took in college, and avoid the temptation to annoy trainees with trick case studies.

At the same time, don't reveal how everything comes out. Obviously, you need to communicate enough information so that trainees understand the main points. But leave some threads hanging to maintain a sense of interest, curiosity and mystery. Don't overdo it; too many hanging threads are frustrating.

Bringing the characters to life makes case studies come alive to learners.

A 'Bad' Case Study

Consider this example of a case study from a training program on quality assurance auditing:

The XYZ Co. is a nuclear technology firm doing business with a private utility that operates a nuclear power station. The firm supplies such things as stainless steel valves and pump parts for the nuclear power station. As an auditor employed by the utility, you are about to participate in a supplier quality assurance audit. You must prepare an audit checklist for the part of the audit that deals with control of nonconforming items. List some examples of checklist items you would want to have in the audit checklist.

What can we say about that paragraph? First of all, is this really a case study? Isn't it actually an essay question? Does it present enough detail to help the learner "participate" in the experience and arrive at a proper answer?

Nothing about it is intrinsically appealing. There is none of what journalists call "human interest" to attract and sustain trainees' attention. There is no story flow to consider, so it hardly can be called a story. There are no people in it or any dialogue for them to speak. The few details that appear are too general. There is no appeal to either eye or ear. Since the case is not complete, it offers no real mystery —

only frustration. Trainers must do better than this if they expect case studies to be effective teaching tools.

A 'Good' Case Study

Consider another example from a course given to quality assurance auditors. This one incorporates all seven of the tips we discussed:

The Tale of the Preaudit Conference

Well, what happened is that we stood outside the vendor's plant entrance for 35 minutes before Doug, our team leader, finally was able to contact somebody in plant management to come and let us in the gate.

We could tell that no one knew we were coming (at least they pretended not to know we were coming) when nobody could tell us where we were supposed to go to meet with plant management. We ended up sitting in the plant QA manager's office while her secretary called around trying to find a conference room for us. The QA manager wasn't there because she had gone on vacation the day before.

While the secretary was calling about our conference room, Doug used another phone to talk to someone in the plant manager's office to set up the meeting. I remember that Doug kept telling them he'd mailed an audit notice to them a good two weeks before. In fact, the preaudit conference was supposed to have been set up by that letter.

We finally got a quick meeting together in a tiny, stuffy conference room. It was 11:05 a.m. when we sat down. My chair was pushed right up against the door. Sweat kept dripping off the end of my nose onto my legal pad.

The plant was represented by Ed Ripley, the assistant plant manager, somebody from the plant quality department (I didn't catch the name), and a couple of people from manufacturing (I didn't catch their names either). Doug tried to tell them what we were there to look at, and who we needed to see. One of the manufacturing people said, "Most of these people you need to see are out on vacation, but we'll try to find some other folks to show you around."

We asked to look at records of manufacturing nonconformances. One of them (I think it was Ripley) told us: "Those records are kept in a busy manufacturing area down on the floor. We're sorry, but we just can't allow you into that area. We'll be glad to bring you specific records if you can tell us exactly what you need." They did agree to provide us with an office to work and meet in.

Doug got very irritated a couple of

times while he was explaining our schedule because he was working from memory ("Damn it, did I say we wanted to visit the metrology lab on Wednesday? — I meant Thursday!"). He had lost his copy of the audit plan, and none of us had ever had a copy. I wish I could remember the name of the person from plant QA, because she was very cooperative. Doug wanted to commend her to the QA manager but we never saw her again, and we never did get her name straight.

Questions

1. *What problems have the audit team created that could hamper the effectiveness of this audit?*

2. *What is the audited organization doing that may be intended to prevent the audit team from gathering certain information?*

Get the point?

This case study won't win any literary prizes, but it does a lot of things right. It names its characters (it omits some names just to make a teaching point). It uses both direct and indirect quotations to put words in the mouths of the characters. It sounds authentic because it provides realistic details of a bad audit experience from the point of view of one of the auditors.

The stuffy meeting room is graphi-cally described. The chronological narration is easy to follow. The case study provides enough information for trainees to answer the two questions at the end, yet some uncertainty remains about what preceded and followed the situation.

By applying these seven tips and adding a little imagination, your case studies will keep trainees awake — no matter how mundane the topic.

Notes:

The Rise of CD-ROM

BY MARK FRITZ

The training field is so laden with acronyms that one might think trainers have a special fondness for them. Even so, that affinity did not help boost the acceptance of the computer technology called CD-ROM in the training community when it was first unveiled in the early 1980s. On the other hand, nobody else embraced it wholeheartedly, either. As a matter of fact, it took nearly 10 years for CD-ROM to catch on in specialized niches, such as data-base storage and document archiving, for which it is ideal.

But CD-ROM has always held tremendous potential for the training industry. It's currently the lowest-cost and highest-density storage medium, a seductive combination for thrifty computer-based courseware developers who also want to create ambitious training programs.

CD-ROM's failure to flourish can be traced to a combination of attitudes and economics. Initially, the biggest problem was that it was too expensive. It was stuck in a Catch-22: People didn't buy the drives because there weren't enough off-the-shelf products available, and companies didn't develop off-the-shelf titles because there weren't enough owners of CD-ROM drives.

But all that changed in 1993, which will probably go down in history as the year the CD-ROM market finally reached critical mass. In 1993, according to Disk/Trend Inc., a Mountain View, CA, market-research firm, shipments of CD-ROM drives jumped to 6.3 million from 1992's 2.5 million. Today, Disk/Trend estimates an installed base of nearly 23 million machines. The firm expects another 14 million drives to ship in 1995 and 18 million in 1996.

Part of what's driving these percolating sales are falling prices for the drives. You can buy one for as little as $99. Because they're so cheap, it's common these days to buy a personal computer with a CD-ROM drive already installed. An estimated 40 percent of all new personal computers are sold that way.

The growing acceptance and familiarity of the medium within the consumer market, coupled with its low price and its attractive features, made it inevitable that CD-ROM would begin to catch on in the training field. Suddenly, it is starting to look like a viable storage and distribution medium for custom-training development, off-the-shelf courseware, and just-in-time training systems.

Successes and Failures

Still, CD-ROM's current popularity is surprising in light of the resistance it encountered when it first was introduced. In the days when a CD-ROM drive could cost $2,000, few companies could justify the expense of using the medium to deliver training. Then, too, it had an identity problem. Many people compared it to interactive videodisc (IVD), which until recently was the most exotic means of delivering training via technology. One of IVD's strengths was its ability to show full-motion video. When CD-ROM offered tremendous data storage — more than 600 megabytes — but not full-motion video, would-be users were disappointed. Instead of looking at it as a unique medium and asking, "What's it good for?" people asked, "Why can't it hold full-motion video?"

Among the early adopters who asked the former question rather than the latter was Federal Express. In 1987 Federal Express launched an ambitious program to deliver training to more than 40,000 couriers and service representatives in 600 locations. CD-ROM was part of the mix. The system used 1,200 personal computers equipped with laserdisc players, which delivered the bulk of the training material. CD-ROMs were used to provide monthly updates.

A company that took early advantage of CD-ROM's ability to store vast quantities of audio material was American Express. In 1989 American Express began using CD-ROM to train telephone-service representatives at its Consumer Card Division center in Fort Lauderdale, FL. Trainees used simulated customer phone calls stored on CD-ROM discs to practice the right way to talk with customers.

In both cases, the companies played to CD-ROM's strengths. Consequently, instead of replacing interactive videodisc — as was endlessly speculated — CD-ROM has carved out its own niche in the training field. While industry observers watched the front door, CD-ROM slipped in the back.

Full Motion

Some CD-ROM trailblazers knew that the technology was not yet good for delivering full-motion video, but they forged ahead anyway. Most of them experimented with Intel's digital video interactive (DVI) video compression/decompression technology. DVI is able to deliver more than 70 minutes of full-motion, full-screen video through CD-ROM, but the cost is high. In 1988, the multiple add-on boards required to use DVI technology cost about $21,000. By 1990, the price had fallen to $9,500 — still a good chunk of money.

Bethlehem Steel, Andersen Consulting, Caterpillar Tractor, GE Government Services, NCR, Nestlé, New York Life Insurance, and Nixdorf have all used DVI for training. Despite the backing of industry giants Intel and IBM, however, DVI has not become the de facto standard for digital video on CD-ROM.

Last year Intel surprised everyone by announcing that it was shifting its emphasis away from hardware-based compression to software-based compression technology. Although the company still offers the ActionMedia II card for DVI decompression, it has sold its high-end DVI encoding/compression-services business to Horizons Technology Inc. in San Diego.

Some industry insiders speculate that Intel realized it couldn't compete with the MPEG video-compression technology. The standard known as MPEG, for Motion Picture Experts Group, is a compression formula positioned to become the uniform standard for incorporating video into CD-ROM. It has an edge because it is an international standard supported by a broad cross-section of the computer industry. And since there probably will be a number of competing MPEG chip manufacturers, their chips should be cheaper than Intel's proprietary DVI chips. If that scenario plays out, full-motion video on CD-ROM could become affordable even for modest-sized training departments.

One DVI user who has switched to the MPEG standard is Carl Nelson, president of VIS Development in Waltham, MA. The firm converts companies' videotape training materials into interactive-video training. A year ago VIS Development was committed to DVI; today it is using the MPEG standard. "MPEG is a big step over DVI," says Nelson. MPEG provides better video quality, better resolution, more colors, and allows for more video storage, Nelson says. And an MPEG decoder/playboard costs half what the Intel DVI board does.

But MPEG video has its own set of problems, the chief one being that it is very difficult to edit. Some argue that CD-ROM may never become the primary storage medium for digital video. It is a medium with severe built-in bandwidth and data-transfer rate limitations. Something better may soon come along.

The upshot is that while some companies have been experimenting with video on CD-ROM, most have been using it in a more obvious way: to store large quantities of data files. The technology is a particular boon to developers of computer-based training (CBT), who find the storage capacity of floppy disks too limiting.

Momentum

Still, the desire to incorporate video remains strong. Fanning that desire is the belief that CD-ROM, boosted by DVI or MPEG video, may be the perfect medium for the new generation of multimedia CBT.

Rising CD-ROM sales figures have not gone unnoticed by custom-training developers and off-the-shelf courseware vendors. Two years ago Comsell Inc. of Atlanta began converting its 250 interactive-videodisc courseware titles to CD-ROM, using

DVI to provide video. The company now offers all its courses on both videodisc and CD-ROM.

Comsell president Steve Roden says clients — particularly new ones — are demanding CD-ROM courses. He estimates that sales of CD-ROM versions of Comsell courses represent about 50 percent to 60 percent of the company's yearly sales. In contrast, two years ago, CD-ROM accounted for just 5 percent to 10 percent of sales.

Roden says he sees some other delivery systems on the horizon, particularly local-area network (LAN) systems that can distribute training through networked personal computers. Still, he says, "CD-ROM will be the medium of choice for the next few years at least."

"All the major players in training will be doing CD-ROM-based multimedia in the next one or two years."

Roden says CD-ROM works well for office automation and PC training, simply because in many cases, the CD-ROM is built into the computer. He says CD-ROM is not appropriate for training applications in which sharp images are essential, such as courseware for technical or medical procedures. For those types of applications, he recommends the better image quality of videodisc.

One big criticism of CD-ROM is its slow response time. A computer might respond in 10 to 20 milliseconds, while a CD-ROM takes a leisurely 300 milliseconds. Roden agrees that the lag can be annoying, but doesn't believe it interferes with learning. A sluggish computer, he reasons, probably will not dissuade motivated trainees from learning what they need to know.

Another company that has embraced CD-ROM is the National Education Training Group (formerly Applied Learning), based in Naperville, IL. NETG has been using CD-ROM for custom-training development for years. And recently the company launched a multimedia CD-ROM series called Skill Builder. The 28 titles in the Skill Builder series cover

popular software applications like Microsoft Excel and Lotus Notes. Hedging its bets, NETG also offers the programs on floppy disks and in LAN versions, but the company reports that the CD-ROM versions are the most popular.

Jim L'Allier, vice president of multimedia development for NETG, agrees with Roden that CD-ROM is edging out videodisc technology. "Videodisc is an aging technology whose user base is dwindling," he says.

L'Allier has also noted a demand for LAN-based training but feels that CD-ROMs and LANs are not necessarily mutually exclusive. He advocates using CD-ROMs and LANs together to maximize the strengths and minimize the weaknesses of each. Trying to send large audio and video files across a network is like trying to force the volume of water held by the Hoover Dam through a garden hose, L'Allier says. A better idea is to store big multimedia files on the CD-ROM drives of the client workstations, while storing the smaller files — containing things such as text information, test questions, and student registration data — on the LAN server.

Another large training company that has begun using CD-ROM as a distribution medium is Wilson Learning Corp. in Eden Prairie, MN. The company recently released the first four of a 20-title series of CD-ROM-based off-the-shelf training courses. The titles cover topics such as teamwork, negotiation, decision-making, personal communications, sales and customer service.

With this series Wilson Learning is putting a new emphasis on training for individuals, says CEO David Ehlen. "The real breakthrough of CD-ROM is that learning can move from the group to the individual," he says. And that's something today's economically unstable society needs. "Individuals have to take responsibility for their own learning," Ehlen says. "There is no such thing as lifetime employment anymore. If you get laid off and need to find a new job, you're going to have to take charge of your own retraining."

Ehlen is convinced that his company has not jumped into multimedia a day too soon. "All the major players in training will be doing CD-ROM-based multimedia in the next one or two years," he predicts. "They will have to, or be dinosaurs."

Indeed, it looks as if trainers, as

well as courseware vendors, may need to take a closer look at CD-ROM. Even standup trainers could take advantage of the new breed of PCs equipped with CD-ROM drives in order to enhance presentations with video and animation clips pulled from CD-ROM disks.

Thanks to the dramatic growth of CD-ROM's installed base, developers can now create multimedia lessons and store them on CD-ROM drives without fearing that no one in the target audience will have the means to access the course. From now on, when trainers talk about lessons on disk, they may not be talking about those floppy things.

Notes:

Certifiable!
Certification Fever Hits the Computer Industry

BY BOB FILIPCZAK

So you've got to hire someone to run the computer network in your company. The candidate in front of you says she is eminently qualified, can troubleshoot any problems that arise, and will get the network "up" again if it crashes. Trouble is, how do you know she can do what she says she can do? If you had someone competent enough to determine whether this candidate could do the job, you wouldn't need to hire anyone. What do you do?

The computer industry is helping companies solve this dilemma by embarking on a journey toward industrywide certification, a training-intensive process designed to give credentials where credentials are due. In some quarters certification is touted as a win-win situation: Employers have external verification that a potential employee can operate a given computer system proficiently, and employees have a portable credential that can give them an edge in a competitive job market.

If that's all there were to computer certification, it would be just another blip on the training screen, an indication that yet another industry has discovered that it's useful to verify the skills of employees.

But there's more to it than that. Certification in the computer industry has expanded beyond the hiring process. In fact, according to a study conducted by Dataquest Inc., the San Jose, CA, research wing of Dun & Bradstreet, most certification-related training is being paid for by employers. That's right, more than 80 percent

of all the training associated with certification in the computer industry goes on corporate tabs. So this isn't a case of hungry job-hunters grasping at a straw that will get them in the door and into an interview. The people being certified in droves already have jobs, and their companies, for one reason or another, are paying to get them certified.

How many people are in a "drove"? Since 1987, 60,000 have passed CNE (certified Novell engineer) tests and 50,000 people have graduated as CNAs (certified Novell administrators), says Jerry Christensen, director of business development for the education division of Novell Inc., the Orem, UT, software developer responsible for putting certification on the map in the information-technology field.

Certification isn't just a rubber-stamp formality nor does it come cheap. A computer technician who wants to get his CNE must pass seven demanding tests. The failure rate is significant: Only 65 percent of those attempting to get the CNE designation manage to do so, even after multiple attempts. The ballpark price tag for the training, books and testing is around $5,000 per person. For an employer picking up the tab, that figure pushes certification from the realm of "It's nice to do" to "We better have a good reason to do this."

A Brief History of Certification

If we're looking for someone to blame for this flurry of certification, it's generally agreed that Novell, the company that developed the most popular computer networking soft-

ware on the market, is the guilty party. It started innocently enough: In the name of good customer service, Novell encouraged its resellers, the businesses that sell its software, to have at least one CNE on staff who could troubleshoot and maintain the product once it was installed.

From there, certification took off because, as Novell's Christensen puts it, "the CNE credential filled a void in the industry." Instead of calling in a reseller's certified engineer twice a week to fix their networks, companies were discovering that they needed a full-time professional on staff. And what did they look for? The Novell seal of approval. That started a certification migration from the world of software distributors to the corporate world. The CNE credential is now becoming a requirement, both for those seeking employment and those already employed, in the world of Novell computer networks.

Certification then spread to other areas of the computer industry. Microsoft, Lotus, and most of the other major software players began certification programs, and it became increasingly important to have credentials from one of these companies.

The Big Why

Some of the reasons for the surge in certification are obvious, but there are still gaps in the picture. Why, for example, are most certifications paid for by employers when it is the *employee* who ends up owning the clearly portable credential? Why are so many *employed* computer professionals pursuing certification? And why should the training industry care about this certification boom — aside from the fact that thousands of classrooms across the country are full of people who want to be certified?

Let's take that last question first. Certification is accepted practice in many professions — accounting, insurance underwriting, etc. And it makes sense that the relatively young computer industry wants to establish some professional standards. Nevertheless, the industry's move into the certification business should concern training professionals mostly because it brings some rather large players into the training field's sphere of influence.

Judith Hale, president of Hale Associates, a Western Springs, IL, consulting firm that recently has drawn up standards for certifying corporate training departments, points out that the training industry could get blind-sided by the formidable forces of the computer industry. In the battle for scarce training resources, "the competition is going to come from places you never thought of before," says Hale. She suggests that everyone in the training business, both internal departments and outside consultants, are competing for the same pool of money. When Microsoft Corp., Novell and Lotus Development Corp. enter the training business, it's not like competing with Joe's Training Consultants & Bait Shop.

The reasons companies are willing to spend considerable sums to train and certify computer professionals already on staff are a little more difficult to nail down. Certainly, a credential is outside verification that an applicant can handle the job, so it increases management's comfort level. Dataquest's findings indicate that managers *feel* that certified employees provide higher levels of service, learn new technologies faster,

and are generally more productive. The words "comfort" and "confidence" crop up a lot when companies and managers discuss why they are willing to pay for their people to be certified.

But there's more to it than that. One of the oldest training issues in the book lurks behind certification in the computer industry: evaluation. Managers — the people who send employees through training — are becoming more concerned with results. Granted, a post-training test of skills and knowledge determines only whether information actually sunk in, not whether the skills will be used effectively on the job. But that's better than nothing.

"If you send somebody to a course, how do you know they actually did anything in that course besides twiddle their thumbs and eat Twinkies?" asks John Mueller, author of *Microsoft Certification Success Guide* and holder of both Microsoft and Novell certifications. The certification test answers

that question, he says.

Marc Waldeck, senior director of business and market development for Sylvan Technology Centers, a Columbia, MD, company that provides a lot of certification testing for software vendors, agrees. Managers want to know that training is effective and "being able to stack up a certification — an independent test — against that training has made them feel a lot better," says Waldeck.

If You Train Them, They Will Certify

Some companies, however, may pay for the training but not the certification testing. They fear that a newly certified employee may take the credential and go looking for greener pastures at another organization; meanwhile the original company loses both the employee and the training investment. According to Alan Hupp, vice president of marketing for Drake Prometric, a Minneapolis-based company that tests individuals

THE FEVER SPREADS

While no generic standard for certification has been agreed upon in the computer industry, the heat from this trend has infiltrated other industries in general and the training field in particular.

In the process of selling certification to everything with a pulse, the software vendors decided they wanted their trainers certified as well. Thus began the certification of trainers, something the training industry at large has wrestled with for decades. At various times, both the American Society for Training and Development (ASTD) and the National Society for Performance and Instruction (NSPI) have formed task forces and committees to study the issue.

In the mid-1980s, a group of impatient NSPI members founded the International Board of Standards for Training, Performance and Instruction (IBSTPI), a non-profit association originally devoted to the idea of certifying trainers as a way to create a more professional credential for those who have made training a career instead of a steppingstone to other positions. IBSTPI established a set of competency standards for trainers, but the initial dream of a formal, widely recognized certification process went nowhere. Until now.

Now powerhouses including Microsoft, Novell, and the Educational Testing Service (ETS) of Princeton, NJ, are using IBSTPI's standards to establish a certified technical trainer (CTT) standard. At this writing, the ink is still drying on the document describing the competencies of a CTT, but it includes parts of IBSTPI's standards:

- Managing the learning environment.
- Demonstrating effective presentation skills.
- Using instructional methods appropriately.
- Evaluating learner performance.

So what's the difference between a competent, run-of-the-mill trainer and a CTT? Consultant Judith Hale of Western Springs, IL, a former IBSTPI board member, says that the primary difference is that these computer trainers will have the backing and recognition of the computer industry, a portable credential that declares the person is recognized as a capable, professional instructor.

In the business world at large, "trainers" are often people who migrate through a training department on their way to something else. This damages the credibility of those who have chosen training as a career, Hale suggests. Transient trainers, she argues, tend to "learn by disease," essentially hanging out with other trainers for a few weeks and watching what they do in the hope that they will "catch it." The CTT designation guarantees that the individual passed tests that examine both training knowledge and classroom skills.

Microsoft's Nancy Lewis, director of education and certification, confesses that when her group set out to establish a standard for a Microsoft Certified Trainer, it didn't know about IBSTPI and the work it had done. When she found out that standards already existed, Microsoft decided to adopt them.

But nothing is static in the computer world. Alternative training-delivery media such as on-line services and distance learning via satellite are already challenging IBSTPI's classroom-oriented standards, says Lewis. Because Microsoft intends to include a lot of certification training on the upcoming Microsoft Network (part of the Windows 95 rollout scheduled for this month), Lewis says additional standards will have to be established for instructors that ensure they can handle distance-education situations.

for various computer certifications, the question for companies becomes: "I need to get them trained but do I need to go the extra mile? Do I need to have that level of confidence, that level of validity?"

Dataquest's research indicates that most companies do want that level of validity. Eighty-four percent of all certification-related training is paid for by companies; so is 79 percent of all certification testing.

Companies that try to protect themselves from turnover by resisting certification can inadvertently create a self-fulfilling prophecy, warns Jim Kryzwicki, senior director of education for Lotus Development Corp., the Cambridge, MA, software developer and also a big player in the certification game. Since the cost of taking the certification tests is only a fraction of the cost of the training and books, an employee may pay for the tests himself. Gratitude for the training is overshadowed by resentment that the company was too "cheap" to go ahead and pick up the bill for the tests. So the employee takes his new credential and hits the road. Maybe it's just a coincidence, but Kryzwicki admits that he used to work for a company that wouldn't pay for certification.

Ironically, says Waldeck, most of the companies that won't pay for certification for their own employees hire only certified computer professionals.

More progressive companies, however, see certification as part of their employees' career development. According to Lauren Hebert, certification program manager for Lotus, some companies use certification as part of a bonus program, a kind of pay-for-knowledge scheme that encourages employees to pursue certification. Other companies, she says, build certification into their promotion and career-development plans.

If verifying applicants' qualifications is one side of the certification coin, then empowering employees you've already got is the other. People know that job security is a relic of the past; a portable credential can stand them in good stead if the layoff ax leaves them in the unemployment line.

And some companies are beginning to think that it's in the organization's best interest to foster a sense of self-directed career development in employees. In this new environment, certification makes more sense than ever. It's no accident that certification

has taken off in the computer field, in which virtual teams form and dissolve rapidly, and employees move from project to project and company to company.

To Vendor or Not to Vendor

But computer certification is not without controversy. As we mentioned earlier, most certification is sponsored by the very companies that sell the software. A Novell-certified network engineer knows her way

---

Some see an inherent conflict of interest in a situation where a company sells you the software, sells you the training, sells you the books, sells you the tests, and then declares you "certified."

---

around a client-server environment, but much of her certified knowledge is product-specific. In other words, she might not be able to fix a network running Microsoft's products or Lotus' software.

Some see an inherent conflict of interest in a situation in which a company sells you the software, sells you the training, sells you the books, sells you the tests, and then declares you "certified." If the failure rates on the tests weren't so high, there would probably be even more complaints about bias.

And it doesn't take much imagination to see that certification is a pretty good deal for software vendors. First, of course, they make money from certification. Then, because the certified people out there in companies answer computer questions, software vendors don't have to spend as much on their own technical-support phone lines, one of the fastest-rising costs of selling software. Companies with vendor-specific certified employees are more likely to keep buying the products of that vendor, especially since they get special discounts and privileges if they have the right kind of certified computer professionals on staff. And finally, when customers have fewer problems with software — because the certified person can fix it or make

it work right the first time — the software vendors have generally happier customers. In case you lost count, that's a win-win-win-win situation.

Ken Kousky is president of Wave Technologies, a St. Louis training company that specializes in training computer professionals for certification. While he acknowledges that much of his revenue comes from vendor-specific training, he is concerned that many of the standards and competencies are being defined by vendors instead of an independent association of computer experts. And he is particularly concerned about the redundancies built into the system: Currently, a computer professional who works with several software products could spend most of her time being trained just to keep herself certified. "If you ran an open-architecture, multivendor network, you would need about 200 days of training to be certified as competent on all the products you're managing," says Kousky. Even after you get certified, you have to keep up with the industry through recertification. (Author Mueller says he's recertified his Novell credentials twice since 1991.)

Kousky is an enthusiastic proponent of a current movement in the information-technology industry toward more general, multivendor certification. Groups including the Information Technology Training Association (ITTA) and Network Professionals Association (NPA) are working to create a more general certification standard. All of the major players — Microsoft, Novell, Lotus and Oracle — are participating in these efforts.

In spite of the vendors' support of generic standards, Kousky worries that they won't let go of their own training and certification organizations. "We've really corrupted the certification market," he says, "because we've made it a profit center" for the software vendors. He may be right: Spokespeople for Novell, Microsoft and Lotus contend that there would always be a need for vendor-specific training and certification, regardless of whatever generic standards the industry might agree upon. Although Kousky's company has profited from the vendor-specific training, he's looking toward the future. "I don't think certification is going to survive long term unless we get some consensus," he says.

Generic certification standards

have already been set up by the Institute for the Certification of Computer Professionals (ICCP), says its executive director, Perry Anthony. This Des Plaines, IL, nonprofit association has been in existence for 22 years, quite a few years before the rest of the industry was bitten by the certification bug.

ICCP offers two certifications: associate computing professional (ACP) and certified computer professional (CCP). ICCP's certification exams are, as Anthony describes them, experience-based. That means you can't take the certification tests unless you've got at least four years of experience in the industry. Both certifications require you to know at least one computer language, and the CCP requires expertise in two specialties — like databases, telecommunication, networks, etc.

Moreover, the ICCP exams have been approved by the American Council on Education, the national organization that accredits colleges. Anthony claims "a lot" of CNEs are now seeking certification through the ICCP, and he considers his organization's credentials a kind of next step for computer professionals who already have their vendor-specific certification.

The trouble is, says author Mueller, the ICCP's certifications don't carry much clout in the computer industry.

Although the association has certified about 55,000 professionals in the last 22 years, those numbers pale in comparison with the 1.6 million people Novell has trained since 1987. Add in Microsoft, Lotus, Oracle and the rest, and it's clear that vendor-specific training has a lot more momentum.

Mueller also asks some hard questions about what ICCP's certification is worth in the marketplace. "If I get a Novell certification or a Microsoft certification, I can tell you what that certification buys me," he says. Depending on whom you talk to, a CNE adds at least $5,000 and perhaps as much as $15,000 to yearly compensation.

Mueller admits that vendor-sponsored training is geared toward the software company's products, but he doesn't see a better alternative. Indeed, he argues that a generic, multivendor certification standard eviscerates the usefulness of the credential.

A Novell-certified professional may not know the *best* way to solve a problem, but he does know the Novell way. And that's valuable knowledge, Mueller asserts. When a CNE calls up Novell for advice about how to fix a network, both technicians are speaking the same language. A more generic certification would replace definitive answers with esoteric, theoretical knowledge, he says.

There doesn't seem to be any end in sight to certification fever. Most of the major players are driving certification further down the line to end users. Microsoft, Novell and Lotus all announced new certifications this year for average computer people like you and me, who just use the blasted contraptions to do our jobs. In the very recent past, being Microsoft certified meant you were very proficient in all their software. These new certifications will be more specific: An insurance claims adjuster might be certified in a particular spreadsheet program, for instance.

In the future, it might become important to have a certification stamp of approval from these computer companies to get your next job. An instructional designer, for example, may need education and experience in developing training, as well as being certified in a particular word processing program, to get a foot in the door of United Glop's corporate training department.

So, on a couple of levels, certification will create ripples in other industries — and the training industry in particular. Everyone with a computer on her desk could be called to be certified as part of staying employable. If that happens, there's going to an enormous need for training.

Notes:

Certification for Trainers: Thumbs Up

BY CHRIS LEE

Official certification. Accountants have it, insurance underwriters have it and public schoolteachers have it. Corporate trainers don't have it, and the occasionally heated debate about whether they *should* has surfaced just often enough over the past few years to sustain the issue as one of ongoing concern.

One of the problems that surrounds any discussion of the pros and cons of certification is what, exactly, one means by the term. It helps to differentiate it from several related concepts that often are used interchangeably and contribute mightily to the confusion. The primary culprits: certification, licensure and accreditation.

The American Society for Training and Development defines certification as: "The process by which a nongovernmental organization grants recognition of competence to an individual who has met certain predetermined qualifications specified by that organization." ASTD also distinguishes certification from licensure (something required by a government agency) and accreditation (something given to a program rather than to a person).

Robert Mager and David Cram refined the definition in "The Regulators Are Coming!" (TRAINING, September 1985): "*Certification* is the process of publicly attesting that a specified quality has been achieved or exceeded. ... If an instructional technologist were to be certified, the certification would imply a public confirmation that certain standards had been met." They further define *standards* as the "description of performance considered to be competent;

descriptions of what competent people do when performing a task."

Certification is a voluntary process, whereas licensure is mandated by law. As Jerry Gilley and Michael Galbraith point out in "Examining Professional Certification" (*Training & Development Journal,* June 1986), certification is the applicable concept for professions in which people can practice without being certified. "In some professions individuals cannot practice without a license. Licensure is a mandatory process administered by a political body with its primary purpose being to protect the public from incompetent practitioners."

The key concept to keep in mind is that certification measures the "competencies" of an individual against a set of predetermined standards.

So, now that we're all talking about the same thing when we use the term, we're ready to ask (and answer) some questions: Who thinks trainer certification is a good idea? Who thinks it's unnecessary? What should trainers be certified to do? Who should take responsibility for certifying them? And what kind of certification system might work best?

To Certify or Not To Certify?

This summer we sent a questionnaire to a random sample of 7,500 TRAINING subscribers. We asked for their opinions on the perennial question of certification and some of the implications that surround it. By the cutoff date of August 25, we received 1,560 usable responses. That gives the survey a 20.8% response rate and a precision estimate of plus or minus 2.5%.

Specifically, we asked: "Should training/HRD practitioners be formally certified (i.e., attested as able to

perform to prescribed standards)?" Those in favor predominated, with 58.9% of our readers voting "yes," and 41.1% "no."

To pinpoint some of the characteristics of those respondents who favor or oppose certification, we correlated responses to this question with several demographic variables. We looked at yea and nay votes according to:

• *Job description* — training/HRD manager, in-house training/HRD specialist or "other" (non-training/HRD manager, consultant, personnel professional, etc.)

• *Size of organization's work force* — small (less than 500 employees), medium (500 to 2,499 employees) and large (2,500-plus employees).

• *Education* — no college degree, bachelor's degree, bachelor's degree plus some graduate work, master's degree and Ph.D.

• *Years of experience* — three or less, four to seven, eight to 12 and 13 or more.

• *Type of organization* — industrial category that represents the organization's primary business.

Most of our efforts to expose a significant pattern came to naught. Only a slightly higher percentage of training/HRD specialists looked favorably on certification than did training/HRD managers: 61.9% vs. 59%, to be exact. Of respondents who worked for small organizations, 60.7% were in favor of certification, as were 58.4% of those in large organizations.

Nor did education seem to exert a strong influence one way or the other. More respondents with master's degrees looked favorably upon certification (62.8%) than those in any other educational attainment category, but compared to the low of 55.2% for those with doctorates, the difference is not particularly significant.

In terms of experience in the training field, those with the least were least likely to be in favor of certification: 54.3% of respondents who had been in HRD jobs for three years or less voted affirmatively. But the curve does not go straight up according to experience. Most likely to favor certification (63.1%) were those in the next-lowest category — four to seven years in the training field.

The same sort of pattern appears when we look at industrial categories: Some differences exist, but nothing dramatic. Most likely to favor certification were respondents in educational services (63.3%) and public administration (62.6%). Least enamored with the idea were those in whole-sale/retail trade-but 54.1% of them still voted affirmatively.

In short, regardless of their demographic characteristics, TRAINING readers appear to favor the idea of professional certification by a margin of about 3 to 2.

Vehemence

Perhaps part of the explanation for the relative consistency of responses is that many people tend to bring long-held beliefs to the debate — beliefs that demographic variables don't account for. Some of our respondents held strong enough opinions on certi-fication to offer additional comments.

From detractors: "No certification system will ever sort the good from the bad," comments a university pro-gram director from Kansas. "Certifi-cation is ridiculous and will just lead to another credentialing spiral restrict-ing services and protecting the 'in group,' " adds a director of staff devel-opment for a state agency. "As a psy-chologist, I have seen its results and don't like what I see."

And from supporters: "It may be difficult to certify all [those] in special-ized fields, but it is necessary to have qualified practitioners," insists an instructional designer for a manufac-turing company. Another respondent supplies a commonly voiced ratio-nale: "The point is that certification reflects the desire for credibility in the training/HRD field."

Seth Liebler, last year's president of the National Society for Performance and Instruction (NSPI), says he has been surprised by the vehemence of opinions on the subject. Two years ago NSPI's executive board set up a committee to study the issue. Its avowed purpose was to examine the pros and cons of certification, and to make recommendations to the board. "The committee took on a life of its own," Liebler says, "and looked at the issue of *how* to certify." Obviously, he concludes, "those who wanted to par-ticipate on the committee were those who were convinced that certification is an excellent idea. But they ended up several steps beyond where the board wanted to be."

Certification has strong proponents and equally strong detractors within NSPI, Liebler says. The organization has not adopted *any* standards or cer-tification procedures for trainers, instructional designers or anyone else. But the committee's activities seem to have created a certain amount of con-fusion about NSPI's official position. Liebler, now a consultant with the Center for Effective Performance, Inc. of Atlanta, says that when clients ask him if he uses NSPI standards, his answer is, "What NSPI standards?"

Whose Job Is It?

Even those who agree that certifica-tion is a good idea do not necessarily agree on the next question: Who should do the certifying?

We asked the nearly 60% of respon-dents who felt trainers should be certi-fied to indicate who should set the standards. Nearly three-quarters of the respondents to this question (71.9%) felt that professional societies could best take on the job; 13.1% put the finger on colleges and universities; 14.9% indicated "other," and wrote in an alternative. The most popular sug-gestions, in order of frequency: both professional societies and academia should take a role; companies that employ trainers should set their own certification standards; "professional experts" should decide the question; and "leave it up to individual discre-tion." One wag even suggested TRAINING Magazine should do it (no thanks).

Whether they favored the idea of certification or not, respondents were asked to react to a list of statements about what certification should en-compass and if, in fact, it is a necessary and/or practical idea. The accompa-nying table shows the percentage of all respondents who agreed with each statement.

The vast majority agreed that can-didates for certification should be required to demonstrate both knowl-edge and skills. But by a slight margin (81.1% vs. 77%), they were more like-ly to favor asking candidates to show what they can *do* rather than what they *know*. This preference falls in line with what we could label a "profes-sional value"; it is not surprising that a larger proportion of respondents agree that performance-based criteria would be a good way to evaluate training professionals.

Although Mager and Cram con-clude that certification itself is an iffy proposition, they, too, agree that test-ing skills would make more sense than testing background knowledge: ". . . If certification is based on an abil-ity to recognize the correct answer to questions about the history or theory of training, that certification is of no value in identifying individuals who are competent in the *practice* of train-ing. . . . For certification to be of any value, it must attest to an ability to *apply* skills that are relevant and valu-able to the craft."

Respondents were considerably more likely to view the idea of certifi-cation as impractical than to dismiss it as unnecessary. Most (71.7%) of those who felt the proposition is "unwork-able in practice" were among the 41% who voted against certification, peri-od. But 28.3% of the respondents who

---

RESPONDENTS' OPINIONS ON CERTIFICATION

Statement	Percent of Respondents Agreeing With This Statement
Training/HRD practitioners should be required to demonstrate mastery of a certain body of knowledge (i.e., essential ingredients of a needs assessment, principles of instructional design, etc.).	77.0
Training/HRD practitioners should be required to demonstrate mastery of a certain set of skills (i.e., write an instructional objective, teach a class, conduct a role play, etc.).	81.1
Certification is a nice idea, but unworkable in practice.	39.1
Certification for training/HRD practitioners is unnecessary.	26.9
Certification would do a lot for the professional image of the training/HRD practitioner.	62.3

agreed that certification is an unworkable idea also voted for trainer certification. Likewise, 13.7% of those who agree that certification is unnecessary support it nonetheless. And better than 25% of those who vetoed certification conceded that it would do a lot for the image of practitioners.

One possible interpretation to draw from these mixed messages: Regardless of whether they are for or against certification, many of our readers neither endorse the idea wholeheartedly nor dismiss it out of hand.

Thumbs Down

We also asked respondents to complete a write-in question: "What is your idea of a workable certification system for training/HRD practitioners?" Now admittedly, they didn't have the space to design an elaborate system of competencies, standards and procedures, but the responses do help round out the picture of what TRAINING readers think of the proposition.

Some feel a certification system would add little to current attempts to evaluate a trainer's competence. Employers, they argue, are better able to appraise an individual's qualifications than any outside credentialing body could hope to be.

"I don't believe there is a workable system. Organizations have their own standards," says a senior trainer from a bank in Arizona. "Let each company decide what mix of education and experience it needs," adds an instructor with a defense contractor in Texas.

And, indeed, respondents who endorse the status quo are in good company.

Carlene Reinhart, a project manager at Xerox Corp.'s Learning Center in Leesburg, VA, says certification is not only impractical for her organization, it is also unnecessary. At Xerox, salespeople "pass through" certain training jobs for a set period while they receive management training themselves. "How would you certify them?" she asks.

And Xerox, like many large organizations, trains its own. Sales and marketing staffers doing a stint in training are required to complete a series of train-the-trainer courses. "We have our own standards. In fact, we have standards for our standards," Reinhart laughs. Xerox would be unlikely to make use of any certification procedure that didn't meet its particular needs, she adds.

At Hewlett-Packard, the training process builds such extensive quality checks into the system, it is almost the equivalent of internal certification, says Mary Humphrey, a program developer for the application engineering training organization. The company offers a variety of both training skills and technical courses for its instructors; its detailed job descriptions for full-time instructors provide a checklist of required skills that are, for all practical purposes, standards; and it carefully evaluates the impact of its courses.

> ## "Certification systems *can* work . . . but not in proportion to the cost and effort that goes into them."

"If we had a serious quality problem, I might worry," Humphrey says. But she feels that HP's internal standards for instructors make certification unnecessary. "Certification in public schools guarantees minimum competence standards. To advance here, you have to meet or exceed expectations."

Many of our respondents also insisted that a trainer's boss is the only person who can truly judge competence. ". . . The training professional's supervisor is the only important 'evaluator' of his or her abilities," was the unequivocal opinion of a director of planning and HRD at an insurance company. "It is the manager's responsibility to hire good, qualified people. I know a lot of 'certified' dummies," comments a director of organizational development and training at a natural gas distributor. "People should be evaluated on their job performance," echoes another training manager from a bank in New York. "To set up [a system for] certification is merely to increase bureaucracy and not necessarily [to] indicate competency for that job [or] company."

Others seem to feel that the whole controversy is a waste of time. "There is no [workable certification system]. Job standards should suffice. Certification hasn't helped other professions like teachers, doctors, etc. The bozos always manage to beat a system,"

concludes a manager of staff development and training at a transportation company in Atlanta. "I do not believe measurable standards could be developed and applied which could provide a proper mix of knowledge and skills leading toward or assuring training effectiveness," proclaims a group director of human resources at an aerospace manufacturer in California.

Thumbs Up

Certification proponents, however, are full of suggestions for workable systems. One training manager for the U.S. Postal Service proposes straightforward testing: "A written examination composed in conjunction with ASTD and major universities [that would test] essential knowledge of training theory and principles."

Judging from other responses, however, this proposal would face a lot of opposition: "[A workable certification system] has to be performance-based, not merely knowledge testing. If we can't demonstrate our knowledge, how can we get others to behave differently?" asks a training executive with an educational services firm. A senior training specialist at a bank concurs: "Observation of skills in use — not testing!"

An ambitious system is laid out by an HRD director in the oil-and-chemicals industry: "Certification standards generated by joint academic/professional, society/business task force. Implemented by employers." What are omitted, of course, are the practical steps for putting such a system into place.

A majority of the respondents who offered ideas for "workable" certification systems had a role in mind for professional groups, primarily ASTD or NSPI. Suggestions included: Establish standards and exams; base standards on ASTD's 1983 competency study; conduct training and testing in cooperation with colleges and universities; and set standards and evaluate competencies in cooperation with employers.

All in all, respondents envisioned myriad roles for professional societies. But they offered no suggestions that the societies themselves haven't explored over the years during their own recurring soul-searching on the topic.

According to executive director Paul Tremper, NSPI is not taking a formal position on the questions of certification or standards. "However, we do have a standards committee that will be looking at those two issues," he adds.

Most recently, in the wake of the competency study that defined trainers' roles, behaviors and "outputs" (what those in the field must produce to perform those roles successfully), ASTD established a professional-standards task force to examine the question of trainer certification.

According to former ASTD president Julie O'Mara, who headed the task force, the committee gathered extensive information about certification before making any recommendations. It conducted a literature search, surveyed both ASTD members and nonmember training executives, "took testimony" from members at the 1984 conference, and conducted a legislation search to track any move to require licensing of HRD practitioners. The upshot: Early this year, the task force recommended to the board that ASTD set standards for the profession.

These standards would be set on the 102 outputs identified in the competency study. Pat McLagan, founder of McLagan & Associates of St. Paul, MN, and technical advisor to the task force, describes outputs as the key products and services delivered by a training and development practitioner. "The criteria for an excellent output are the standards," she explains. "In evaluating an instrument, for example, one criterion for excellence would be that it exhibits good psychometric design."

A lot of the fear about setting standards, she says, stems from the mindset that dictates tying them to tasks: MBO-type "objectives" with measurable criteria. Yet subjective criteria are essential to the quality of the product or service produced by knowledge workers, she contends. Basing standards on outputs actually encourages practitioners to come up with creative ways to produce them, rather than following prescribed steps.

Standards are certainly a step toward certification, O'Mara says, but

"they are assessment tools without actual certification." When are ASTD's standards likely to appear? It depends on the budget for fiscal year '87. If further study is funded, the professional development committee will begin to examine methods for establishing standards next year.

So while ASTD has not closed the door on the possibility of certification, it is certainly not jumping into the fray — and for good reason. Any kind of certification process would demand a substantial investment, and the society is moving cautiously. "A standards effort would take [resources] away from other projects, in both administrative time and money," O'Mara points out "Is there a great enough return on the investment to do that?"

Good question. A respondent to our survey provided one answer: "[Certification systems] can work... however, I don't believe they do in proportion to the cost and effort that goes into them."

Notes:

Making Competencies Pay Off

BY TIMM J. ESQUE AND
THOMAS F. GILBERT

The notion of "competencies" has gained a great deal of currency in the training world. Some advocates go so far as to suggest that it should be the basis for all human resource management. The idea is to define a set of competencies for each job in the organization — a list of things that the jobholder must be able to do. These job-specific competencies become the basis for hiring, developing and compensating employees within those jobs.

The danger here is that the term competencies can lead people to err by focusing on behaviors instead of on accomplishments. It is really the accomplishments of the job performer — the results the person produces — that have value to the organization. The specific behaviors that go into producing those accomplishments are important, but they are a secondary concern. Unless we begin our analysis of a job by determining the valuable accomplishments we want the performer to produce, we're likely to make mistakes about which behaviors are really important (see box page 55).

Since competencies have become a popular tool, let's see if we can clarify how to use them productively for employee development. Specifically, how can we use the notion of competencies to improve the current and future performance of employees? Before we can answer that question, we'll need to clarify what we understand to be the purpose of developing lists of competencies.

The Purpose

Regarding current performance, the purpose of defining competencies is to give people information about what they need to do to prepare themselves to succeed at their current jobs. Employees are provided with a list of competencies associated with their jobs. They are expected to work with their supervisors or peers to determine which of the defined competencies they already possess and which they need to acquire. Presumably, if they acquire all of the competencies associated with their jobs (or at least the "right" ones), they will succeed and the organization will benefit.

Regarding future performance, competencies are supposed to serve a similar purpose. "Future performance" can refer to continued success in the same job when the requirements for that job are changing, or simply to performance in a different job that the individual plans to hold in the future. Theoretically, an organization that does a good job identifying emerging competencies will benefit because its employees will be better prepared to succeed when their jobs change or when they change jobs.

In either case, present or future, the point of defining competencies is to provide information to help a person prepare to be successful in a job.

Now we can be clear about the effective use of competencies. Competencies are being used effectively when individuals continually succeed at their jobs and, as a result, the entire organization benefits.

Drawing up lists of competencies for each job in an organization is not very difficult, but how can we be sure that because these lists are provided, individuals will succeed in their jobs and the organization will benefit? What really has to happen in order for competencies to have an impact on the *organization's* performance? We suggest that the following requirements need to be met:

1. The information conveyed by competencies must accurately describe how individuals can prepare to succeed at their (current or future) jobs.

2. Individuals must, in fact, acquire the competencies needed to succeed at their jobs.

3. Individuals must be able to exhibit these acquired competencies in the appropriate sequence at the right times.

4. Individual success on the job must be defined by the requirements for success of the organization. In other words, if the organization is not succeeding, then individuals by definition are not succeeding either.

When a list of competencies is defined and put to use, and it meets all four of those requirements, we can say that the organization is using competencies effectively. But we still haven't defined exactly what competencies are. So let us suggest the following operational definition: Competencies are *behaviors that assist the performer to overcome known barriers to achieving the performance standards.*

The question becomes, how do we identify competencies that meet our requirements and fit that operational definition?

Developing Effective Competencies

The table on page 54 describes a process for identifying competencies that, if acquired, will help overcome known barriers to successful performance. Next to each step in the process are some questions that need to be answered.

Let's apply the steps in the table to a simplified industry example. Suppose we were going to identify competencies for the design engineers at a paper clip company. We begin by asking: What is the mission of these engineers?

Design engineers do a variety of things, but their ultimate output, for contributing to organizational goals, is new (or modified) products. They produce paper clip designs — and in order for the designs to contribute to the company's goals, the paper clips probably need to be easily manufacturable, meet customers' quality requirements, and be ready for production according to some schedule. We have just defined the mission of the design engineers and some criteria to evaluate their success.

The next step is to identify major outcomes (or accomplishments) that result in achieving the mission. We're not talking about a list of tasks here; we want to know the subproducts that lead to the ultimate product. Some of the things the engineers produce are design specifications, product test plans, product performance reports and so on. We are only interested in outcomes that are necessary and sufficient to achieve the mission.

For each of these things the engineers produce, we need to be specific about how we would know if an engineer (or team) had produced it, and if it were any good. Let's look at design specifications as an example.

Several people are going to use the design specs later, so the document needs to include the information needed by all of the different users. It has to be written so that each of those users interprets it the way the design engineer intended. It also probably needs to provide evidence for the customers that the resulting product will meet their stated requirements — and how that will be demonstrated.

Next we want to establish how we can tell, when evaluating design specs, if each of the requirements has been met. For example, we know who will use the specs later, so they can help us design a checklist of the types of information the specs must contain.

How will we know if each user interprets the specs as intended? One way we'll know is if somebody uses the specs to do something that the design engineer didn't intend. That won't prevent the problem but it will tell us, after the fact, if a requirement was met. It might be better to have a specs review meeting, where the users ask questions of the design engineers whenever anything is not crystal clear.

The length of these meetings and the number of spec rewrites required afterward might be an excellent measure of this "interpretation" requirement. It is best to be as clear as possible about how success will be measured for every single requirement.

Experienced design engineers and their managers should have some idea about how well these requirements have been met in the past. A performance standard should be identified for each measure of an outcome requirement. The standard should represent how well the best performers have met the requirements of each outcome.

That standard, derived from the very best performers, becomes a realistic goal for every design engineer. Why? Because this process we are going through is meant to remove the barriers that prevent achievement of the desired standards every time a product is designed.

That brings us to barrier identification. Why is it that some design specs get interpreted differently from the

A PROCESS FOR IDENTIFYING COMPETENCIES THAT REALLY MATTER

No.	Step	Questions to be Answered
1	Define the mission of the job.	a. What is the ultimate product or service that results from this job? b. Is this the product or service that best describes how this job contributes to the goals of the organization? c. How would I know if the mission had been achieved (what are the success criteria for achieving the mission)?
2	Describe the major outcomes (accomplishments) required to achieve the mission.	a. What are the necessary and sufficient outcomes that result in achieving the mission of the job?
3	Define performance standards for each major outcome.	a. What are the requirements of success for this outcome? b. How can each requirement be measured? c. How well do the best performers perform against these measures today?
4	Identify known barriers to achieving the performance standards.	a. What has prevented people from achieving the standards in the past? b. Which barriers, if overcome, will provide the greatest performance improvements?
5	Determine which barriers will be best overcome by training the performer.	a. Would the barrier best be addressed by: • clarifying performance expectations? • providing performance feedback? • providing better tools (or job aids)? • teaching the performer certain behaviors that will assist in overcoming known barriers to achieving the performance standards?
6	Develop (or buy) and deliver training.	a. What is the briefest training that will allow the performer to overcome the targeted barrier? b. Could a job aid be provided instead of training?

original intent? Maybe different design engineers use different language to describe the same things. Maybe some users of the specs have their own ideas about how the product should be made, and they choose to ignore parts of the specs. Maybe every design spec document looks so different that the users don't learn anything from one to the next.

By discussing these issues with the design engineers and the users of the specs, and by reviewing some of the specs, we can generate a list of potential barriers.

It is a good idea to go through some process to shorten the list to those few barriers that people seem to agree on. Eventually you will have identified barriers pertaining to each outcome (or even each requirement). It probably isn't possible (or desirable) to act on every barrier at once, so you want to identify the ones likely to provide the biggest bang for the buck.

Those barriers identified as needing immediate attention should then be examined in light of the questions in Step 5 of the table. Not every barrier means that design engineers lack a competency. In the case of interpreting the design specs, it is possible that design engineers have never had the chance to receive input or feedback from the users of the specs. All that may be needed is a review meeting to give design engineers the opportunity to hear how the users interpret their work.

Then again, maybe the design engineers have gotten this feedback, but they all have their own personal style for developing specs and that is causing a problem for the users. In this case we might want to get the engineers to behave more uniformly in regard to the format and language they use.

This would seem to be a competency issue for design engineers, as we've operationally defined competencies. But even in this case, we don't want to jump to the conclusion that training courses are warranted. If some simple rules for formatting the specs were clearly stated, would the design engineers really need training, or would they just need to review those rules before they write their next spec document? This general line of thinking should be applied to each barrier to determine the most effective (and cost-effective) way to remove it.

Out of this analysis, a plan emerges for overcoming the barriers that limit performance. To remove some of

---

COMPETENCIES VS. ACCOMPLISHMENTS

BY THOMAS GILBERT

In a 1978 book called *Human Competence: Engineering Worthy Performance*, I defined competence as the worthy outputs of behavior. I asserted that competence has to do with the accomplishments that certain behaviors enable us to produce, and not with the behaviors themselves.

Recently there seems to be more discussion about "competencies" than competence. The word competency typically implies "behaviors exhibited when the performer is performing well." But what does it mean to perform well? Organizations are primarily interested in behaviors or activities that have value — that are worthy. The only way to tell if activities are worthy is to look at the outputs that result from them: a well-made product, a big sale, an excellent safety record, a delighted customer.

Thus, worthy performance is evidenced by people's accomplishments, not by their behaviors. Unfortunately, the use of the term competencies seems to be putting the focus on behaviors at the expense of accomplishments.

It is argued that in order to achieve valued accomplishments a person must exhibit a certain set of correct behaviors (or competencies). This is most certainly what you will be told if you begin analyzing a job by asking experts how they do it.

But in 30 years of observing exemplary (and nonexemplary) performers, I have not found this to be the case. In fact, I have found a surprisingly low consistency in how exemplary performers do their jobs. In other words, two exemplars are likely to exhibit quite different behaviors in the course of producing their masterful results.

I came upon a classic example in a company that sold forklifts. One exemplary forklift sales representative spent much of his time cruising through the countryside looking for abandoned warehouses that might be opening in the future. Another spent his mornings on the phone tracking down leads. Still another top sales rep (who hated phones) sorted through all manner of paperwork — building codes and the like — looking for prospects.

All three were distinguished from the rest of the sales representatives by one thing: Their prospecting was excellent, and it led to sales, an accomplishment highly valued by this company — and most others.

The best way to improve performance is to begin by observing it: Determine which performers are really achieving worthy accomplishments and understand why. But for a variety of reasons, it is often difficult to make direct observations of performance the first step of a job analysis.

When this is the case, the method described in the accompanying article is the next best thing; you are still beginning by identifying the valued accomplishments and focusing on overcoming barriers to those accomplishments.

The popularity of "competencies" (and loose definitions) seems to lead many organizations to focus solely on behaviors when analyzing performance. This can greatly reduce the effectiveness of training and other performance interventions.

We are not suggesting abolishing the term competencies. Training professionals need to be ready and able to communicate in the language of their clients, and many clients are using the C-word these days. The process we present here is described in terms of competencies so that you can respond to clients who ask for competencies. Obviously, the same method can be used without anyone ever mentioning the term — whenever your client is simply looking to improve performance in a way that really matters.

Just remember: To be effective, accomplishments first; behaviors second.

these barriers, the design engineers will have to acquire certain competencies. But now it will be clear exactly how acquiring each competency will lead to the achievement of organizational goals. Using this process, we are able to identify competencies that are linked to important business goals; therefore, they are measurably worth the effort expended to develop and apply them.

Tips For Developing Useful Competencies

Generating a list of competencies is easy. Identifying a set of *useful* competencies is harder. Here's how to avoid a few of the most common pitfalls.

The first obstacle to a successful analysis is defining the mission. Through decades of conditioning, most of us have learned to analyze work in terms of jobs. But when you try to paint a picture of a job, you are likely to include lots of work (or activities) that do not directly result in valuable outcomes; that is, most jobs involve a lot of tasks that don't really contribute to organizational goals.

Useful mission statements are usually associated more with specific business processes than with whole jobs. Invariably you find that more than one job contributes to the success of a mission.

Returning to the paper clip example, the mission of producing a paper clip design that is easily manufacturable, meets customer requirements, and is completed on schedule is largely the responsibility of design engineers. However, responsibility for designing a product is often shared by a team of design engineers, and many other jobs play a role in the success of this mission.

For example, for every new paper clip design, one or more people from marketing will interrogate the customers who define the requirements for that product. People from manufacturing may also play a role in the design process to ensure that the end design is manufacturable (in very measurable ways).

When we set out to find a clear mission, we are more likely to find it in a process than in a job (in this case, design engineering or product development as opposed to "design engineer"). It is the process with a clearly stated mission that provides our link to organizational objectives and, ultimately, business impact.

You will probably begin this whole analysis by focusing on a specific job, and that's fine. But if you are proceeding correctly, it is likely that you will soon find yourself describing a process — and that other jobs will come into play. In fact, some of the key barriers to success that you identify will likely involve these other jobs in addition to or instead of the one you started with. Avoid getting hung up trying to remain focused on a particular job. That several jobs play a role in the process just means there are more opportunities to identify and overcome barriers to success.

The other major consideration for a successful analysis involves the training professional's role in the effort. Because this analysis is going to identify more than training issues, you would like your clients — the people who perform the jobs you're analyzing, and their managers — to feel as much ownership for the initiative as possible.

The clients need your help to do this analysis, because it requires discipline to focus on outcomes and measures before jumping to conclusions about barriers and solutions. But in the end, you will be better off if they consider the end product their own work.

The analysis allows the clients to discover that there are lots of barriers to success that are not under the direct control of the performers (design engineers in our example). As they make these discoveries, it is imperative that they seek ownership for these barriers from people who can do something about them. In most cases, that means line managers and executives, not the training professional.

Keeping those two considerations in mind will greatly enhance your chances of developing useful competencies.

Notes:

Competency-Based Training vs. Criterion-Referenced Instruction: What's the Difference?

BY RON ZEMKE

For several years now we have been subjected to considerable rhetoric about the potential power of something called *competency-based training*. In a nutshell, CBT refers to the idea that if you want to teach someone to do something (like a job), you start by figuring out exactly what things successful performers do (what it looks like when it's done right), then train the learner until he or she is able to do all of those things.

Actually, it's not quite that simple, as we'll see. But the strength with which the notion of competency modeling has taken hold in the world of human resources development (HRD) needs no more illustration than the release last June of the American Society for Training and Development's (ASTD) report on the results of its two-year study of the necessary competencies of a training or HRD professional — a study that involved several rounds of survey work and a cast of thousands.

The outcome of this survey, directed by consultant Patricia A. McLagan of St. Paul, MN, is a litany of 31 competencies, 15 HRD "role profiles," four "role clusters" and 102 "outputs [which] people in the training and development field must produce in order to function with excellence." It is an impressive report, and most working trainers indeed could benefit from browsing through it.

The Association of Information Systems Professionals (AISP) recently launched an effort to come up with a similar document that will "identify and define some of the positions and required skills which comprise the office-information-systems profession."

In short, everywhere you go these days you run into someone defining the "competencies" you'll need when you get there.

Valuable as this may be, one question deserves to be answered. In its naked form it arises whenever you hear someone say, "I believe in training that is competency-based and criterion-referenced." The question is, has this speaker just distinguished between two different things, or is he being entirely redundant?

Is the competency-model approach to designing and developing training in fact an entirely new breed of cat? Or is it more the repackaging of well-known and widely used approaches, with a couple of twists and a new name? We have asked this question frequently of card-carrying members of the competency crowd. There is a certain quicksilver element to most of their answers.

CBT Is . . .

Others have noted that there is a remarkable lack of consensus about what a "competency" is and how directly or indirectly the defining of one should be expected to affect a training effort. William G. Spady, a researcher with the National Institute of Education, who has followed the public-school version of the compe-

tency phenomenon — the Competency-Based Education (CBE) movement — since the mid-1970s, has called CBE "a bandwagon in search of a definition."

"Like most self-respecting fads in American education over the past few decades," Spady writes, "this CBE bandwagon cannot be accused of having put its conceptual house in order before launching on its uncharted parade route and accumulating a vast and lively following . . . the adherents and practitioners of current . . . CBE efforts are marching (or parading) in different uniforms to different drummers playing different tunes.

Spady himself managed to propose a definition of CBE that still is being cussed and discussed in academic circles fully seven years after it was penned. According to him, CBE is "a data-based, adaptive, performance-oriented set of integrated processes that facilitate, measure, record and certify within the context of flexible time parameters the demonstration of known, explicitly stated and agreed-upon learning outcomes that reflect successful functioning in life roles."

Okay, you wouldn't want to set that to music or have it tattooed on your hip, but slog through it a few times and you'll discover that it does offer some guidance. Lurking within Spady's definition are six elements that pretty much spell out the critical parameters by which an instructional effort might be judged CBE or non-CBE. These same six distinguishing features also may serve as a candle to help us illuminate the competency idea as it applies in the training and development world.

1. *Statement of competencies* — the explicit statement of desired outcomes or indicators of successful performance of some activity. These are distinct from statements of cognitive, manual or social capacities.

2. *Use of time* — within a CBE framework, time is used flexibly. The focus is not upon classroom time or instructor time, but upon the time needed by the learner.

3. *Delivery of instruction* — learners are free to choose from a variety of learning activities and experiences. There are, theoretically, no limitations on the media/method mix a learner and an instructor can invent and/or negotiate.

4. *Measurement of learning* — pre- and post-tests are administered to avoid relearning information and to

assess mastery of the competency.

5. *Certification of attainment* — certification depends solely upon verified demonstration of the specified and agreed-upon competencies or indicators.

6. *Program adaptability* — program decisions are based on student performance. The program is finished when the learner can demonstrate the competency.

Spady's definition is generally acknowledged to have withstood the test of time and the torment of debate well enough to be accepted in the education world as a reasonable standard for comparison. Such has not been the case in HRD. Competency-based training enthusiasts tend to cloud their definitions with ambiguity and guard their processes with the jealousy of video-game designers.

Occasionally, however, the veil of mumbo-jumbo can be pierced and some light shed on the similarities and differences of the competency concept as advocates in the HRD field are currently using it.

William E. Blake, author of the *Handbook for Developing Competency-Based Training Programs* (Prentice-Hall, 1982), describes competencies as "... specific, precise student outcomes ... that have been recently verified as being essential for successful employment in the occupation for which the student is being trained."

A very different approach, one we have dubbed a "critical traits" tack, is practiced by Boston-based McBer and Co. "To us," says George O. Klemp, vice president of the consulting firm, "competency is a description of the qualities an individual brings to work or life pursuits that make him effective."

Patricia McLagan, designer of the ASTD competency study, takes a more "situational" approach to defining competencies. To her, a competency is a capability of an individual which relates to superior performance in a role or job. It may be a knowledge, skill, intellectual strategy or a cluster of all three.

CRI

In an effort to come to a more concrete understanding of how the competency-based training concept works, we can change tacks and attempt to compare and contrast competency-based training with an older and more widely agreed-upon approach: criterion-referenced instruction.

Robert W. Mager, who, with colleague Peter Pipe, has done much of the refining and a lot of applying of the concept, defines CRI as "... a way of organizing instruction in which pre-specified performance criteria are achieved by each qualified learner (i.e., instructing until the student learns rather than until the bell rings)."

The key distinguishers of CRI are *flexible time* — the training takes as

---

According to Bob Mager, CRI and CBT "are just different terms for the same thing."

---

much time as the learner takes — and a focus on performance rather than on subject matter. The appropriate measures to determine if the individual has learned the material are measures of what he or she can *do* as a result of the training, rather than what he or she "knows."

A number of characteristics are often associated with CRI, but do not actually define it. CRI is often self-paced and student- or learner-controlled. That characteristic, says Mager, is not definitional even though it is often present. "To say that CRI is synonymous with self-paced or learner-controlled instruction is the same as suggesting that four-wheel drive is a defining characteristic of an automobile," he insists.

And the Difference Is . . .

How do CRI and CBT differ? According to Mager, they don't. "They are really different terms for the same thing, or so it seems to me," he says. "You will hear the terms 'competency-based education,' 'mastery learning' and so on used interchangeably and more frequently in education circles, but I haven't been able to discern an operational difference between what people in training call competency-based training and criterion-referenced instruction."

John Daniel Lyons, director of training for Goodyear Tire and Rubber Company of Akron, OH, agrees with Mager. Testifying in Washington last year before the House Subcommittee on Employ-

ment Opportunities about a highly regarded competency-based apprenticeship program Goodyear established, Lyons said, "Competency-based training is also known as performance-based training, criterion-referenced instruction, performance-oriented training, objective-based training and mastery learning. These terms are essentially equivalent...."

As far as Lyons is concerned, attempts to pinpoint minute distinctions among these terms are a waste of time. "Let's say that one could actually draw a distinction between competency-based training and criterion-referenced training and whatever else you would care to distinguish. Except in some irrelevant academic sense, those distinctions would be immaterial. As practitioners, we know that what we do varies so much between applications — from situation to situation — that the distinctions between methods are really lost," he insists.

None of the competency-based training advocates we've talked with are eager to try specifying differences between CBT and CRI. Nor are the CRI folks enthusiastic about taking on the charge in reverse. Still, we found it revealing to chase both sides around the bush.

Ask a criterion-referenced instruction advocate what she thinks about competency-based training and she answers, "I don't know. Tell me what it is and I'll tell you what I think."

The typical CBTer's response: "Criterion-referenced who?" When prodded, one CBT advocate was willing to concede — without attribution — that at least for "lower-level skills there really is no practical difference." But, he continued, as "one moves to more cognitively complex performances, they aren't at all the same."

Indeed.

Viewed in the context of life's important issues, of course, this whole CBT-CRI business does not exactly stack up against, say, the national debt or the question of why there is not a single Mexican restaurant in Minneapolis that rates above a B-Minus.

That is pretty much the attitude Mager takes toward the problem of words meaning whatever the user decides they mean. "The fact that there is no operational difference between the two (CRI and CBT) may be less important than the fact that different words 'work' in different environments," he says. "At Florida

Power they call our work Flex-Learn instead of CRI. They are more comfortable with the former than the latter. Perhaps the important thing to note is that a valuable idea is being called to people's attention, and not that two different names are being applied to the same useful idea."

A charitable view that, but one we suspect will wear poorly — especially on CBTers. But for this round, at least, we have to conclude that CBT, whatever else it may be, is primarily a synonym for the less-mysterious idea of criterion-referenced instruction.

Ooh, we're going to get letters.

Notes:

Engaged: The Nature of Computer Interactivity

BY BOB FILIPCZAK

"Colonel, I've got something to report," the nervous Pfc. stammers.

"Speak freely, soldier," the superior officer barks.

"It's about the new training, sir. You know, the new tank simulators here at Fort Knox. Well, the men have been really impressed with the realism of the tank battles, especially the enemy tanks the computer generates." He pauses. "They're learning a lot, getting quite proficient, by using this new technology." Another pause. "But it seems a couple of the trainers who have the keys to the room are letting soldiers in on off-hours, sir. In fact, the trainers themselves have been coming in on Friday nights and weekends for mock battles. Not only that, sir, the trainers bring in their families and one family competes against the other. We have an 8-year-old who is probably the best tank commander on the base."

"So what's the problem, soldier? That shows initiative, backbone and ambition. Our men can't be too well-trained, can they?" the colonel inquires, brows furrowing.

The young Pfc. hesitates. "But they're not bucking for promotion, sir. They're having fun."

That may not be exactly how the conversation went, but the events actually occurred, says Bob Clover — one of the trainers with the keys — who was site coordinator at Fort Knox, KY, back in the early days of computers and simulators. Now he works for the Institute for Defense Analysis in Alexandria, VA, but he remembers fondly the popularity of the tank simulators among his trainees and his children.

Imagine for a moment what it would be like to have overeager learners — and their families — sneaking into your company on weekends to get at your training courses. That's the promise of interactive training: It can be so good, so engaging, so much fun, people only half-realize that they are learning valuable job skills while they take the course.

No, we're not really suggesting that whole families will flock to a sales-skills course as they will to a tank-battle simulation. But when it's done right, self-paced interactive training can be the most effective way to train. When it's done wrong, it's boring, useless, and an expensive waste of time. The key ingredient in computer-based training — or multimedia-based training — is interactivity. But what exactly is this X-factor? And where can we find it?

The Ghose in the Machine

For the purposes of this discussion, we are focusing on the kind of interactivity instructional designers try to build into computer-based training (although some of the same principles apply to the classroom as well). When they do it successfully, learners interact with the computer in a meaningful way that engages them *and* imparts some knowledge or skills.

The concept of interactivity has been around a long time. In fact, Socrates was an early architect of interactivity, says Gloria Gery, president of Gery Associates, a consulting firm in Tolland, MA, and author of *Making CBT Happen*. The give and take of Socratic dialogue is as interactive as we humans can get.

However, Gery contends, the classroom is not always the ideal setting for Socratic dialogue. Only one person in the class can answer the instructor's questions; everyone else is only partially engaged, thinking to themselves how they would have answered without really being accountable. When the computer is acting as the inquisitor, says Gery, the learner must answer the question, and there's no escaping accountability for those answers.

Since Socrates's name has already come up, we might as well admit that discussions about the nature of interactivity easily digress into philosophy. That's why we pestered a meditative Silvasailam Thiagarajan, a.k.a. Thiagi, who heads Workshops by Thiagi, a simulation and game-design consultancy in Bloomington, IN. While Thiagi trains mostly in classrooms, his ideas about interactivity apply equally to a computer-based environment.

Thiagi draws a distinction between "pure" interactivity and "pseudo" interactivity. Pure interactivity is like a conversation in a bar, he says: There's lots of uninhibited banter, interruptions are frequent and forgivable, and no one controls the conversation. (No one is *able* to control the conversation.)

That, however, is not an effective model for instruction, says Thiagi. Instead, he prefers "guided discovery," a model that gives learners opportunities to talk, interrupt, and control the learning, but still sticks to the objectives for the training.

Risk In a Risk-Free Environment

If there is one factor that separates truly interactive training programs from the page-turners (a derogatory term for noninteractive CBT that forces you to read screen after screen of text) it's risk, says Michael Allen, president of Allen Interaction, a Minneapolis consulting firm that teaches clients to develop interactive multimedia training.

Allen has been wrestling with interactivity issues for many years, first as the director of the PLATO project at Control Data Corp. and later as the creator of Authorware, one of the most popular authoring programs. When he evaluates a CBT program, he says, "I look to see if the user is put at any risk." Can users lose something or have something unpleasant happen to them? When there is no risk of consequences for the learner, he points out, the mind runs on idle.

Any number of things can be consequences, says Allen. One is making learners start over if they answer too many questions incorrectly. In a simulation developed by 3M Co. of St. Paul, MN, for example, users are given a bunch of materials and a variety of the company's adhesives. They are supposed to put them together to build a bridge that a cartoon elephant will cross. If they use the wrong adhesives with the wrong materials, the bridge won't hold, the elephant falls into the chasm, and the user has to start over. That's the risk, the consequence of not learning.

This talk of inserting an element of risk into interactive multimedia training may seem to contradict the oft-touted advantage of computer learning as safe and nonthreatening. But Allen contends that the risk-free nature of CBT has been misinterpreted. Computer learning is safe in the sense that learners can't be humiliated in front of their peers, he says. In classroom situations, even as adults, many of us hesitate to answer questions in front of a group unless we are certain we are right. Computer environments can challenge us, put us at risk on an intellectual level, without making us ante up our self-esteem in the interest of learning.

There are other risks employees don't need to face in order to learn. Neil Silverstein, training manager for Duracell International Inc., the Bethel, CT, battery manufacturer, is developing a battery-technology multimedia course in which employees build their own batteries in a simulated environment. In the simulation, learners have a lot of chemicals at their disposal. If they incautiously experiment with substances, say, mixing lithium and water, they create an explosion.

The computer environment teaches an important lesson without anyone getting hurt, explains Silverstein. He's fairly certain that employees who go through the simulation will never try the lithium and water cocktail again. "You need to let the users make mistakes because that's how people learn," he says.

Risks are also built into a program developed by Federal Express Corp., the Memphis, TN-based courier. In this program, trainees see a simulated conveyor belt carrying packages past them, explains Bud Demetriou, manager of training and testing technology. They must choose the right packages, based on addresses, to put in their vans. If they aren't careful, they will get the wrong parcels. If they aren't fast enough, they may miss some. Those are the risks.

Some simulated consequences can be more severe than others, says Lori Southerton, senior multimedia and Internet consultant for Medtronic Inc., a medical-device manufacturer based in Minneapolis suburb Fridley, MN. In one of her company's multimedia programs, the user has to follow the right procedure for programming a pacemaker just put in a patient's chest. If you do it wrong, says Southerton, you lose the patient.

Keeping score is another way to attach consequences — and thus ensure interactivity — in computer learning environments, says interactive pioneer Allen. You don't lose patients or blow up laboratories, but competing against yourself or the scores of others who have taken the course still introduces an element of risk. To competitive types, the risk of losing is sufficiently compelling to encourage them to learn.

Even competing against the clock can be engaging, says Clare Walsh, an instructional designer for InterCom, an interactive training supplier in The Woodlands, TX. For a health club's employees, she developed an interactive program that combined the elements of keeping score with some of the aforementioned elements of risk. In her simulation, the employee has to keep the customer alive as long as possible with a regimen of suggested exercises and dietary proscriptions, essentially attempting to stall a predetermined arrival of the Grim Reaper. (Funny how death, the ultimate risk, shows up in many of the truly interactive programs.)

MORE INTERACTIVITY: THE SHORT COURSE

The trouble with any discussion about the nature of interactivity is that it soon becomes a philosophical treatise on humans, machines, questions, answers, and the meaning of existence. Blame Socrates. For those of you busting your backs to make computer-based instruction more interactive for learners, however, some concrete tips might be helpful.

• Limit video clips to 30 seconds, says Steve Bainbridge, director of multimedia for Wilson Learning, the Eden Prairie, MN, training supplier. If the video goes on longer, you'll lose users' attention — unless the footage is particularly riveting.

• Make users *do* something every 15 to 30 seconds. "The idea is to get people to interact several times each minute," Bainbridge says. And if you can get their synapses firing along with the interaction, he says, all the better.

• Observe while users beta-test your courseware. If you are used to a classroom environment, you probably unconsciously pick up messages from trainees' body language. That's why Bainbridge insists that his developers watch customers try out training courses in the field. You see when they are bored and see when something you've done turns the porch lights on, he says.

If you're really brave, says Lori Southerton, senior multimedia and Internet consultant for Medtronic, a Minneapolis medical-device manufacturer, beta-test your courses with your kids. She takes programs home and lets her 8-year-old son test-drive them. If it's not engaging, someone from the Nintendo generation will toss it aside pretty darn quick.

• Understand that not everyone needs the same level of interaction. Computerphobes will get intimidated, says Southerton, if there's too much interactivity. They can also get confused if there's too much going on in front of them. Advanced users, on the other hand, will get bored if you don't have enough on-screen activity. Walking that fine line and getting just the right amount of interactivity is the real trick.

Michael Allen, CEO of Allen Interaction, a Minneapolis consulting firm, attacked this problem by designing five different paths users can take through his training course for Windows 95. Each path has different levels of interactivity, ranging from a simulated environment in which users are encouraged to try things on their own to a carefully coached scenario with lots of demonstrations of the skills the course is designed to teach.

WITH A LOT OF HELP FROM MY FRIENDS

This article about interactivity may look like other articles you see in TRAINING Magazine, but it's a little different: It is the product of the process it's describing. With a lot of help from my friends, I decided to try a little experiment in interactivity.

Instead of going through the usual process of researching and writing an article, I decided to make the procedure interactive — like a good computer-based training program. Now, there was no way I could involve every reader in this process, so I recruited about 20 people from the TRDEV-L newsgroup, an Internet-based discussion group dedicated to training and development issues. Volunteers from this group helped me research and write the article.

Here's how it worked:

I told the group, which became known as the "Focus Group" in e-mail messages, the subject of the article and the general direction I wanted to go. I asked for questions they would like me to put to the experts I would interview. I also gave group members the parameters of the process — deadlines for reading and answering their e-mail for several days — as well as the opportunity to un-volunteer themselves. Only a few dropped out, either because the topic didn't interest them or because they would be out of the office on those particular days.

During my interviews with experts and practitioners, I asked some of the questions submitted by the group as well as my own (hey, I wasn't about to give up all control). After the interviews were completed and the notes assembled, I started writing.

Instead of an intense couple of days writing start-to-finish, I wrote this article in chunks and submitted them to the Focus Group, always concluding the e-mail message with the question: Where should we go from here? I usually gave a choice of two or three different directions the article could go, as well as the choice I feared most: "Some other direction entirely."

Mercifully, the group never picked that one and instead helped me frame and focus the information I had gathered. The group did, however, point out some areas I had missed, areas that could easily inspire other TRAINING Magazine articles.

So how did this process affect what you're reading? I started out by sending the group two alternative introductions. The one you see — about the tank simulators at Fort Knox — was chosen almost unanimously by the group. The next section used to have two more paragraphs in it about how it's important to create a dialogue with the computer, but the group cut them. The sidebar ("This Is Just a Rehearsal") used to be part of the main story, but almost everyone agreed that the story was getting sidetracked, so the consensus was to take it out and box it.

In the end, the group focused the article, changed its direction, and generally dispelled my preconceptions about what readers really want in a magazine article. The primary message was: Stop playing around and get to the meat of your message.

The process was fun. In the spirit of interactivity, it was also somewhat risky, at least for me. It was an experiment and, I think, a successful one.

The members of the Focus Group combined great humor with terrific insight and an uncanny ability to overlook typos and grammatical errors in the drafts I fired at them. Special thanks to Celia Bastis, Don Elkington, Meg Stephens, Ron Fulkert, Kelly Grogan, Meredith Cash, Kathleen Kelm, Normand Tanguay, Charles Balan, William Crimando, Dave Ferguson, Dan Thompson and Dan Barkowitz.

— Bob Filipczak

Don't Worry, Be Stupid

Allen has another bone to pick with much of the interactive training he's seen: The feedback the computer gives trainees is too protective of the presumed sensibilities of the learner. "There has been for some time this tendency to be so sweet and warm with respect to hand-holding the users that if they should ever by happenstance enter an incorrect response, then you kind of gush forward with, 'Oh, we're so sorry you made this mistake. Now don't worry. Everything is going to be fine,' " says Allen.

Again, he blames devotion to the idea of risk-free learning for producing feedback that is meaningless and boring. In one off-the-shelf course Allen recently developed, *Breeze Through Windows 95*, the feedback is anything but boring. After committing the same error a number of times, the user is regaled by animation showing an old man, smoking a cigar, who compares the error to sticking the lit end of a stogie in your mouth. "My feeling about it is, if people do something stupid, you ought to say so," says Allen.

But there's a fine line between feedback that's too soft and cracks that are too judgmental, says Robert Zielinski, co-founder of The Human Element, a Bloomington, MN, consulting firm that develops interactive multimedia training. Today we are faulting on the side of being too careful, he says, using candy-coated buzzers to show trainees that they are wrong without hurting their feelings. He prefers to put learners in computer-aided simulations and give them a problem to solve. That way, feedback can be corrective rather than judgmental, or even completely neutral. For example, if a user changes the timing on a simulated engine, and the engine behaves differently, then the user must figure out what it all means.

Sometimes, however, it pays to just scare the pants off them. Steve Bainbridge, director of multimedia for Wilson Learning, an Eden Prairie, MN, training supplier, has been developing interactive multimedia training since the days of "interactive videodisc" training in the early '80s. One of the sales-training courses his company has just completed includes a feedback device that hits salespeople where they live.

The course is designed to help salespeople sell to high-level executives and CEOs. If the trainee uses a traditional product pitch, or questions the executive about industry trends (something the saleperson should know from doing his homework, Bainbridge explains), the CEO gets mad, harangues him, and throws him out. "Those are the salesperson's worst fears, and we play them out," says Bainbridge.

Feedback should also make the

learner more accountable, says Allen. If the computer coddles the trainee too much, he suggests, "that almost says that the student is faultless and the whole responsibility for learning is on the designer."

Brain Surgery By the Numbers

A long-accepted element of the interactivity equation is learner control and navigation. But that invariably leads to the question: How much is enough? Some designers, like Duracell's Silverstein, say that as a general principle, the learner should be given as much control as possible.

"Adults need to be in control of their situation, period," says Silverstein. He points out that no designer — no matter how good — can accommodate the preferences of every learner. Handing the controls over to learners allows them to customize the course on the fly and get more out of it.

When you get into specifics, however, learner control is often subject to the content of the course. If you're teaching a linear process, you can't let trainees jump wherever they choose, hypertexting from topic to topic and dabbling in random bits of training.

"There are times — particularly when we are trying to educate [customers] on a process — we need to force them through a series of steps," says Medtronic's Southerton. Remember what kinds of products her company develops; you're going to

feel a lot better knowing the medical technician who is programming your pacemaker learned all the steps in the right order.

Consultant Zielinski agrees. "You don't want someone hyperlinking their way through brain surgery," he says. When learners have to know Fact A before they can understand Principle B, instructional designers can restrict some of the directions in which a learner can proceed. In general, most designers suggest letting learners control which modules to take and in what order. But once learners are in the module, make them go through it in a linear fashion.

Just as important as control, says Southerton, is navigation. All of Medtronics' 30 multimedia programs have Perpetual Navigation, an icon that tells users where they are, where they've been, and how to escape. It even tells them how far they are into a particular module.

The ability to escape from a training program is important at Federal Express, says Demetriou. Many employees take courses at their desks and can be called away suddenly. They have to be able to get out of the program. It's helpful if the system puts some kind of bookmark where they left off, he says, so they can find their place without too much hassle.

The navigation in most programs, especially page-turners, really frosts Southerton. "It's next, next, next, next," she says. "Well, from a user's

standpoint that's really boring. I always jump to the end because I don't care about all that garbage. Every time I get stuck in a video, I want to quit and go somewhere else."

The Learning Environment

If interactivity is the quest of effective computer-based training, then simulation is the Holy Grail of interactivity. Although there's little agreement on the definition of a simulated environment, we tend to know it when we see it. It's no coincidence that almost every example of effective interaction mentioned thus far has been a simulation or a simulated environment. "The most powerful learning environments are simulators," says consultant Gery.

But only when the learning is "designed into" the environment. Simcity, a popular game in which users plan an urban landscape from scratch, is still one of the best examples of how compelling a simulation can be, but it has serious limits as a teaching system, says Gery. It's easy to plateau at a certain level and be unable to improve your score. There's nothing built into the simulation that helps you get better.

Multimedia veteran Allen agrees that simulation provides one of the highest levels of interactivity. But, he points out, without the right kind of coaching or guidance, a simulation can bog down learners. He compares the effect to that of experimental class-

---

THIS IS JUST A REHEARSAL

If all the world's a stage, then interactivity can be an important player in the brain's theater of learning. Some suggest that if multimedia developers used more of what learning theorists know about how adults acquire skills, interactive programs would suffer fewer catcalls from users.

Enter stage right: Ruth Clark, an instructional psychologist who heads Clark Training and Consulting in Phoenix, and the author of *Developing Technical Training*. She is currently working on a book about cognitive processing of information as it relates to learning and how it gets expressed in job performance.

According to Clark, learning-theory research suggests that information enters human memory in two ways: maintenance rehearsal and elaborative rehearsal. Most computer-based learning, she says, uses maintenance rehearsal — repetition of information learned — to get the stuff into long-term memory. "Many people build that in as interaction. They'll ask a question that's essentially a regurgitation of information just given, and that does not result in learning," Clark emphasizes.

What does result in learning, she says, is elaborative rehearsal: You transform the knowledge you're trying to insert into the learners' heads by associating it with what they already know.

She illustrates the difference: A company was teaching its employees about object-oriented programming (OOP) by having an expert lecture at them about the four benefits of this new tool. The expert was asked to make the lecture more interactive, so he added questions. He explained the four benefits of OOP, and then asked the class to name the four benefits of OOP. More maintenance rehearsal, says Clark, and not terribly effective.

Finally, Clark suggested breaking the class into groups and asking each group to discuss how they could use OOP on projects they were actually working on at the time. That's elaborative rehearsal, says Clark, as opposed to volleying facts back and forth between instructor — or computer — and students. When the mind rehearses the knowledge elaboratively, she says, learning research demonstrates that it's much more likely to wend its way into long-term memory. — **B.F.**

---

rooms popular in the late '60s: An information-rich environment was available, but students didn't learn anything because there was no direction, no problem to solve, and no learning goals to strive for.

Allen solves the problem by including a computer coach in a simulated environment. In his Windows 95 trainer, one on-screen coach is a thermometer that shows users when they're getting warmer — closer to accomplishing the task. Zielinski suggests that presenting users with a problem, then dropping them into a simulation that requires them to solve it, creates the kind of interaction that immediately engages them.

The Media Ain't the Message

Now that we've sort of evolved from computer-based training to multimedia-based training, has truly interactive courseware become the rule?

True, multimedia engages more senses, so trainees should be more involved in what's going on in the course. Unfortunately, more media don't necessarily equal more interactivity, just as more interactivity doesn't always result in more learning. If the flurry of media don't get the trainees responding to and thinking about the material on the screen, the learning won't take.

Trouble is, media are seductive, says Gery, "and all the good work around instructional design, on relevance, on representation, on engaging thought, sometimes gets subsumed because people like playing with the media."

Duracell's Silverstein says he never includes a medium in a course just for the sake of including it. "Everybody can make nice pictures," says Silverstein. "But we have to remember that training is what we do," he says.

And it's easy to take your eye off that ball, concedes Ruth Clark, an instructional psychologist with Clark Training and Consulting in Phoenix. Learning is not a function of the media used in a course, she says. It's a function of the instructional methodologies used to build the course. Similarly, she says, you can't evaluate a multimedia course on the basis of how it looks. "You're not evaluating learning outcomes, and as long as you don't do that, one [course] is as good as another."

The best you can hope for with the new media you can now employ, says Gery, is to add depth and more concrete details to the programs. "I'm not saying, by the way, that media can't add value. A really good media representation of an object will permit much more direct manipulation and require much less transformation in thinking," says Gery.

> ## "You need to let the users make mistakes, because that's how people learn."

Making the Leap

Can average classroom trainers make the leap to interactive computer-based training effectively, or will they have to be, God forbid, retrained? Maybe a good first step is to convince classroom instructors to be more interactive in the classroom, says consultant Thiagi. Often that means putting them through the equivalent of a 12-step program so they can kick their addiction to lectures, he jokes.

But some traditional classroom skills do transfer to developing interactive multimedia training. George Ferguson, a senior consultant in leadership, education and development for Hoechst Marion Roussel Inc., a pharmaceutical company in Kansas City, MO, incorporates what he learned about trainee preferences as a stand-up trainer into CBT programs. He tested material he intended to use in interactive CBT with live classes just to see how students reacted, what questions they asked, and which directions they went.

In that way, Ferguson says, he was able to anticipate the learning paths trainers preferred and to include them in CBT. "When I was designing, what I was doing was visualizing myself in the classroom, giving the information, asking the questions. So I guess there's an understanding about how to ask questions. There's an understanding about how adults learn," he says.

Duracell's Silverstein agrees. He tells trainers that their classroom skills are 100 percent transferable to a computer-learning environment. All you have to do is learn the technical skills of using an authoring system, he says. "Design is 70 percent of the game. Or maybe it's 80 percent."

Thiagi, however, suggests that other instructional skills may be more important for CBT developers. Instructors who are best at working with individuals, not whole classrooms, will probably excel in a computer environment, he says. Instructors who are good at coaching or tutoring, he adds, probably have the right set of skills.

When Wilson Learning pioneered its interactive videodisc training, Bainbridge says, it asked its best, most experienced instructor — who was well-versed in one-to-one instruction — to consult on the project. "You're really trying to clone your very best one-on-one instructors," says Bainbridge.

But trainers have to learn to think out of the box, says Lance Dublin, CEO of the Dublin Group, a computer-training consulting firm in San Francisco. "Educators are trying to find a way to replicate an old model, which I think is old-paradigm thinking," he says. And they need to look to other models and other areas of expertise if they really want to learn about interactivity.

Salespeople, marketing people, advertising and broadcast-television professionals know how to hook an audience, says Dublin. Trainers can learn from them. Look at the Publisher's Clearinghouse sweepstakes mailings, he suggests. The people who design those contests know that if they can get you to interact with the packet — finding the right stamps, transferring stickers from one page to another — you are more likely to pay attention to what they are selling.

Bainbridge, who is also a part-time marketing person, agrees that some of his presentation and selling skills have helped him develop hooks that draw people into his training programs. So, odious as it may sound, trainers may want to take a trip to the marketing department and find out how those people hook an audience. But take some pepper spray, just in case.

VR, AI, and the End of Interactivity As We Know It

The nature of interactivity doesn't change — even though faster, slicker, brighter tools can make training presentations more attractive. Even so, some contend that advances such as virtual reality and artificial intelligence will turbocharge the engagement power of a simulated environment.

Duracell's Silverstein believes that virtual reality will become the next training medium. "The handwriting is on the wall," he says. "I'm kind of scared because now I've got to become a virtual-reality programmer."

He's planning to build a virtual-reality manufacturing simulation so employees can learn to run machinery without shutting down the line for training.

Federal Express may create a virtual van, a training simulation for couriers who drive trucks, adds Demetriou.

If all this talk of interactivity reminds you of your excursions on the Internet, there may be lessons we can learn there, too. The Internet, says consultant Dublin, is a good example of an interactive environment in which no one even thinks about interactivity as an issue. Much of the Internet was set up so that humans could interact, via computer, with other humans and other computers. The interaction was so natural that interactivity became the norm, and people didn't think about it, they just did it.

The point of multimedia training, Dublin says, is not to create an interactive environment for its own sake, but to create a dynamic educational construct where people learn and interactivity is . . . well, it just is. "In the learning environment of the next decade, interactivity becomes a nonissue because interactivity is a given," he says.

Dublin quotes from David Kline and Daniel Burstein's book, *Road Warriors: Dreams and Nightmares Along the Information Highway:* "[People] do not want technology nor do they want interactivity per se. They want an immersive, emotionally compelling or truly informative experience."

Notes:

CORPORATE CULTURE

Raiders of the Corporate Culture

BY CHRIS LEE

It's one of those concepts that evolves over years or even decades, remaining submerged just beneath the surface of public awareness until a simple, yet unpredictable, catalyst brings it into focus. Often, the interrelated swirl of events makes it nearly impossible for those caught in the mainstream to pinpoint that specific "spark."

Not so with the current fascination over corporate culture. Although a wide range of social and economic events over the last 20 years certainly contributed to the strength with which the idea has taken root in the hearts and minds of corporate America, Thomas Peters and Robert Waterman's best-selling *In Search of Excellence* is the logical nomination for catalyst in this case.

A largely anecdotal and common-sensical description of what some of the most successful American corporations *do right*, the book has created an avalanche of demand for "excellence" — excellence in productivity, customer service, management and training.

How do you define excellence? And, once it's defined, how do you attain it? Not simple questions, but ones that are inextricably tied up, according to suddenly prevailing opinion, in the concept of corporate culture.

Why should HRD types attend to the current hoopla over culture? For one thing, it provides a means of taking a holistic look at your organization. What, exactly, are its espoused values? What assumptions go without saying? What factors perpetuate, for good or ill, its prescribed way of doing business? Without a finger on the pulse of your company, culture mavens argue, you are operating in a vacuum and will be hard put to design or deliver effective training programs.

An understanding of corporate culture also can help you excel as a change agent in your organization. When external factors — an economic downturn, new technology, competition, deregulation — put a company's traditional operating methods in jeopardy, fine tuning or even drastic change may be necessary. Witness the new emphasis on marketing, sales and customer service in the telecommunications and financial industries. It's a whole new ball game for Ma Bell, American Express, et al, and a golden opportunity for HRD to become an integral part of a reworked strategy.

What Is It?

The more the notion of corporate culture is bandied about, the more likely that it will turn into one of those terms that means everything — and nothing. And for the pragmatic trainer who suspects the concept is more than slightly akin to the emperor's new clothes, the current trendiness of "Culture" may supply the impetus needed to dismiss the whole idea out of hand. Therefore, a few definitions are in order.

Peters and Waterman define corporate culture as shared values, conveyed by the organization's stories, myths and legends. In the companies they characterize as "excellent," they point out, these shared values are as crystal clear to the CEO as they are to the production-line worker.

In another best-selling treatment of the subject, *Corporate Cultures* (Addison-Wesley, Reading, MA, 1982), Terrence Deal and Allan Kennedy differentiate five elements that are key to understanding a corporate culture: Business environment, or the external marketplace that defines what a company must do to be a success; values, which define "success" and form the heart of the culture; heroes, who personify the values and act as tangible role models for success; rites and rituals, which spell out the kind of behavior expected from employees; and the cultural network, which carries the values and heroic mythology.

Such understanding is crucial, Deal and Kennedy maintain, because "[companies] that have cultivated their individual identities by shaping values, making heroes, spelling out rites and rituals, and acknowledging the cultural network have an edge. These corporations have values and beliefs to pass along — not just products. They have stories to tell — not just profits to make. They have heroes whom managers and workers can emulate — not just faceless bureaucrats. In short, they are human institutions that provide practical meaning for people, both on and off the job."

Edgar Schein, a professor of organizational psychology and management at MIT's Sloan School of Management, contends that the concept is grounded in something deeper than "shared understandings" or values. He defines organizational culture as "a pattern of *basic assumptions* which a given group has invented, discovered or developed in learning to cope with its problems of external adaptation and internal integration, which have worked well enough to be considered valid, and, therefore, to be taught to new members as the correct way to perceive, think and feel in relation to those problems."

Schein's three-tiered model of culture begins with visible artifacts (those things in an organization that are easily seen — architecture, dress, training materials — but difficult to analyze), progresses to the "whys" of those artifacts or the espoused values of the group, and goes still deeper to basic assumptions — the non-debatable values of a group; the axioms that are taken for granted.

According to Schein's model, basic assumptions are the invisible, preconscious underpinnings of a culture that actually determine both values and overt behavior. "This is where culture lies," he says. And the nature of basic assumptions is what makes the study of organizational culture extremely complex.

In a 1981 paper, "On Organizational Culture," Schein emphasized caution for culture faddists who would use the idea to explain everything in sight.

"If we look at the recent use of the concept in reference to management style differences between countries or, more significantly, behavioral differences between organizations, we see less concern for ethnographic rigor and virtually no concern for explaining what we mean by the concept of culture.

"If this trend persists," he continues, "we will have one more concept that purports to explain almost everything but that, in the end, explains nothing because it does not explain itself."

The Training Research Forum (TRF), an informal group of HRD practitioners that has been meeting for 15 years to discuss a wide range of subjects of interest to its membership, addressed organizational culture last fall. TRF's avowed objective is "to increase and substantiate our economic value to our organizations." The title given to the fall meeting, "Organizational Culture — Why Bother?" reflected the skepticism the subject might engender in a group of pragmatic practitioners.

Mel Tumin, a professor of sociology and anthropology at Princeton University and author of numerous works on social and cultural issues, led one of the TRF sessions. Tumin contends that the concept of culture, in the deep, rich, anthropological sense, cannot be applied to the shallow environment of the corporation.

"Rich cultures integrate over a long period of time," he explained, "and this is not the way organizational culture is being talked about. Peters and Waterman are talking about a culture of *means*, not ends. You can change the operating rules in an organization to reflect sound goals, sound processes and sound relationships — a useful concept, but not an anthropological culture."

Tumin, in fact, doubts the efficacy of attempting to create a "culture of commitment" in a company. He posits a continuum of individual performance within an organization that has compliance on one end (what most companies get through coercive means) and commitment on the other (the most difficult to come by and pos-

sible only when the culture's means and ends are one and the same).

Religions and families are examples of cultures wherein the means and the ends are one, Tumin explained. "You get *commitment* when rewards go with membership, not on the basis of performance."

In an organizational culture, he adds, you've got diverse means that result in diverse ends — and you can't judge the effectiveness of the "culture." One constant is the nihilism of the bottom line — employees know they will not be rewarded for membership, only for performance. Given that any rational employee will operate in his own interest, to the extent possible, Tumin suggests one route by which an organization can create commitment: Maintain an environment in which the employees' self-interest and the common good are one.

"Trainers are thrilled when management comes to them looking for a training program to 'fix' a problem. But the worst thing you can do is try to 'fix' it."

How's Your Culture?

The urge to tinker with culture is based on two assumptions: 1) excellent companies have strong cultures and 2) a company's culture can be changed.

Peters and Waterman reinforced the idea that strong cultures equal excellent companies (companies that innovate continuously and make money doing it) in the now-famous eight attributes that summarize their characteristics.

1. *A bias for action.* "These companies may be analytical in their approach to decision-making, but they are not paralyzed by it. Standard operating procedure is 'Do it, fix it, try it.' "

2. *Close to the customer.* "These companies learn from the people they serve ... Many ... got their best product ideas from customers. That comes from listening, intently and regularly."

3. *Autonomy and entrepreneurship.* These companies foster leaders and innovators — "champions" — by encouraging practical risk-taking and

supporting good attempts, even when the attempts fail.

4. *Productivity through people.* "Excellent companies treat the rank and file as the root source of quality and productivity gain."

5. *Hands-on, value driven.* Excellent companies pay "explicit attention" to values and "their leaders have created exciting environments through personal attention, persistence and direct intervention — far down the line.'"

6. *Stick to the knitting.* "The odds for excellent performance seem strongly to favor those companies that stay reasonably close to the businesses they know."

7. *Simple form, lean staff.* "The underlying structural forms and systems in the excellent companies are elegantly simple....Top-level staffs are lean...."

8. *Simultaneous loose-tight properties.* "The excellent companies are both centralized and decentralized ... they have pushed autonomy down to the shop floor or product-development team. On the other hand, they are fanatic centralists around the few core values they hold dear."

The companies that demonstrate these qualities, IBM, Hewlett-Packard, 3M, Delta Airlines, Disney Productions, Procter & Gamble and others, measure up on Peters and Waterman's yardstick of "excellence." Their message, although surprisingly non-prescriptive, comes through loud and clear: "It works for these guys; it'll work in your company, too."

Many CEOs are taking heed: They want to set their own companies upon the eightfold path. Why have so many managers adopted the word according to Peters and Waterman? One possible explanation is offered by Richard Wilson, vice president of marketing for Zenger-Miller, the Cupertino, CA-based training company that recently introduced "Toward Excellence," a program built around the *In Search of Excellence* principles.

"The common knowledge and logic in the book confirmed a lot of biases for many executives," Wilson says. "It confirmed things they always wanted to do — 'Management By Walking Around,' for example — but never felt comfortable doing. Now it's easier for them to change the system — they can point to the excellent companies and the book for substantial justification."

But when these same managers begin to talk about building a culture of "excellence" in an existing organization, the waters begin to get murky. "You can label it 'building a new culture,'" says Ed Schein, "but, in fact, you are enhancing and building on the strengths of the existing culture."

Rosabeth Moss Kanter, author of *Change Masters: Innovation for Productivity in the American Corporation* (Simon & Schuster, Inc., 1983), questions the utility of the concept itself in terms of change. "Saying, 'We want to change the culture of an organization,' is not saying anything useful," she told TRAINING. "The culture is a function of the organization's structure, so you work within the structure to change work practices, policies, job behaviors, rewards and communication."

In *Change Masters*, she describes the "five building blocks of change" that she has seen organizations use to manage change and meet new challenges.

1. *Departure from tradition.* Whether by plan or design, activities occur that "deviate from organizational expectations" and "permit entrepreneurs to step forward. . . . Look for the already existing innovations that signal ability to make [a] shift," she recommends, "and then use these as the organization's own foundation for solving its problems and designing a better system."

2. *Crisis or galvanizing event.* "The critical point for the people involved is that the event or crisis has a demand quality and seems to require a response. . . . [An] effective response to crisis may depend on the tradition-departure factor."

3. *Strategic decisions.* "New strategies are defined that build new methods, products, structures, into official plans."

4. *Individual "prime movers."* "The job of prime movers is not only to 'talk up' the new strategy but also to manipulate those symbols that indicate commitment to it. . . . A few clear signals, consistently supported, are what it takes to change an organization's culture and direction: signposts in the morass of organizational messages."

5. *Action vehicles.* "The actions implied by the changes cannot reside on the level of ideas, as abstractions, but must be concretized (sic) . . . Changes take hold when they are reflected in multiple concrete manifestations throughout the organization."

And that's where training can play a crucial role. Training, although far from the only change strategy, can act

---

CASE IN POINT

BY CHRIS LEE

"Corporate culture" is an easy term to bandy about, a difficult concept to get a solid handle on. *In Search of Excellence* has been criticized by fans of hard data and "solid research" for its heavy reliance on anecdotes to make its points, but culture is an "umbrella" concept — and an abstraction. If you want to draw a picture of it, the alternative to generic "managementese" almost has to be anecdotal examples of the sorts of things found beneath the umbrella.

One way to get the flavor of what corporate culture is and what it means to change a culture is to look at a company whose culture is changing.

GTE Corp., already rocked by deregulation of the telecommunications industry, was hit with another zinger late last year when its president, Thomas A. Vanderslice, resigned. Vanderslice was recruited from General Electric Co. by GTE chairman Theodore F. Brophy in 1979 to help prepare the company for the brave new world of competition. But this "agent of change," as *Business Week* characterized him, seems to have overhauled himself out of a job.

Vanderslice resigned four years into a five-year contract at least partly because of a cultural clash: "As might be expected of any agent of change, Vanderslice had a management style that contrasted sharply with that of many executives already at the company," reported *Business Week* ("Turn-over at the Top," December 19, 1983). Yet the changes he made appeared productive: Sales per employee rose 40% from 1979 to 1982 and profits were up.

Telecommunications accounts for 70% of GTE's business and, although the company has not been in the throes of divestiture like AT&T, the changes in its marketplace are equally revolutionary. The well-publicized struggles of AT&T created considerable readiness for change on the part of GTE employees — it was obvious something had to happen. And Vanderslice was a visible and concrete something. His departure will no doubt have a momentous effect on the cultural changes in progress at the company.

GTE is a conglomerate that includes operations as diverse as a light-bulb manufacturer and a high-tech micro-circuit manufacturer, as well as telephone companies — each with its own cultural norms. In fact, it is such a diversified organization that another question enters the fray: Does it make sense to try to create some sort of "unified" GTE culture?

One cultural vehicle GTE has used across its five groups of companies is the "Best Program." A year and a half ago, all 45 strategic business units were asked to systematically analyze their operations by identifying two or three major competitors and the benchmarks of comparison with those competitors, i.e., what their competitors do better, to get a measurement of how they stack up. They then identify the major gaps and give management a plan for a strategy to close those gaps within two or three years — or justify why GTE shouldn't sell them off.

The message that gets across is that each company has to define the business it is in and its market. The Best Program has been taken seriously, a company spokesman says, because Brophy takes it seriously.

Since Vanderslice left GTE, the company has reorganized to eliminate the position of president. Two chief operating officers now head GTE's businesses, divided according to regulated and unregulated companies. One of Vanderslice's protégés from General Electric heads up the unregulated side of the businesses; a GTE veteran heads up the regulated side.

What happens next is anybody's guess. But GTE's experience over the next few years may become a classic case in the study of corporate culture: the story of a company's efforts to orchestrate cultural change to meet the requirements of a new environment.

as an action vehicle that helps integrate the new structures, skills and methods.

Doing It

One organization Kanter has helped through the change process is Honeywell Information Systems, the international giant's $2-billion computer business. When James J. Renier took over the presidency two years ago, he wanted to get the culture in line with his new business strategy, says David Dotlich, manager of corporate human resources development. Renier, who is no stranger to the inner workings of corporate culture and its importance in creating a productive work environment, decided to work through the human resources subsystem to effect the needed changes.

And Honeywell's computer business was in need of change. "It was bought from General Electric 25 years ago," explains Dotlich, "and was never 'Honeywellized.' It was a poor performer and the employees were cynical and distrustful. Renier wanted to build a cultural effort that would produce trust, cooperation and teamwork."

Honeywell's change efforts have included a communication program to emphasize teamwork and define values; a "cultural boot camp" which brought 25 top managers together for six days to examine how to change the culture; participation in Executive Challenge, an out-in-the-woods program that seeks to build trust through teamwork activities; and training programs to let managers and employees at all levels know what kind of behavior is expected and rewarded.

In addition to emphasizing team building, Honeywell used what Dotlich calls intervening symbols, such as who gets promoted and demoted, and factory tours and speeches by Renier. All of these activities were aimed at getting employees to share, instead of protect, information and to treat each other with respect, Dotlich says.

According to Dotlich, a key element in Honeywell's cultural adjustment is — you guessed it — an eight-step formula.

* Define your philosophy or values.
* Assign resources to your cultural change effort — people, time and money.
* Be sure you have top-down commitment.

* Be sure you have bottom-up support.
* Use a hierarchical approach to attack all levels of the organization simultaneously.
* Build the program into your human resources subsystem — training, selection, compensation, etc.
* Use a learning replication model — start small and build from there.
* Be patient.

Since Honeywell's cultural change process has been in motion for the past two years, Dotlich speaks to that last point from personal experience. At this stage, he says, he does see a change. "You get some of the results intuitively — the stories people tell, the joking." And then there are the concrete changes: reduced turnover and a dramatic flip-flop from a $150-million loss in 1982 to a $100-million profit in 1983.

Fire Fighting

For some organizations, cultural change is more than choosing to redefine a business strategy — it has become a matter of survival. Thanks to government intervention, both the banking and telecommunications industries are facing a marketplace as unfamiliar to them as a moonscape. Their strategies for dealing with change reveal some interesting quirks in the cultural arena.

While many financial institutions are struggling to create a culture to meet the newly competitive nature of the banking industry, one giant in the business is looking backward in order to cope with the changes. The 80-year-old Bank of America traces its cultural heritage back to founder A.P. Giannini — who built a small local bank into a financial giant through the conviction that "every man deserves a teller."

Bank of America's heritage has proven a firm foundation for its reassessment of corporate values, says Jean Coyle, vice president of management development. "We articulated our values in four key dimensions — strategy, marketing, people and technology — that we can trace back to the founder. Those values have been alive since then, but they got out of kilter as the bank became regulated. As we've become deregulated, we've polished them off and they are back in the forefront again."

The bank has given more than lip service to its rediscovery of key values. With the help of Stanley Davis

and Howard Schwartz, consultants with the Management Analysis Center (MAC) in Cambridge, MA, top management defined the values that needed particular attention. The bank used a natural vehicle, its management-development program, to bring about the desired changes in behavior, Coyle says. Twenty-five-hundred managers have already attended the week-long training program, which leans heavily on role play and case studies to increase the odds of internalizing the newly learned skills.

The impetus for cultural change at Bank of America came from the top: president Sam Armacost and executive vice president of personnel Robert Beck decided it was their job to make change occur. In another industry that deregulation has sent reeling, the training function took a decidedly proactive stance to meet the change head-on.

When Michael Mazzarese took time out during December to talk to TRAINING about the changes in store for AT&T Communications (formerly AT&T Long Lines), he was, appropriately enough, surrounded by boxes in preparation for an office move. Formerly a manager in the curriculum-development division, Mazzarese knew he would be responsible for supervisory training and research and development for management education in the new Headquarters Learning Center, but he was unsure of his new title.

"It's a study in Zen," he laughed. 'Today it is, tomorrow it isn't, the next day it is. Things should settle down in about six months."

The AT&T group, regardless of title, has been preparing for the divestiture for the past year. "A year ago, we were still waiting around for January 1, 1984 — waiting to be told what to do," Mazzarese said. "That's okay in a regulated environment, but we finally said, The Fairy Godmother is not coming. Let's get started and do *something.*'"

The "something" they came up with is a model to help define the "outputs" of an excellent manager — the things such a person produces and does — and the skills and competencies needed to produce those outputs. The items they have defined, with the help of Patricia A. McLagan, president of St. Paul, MN-based McLagan & Associates, Inc., tend to emphasize business goals and teamwork. The model, still under development, changed the emphasis of management outputs and the training required, says Mazzarese.

"Now that we have the model, we can match training methodology and content to it," he explains. But they did not wait for research on the model to be completed before developing and delivering training. "We never had a supervisory-skills program before and we needed to supply one as soon as possible. Judging from the requests we were getting, the people in the field were panicking. At least now we have a common vocabulary — it may change, but at least we have something."

The massive upheavals at AT&T also have introduced cultural change into the training function. The "Headquarters Learning Center" label is intended to convey the idea that training, in the formal sense, is only one option for learning and development. "We're changing training from a one-shot deal to a continual process," explains Mazzarese. "Learning is part of the job — not nonproductive time — where you learn from your mistakes. Learning should not be seen as a way to remedy a deficiency, but as a way to improve skills."

The new proactive stance of the learning center has not gone unnoticed at AT&T: "We've changed our image from 'personnel types' — we're not trying to drum up business," Mazzarese says. "We got a call from our data processing group last June and they said, 'We need some training.' We said, 'Okay, you'll have it in two weeks.' Their response was, 'Whoa. We don't even have the employees selected yet.' Before, you see, it was always two or three months [before programs were ready]. It's a great pleasure to be part of this change," he adds.

Words of Warning

According to Tom Peters, some of the best purveyors of corporate culture are inside "universities" of employee training — like those at McDonald's, Disney Productions, Dana and the newly established Apple University. So what are trainers with considerably fewer resources and less tradition at their command to do?

Don't, says Peters, supply a quick-fix training program. "Trainers are thrilled when management comes to them looking for a training program to fix a problem. The worst thing they can do is try to fix it," he says.

"The best way to hang yourself," counsels Larry Bennigson, a senior vice president with MAC, "is to use off-the-shelf training and management-development programs — the materials that already exist in your company — when you're trying to change. [This material] has values imbedded in it that are not relevant to your new situation."

Another mistake he cautions against is a "hit-and-miss process of bringing in outsiders." Most companies attempting cultural change do find outside assistance necessary to get them past the insider's myopia. But, Bennigson emphasizes, "at the time of a strategic change, it's important that the messages are redundant, that they come from the organization's structure. The CEO's speeches, the performance measurements and the training and development programs must be consistent. If you use old programs or outside speakers — regardless of how popular or entertaining they are — they will be carrying the wrong message.

The lesson to be learned from the Chinese character for change seems worthy of mention here: It signifies both danger and opportunity. Given the force of the current winds of change, trainers can't afford to ignore the implications inherent in the concept of corporate culture. As Peters says, "Since managers have realized they are 'In Search Of . . . ,' it's a time of great opportunity."

Notes:

Creativity Training Gets Creative

BY MARC HEQUET

A utility executive and a 10-year-old are playing with ring-shaped magnets, arranging and rearranging the rings on a wood dowel. Sometimes, magnets on the dowel attract and stick together tightly. Sometimes, adjacent magnets repel. Then the upper ring hovers suspended above its neighbor on the upright dowel.

"Do you know anything about electricity?" the boy asks the utility manager.

"Yes, as a matter of fact, I do," chuckles the exec. "Why do you ask?"

"It seems to me," says the boy, studying the magnets on the dowel, "that you could replace a hydraulic suspension system with a magnetized system like this, and it would last forever. There are no parts to wear out."

The executive is stunned. "That's a great idea," he says. "That's a multi-billion-dollar idea. Do you mind if I use it?"

The kid shrugs. "Nah. That's all right. Go ahead. I've got lots more ideas."

A scene from a cute Hollywood movie? No. This is Dallas-based creativity consultant Ann McGee-Cooper's memory of an interaction between a real child and a real utility executive who worked together during a creativity program. McGee-Cooper cloisters half a dozen gifted, outgoing youngsters from a Dallas school with up to 30 top managers in daylong sessions. The adults vent their business problems — and the kids give advice.

Why kids? Fresh brains. "We bring them in because the expert knows the old paradigm," says McGee-Cooper, "and when you know all the rules to the old paradigm it's hard to get to the new."

Adult participants say having the kids around works. "They didn't have any preconceived ideas," says John Janak (not the executive in the magnet story), executive vice president of Texas Utilities Mining Co. in Dallas. "They would throw out possible solutions to problems that on the surface didn't make sense. But when you started thinking about it, maybe a piece of it made sense. It caused you to think in different terms."

And the kids? In her evaluation after one session, 11-year-old Cathy wrote: "I was surprised that the managers had a sense of humor and were funny. My dad is a manager in a large business but he comes home real serious and grumpy." Added another 10-year-old: "The guys [managers] had lots of good ideas. I hope they won't be afraid to try them."

"Lots of good ideas" is precisely what the creativity training industry claims to generate for its clients. Whether the magnetic suspension idea would work in practice isn't the point. What matters is that it illustrates the vaunted paradigm shift that creativity consultants try to effect.

Creativity trainers are becoming ever more creative in that quest. Kids in the conference room is only one tactic. Other trainers use storytelling, dance, even drumming to draw the workplace drones out of their accustomed hives and into flights of imagination that — the creativity mavens argue — will boost productivity, solve job problems and fulfill employees as human beings.

To which critics of the creativity parade reply: Harrumph!

"Do you want your surgeon to be creative? Do you want your nuclear power plant operator to be creative? Your airline pilot? Uh-uh," says Joe Harless, an experimental psychologist and president of Harless Performance Guild in Newnan, GA. "I want them to be systematic. Creativity is technically the behavior of individuals in unpredictable and unanticipated ways. In 99.9 percent of the jobs in America we don't want people to be creative. What we want them to do is replicate what's been successful before.

"If we sheep-dip half the people in the world's business and industry in so-called creativity training, we jolly well might be doing more harm than good," he contends.

Recession Proof?

Be that as it may, creativity training is capering along at a pretty good clip. It began to draw greater attention in the late 1980s, and growth in the area seems to have continued, affected by the recession only a little if at all. Consider:

• TRAINING Magazine's *Industry Report* shows that the number of organizations with 100 or more employees that offer creativity training doubled from 16 percent in 1986 to 32 percent in 1990. That percentage retreated an insignificant 5 points in 1991.

• A Conference Board survey of 2,600 companies released last June showed 32 percent offered creativity training in 1990, up sharply from 22 percent the year before.

• The Center for Creative Leadership (CCL) in Greensboro, NC, says attendance at its programs grew 65 percent over the past three years. Significantly, 25 percent of attendees in 1990 were senior executives, up from just 5 percent three years earlier. In 1989, the CCL conducted creativity training programs for 47 corporate clients under contract. Through the first three quarters of 1991, it had already conducted 65. CCL has experimented with offbeat creativity training methods such as drumming and fables.

• Attendance by corporate clients at presentations on creativity by Buffalo State College's Center for Studies in Creativity jumped from 8,000 in the 1986-87 academic year to 19,000 in '88-'89 before declining to 13,000 in '89-'90. According to the college, the decline does not indicate drooping interest. Instead it reflects the center's changing mix of client companies.

• In January 1991, DuPont de Nemours & Co. of Wilmington, DE, established a Center for Creativity and Innovation that dispatches teams within the corporation to help solve problems, circulate creative ideas, and give in-company grants to people to pursue other creative ideas. "We're in a highly competitive environment and in order to outperform our competitors we're going to have to think and act more creatively," says David Tanner, director of the center.

• Dr. Edward de Bono, a physician turned creativity consultant, says his curriculum is so much in demand that he will license it for the first time to about 50 other trainers beginning in 1992.

Even when the recession does crimp budgets, some companies find a way to obtain creativity training. When money wasn't in the budget for McGee-Cooper's full creativity session for everyone in Texas Utilities Mining Co., she worked with the company to repackage its safety training with elements of her creativity program and trained employees to deliver it.

Creativity training has been criticized in some quarters as difficult to justify. So why isn't it the first to go in widespread corporate budget crunches?

"Organizations are realizing that a recession is short-term and they need to be thinking about the long-term," says Stan Gryskiewicz, senior fellow at CCL. "Usually creativity is on the front end of new products or new processes. What better time than in a recession to think about what your products are going to be three to five years from now?"

Another reason for continued spending on creativity training is that managers see it as closely related to the total quality movement. More companies value employee ideas on productivity, product improvements and customer service. How better to cultivate those ideas than with creativity training?

Still another explanation: The recession itself has increased demand for creativity. After years of corporate downsizing, further budget cutting isn't as simple as it once was. "Cost cutting isn't just putting down figures on a paper," says creativity guru de Bono. "It really involves some creative thinking about what you're doing."

Critics are skeptical about the need for training in a human trait as funda-

mental as creativity. "If you hired me to improve motherhood I would start with motherly love," says consultant Tom Gilbert, president of Hampton, NJ-based Performance Engineering Group. "But we already have an awful lot of that, and I wouldn't know how to improve it."

And is there a hint of desperation in the scramble for creativity skills? "If creativity training is [selling] well in recessionary times, I have an alternative hypothesis about why that's true," says training veteran Harless. "When they're in trouble and facing punishment in the unknown, people tend to grasp at straws."

"Lots of good ideas" is precisely what the creativity training industry tries to generate for its clients.

The Creativity Spectrum

Several different approaches to creativity training have emerged. At one extreme are behaviorists like Gilbert and Harless, both HRD Hall of Famers, who more or less bypass the subject of "creativity" altogether and look directly at their clients' goals. They research how others have successfully achieved those goals, and then try to help their clients emulate that success-producing behavior. Does a client want, say, more inventions? What have other companies done to produce more inventions? Go and do the same thing, they say.

Toward the middle of the creativity training spectrum is the widely known technique of brainstorming, as well as the familiar sequence of divergent thinking-convergent thinking-action planning: Kick it around, develop ideas, bring the ideas together, develop a plan.

Some other middle-of-the-road approaches are metaphoric thinking and two devices identified with de Bono: lateral thinking and the "Six Hat Method."

An example of metaphoric thinking from DuPont: The big chemical maker was pleased with its flame-retardant Nomex fiber, but couldn't get dye to adhere to the tightly knit

surface of the white substance. That precluded Nomex's use for military camouflage. Nor could DuPont imagine clinic-white airplane interiors selling very well.

Company scientists tried thinking metaphorically, a process in which one compares the elements of a problem to other things. One scientist asked what else was like the hard-to-penetrate surface of the Nomex fiber. Well, the surface of the earth is hard. How do we penetrate it? With mines! That led the DuPont researchers to develop a way to fix large organic molecules under the surface of the Nomex, in the same way that timbers prop up the roof of underground mines. The molecules leave space into which dyes can penetrate.

Another teachable middle-of-the-road creativity technique is lateral thinking, so labeled by de Bono in 1969. Lateral thinking is thinking that jumps sideways instead of boring straight ahead. A real-life example, again from DuPont: What could be a new use for Lycra spandex fiber, already used in bicycle shorts and women's bathing suits and undergarments? Lateral thinkers at DuPont wrestled with this one using de Bono's "escape" or "reversal" form of lateral thinking: All Lycra spandex products so far are for people. What about Lycra spandex products for non-people? Doll's clothes? Racehorse warm-up suits?

After a certain amount of lateral thinking, DuPont now says it has a non-people spandex product in the pipeline. What is it? DuPont won't say — except that it's not doll's clothes or horse sweatsuits.

Another de Bono technique is the Six Thinking Hats: White for objective information, red for hunches and intuition, black for logic and caution, yellow for "logical positive" feelings, green for creativity and blue for "control of the thinking process."

The six-hats approach encourages a group of people to think in parallel about a new idea, rather than at cross purposes. It works like this: The leader might first ask everyone to don the imaginary white hat to elicit information about an idea uncolored by feelings, then the red hat for hunches and intuition about what might work, then black for constructive criticism, and so on. The approach is one way to outflank the familiar standoff between perpetual naysayers and eternal optimists.

Examples of de Bono's own creative thinking: Why don't automakers buy downtown parking ramps in major cities — and let only their models park in them? Why don't automakers guarantee that they'll buy back their cars after a certain fixed period, thus solidifying customer loyalty and accelerating the pace at which buyers return for a new vehicle?

Another creativity training guru is Ned Herrmann, a former General Electric trainer. The Ned Herrmann Group, based in Lake Lure, NC, applies Herrmann's "whole brain" model and brain dominance technology to assess thinking styles and train clients accordingly in thinking skills to which individuals are best suited.

Still another is Roger Von Oech, who first became successful in Silicon Valley with the idea of dodging hang-ups that inhibit thinking. When all else fails at working loose from such snags, he suggests *A Whack on the Side of the Head* — the title of his best-selling 1983 book.

Then there are the newcomers. Emerging ideas in creativity training include approaches such as the fables of Minneapolis-based Vara Kamin and the drumming of St. Louis percussionist Gary Muszynski.

Kamin, a former magazine writer, says she realized the power of fables when she and her husband began reading to each other at bedtime to calm themselves after listening to troubling news reports. She now makes presentations and leads exercises based on her fables for corporate clients.

Louis Coffey, a partner in the Philadelphia law firm of Wolf Block Schorr and Solis-Cohen, attended a two-day Kamin program at Omega Institute in Reinbeck, NY, last summer. "What she does first of all," he says, "is create a very safe atmosphere, an emotionally, psychologically safe, warm, nurturing atmosphere in which people feel free to articulate their feelings."

That may sound a bit cuddly for business purposes, but Coffey, for one, has no qualms about writing off the session as a business expense. Kamin's fable "The Mirror Without A Wall," for example, is about beauty. It made lawyer Coffey realize that he finds beauty in a well-crafted legal document. Another lesson: "Different people find beauty in different things," says Coffey, "and it's important to be open and sensitive to that in

dealing with clients and other parties that I negotiate with."

Kamin designs her exercises to have an impact on people's lives, including their work lives. "Having a small 'Aha!'" says Kamin, "can change the direction of the way in which you do things."

At the same time, the fables of Kamin — trained as a registered nurse but not as a psychotherapist — may arouse some troubling emotions. "I was very skeptical and got a real surprise," wrote one participant in an evaluation. "It really brought some feelings to the surface. But, God, what do I do with them now?"

Is there a hint of desperation in the scramble for creativity skills?

Percussionist Gary Muszynski uses music as a metaphor for business in team-building, creativity and leadership development exercises. "When people are learning how to play as a tight, efficient ensemble, some of the same issue blocks come up," says the St. Louis-based trainer. As his participants jam on a Nigerian *udu* drum, marimbas and other percussion instruments, says Muszynski, they learn to overcome their inhibitions and find where they fit in — musically and back at the workplace.

Creative Accounting?

All this seems to stray pretty far afield from the accounting department, where stuffy budgetmeisters might remark that some of it sounds like fun but what's the payback?

Behaviorists such as Harless fault creativity training when there is no way to measure its effectiveness. In many cases, they say, training in such "soft skills" produces little change in the workplace. "If there's no change on the job, in my lights, you may have made people feel good but you haven't produced anything of value," says Harless.

Adds Gilbert: "People sit and listen, but they go home and they aren't changed."

Creativity training proponents, however, do make claims of measurable success. One study conducted by Roger Firestien, assistant director at

Buffalo State College's Center for Studies in Creativity, shows that groups of subjects trained in creative problem solving generated significantly more ideas than those in a control group that received no training. Training recipients also participated more in problem-solving discussions; they criticized ideas less and supported ideas more.

Indeed, says Firestien, a defining characteristic of good creativity training is that it's backed by research. "A good creativity program is not only going to give you divergent techniques to generate ideas but it's also going to give you techniques to evaluate and refine those ideas," he explains. "And that's crucial. We can call our clients up and ask what they're using and how they're using it, and they can specifically tell us what they're doing and how they're using it instead of saying, 'Well, I feel real good after I attended your program.'"

In many cases, however, documentation of the positive effects of creativity training becomes a little fuzzy because it is two or three steps removed from the training itself. Nevertheless, some impressive numbers show up in association with creativity training.

Frito-Lay, the Plano, TX-based unit of PepsiCo, says a cost-management program done in conjunction with creative problem-solving training saved more than $500 million in the five years from 1983 to 1987. Meanwhile, profits grew at a compounded 12.7 percent annual rate, twice as fast as sales.

At DuPont, creativity center director Tanner credits creativity training with a $30 million saving. About two years ago a new industrial technology worked in the lab but faltered after it was transferred to a manufacturing plant. A team of DuPont's best engineers were stumped by the problem. After six months, creativity trainers came to the rescue with their thinking techniques. The technology now is back on track, says Tanner, who declines to identify it.

At Texas Utilities Mining Co., which used McGee-Cooper's techniques for safety training, one power plant completed 5 million worker-hours without a lost-time injury, and a surface coal mine recently reached 4 million worker-hours without a lost-time injury — both noteworthy achievements in those industries. Not least important, the company's workers' compensation premium payments have dropped to $55,000 per month in 1991 from $135,000 per month in 1990, says Janak.

Linking such achievements directly to creativity training is all but impossible. Dallas consultant McGee-Cooper says reduced medical expenses and lower absentee rates are associated with her work. But she claims no direct link. "We can't prove — and we don't even try to prove — that this would not have happened without us," she says.

However, McGee-Cooper does say she offers to waive her fee if the client isn't happy. Nobody has taken her up on it, she says.

Creativity training programs do require patience. Early on, Texas Utilities Mining Co.'s Janak had his doubts about McGee-Cooper's regimen: Nerf balls, toy trucks and slingshots around the office; meditation; "joy" breaks. His pilot group met with McGee-Cooper half a day once a month for 10 months. "It was probably the fifth or sixth month that all of us in that pilot group got comfortable with the process and got rid of a lot of skepticism," says Janak. "We were a pretty tough bunch."

Arguably, creativity training is about changing corporate culture — perhaps changing into a culture that can take a pratfall and run with it. Remember 3M's Scotchgard story? In the 1950s, as 3M researchers worked on developing a synthetic rubber for jet aircraft fuel hoses, a beaker of the stuff broke and goop splashed on a lab technician's tennis shoe. No standard cleaning solvent could remove it. The substance never made it in jets. But a few incarnations later, it became the well-known product that protects fabrics against soiling.

A narrow-minded corporate culture might well have scotched that discovery, says chemist Patsy Sherman, 3M's technical development manager and coinventor of Scotchgard. 3M's culture of encouraging creative applications nurtured it.

Even so, Sherman is skeptical that creativity is a trainable skill. "I think problem solving is routinely taught by all our companies in various ways," she says. "But the area of creativity per se is much more difficult to teach."

As oddball new techniques stretch the envelope of creativity training, perhaps the best advice for trainers is to keep an open mind. Should you hire a 10-year-old kid to kick your people out of their ruts? The answer probably requires some thinking — *creative* thinking.

Notes:

How To Customize Off-The-Shelf Training

BY BOB FILIPCZAK

Who's got time to cook anymore? OK, so maybe on weekends you put together a dinner of fresh tomato-basil spaghettini followed by tiramisu and a latté. But when you've done a full eight hours or more at work, you're more likely to reach for that can of Campbell's soup. Sure, you might add some oregano or garlic salt or pepper to whatever slops out of the can, but the real mission here is to get food into your family's stomachs before you collapse for the evening.

Time and energy are even more precious commodities at work these days. We've been hearing about the reasons for years: downsizing, doing more with less, being lean and mean. While TRAINING Magazine's research (See *Industry Report*, October 1992) shows that training departments haven't borne more than their share of the cuts, they've certainly felt the ax in terms of reduced staffing and budgets. Consequently, when a manager approaches the training department with a request for training on, appropriately enough, time management, the harried director of training often looks for an off-the-shelf course.

Saving time is not the only reason trainers are drawn to packaged training. Using off-the-shelf courseware staves off a deep-seated fear of redesigning the wheel, of building a course from scratch only to discover some professional training company has a better program that has been proven successful time and time again. An outside supplier probably would have saved money and, ultimately, time.

Expertise is also a key consideration for many who buy off-the-shelf training. Susan Keen, a management and professional development specialist for Sunquest Information Systems, a software company in Tucson, AZ, says she investigates packaged training courses when she doesn't have the internal expertise to design the program. Most training suppliers do extensive research into a subject before designing off-the-shelf courseware, something Keen says she has neither the staff nor the time to do. Pure expedience — she needs a course right away — is usually only the secondary reason she considers packaged training. Her first concern is getting a course that has been well-researched and proven to work in pilot tests and with other clients.

Adjusting the Spokes

Off-the-shelf courseware saves you time and money, is the product of extensive research and testing, and has a proven track record. So why customize it? Good question.

There's a fair amount of anecdotal evidence to persuade you that customized training is more effective than packaged programs, but harder evidence is sparse. A typical example: Ed Mohebi, chief operating officer of Cogent Technology Training, a Seattle software training company, says one of his clients estimated a 20 percent increase in skill transference after Cogent customized a packaged course. But that's only a guess.

Rachael Tayar, chief of training services at the Department of Health Services for the state of California in Sacramento, taught an off-the-shelf business writing course to employees both before and after she customized it. Her gut feeling is that the customized version was more effective and that the trainees got more out of the program because she used examples of poor writing taken directly from the employees' departments. But she didn't conduct any statistical research to validate what she intuited.

A lot of the reasons people customize training fall into the common-sense category. It just stands to reason that if you use engineering examples when teaching engineers the principles of good business writing, the training will stick better than if you use office automation examples. And if the training is more relevant in the classroom, common sense also dictates that the training will transfer back to the job better. Which is, after all, the objective of the entire exercise, isn't it?

And, to be honest, who can resist the temptation, without reinventing the wheel, to adjust the spokes a little?

Jim Kouzes is chairman and CEO of Tom Peters Group Learning Systems, a Palo Alto, CA, consulting firm that sells off-the-shelf training programs. Kouzes adds one more factor to the customization equation: the customer. As our economy evolves beyond customer service to customer intimacy, he says, companies will deal with customers as individuals instead of demographic groups. As he points out, Julie Nixon and Grace Slick are part of the same demographic niche, but you probably won't sell them the same set of goods.

Part of customer intimacy is tailoring products for individuals, says Kouzes. Levi Strauss, for example, is now testing the market for custom-tailored jeans. You go to a Levi's store, get your measurement taken and, presto, within weeks you receive made-to-fit-you Levi's jeans. Likewise, says Kouzes, training must be increasingly customized to meet the needs of the ultimate customer: the trainees.

Joe Lipsey, manager of corporate training and development for Mutual of Omaha in Omaha, NE, says that training departments in general don't do a very good job of reaching their customers by addressing the specific issues important to trainees. He suggests that adjusting training to fit the customer is a matter of accountability, that trainers who don't deal with the precise problems of the trainees are shirking their responsibilities.

Teaming Up With a Supplier

Once you've decided to customize a training course, where should you begin? Most experts and practitioners agree that the process begins with a traditional needs assessment: What's the problem? Is training the right solution? If so, what does the audience already know, what does it need to know, and what kind of training will bridge the gap?

Another camp in the customization debate suggests that the first step is finding the right supplier and establishing a long-term relationship. You save time if the company selling you the training also does some of the customization work for you. The training company comes in, asks some questions, does some interviews, and modifies a course for you, rather than just dropping workbooks and videos on your desk and letting you figure it out.

In fact, many suppliers of off-the-shelf training discourage practitioners from customizing a course without input from the company that designed the training. Sometimes the issue is copyright infringement and the desire to protect intellectual property, which we'll address later. But suppliers' careful research and testing can be undone by well-meaning trainers who don't understand the

methodology behind the packaged training. Cutting a lot out of a course or patching together a bunch of courses are two ways to compromise the objectives of packaged training.

Even so, there are trainers like Mike Perry, a site training administrator for Texas Instruments in Dallas, who prefers to get his hands on packaged courseware and customize it himself. He's impressed with training companies that will send him material on a CD-ROM so he can pick and choose what to include in the course. "I find that it's faster — as long as it's an easily customizable thing — than me trying to teach them exactly what I want," says Perry.

Rich Wellins, senior vice president of programs and marketing for Development Dimensions International (DDI), a training supplier with headquarters in Pittsburgh, also encourages companies to let DDI customize off-the-shelf products to keep the integrity of the training intact. His company does some needs-assessment work and alterations, when requested, as part of the relationship between customer and supplier.

DDI has "almost developed a packaged approach to customizing," says

Wellins, with its "tailored to fit" program. The program allows for changes that range from putting the client company's logo on the materials to adjusting the skill practices to better fit the company's environment — in other words, hospital examples for health care companies or factory scenarios for manufacturing facilities. Wellins considers a fully customized course one that involves a radical overhaul of the program or combining pieces of two or more DDI programs.

Exercising Options

There is no universal agreement about what it means to customize an off-the-shelf training program. Customizing is often a matter of degrees, ranging from changing the logo on the cover of the workbook to reshooting video footage that reflects a particular company's problems.

Wellins contends that making purely cosmetic changes to packaged programs can be effective. Often, the off-the-shelf program fits quite well with the needs of the customer and just a little tweaking is needed.

Kerri Reid, a training specialist for the Federal Judicial Center in Washington, DC, has spent up to a

---

MASSAGING THE MEDIA

If you're planning to customize a course, you probably want to figure out how easy it will be to customize it before you buy. There seems to be a consensus that text-based materials like workbooks, overheads and handouts are the easiest to alter to fit your company's mission, vision or industry. And if the text is sent from the supplier on disk, it's even easier to change.

"Getting something on a disk that is compatible with your current operating system is like dying and going to heaven," says Susan Keen, a management and professional development specialist for Sunquest Information Systems, a software company in Tucson, AZ.

Customizing computer-based training can be tricky, especially if you want to do it yourself. Most CBT is developed using authoring software, so if you don't know how to operate an authoring system, and particularly the authoring system that was used to assemble the packaged training program, customizing a course that runs on computer may be difficult. In the hands of someone who knows the appropriate authoring system, making changes can be pretty straightforward.

A lot of attention is currently centered around multimedia training in general and courseware stored on CD-ROM in particular. That second part of the acronym — ROM — stands for "read only memory" and that means whatever is on that disk is unalterable. So if you want to customize the training on a CD-ROM, you're either going to have to do it with software on the hard disk of the

computer or remaster the CD-ROM disk itself.

In the past, altering a CD-ROM seemed unthinkable, but with CD-ROM recorders plummeting in cost and rewritable optical disks becoming more prevalent, this may not be such an insurmountable obstacle in the future. As it is, though, the CD-ROM you buy is pretty much what you get.

The most expensive media to change is video. It's not hard to record or duplicate a tape, but reshooting footage can quickly turn into a nightmare if you're not familiar with the intricacies of video production. Just the shoot — setting up a site, hiring actors and a crew, adjusting lighting, and doing a number of takes — is a complicated and costly affair. Tape editing, where you put your customized scenes back into the original video footage, is also an expensive and labor-intensive process.

The advice from those who have been there boils down to this: If you want to customize a video to fit your corporate culture, be sure you know in advance what you're in for. Kerri Reid, training specialist at the Federal Judicial Center in Washington, DC, actually reshoots whole videos — not just segments of them — for her audience. But she also has a staff of video technicians to handle this kind of major customization. Reid rewrites the scripts, based on the principles of the original video material, and hands them over to the technicians to reshoot. — B.F.

---

year completely reshooting videos in an effort to customize a canned program for her audience. Her main problem with packaged training is that most of it is designed for private industry and doesn't translate to the public sector very well. For example, profit is the bottom line emphasized in many training programs, a concept irrelevant to her audience.

If you've decided to customize a packaged program on your own — and you've done your needs assessment — your next step may be to look at the student exercises, case studies and role plays. Practitioners use participant-focused events, in which trainees actually do something besides just listen to a lecture, as likely targets for customization. And that makes sense: This is where the rubber of a training course meets the road of actual skills practice. So altering the student exercises in workbooks, handouts, overheads or computer-based training is an effective way to customize a training program.

Mary Walter, principal of NewLeaf Consulting in Atlanta, often customizes canned training programs for clients and goes for the exercises first.

She customizes with an eye toward "option-optimization," adding three or four exercises that will deliver the same point for every exercise the canned program suggests. That way, she says, trainers can customize on the fly, adjusting to different audiences with participation appropriate for each circumstance. In case audience members show significant reluctance to talk to each other, for example, Walter offers optional exercises that will reinforce the learning points, but allow participants to work on their own. Her definition of customization is fairly simple: "giving myself more options than they give me."

Reid likes going after the student exercises first, because it gives her the chance to get more of her peers involved in the customizing process. She picks an exercise out of a training program, faxes it to 10 other trainers who work for the federal courts, and asks them how they would change it to make it more specific to the organization.

Sunquest's Keen agrees with this strategy. She often contacts people in the target audience and "vacuums their brains" for ideas on how to make the student material more relevant. If you can limit the customization of a program to just the exercises and leave

the rest of the course alone, she says, you'll be in good shape.

Customizing for the Individual

In addition to altering student exercises, other strategies can also make packaged training programs more relevant to your audience. Scott Parry, chairman of Training House, a Princeton, NJ, supplier of off-the-shelf training courseware, encourages his customers to "take it out of the can" and customize the training for each participant.

Who can resist the temptation, without reinventing the wheel, to adjust the spokes a little?

On the flip side, he also encourages participants to customize their own training. "The ultimate customization — the last-analysis customization — is on an individual basis, as each participant is ultimately the best person to decide what is relevant in his or her work area," says Parry.

Trainers can encourage this individual buy-in by asking each trainee to come up with an action plan, an outline or document that states as precisely as possible how the training will be applied back on the job. Parry says he tells participants to consider the training course a kind of cafeteria plan, a collection of skills and knowledge from which they should pick and choose to assemble the action plan that they will take back to their supervisor. But not everything in the collection will be completely relevant, he warns, so trainees shouldn't just take one of everything from the cafeteria line.

Parry also uses a method he calls "critical incidents." He encourages trainees to come up with real situations from their own work that demonstrate the training concepts and to discuss these incidents with the other participants. The instructor then collects these examples and points out the similarities to the group. Moreover, says Parry, trainees themselves can become important sources of case studies and role plays for future training sessions. He's even

seen ambitious trainees go off and develop case studies on their own time. These, too, can be included in future training sessions, creating an environment in which customization of an off-the-shelf program becomes an ongoing process.

Finally, Parry encourages clients to use both internal trainers and key managers to co-facilitate his packaged training. This partnership makes training more effective in two ways. First, the internal trainer can translate generic language into company-specific terms that make more sense to the trainees. Second, by including a key manager as co-trainer, trainees see that the managers — sometimes an obstacle to implementing training back on the job — are supporting the training. "It lends a lot more credence," says Parry, because trainees think, "It's no longer a canned program, because it's being delivered by our key managers."

Action Learning

Another way to customize a packaged training program is to incorporate action learning principles, says Mutual of Omaha's Lipsey. Action learning is a training method that brings real problems into the classroom; participants learn to apply new principles or techniques by solving these real problems. If, for example, you were using action learning to train managers in strategic planning, the group would assemble a real strategic plan during the program. This plan wouldn't be hypothetical; it would be the plan the group would implement in the future.

In this way, Lipsey customizes each packaged program by having participants bring real problems to the class and solve them while they learn. "You find out where they are having problems, what they are trying to accomplish, what their success factors are," says Lipsey, and then you incorporate those into the course.

Action learning, which his company now uses to customize all off-the-shelf courseware, also addresses issues like transfer of training and validity. Lipsey says he doesn't worry about training transfer because participants actually do the work; the training becomes what he calls a byproduct of the process. As far as validity is concerned, Lipsey says "if our customer says this works for them, that's enough validity for me." A work group that goes through a class using action-learning principles also signs a contract that makes members accountable for using what they've learned back on the job.

One quirky way to customize an off-the-shelf training program comes from Ann Petit, author of *Secrets to Enliven Learning: How to Develop Self-Directed Training Materials.* She puts a little life into a packaged course by changing the name and trying to make it fun. She took what she described as a deadly program on how to do a needs assessment and renamed it "A Ferndale Tale." She rewrote the needs assessment exercise as a story about a French restaurant in Ferndale, CA, and set up the room to look like a bistro, including croissants and French music. If you don't put a little life into a course, says Petit, "people come into the room and there's an agenda and they sit down and they want to die" of boredom.

It's All Mine Now . . . *Not*

Just as there are many useful ways to customize a packaged training program, there are several ways it can be done badly, and a couple of ways you can get in trouble. The most contentious arguments about customization are over copyright and intellectual property rights.

Suppliers accuse some trainers of buying a training program, altering it to fit their needs, and then reproducing the materials ad infinitum because the trainers think the program now belongs to them. Suppliers contend, however, that the training principles and ideas remain their own intellectual property, protected by copyright laws. Some training departments, they insist, try to get around paying for a course by altering the product a little and claiming that the program is now their original work.

When Parry's company surveyed customers about copyright infringement, 35 percent *admitted* to wrongful copying of training materials. A 1987 study sponsored by the Training Media Association and conducted by Lakewood Research, a subsidiary of TRAINING's publisher, Lakewood Publications, found that more than 30 percent of training videos are illegally copied. Kouzes suspects the numbers are similar for training software and packaged programs. He says that the training industry is rife with people

who would never even contemplate stealing a car but who readily steal training programs.

To be on the safe side, Audrey Choden, president of Training by Design, a Kansas City, KS, firm that customizes other suppliers' canned training for corporations, always checks with the supplier of the training to find out what kind of rights the customer has to alter the material. She also advises trainers who customize to check with their legal departments and with their suppliers when they make changes — just to be sure they stay out of legal hot water.

One of the prevailing methods for customizing training is, for want of a better term, a pick-and-patch approach. Let's say you find two packaged programs you like, and you take what you think is the best stuff from both and patch them together to make one course. Choden says a significant number of the requests she gets for customization are from companies that want her to make a hybrid course from two or more packaged programs.

Other practitioners admit that combining the best parts of multiple programs or approaches is a common way to create a new training course. Aside from the aforementioned copyright violations this approach invites, Kouzes of the Peters Group contends that this creates less effective training. "The worst customization I have seen is when something isn't designed as an integrated whole. There's no system to it, there's no sense of integrity or wholeness to it. It's stuff that's stuck together," says Kouzes.

For the sake of argument, he suggests applying the pick-and-patch approach to car assembly. Imagine what you'd end up with if you took the best transmission from one company, the best engine from another, the best chassis from another, and tried to assemble a car from these high-quality but incompatible parts. Likewise, making a milk shake training course of principles from Margaret Wheatley, Peter Block, Warren Bennis, and his own theories is probably not a very effective approach, says Kouzes.

Another even more prevalent reason to customize training, especially lately, is to trim hours or days from courses to save time. Many experts and practitioners agreed that "cus-

tomizing" a two-day course down to a two-hour course is becoming commonplace. The danger, of course, is that you end up just dumping information on hapless trainees and essentially wasting those two hours.

Choden has noticed a tendency to chop all the exercises out of programs to save time. "The question is, what do you want to achieve with this training? Because if you've taken out all the skill building — which takes time — and you've taken out some specific things to help them transfer the learning, the program just isn't effective at all," says Choden.

If you cut a program to fit a time slot, consultant Walter advises, also cut out some of the objectives. In other words, if you start cutting the time, you have to cut some of the meat of the course if you want the remainder to be effective. And being both effective and cost-effective is what customized packaged training is all about.

It's not that the training sold by many training companies isn't good enough; there's just this tendency to tweak and edit it so it's even better. The suit analogy comes up quite often; a suit off the rack may look pretty good, but when it's altered to really fit you, it looks that much better. Laura Lind-Blum, coordinator of contract training for the Community College of Vermont in Waterbury, added this to a computer on-line discussion of customizing packaged programs: "Sometimes (I'll admit it), I customize an off-the-shelf training program to 'make it my own' . . . I think there is something about human nature that causes us to believe on some level that we can do it a little bit better."

As the movement toward one-to-one customer intimacy increases demand for customization, technological improvements will make it easier and quicker to accomplish. What happens when everything — text, visuals, video — is on disk and it can be mixed together by someone who isn't even one of the computer cognoscenti?

DDI's Wellins postulates a future that looks like this: "Nothing will be shelf product. When customers order, their workbooks and materials will be produced within 24 hours and shipped to them with their logos, their exercises, everything that would make it relevant to their organization."

DISTANCE LEARNING

Putting the Learning into Distance Learning

BY BOB FILIPCZAK

When people stopped talking about videoconferencing and started talking about distance learning, the easy assumption was that this was just another cosmetic change, another label to attach to some technology to ratchet up the hype. It wasn't. The new term heralds an important change in thinking about how people learn and, more specifically, how we can teach them things when we're not in the same room with them.

Not that the hype has disappeared. Everybody wants to market his latest and greatest training product under the label of distance learning. Order a workbook and video from a training supplier, it's distance learning. Plug a CD-ROM into your computer to learn how to use Windows 95, it's distance learning. Answer a matchbook-cover ad for a correspondence course that teaches you to become a brain surgeon in your sleep, it's distance learning. Mister Rogers shows your kid how to button a cardigan, it's distance learning.

The kind of distance learning that concerns us here is the type that connects people with other people via technology, what some experts call interactive distance learning. "Interactive" is a term associated mainly with computer-based training (CBT), of course, but in this case it means getting people — and often video images of people — into the same electronic space so they can help one another learn something.

For our purposes, distance learning is an event or a process that involves direct two-way communication between people; it doesn't include traditional correspondence courses or the CBT software you got in the mail. It *does* include audioconferencing, videoconferencing and docuconferencing, a relative newcomer to the distance-learning arena that allows many people to collaborate on a shared document via computers separated by a few feet or several time zones.

The real story lies in a gradual shift in thinking about how distance learning ought to be done. In the past, we used videoconferencing to emulate a classic classroom situation: Groups of people sit in rooms and listen to experts talk. If we couldn't get everyone in the same room for whatever reason, splitting them into several groups connected by some kind of video link seemed the next best thing to being there.

But in a lot of cases, getting the technology to work well took so much time and energy that nobody had the wherewithal to wonder whether replicating the experience of a live lecture was good enough. How much learning actually was taking place? That question was asked only in relation to the learning that occurred when the same instruction was delivered in a single-site classroom. According to Carol Twigg, vice president of Educom, a Washington, DC-based consortium of 600 colleges and universities trying to transform higher education through information technology, much of the research about distance learning over the last 50 years has shown that there is "no significant difference" in the effectiveness of distance learning compared with face-to-face instruction.

Now, that can be good news or disappointing news, depending on how you look at it. If your videoconferencing system is reaching scads of people who no longer have to fly into a central training facility, and the instruction is equally effective, then you've saved lots of time and money. As J. Olin Campbell, a researcher for the Center for Innovations in Engineering Education at Vanderbilt University in Nashville, TN, writes in an e-mail message about distance learning: "As to travel and time savings ... the learners' time is typically the most expensive component of training programs in business. So businesses want to cut travel costs, but also learning time."

But suppose you're being pushed to make all of your training *more effective* — not just cheaper, faster and more efficient. In that case, "no significant difference" in effectiveness doesn't help you.

Lecture Busters

The genuinely interesting discussions of distance learning aren't about technology anymore. The gee-whiz talk about two-way video, audio and data links between instructor and trainees is giving way to questions about the usefulness of delivering lectures to people in 10 cities instead of one.

Alan Chute, managing partner of AT&T's Center for Excellence in Distance Learning in Cincinnati, defines distance learning as "a system and a process that connects learners with distributed resources." His definition has been adopted officially by the American Council of Education as well. "Distributed resources" may sound a little clunky, but the point is that we're no longer talking simply about connecting people in one classroom to a lecturer in another.

Chute admits that, in the past, distance learning has relied on the classroom model. "What's difficult at this particular place and time is that there aren't many good models out there for people who are doing [distance learning] in an innovative way," he says.

Hank Payne, manager of the Federal Aviation Administration's distance-learning program at the FAA Academy in Oklahoma City, puts a sharper edge on the point. "Emulating the classroom should be the lowest possible level of acceptance," Payne says.

Are we telling you that distance-learning pioneers have discovered new teaching techniques that will render classroom training obsolete? Well, no, though some talk that way. What they have really discovered is the same dissatisfaction with the lecture method that has permeated adult-learning literature and train-the-trainer workshops for decades. The distance-learning crowd is awakening to the fact that classroom instruction need not be synonymous with lecturing.

Let's put it more bluntly. As the novelty of the technology fades, it becomes harder to ignore the fact that distance learning usually amounts to several rooms full of people sitting in chairs and watching somebody lecture on a video screen. And it gets harder to pretend that this is somehow more fascinating than watching somebody lecture in person.

The hot term in distance-learning circles is "learner-centered" instruction, as opposed to content-centered or instructor-centered learning. It may be that reports of the death of the hour-long lecture via satellite are greatly exaggerated, but more and more people in the field are beginning to talk like Educom's Twigg: "To make distance learning, or any kind of learning, more effective," she says, "you

really have to change the nature of the instructional process."

As always, it's a matter of getting the learners more actively involved in the training experience — of giving them something to do besides listen to somebody else talk. At the FAA Academy, distance learning is delivered via one-way videoconferencing, but trainees are armed with electronic response pads. The instructor in Oklahoma City delivers technical training to as many as 10 sites, and the students at the sites can react to questions, or ask questions of their own, using the response pads. The pads look like calculators but are also equipped with microphones; the instructor can ask the whole "class" a question and get instant feedback on how well everyone understands the material at any point. The instructor can even administer a quick 10-question quiz every once in a while. Frequent checks of understanding are vital, of course, since the instructor can't see the students or the puzzled looks on their faces.

Questioning, probing and interacting with learners in a classroom environment is not something that instructors can be counted upon to do naturally, says Payne. And that applies especially to distance learning. "We decided, based on research and going out and talking with the people who are doing this, that you have to force interactivity," Payne says. The FAA Academy has a weeklong training course to help its instructors learn how to use distance learning, both technologically and interactively.

Even in the academic world, citadel of the lecture method, distance-learning enthusiasts are seeking ways to increase student participation and interaction. Albert Ingram, assistant director for instructional technology at the University of Medicine and Dentistry of New Jersey in Newark, says that the key to successful distance learning lies in changing the way courses are taught. "When it's successful, it's because the faculty make it a lot more interactive than the usual classes," says Ingram. "If you're just

---

DISTRIBUTED RESOURCES

As this story is being written, a train full of Eastern European women is traveling from Poland to Beijing, China. The passengers are on their way to the Fourth World Conference on Women, sponsored by the United Nations Development Program.

So what, you ask? Well, for distance-learning enthusiasts, this train is particularly interesting. A description on the World Wide Web homepage that is tracking the train's progress reads: "An exciting element of this extraordinary journey is the intensive program of seminars and skill-building workshops that will take place while enroute. The train will even be equipped with a mobile satellite for on-board, on-line computer training." That's right, this is a training train.

The other reason we mention this unusual little experiment in mobile distance learning is the fact that you can, indeed, learn all about it on the World Wide Web, the fastest-growing and most popular medium on the Internet. By "going" to this web site (http://www.undp.org/bexpress/beijinge.htm), you can find out the schedule of the Beijing Express, what kind of training the women will be getting, a brief biography of the trainers, a map of the 5,734-mile journey and more.

If you're interested in distance learning, you should probably spend some time surfing the Internet. It can be a little overwhelming at first, especially if you go to the search program Yahoo (http://www.yahoo.com/search.html) and type in the search words "distance learning."

To avoid information overload, you might start instead at the homepage maintained by AT&T's Center for Excellence in Distance Learning (http://

www.att.com/cedl/). This site will tell you plenty, of course, about products and services offered by AT&T, but there's more. The homepage offers a collection of articles and research done by, among others, Alan Chute, the managing partner of the CEDL. It also has connections to universities that provide even more information. One link will take you to the University of Wisconsin's Distance Education Clearinghouse (http://www.uwex.edu/disted/home.html). While you're there, check out a document called "Lessons Learned."

Another web site that recently came on line is the literature section of the International Centre for Distance Learning (http://acacia.open.ac.uk/). This is a database of references and abstracts for over 7,500 documents.

If searching or surfing isn't your style, and you'd just like to discuss distance learning with others, you can always join the Distance Education Online Symposium (DEOS-L), one of the more active listservs focusing on issues of distance learning. DEOS-L has approximately 2,100 participants from 51 countries. Just send e-mail to: listserv@psuvm.psu.edu with the message: subscribe DEOS-L Your Name.

If you don't have e-mail or an Internet connection, but you're interested in finding out more about distance learning, invest the time and money it takes to get on line. Some of the most innovative, cutting-edge stuff on the subject is being published as you read this article. Just like the train going from Warsaw to Beijing, the subject of distance learning is a moving target, continually crossing borders and emerging into new territories.

— B.F.

doing the same thing, except in two different classrooms [instead of one], you wouldn't expect much of a difference. And I don't think you get it. If you start getting learners involved and having them do different sorts of activities, then maybe you do see a difference."

New Habits?

Sometimes the newness of distance learning can be used as a lever to pry even a longtime, dyed-in-the-wool lecturer out of old habits. In a prior job at a medical school, Chute says, he tried hard to get the faculty to change the way it ran its classes, but the doctors were stubborn about forsaking their 55-minute lecture technique. Here was Chute, a young Ph.D. who specialized in instructional design, trying to tell sage physicians how to teach their classes more effectively by involving the students. Predictably, the advice didn't go over well.

But then the school started experimenting with distance learning, putting these same doctors in front of cameras and beaming the classes to remote sites. All of a sudden, the know-it-all doctors were in a new situation where they couldn't rely on their educational preconceptions. That's when Chute started helping them redesign their courses, including more opportunities for questions and dialogue with the learners. Consciously or unconsciously, the doctors took some of the techniques they learned in the distance-learning courses back to the classroom, says Chute. And they became more effective instructors.

In some university settings, distance learning is actually being touted as a tool for faculty development. For instance, relates Joan Mattila, program manager for PictureTel, a hardware and software manufacturer that provides videoconferencing systems for distance learning, Boston University has begun beaming some of its engineering classes to employees at United Technologies Corp., a manufacturing conglomerate in Hartford, CT, that includes Pratt & Whitney and Sikorsky. When learners in private industry started mixing it up with engineering students and university faculty in the same electronic classroom, everyone benefited. All of a sudden, engineering professors didn't have to scramble for real-life examples of the principles they were teaching; they could just ask the engineers at

United Technologies. For their part, the private-industry engineers were able to access the latest research and theories in engineering. And sometimes, says Mattila, the engineers made things more interesting by challenging the instructors on whether some particular theory reflected reality.

"It's kind of silly. We know that adults don't learn for eight hours. They can't. That's not how any of us learn."

Multimedia

Chute sees an increasing interest in using multiple media in distance learning — before, during and after the actual training event. Again, most of the techniques are borrowed from other types of learning activities. For years, companies intending to fly in employees from all over the country to a big training session in Chicago, say, have used computer-based training modules as a preliminary step. Some time before the class, the company delivers the CBT package to the trainees, either by snail mail or over a computer network. The CBT can assess the trainees' present level of knowledge — and it can raise the bar on how much they know before they enter the classroom. The same technique now is being employed prior to distance-learning events, Chute says. In some cases, on-line discussion groups substitute for or supplement the CBT: Trainers and participants send e-mail to each other about what the class will be covering.

The advantages are obvious, Chute points out. In any training class, if you don't want to lose part of the group, you're forced to teach to the lowest common denominator. By using technology to deliver some pretraining, you can raise that denominator and make the distance-learning class more effective.

After the course, technology can also help. "We all know that if training is left unreinforced, it's attenuated quickly," says Chute. Once back on the job, far-flung learners can set up a computer newsgroup in which they can continue a running discussion

with the trainer and one another. The group may even decide to schedule a follow-up training session. Because you don't have to fly all the trainees to a central site or ship your trainer out to multiple sites, scheduling a follow-up class is considerably less intimidating.

Cram Sessions

One of the drawbacks of bringing trainees to a central site for a class is that the event usually turns into a cram session, says the FAA's Payne. Because the organization is paying for the flights, lodging, time off the job, and all the rest of the costs of bringing employees in for training, it often tries to make the most of the investment by sticking them in a classroom for eight or 10 hours a day, sometimes for several days in a row.

"It's kind of silly," says Payne. "We know that adults don't learn for eight hours. They can't. That's not how any of us learn." Nevertheless, he says, "We feel compelled to do something with them for eight hours. So what do we do? We put them in a classroom. And we know full well that their ability to take in new knowledge is really limited."

With the distance-learning system the FAA is testing, Payne says he can break up the courses into three-hour modules that can be delivered over an extended period of time, instead of cramming information into trainees for three days and expecting them to retain it.

Another issue is speed. Steve Molik, multimedia coordinator for Owens Corning in Toledo, OH, says his company is also starting to experiment with distance learning using a two-way video and two-way audio system set up by PictureTel. In the pilot stage, Owens Corning was doing a lot of safety training centered on regulations of the Occupational Safety and Health Administration. The company could get a class on line fast — sometimes within two hours of hearing about a new rule — and therefore sped up the process of distributing the most recent information on regulations and safety practices. Employees at the initial 38 distance-learning sites don't have to wait either to be flown in for training or for a trainer to show up at the plant somewhere down the line.

Owens Corning is building a new world headquarters, scheduled for completion in July 1996, with a dedicated distance-learning facility. Molik says the corporate goal is to deliver 80 percent of all training over the video-conferencing system by the end of five years.

The FAA Academy's goal is to deliver 40 percent of all the training it currently does on-site by the year 2000, according to Payne. That would be between 10,000 and 12,000 hours of training going out over the distance-learning network every year.

Problems, Problems

All is not sunshine and roses in the land of distance learning, of course. When we mentioned earlier that technology isn't the main issue anymore, that doesn't mean it isn't an issue.

Videoconferencing can happen in one of two ways: broadcast via satellite or transmitted over terrestrial lines. When it goes via satellite, like it does at the FAA Academy, the video is of excellent quality, without the herky-jerky motion you can get when using buried, high-bandwidth cables. On the other hand, the amount of satellite time and space is not growing with demand. In fact, satellite time is becoming a rare and expensive commodity.

Terrestrial lines are both cheaper and more plentiful than satellites. Most of the growth in videoconferencing has occurred because organizations are able to run their video over what are called ISDN lines, cables that can carry much more information than regular phone lines, but not quite as much as fiber-optic cables. The Owens Corning system, as well as most university distance-learning systems, currently operate over ISDN lines. When fiber-optic lines become available, most videoconferencing will upgrade to that medium. With ISDN lines, the video gets compressed before it goes through the cables, causing a slight delay between delivery and reception.

This delay creates timing problems for trainers. At the School of Medicine and Dentistry of New Jersey, Ingram warns instructors that if they tell a joke, they may have to wait a "beat" before finding out if students thought it was funny. Ingram also warns that with ISDN lines, the more motion you interject into the instruction, the more jerky it comes across to the remote sites. His school broadcasts a very popular class on open-heart surgery, where students actually get to watch the surgery live. For this course, Ingram says, the video has to be sent over fiber-optic lines.

There are also etiquette issues in distance learning. For example, Ingram says that instructors often run into problems with students at remote sites talking among themselves in a

---

"We decided, based on research and going out and talking with the people who are doing this, that you have to force interactivity."

---

way they wouldn't if the presenter were actually in the room. In such a case, he says, the instructor needs to bring them back on the subject using audio — a nice way of saying the professor has to yell at the students.

On the other hand, Molik says trainees at Owens Corning tend to display the opposite reaction: "Because you're at such a distance and you're not sitting right across the table from each other, you find yourself paying attention. You can't afford to have side conversations because you'll miss something."

One simmering debate in the distance-learning world concerns whether to have a group of "live" students in the room with the instructor during the broadcast to the remote sites. The FAA chose not to include live students in its sessions, Payne says, because of reports that when one group of trainees is in the room with the instructor and others are watching on video, both groups wind up feeling alienated. The trainees at remote sites feel as if the instructor is talking only to the live audience, while the live group feels that the trainer is playing to the camera. "So they all feel slighted," says Payne, "and the poor instructor, it doesn't matter what he or she does."

The biggest reason distance learning falls short of expectations, according to PictureTel's Mattila, is because companies and educational institutions focus solely on the technology. She decries the practice of just pumping the same tired old lecture over a videoconferencing system, instead of looking at hard issues of learning objectives and moving toward a more learner-centered environment.

Of course, the reason distance learning is such a hot topic right now is that it provides what training departments are desperate for: cheaper, faster, and sometimes more effective training that can reach a bigger audience. In short, more training bang for the buck.

"If you give most people a choice," says Payne, "they will opt to meet in a class. But we're not talking about a choice here. We're talking about going to this because we have to. We have to find ways to reduce our overall training costs, and this is one way we can do it."

That's the no-brainer for companies interested in distance learning. It hits the bottom line of an organization in a way that is both convincing and exciting. The technology is here and it works. The next step in this evolution is to demand the same sort of accountability for *learning* results that we ought to demand of any other training medium.

ELECTRONIC PERFORMANCE SUPPORT SYSTEMS

Should Every Worker Have A Line In The Information Stream?

BY MARC HEQUET

Marty was fuming over some minor corporate backstabbing. "Calm down, Marty," said Chris. "The Chinese have a proverb: 'Those who sit by the river and wait long enough will see the bodies of their enemies float by.' "

Marty calmed down. But it hurt, that pompous cold comfort from a friend. Later, lost in a computer program, Chris wailed for help over the divider.

"Grasshopper," Marty replied in the even-toned parlance of the wise old monk on the "Kung Fu" TV series, "if I throw you a fish, you will eat for a day. But if you learn how to fish, you will never be hungry."

Score that round for Marty. And we could argue that he did the right thing. How can you get your own work done when you're bailing other people out?

Marty's wisecrack rings true up and down corporate corridors. When workers get stuck, it wastes time — their own and that of the nearest available veteran on whom they call for help. The head-scratching and standing around also waste money. Ford Motor Co., Xerox Corp. and Sprint Corp. estimated in 1992 that calling on co-workers for help on PCs alone cost from $6,000 to $15,000 per computer per year.

What Chris and other workers need when they're stuck, some say, is an electronic performance support (EPS) system. Such systems are already up and running in workplaces around the world.

EPS advocates see a great future. If a person can call on all the specialized information he needs to do a job, at the moment he needs it, "we see that as a really powerful concept that can change the way businesses operate," says Alan Cohen, performance support and education technology manager with Somerset, NJ-based AT&T Learning Services.

What Is It?

Think of EPS this way: You're Pinocchio and the EPS is Jiminy Cricket, sitting on your shoulder and whispering advice in your ear as you career through the adventure that is your job.

Suppose Chris gets stuck. What's corporate policy on this case? What's standard procedure for responding to this inquiry? What's the right way to process this order?

At a workplace using an EPS system, Chris can punch a few keys and call up a computer-based mother lode of know-how on performing the tasks at hand.

Instead of thumbing through manuals, Chris can hit a few more keys and bring up the correct manual page electronically on the screen. The EPS outlines policy and procedures, and shows a few similar cases as guidance. It offers computer-based training to build Chris' confidence. An expert system offers guidance on ticklish decisions. There may even be video segments. And it's all updated regularly.

In short, EPS is an all-purpose refer-ence that workers can access while they're running other software as they do their jobs. It can be a godsend for workers in a variety of jobs. Customer-service representatives have quick access to questions that come in from left field. Roving sales reps can wow clients by downloading information from EPS networks and/or CD-ROMs into their laptop computers before leaving on their rounds, or even by modem while they're on the road.

Suppose a client asks, "How do you solve such-and-such a problem?" The intrepid rep can snap an adapter in place, fire up the laptop, and show the client a dazzling array of product specifications, electronic paperwork, and even side-by-side comparisons of the competition's price and other features.

And what if there's a question the rep can't answer? Instead of making something up or thrashing through a steamer trunk full of manuals, the cool consultant pushes a few keys on the laptop and the answer scrolls into place.

Do People Like It?

Companies with EPS systems report very favorable reactions from workers using them. "Great package," one worker told the hot line for AT&T's Performance Management Assistant, which helps managers set goals and objectives for themselves and for their direct reports. "I love it. It's extremely helpful." Said another: "The online help is great. A big help." And still another: "Best thing to come out of AT&T in 14 years."

Deloitte & Touche, the big accounting firm based in Livonia, MI, rolled out a system for its consultants, and accolades rolled back in. "I've never gotten a 'thank you' in this job," gushes Paul Radding, a senior manager at Deloitte & Touche and the architect of its EPS. "But since people took delivery on this system I get voice mail every week saying, 'Thank you. Give me more.' "

On the other hand, neither companies nor individuals appear in a mad rush to acquire EPS systems. "I don't think you're finding people lining up all over the world to get on this bandwagon," says Randall Jensen, a Dow Chemical Co. performance technologist. Jensen has been trying to explain the concept to thousands of Dow employees who are going online with an EPS that supports them on regulation, product servicing, shipping, safety and the like at 50 Dow plants globally.

"It challenges a lot of the things that people have already bought into — for example, classroom training," says Radding. "Most people didn't get it until they used it themselves."

Your chance could come soon. Deloitte & Touche consultants delighted with EPS are designing it into the software they create for clients. And AT&T is considering marketing its Performance Management Assistant outside the company.

Who is using EPS systems?

• Deloitte & Touche installed an EPS in 1993 for 4,000 of its information-technology consultants in 15 countries. The consultants develop planning, systems-integration and project-management software for clients.

• AT&T's Performance Management Assistant helps 3,500 managers set goals linked to business-unit performance, both for themselves and for their direct reports. It also acts as a performance-appraisal tool. AT&T's Global Information Solutions unit (formerly NCR) uses another EPS that supports instructional-system design and technical documentation.

• Aetna Life & Casualty Inc. has a handful of EPS systems. The company's AMP Facilitator coaches 45,000 managers in the use of the Aetna Management Process (AMP), a planning tool that aligns day-to-day decision-making with overarching corporate goals. Aetna's Reference Base supports 1,000 computer troubleshooters at 350 locations. A third system, Basic Anatomy, helps bodily-injury claims representatives read medical reports. A fourth, called InfoBase, guides pension analysts in Aetna Life Insurance & Annuity Co. (ALIAC).

• U.S. West Learning Systems uses a system that helps trainers design and create training materials and analyze training trends.

Users see some startling returns. Formerly, Aetna held a two-week training program for all of its computer troubleshooters at a cost of $3,000 per individual for travel and lodging expenses alone. Now its ITA Reference Base has replaced the classroom course. One internal developer created the EPS in about three months, and the company runs it on existing equipment. The total development cost, estimates Aetna, was about $20,000 —

meaning ITA Reference Base paid for itself in just weeks.

Aetna says its Basic Anatomy EPS, which supports medical-claim representatives, cost $33,000 to develop and saves $49,000 per year.

IDS Financial Services Inc. of Minneapolis says an EPS teaches customer-service representatives to move money between mutual funds in an hour, replacing 15 hours of classroom training. "Time to competency" for new reps was cut from two or three months to four weeks, and error rates are down 50 percent.

> **You're Pinocchio and the EPS is Jiminy Cricket, sitting on your shoulder and whispering advice in your ear.**

How To Build One

Training managers shouldn't start laying off trainers, however. EPS needs them at the front end of the process, in planning the system. Trainers know how people learn and how to deliver information effectively.

Nevertheless, expect some problems getting trainers onto the EPS design team and some frustrations while they're there. Trainers may need to throw some elbows to get their concepts incorporated into the system. Information-system designers are used to doing things their way, and user-friendliness isn't always at the top of their priority list.

Stan Malcolm, manager of learning technologies for Hartford, CT-based Aetna and an enthusiastic advocate of EPS, says a member of his training staff came back from a design meeting to report a great victory. "I got the words 'performance support' into the project plan," the trainer reported. That meant the computer jockeys acknowledged they were designing a system for people who need more prompting than your average computer programmer. Says Malcolm: "That was a breakthrough."

At AT&T Learning Services, technical people grew impatient when discussion dragged on about what an EPS computer screen icon should look like. "In the beginning we spent a lot of time thinking about metaphors,"

says Peggy Wilhelm, AT&T Learning Services project manager for its Performance Management Assistant EPS. "Some people on the team felt we might be wasting time."

But symbols are important, perhaps crucial. What should the on-screen symbol for a checklist be? An early suggestion at AT&T showed a rectangle with an "A+" and a checkmark on the bottom. Some on the design team worried that users would get the idea they were being graded. "It communicated too much judgment," says AT&T's Wilhelm. Instead, the program now carries a "Q" over a checkmark.

Rapid prototyping is a must, EPS advocates emphasize. What use is a long, elegant, exquisitely engineered process that results in a single prototype — if people think the prototype is clumsy and stupid and they hate using it?

AT&T pushed out prototypes of its Performance Management Assistant so early that some keys were dead; programmers hadn't gotten that far yet, says Jane Takacs, AT&T Learning Services Performance Support Technologies Group manager. When an employee testing the system hit one of the dead keys, Takacs would whip out a piece of paper showing what the screen was supposed to look like.

Takacs' job, essentially, was to seize people wherever she could find them — real prospective users — and plop them down in front of the latest version to find out what they thought. She used a computer-industry method to record user response to early prototypes: a mike-equipped camcorder mounted on a tripod and aimed at the screen. As users explored the system, Takacs asked them to talk about what they were doing. One of her ground rules: If they get stuck, give them at least two minutes to fiddle on their own before intervening and offering help. "We tried to emulate the real world," says Takacs.

Her advice to EPS designers during this phase: Think of it as a work in progress. The good news is that suggested changes eventually slow to a trickle. You'll reach a point where you know you're getting very close to a rollout version. "After the fourth application, it kind of reached a saturation point," says Takacs. "We weren't getting any new information from the people using the fifth and sixth and seventh prototypes."

Designers took feedback seriously

and made changes. For example, users were stumped at first when they reached a screen area in which they were to write a performance appraisal. It looked like a space where they should be able to write, but when they keyed in letters, nothing showed up. They were forgetting to hit an "add" button. Designers responded with a more prominent prompt to hit "add" and then write.

Another recommendation from EPS veterans: Stay modular, because you're going to have to update. "You find out three months down the road that you really need to add a few things," says Karen Kocher, an Aetna training administrator. "We were close to saying, 'Forget modules. Let's just build this one massive system.' Looking back, if we had done that we would have been in a world of hurt." Designers are reluctant to build modular systems, she says, because "people don't want to send out something they feel is incomplete." But the thing to remember about your vision of producing a complete, finished system on the first try is that it is a mirage. Your creation will require updating. Make it modular.

What Can Go Wrong?

Design work may be all for naught should people find an EPS too hard to use. "If it's easier to go pick up a book and look it up," says Aetna's Kocher, "that's what people will do."

EPS advocates have their little ways, though. At ALIAC, Kate Butterworth, hired to ramrod an EPS for pension analysts, has taken the analysts cold turkey: Aetna ships them no more printed manuals. "It makes it easier," says Butterworth, "if you don't give them a choice."

Age may make a difference in who embraces an EPS system and who resists. "The younger ones take to it faster than the older ones," says Butterworth, who is 24. "I think younger people are exposed to the computer very early. They're getting it in college if not in high school."

A common EPS rollout problem is simply getting the software to run on a variety of computers throughout an organization. Sometimes the answer turns out to be exasperatingly obvious. One computer wouldn't run an EPS because its memory was all but completely taken up — by a computer-based bridge game.

EPS requires lots of memory, so beware using it on older computers.

When an Aetna computer goes down, standard procedure calls for a troubleshooter to access the company's Reference Base on a nearby computer and jigger the problem machine back to health. But when troubleshooters power up some old machines, the EPS swamps them. The old units don't have enough memory. "Then they've got two PCs not working, and two problems to fix," flinches Aetna's Kocher. "That doesn't make them happy."

Complaints from users provide useful advice for the inevitable upgrade. Why no spell checker? asked EPS users at AT&T. The next version will have one. Other AT&T users wanted built-in e-mail to send performance appraisals to the person reviewed. Still others suggested more space on the electronic form for writing up a person's performance. At ALIAC, senior pension analysts wanted more information, such as up-to-date comparisons on how Aetna portfolios are performing against competitors. They'll get it in an update.

But some complaints run counter to the purpose of an EPS. Another ALIAC gripe: Why can't we print out? The answer: EPS information is updated weekly. What you print out and post today may soon be out of date.

Enthusiasts say that, in certain areas, EPS has the potential to render training all but obsolete.

Many EPS problems stem from computer illiteracy. Workers lacking basic computer know-how will struggle with an EPS. "When people call our EPS hot line, nine out of 10 times it's not our system but the underlying software, so we put them in touch with the general help desk of our firm," says Deloitte & Touche's Radding.

Of course, you'll never satisfy some people. One I-want-it-yesterday type at AT&T called the EPS hot line when pressing "print" produced no immediate result. It turned out everything was fine. The printer just wanted a moment to mull the graphics.

What's It Mean For Trainers?

Just-in-time learning will take some getting used to. That much became obvious as Deloitte & Touche presented the EPS concept to its clients. "It took us a while to explain our own vision of what performance support could do for you," says Radding. "A lot of people put together a five-day training course, not realizing that instead it could be a two-day course with three days of computer-based training."

Training, remember, is still at least one step removed from actual performance. "We may do a very good job of having people accomplish instructional objectives in the classroom, and they may be able to walk out the door tested and with demonstrated competence," says Dow's Jensen. "But what do they do when they get back on the job?"

Enthusiasts say that, in certain areas, EPS has the potential to render training all but obsolete. "The goal is no training," says Aetna's Malcolm. "The crux of the performance-support point of view is to flip-flop where we've been traditionally — trying to fill people up with knowledge and skills, and then put them to work. The notion of performance support is, Let's give them real work to do and provide them with the support to learn while they work."

At the same time, however, even its promoters acknowledge that overreliance on EPS would be a danger. If a company gives up traditional training for just-in-time training — what happens to just-in-case learning? Who will pass along the unwritten rule that you should never compliment the CEO on his tie because he hates flatterers? What will replace the dead-earnest look in a good trainer's eye when she explains that this company is about helping people, and here's how you do it in this case, and here's how you do it in that case?

What will happen to customer-service heroes when front-line workers are guided step-by-step through electronic paperwork and given only a few choices — with no exceptions to the rules? Even if they are allowed to break the rules, will workers get lazy and stop thinking on their feet? Will it be easier to choose the default option?

What about the merits of classroom learning? Isn't there a kind of liberal-arts aspect to much corporate training that EPS blocks out? What about learning things that you don't need to know right away, but will need to know someday — someday when an EPS system isn't right at hand? Will EPS barricade workers from each other and take away networking opportunities that in-person training offers?

These question don't have answers yet. EPS advocates say current systems do allow for innovation. But some have concerns. "Unless you're using an expert system, it's really just teaching you some task-specific problem-solving," says Jim Dods, education specialist with U.S. West Learning Systems. "It isn't teaching you how to think."

That may cut to the heart of the matter. Do we want workers who have fast, ready-made answers, or workers who can think?

"My fear is that EPS will be used in lieu of learning," says Aetna's Malcolm. "In a typical corporate-education setting the goal is not learning. The goal is performance. For some people, learning isn't an issue. They say, 'Who cares if people learn or not, as long as they do the job?' "

The consensus among trainers who have developed EPS systems is that they can be a big help in some settings, but they are only tools — and certainly don't replace human trainers outright. Face to face is the only way to teach some subjects — and trainers also belong on the design team of any EPS that's going to work.

It comes down to this: Do you want clueless workers waiting by the computer screen to see what floats by? Do you want them bugging co-workers to throw them a fish? Or should every Grasshopper get a Jiminy Cricket on the shoulder, and a line in the information stream?

Notes:

EMPOWERMENT

If Empowerment Is So Good, Why Does It Hurt?

BY LAWRENCE HOLPP

In a robotics lab deep in the bowels of the Massachusetts Institute of Technology, squats an ungainly collection of nuts and bolts that looks like an ancestor of Luke Skywalker's little buddy R2D2. Students have programmed it to wander around the lab at night picking up empty soda cans and depositing them in the recycling bin. At the end of its rounds, the industrious gizmo parks itself in the corner and shuts down. All rather sophomoric, except for one thing: Without a central program, human intervention, or constant redoing of its program, the robot manages its routines flawlessly each night.

To do more with less, to do it without tight controls, to instill the principles of outstanding and consistent performance. . . . If we substitute "teams" for that robot and any number of tasks for the chore of picking up cans, we could be talking about the goals underlying the present corporate drive for employee empowerment.

In many companies, though, empowerment goes down like organizational castor oil. What it has in common with that old panacea is that we think it's good for us even though it tastes terrible. We take it when we're bloated and need to lean out fast. It treats the symptoms while ignoring the causes. Holding our noses, we swallow it all at once, glance obliquely at the outcome, and try to forget it until the next time we'll need it.

Nobody wants to admit they have a problem with the complex process of empowering teams, but nearly everybody does. The causes are legion:

• A large health care organization decides to create self-directed teams but fails to involve the physicians. Result: The docs don't show up for case-management reviews, decisions are postponed, patients wait for service, and the teams are discouraged to the point that they disband.

• The president of a bank holding company falls in love with the idea of empowerment and tells his training manager to get on with it. Six months later teams have been formed, training begun, and the roles of supervisors challenged. Problem: Vice presidents weren't brought into the picture, and now they're resisting, with questions and suspicions, the changes proposed by the teams. The teams can't tell if the empowerment campaign has any real support. Suddenly all sorts of problems have been created where none existed before.

• With the best of intentions, a start-up manufacturing plant devotes a great deal of time and money to selecting the "right kinds" of employees, teaching them to work in teams, and training managers to operate in a team environment. The missing link: The plant fails to measure team progress. Instead of setting goals for their teams and holding them to achieving those goals, managers close their eyes, cross their fingers, and hope that everything will work out. It doesn't. Finally, an old-school executive from corporate headquarters has to be called in to take control.

In each case, management wanted to do the right thing. The decision-makers understood that empowerment involves more than lip service — that it requires both commitment and resources. The errors were not strategic, but tactical. These organizations failed to think through the process, reflect on potential problems, ask a few hard questions about their goals, and spend the time to consider how these goals would be received and interpreted by employees.

For many trainers and consultants, the intuitively correct solution is to go back to the cultural drawing board. With rulers, markers, charts and tape, we want to work with executive groups, boards and management teams to reengineer not processes, but visions, goals, missions and values. We want to tinker with executive teams until they are running like clocks, aligned and on time. We want to involve the work force through focus groups in which we can enlist their spirits, plunge our hands into their historical experience, and come away with confirmation of our grand plan. We then want to roll out this plan with fanfare, free lunches, a video, and an inspiring speech by the CEO.

But welcome to the '90s. Life's not like that anymore — at least, not in my experience. I haven't facilitated a vision workshop in four years that's lasted longer than a day. I can't get managers to sit through any kind of training session more than two days long. I'm forced to employ every gram of persuasion I have to get work-team members to drag themselves away from their computers and sit down to meet once a week. When I say that empowerment takes years, eyes cloud over and someone from Cincinnati pipes up that his team was totally empowered in a week, everyone was very happy, and what's the big deal?

Maybe things are different in your company. But assuming they're not, perhaps we need a new paradigm for the kind of intervention that makes empowerment work in unfavorable or indifferent environments. The old models of realigning organizational cultures through a kind of long-term therapy are out the window. What we need is a simpler approach.

Which brings us back to the robot janitor at MIT. The deep thinkers at that university have abstracted a set of principles that govern the error-free, yet simple programming that propels this tin heap:

• Do the basics first.
• Learn to do things flawlessly.
• Add tasks only as previous tasks are mastered.
• Make the new tasks work as flawlessly as the basic ones.
• Repeat, ad infinitum.

I submit that those principles offer

a good outline for making empowerment work.

Do the Basics First

Begin with a definition and a set of goals. Have a plan that is clearly articulated to the teams involved.

It's amazing how many organizations simply skip this step or leave it to the human resources department to take care of. Try as they might, HR people are not up to the task of relieving management of its basic responsibilities.

Empowerment requires a specific, operational definition. Here's one that has proven useful to a number of organizations:

Empowerment is a process for helping the right people at the right levels make the right decisions for the right reasons.

This definition asks a lot but it also provides a lot. For one thing, it suggests a number of questions that need to be asked and answered to the satisfaction of everyone involved.

Right people. Who should we target to begin an empowerment effort? Is there some way to determine which groups are best suited for empowerment and self-direction? Can anyone be empowered or only certain people? How do we deal with those who don't seem to want to take responsibility?

Right levels. What kinds of decisions should people be making on their own? What are the boundaries? How much authority can we push down the line, and how quickly can we do it? How do we track the effectiveness of delegation? How do we make sure things are getting done? If we're forming a team, who does the team report to? What are the differences between managing team performance and managing individual performance? How do we deal with people's expectations to be recognized and promoted as individuals? Can responsibility and authority be an adequate substitute for a management job title? If so, how?

Right decisions. What are the right decisions? What are the boundaries of decision-making? What should people be tackling right now? Three months from now? A year from now? What role will management play in decision-making? What if we see a team making a bad decision? Can we intervene without sinking the team?

Right reasons. How much knowledge and education does the team really need to make good decisions? What's our investment in training going to be? Can we really afford it? Is this a long-term business strategy and are we willing to make a commitment to not jerking people around? Do we really understand what we're proposing to do, and do we seriously believe in it?

By answering these questions, managers can begin to get their hands around the scope of their empowerment strategy. They can avoid a lengthy and perhaps redundant sociotechnical analysis while nonetheless airing the key issues and making some important preliminary decisions. It may be impossible to get empowerment right the first time, the maxims of total quality notwithstanding; but it's inexcusable to avoid asking the right questions.

THE PREMATURE TEAM

BY LAWRENCE HOLPP

What happens when you uncork a team before its time? Some years ago, at a pharmaceutical plant, a longtime supervisor on the third shift finally retired. Since he'd had the reputation of being an autocrat, everyone felt that here was an opportunity to try out some new ideas about teams and participation. Management decided to get this retiring supervisor's crew of four maintenance mechanics to operate as a team without a supervisor.

The plant manager, the production manager and I (the consultant in the picture) met with the mechanics to discuss the situation. We collected all the problems and obstacles they saw in this new arrangement. We listed the issues, one at a time, until they were all on the table. Then the plant manager addressed as many of their concerns as he could. When he or the production manager couldn't provide an immediate answer, they promised a quick follow-up. Thus ended the meeting. We congratulated ourselves on having established an empowered, self-managed work group (though we didn't use that expression), in one quick and efficient meeting.

Within a month, the four men on the third shift, who used to work, play and socialize together, were at each other's throats. Crisis followed crisis, with managers being called in, often out of their sleep, to resolve issues that would only crop up again and again in slightly altered forms. For instance, a dispute would arise over who should clean the tool crib. Using our flip chart and calendars, we laboriously worked out a three-month schedule. The next week the mechanics would complain that they couldn't agree on who would write up parts orders.

After several months of this, the second-shift supervisor began to give the third-shift team its instructions for the evening, and the first-shift supervisors reviewed the night's activity with them. After a while, one of the mechanics was appointed "lead" and functioned as a supervisor in nearly all respects. They were still called a team, but the mechanics were supervised, their work was controlled by others outside the "team," and the responsibility for most significant functions remained in the hands of management.

Having told this little story many times, I've gotten lots of excellent advice: We went wrong in not following up with the crew, in failing to train them and so on.

But the real lesson, I think, is that the popular bromide about how workers make many "management decisions" in their private lives, and therefore can easily take over management responsibilities on the job, is a vast oversimplification. Yes, most workers can balance a checkbook, mow the lawn when the grass gets high, and select a contractor to put on a new roof. But in reality, those skills do not translate easily into the ability to work as a team to coordinate budgets, plan preventative maintenance, deal with vendors and suppliers, or select new team members. These represent a new set of tasks being done in an unfamiliar environment. Ensuring flawless performance, or performance of any quality at all, takes time, planning, and a measurement system that tracks each step of the learning process.

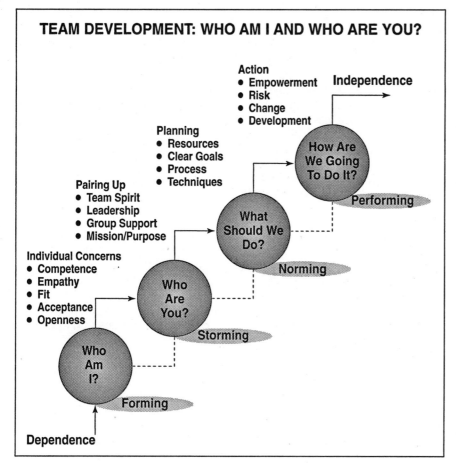

TEAM DEVELOPMENT: WHO AM I AND WHO ARE YOU?

Action
- Empowerment
- Risk
- Change
- Development

Independence

Planning
- Resources
- Clear Goals
- Process
- Techniques

How Are We Going To Do It?

Performing

Pairing Up
- Team Spirit
- Leadership
- Group Support
- Mission/Purpose

What Should We Do?

Norming

Individual Concerns
- Competence
- Empathy
- Fit
- Acceptance
- Openness

Who Are You?

Storming

Who Am I?

Forming

Dependence

Learn to Do Things Flawlessly

Treat every delegation of some new area of authority and responsibility as if it's your last. Don't move on until the team has got the new task down cold.

There's no great mystery in handling the basics: housekeeping, vacation planning, shift coverage, even phone coverage. But the team will find it more difficult to manage things like rotating jobs, maintaining standards, and taking responsibility for results. Allowing the team to move on to the next task before it has mastered the present one condones half-baked performance and lowers standards.

At GE Capital Mortgage Insurance in Raleigh, NC, team-development coordinator Robert Phillips has devised a system to ensure that each department responsible for pushing empowerment into the ranks has a written plan in place. It's neither complicated nor even particularly demanding, but it does require each manager to think through the tasks that will be delegated, explain how that task is currently handled, and set a goal for when it will be assumed by the team.

"We don't want to dictate what each team should be doing and when," says Phillips, "but we feel that each team should have its own plan for empowerment and that it should be a written plan, not just a general goal."

The GE scheme consists of a matrix that lists the kind of tasks that teams will be asked to assume during the next few years. A generic list is provided that helps managers think through a broad range of actions, but each list must be customized by management and staff working together to build the final document. Once the list is built, management needs to ask itself two questions: Who is currently responsible for this task? And what role will the team play in this task when the empowerment process is complete?

For instance, in a newly formed team, hiring currently would be the responsibility of management. The goal might be that one year from now, the team will make hiring decisions entirely on its own. As an intermediate step, six months from now the team and management should be sharing joint responsibility for hiring new members. Firing, on the other hand, will remain permanently a management responsibility. By charting out such plans for all of the tasks the team will (and will not) be expected to take over, everyone understands from the beginning what the "empowerment" process will mean and how it will work.

Add New Tasks Only As Previous Tasks Are Mastered

Until the team has demonstrated competence in a task, new tasks should be delayed. Mastery, consistency, control, uniformity and direction are words seldom associated with either self-managing teams or empowerment. Nevertheless, to ensure that empowerment goals are met and that the process moves along at a steady pace, performance management is critical.

When your teams start complaining because management doesn't want them hiring, firing, budgeting, or doing the company's strategic plan until they are capable of getting their day-to-day work done with consistency and quality, you may interpret that to mean that they do not, as yet, have a realistic sense of what performance management is all about.

At Thrall Car, a manufacturer of railroad cars in Cartersville, GA, the importance of managing team performance became clear after a year of letting teams feel their way. At that point, some teams had made significant progress while others foundered, still uncertain of their mandate and expectations. The lagging teams needed some sort of structure to help them move ahead.

Thrall Car's steering committee drafted a set of job descriptions that clearly laid out duties and responsibilities in each of several key areas: quality, administration, safety and housekeeping, team function, production, and tools and materials. For instance, under "team function," a catch-all category covering such things as meetings, self-management and communications, the basics were spelled out in detail: "Teams will meet weekly, for no longer than 60 minutes, to address team duties and problem-solving issues. An approved agenda and structured meeting format are required .... Teams will address and counsel any team member whose performance or conduct (such as attendance, quality, safety, work habits, etc.) violates company rules or hampers the smooth function of the team." And so on.

If this sounds a bit draconian — or even contradictory, since the point of the whole effort is supposed to be to get people to manage themselves instead of just following rules — consider the common alternatives: frustration, poor performance, and, sometimes, the dissolution of the empowerment vision itself. A good maxim of empowerment is that it's always easier to loosen up than to tighten up. Power delegated all at once is more difficult to take back than when it's given piecemeal, connected to performance and achievement.

Make The New Tasks Work As Flawessly As the Basic Ones

As levels of empowerment build up, the speed at which the process moves increases. Maybe there's a physical principle that accounts for this, something associated with Newton's laws of motion. It isn't nearly as difficult to get maturing teams to take responsibility for complex assignments as to get beginning teams to do their timekeeping or basic office management in the first place.

The figure on page 93 depicts the process by which a group of people develop into a team. As the figure suggests, team development is a matter of personal development as well. Each team member has to get some positive feedback from the others during the initial "forming" stage, for instance, or the team will be reluctant to proceed through the other stages.

A great deal has been written about the difficulties of moving a team through the forming/storming/norming/performing process. But the good news is that once any *task* has moved through this process, it will be easier to move another one through. This is because the personal relationships, including trust and cooperation, already have been cemented. In other words, once you have made the journey from isolation and individuality to team performance, even on a simple task, it becomes easier and faster to repeat the journey with subsequent tasks — including more complex ones.

Repeat, Ad Infinitum

The real benefits of empowerment are seldom felt early on in the process. In fact, the costs of hiring the right people, training them, and working closely with them long enough to get them comfortable with the range of management duties they are expected to perform can be costly. The payoff comes later on when, with little supervision, they are able to take a task and make it part of their work.

To maintain this process is, for management, a lot like dancing with a 500-pound gorilla: You don't stop when you're tired, you stop when the gorilla is tired. Teams don't get tired of having control over their work, and a process of empowerment, once begun, is difficult to withdraw.

Notes:

Prove It! Does Your Training Make A Difference?

BY BEVERLY GEBER

Trude Fawson first noticed the renewed fascination trainers have with course evaluation as she tried to worm her way into a packed seminar room during a conference in San Francisco last April. The unlikely title of the SRO session was "Cost-Benefit Strategies for Conducting Level 4 Follow-Up Evaluations." Fawson, manager of needs assessment and evaluation services within the AT&T School of Business, was the presenter.

Like any diligent classroom instructor, she had arrived early, before the previous session ended. What she found was a statuary of people crowding the door, protecting their positions so unbudgingly that the exiting participants from the other session could barely edge out.

By the time Fawson's presentation started, 150 people were crammed inside a room set up for far fewer. Curious, she asked why the throng hungered to hear about a topic that had generated only tepid interest at previous conferences. After all, doing Level 3 and Level 4 evaluation is the trainerly equivalent of flossing your teeth. You *know* you're supposed to do it, you *know* it's good for you, you *know* there might be dire consequences eventually if you don't, but let's be honest: How many people floss each day unless their dentists have warned them that their gums are flabby and their teeth are starting to wobble?

What Fawson discovered at the annual convention of the International Society of Performance Improvement is that a lot of dentists appear to be populating the line-management ranks at companies these days, and

they're squinting suspiciously at the training department's gum line. The message these managers are delivering is that the training department had better be able to show concrete evidence that training is achieving its goals of changing behavior on the job (Level 3) and contributing to the bottom line (Level 4 — see box on page 94). And they want to see results not just for the easy-to-measure technical training courses, but for soft skills as well.

That was the explanation Fawson's participants reported most often for jamming into her session, but it wasn't the only trigger. Other attendees pointed to the influence of the quality movement and its emphasis on measurement. Some mentioned the pressure exerted by cost-cutting measures, which forces training departments to use money more wisely. Still others told of the rise of technology, which has eased much of the burden of data-gathering for evaluating programs.

It all adds up to a keen interest in evaluation in general, and in Level 3 and Level 4 evaluation in particular. Some large organizations have gone so far as to establish new evaluation units within their training departments. Fawson's unit at AT&T, for instance, was created two years ago. Motorola Inc. also formed its evaluation unit about two years ago, and recently responded to rising interest in the topic by adding a module on evaluation to the course it gives at Motorola University for trainers from customer companies who want to learn Motorola's secrets.

TRAINING's 1994 *Industry Report* also indicates great interest in evaluation. Of the respondents from organizations with 100 or more employees, 83 percent said they do a Level 1 eval-

uation of at least some courses (measuring trainee reactions); 66 percent said they do Level 2 (testing); 62 percent said they have done at least some Level 3 evaluation, and 47 percent reported doing Level 4 evaluation. What's more, of those who do at least some checking at Level 3 or Level 4, respondents said they do Level 3 evaluations on 45 percent of their courses and Level 4 probes of 44 percent of their courses. Those latter numbers, in particular, seem mendaciously high to many observers, and could reflect respondents' flossing guilt rather than their actual practices. But the numbers definitely imply interest in the topic.

A Paper Nightmare

For years, leading lights in the field have preached that if job-related training is to be done correctly, the training department ought to do Level 3 and Level 4 evaluation of at least some courses. Trainers hearing the sermon would nod dutifully, go back to their companies, become overwhelmed with the workload, and rationalize that Level 1 or Level 2 evaluations were sufficient.

There were good reasons to neglect doing deeper evaluations. For one thing, very few higher-ups wanted it done, perhaps out of ignorance that it could be done. For another thing, rigorous Level 3 and Level 4 evaluations are time-consuming and expensive. Measuring changes in on-the-job behavior can't be done properly in a slap-dash manner. It takes time and a chunk of the training department's budget to do it properly.

Fawson recalls that years ago, her division of AT&T attempted to do Level 3 and Level 4 evaluation of an important course, but gave up after trying to assess just the first two groups of trainees. "It was a paper nightmare," she says.

But lately there has been a turnabout in attitudes toward evaluation. Marc Rosenberg, district manager for education and training in AT&T's corporate human resources department in Somerset, NJ, thinks that part of the change can be attributed to a growing maturity in the training field as trainers realize that their charge is to effect results, not just to put people in chairs. "Learning is nice, but it's inadequate," he says. "Learning that doesn't change the business isn't useful."

Some of this evolution reflects more professionalism in the field, says

James Hite, a training manager with Northern Telecom's Learning Institute in Nashville, TN. Although people still enter the training department with no experience in human resources development, Hite says, there are more and more college graduates with advanced degrees in HRD who are signing on. Most of them are well-schooled in fundamental concepts such as the Kirkpatrick model.

Of course, this is not the whole reason for the evaluation renaissance, or even the greater part of it. Even the most conscientious, "professional" trainers have found it all too easy to sacrifice the long-term benefits of evaluation to their current workload.

What really fueled the surge of Level 3 and 4 evaluation at Northern Telecom, Hite says, was the company-wide push for continuous improvement. All over the organization, departments started to measure themselves in new ways. So it was natural for the training department to begin calculating results that were more meaningful than the number of happy trainees or the total training hours delivered.

Being able to demonstrate to line managers that training was making a difference on the job was in line with the training department's effort to be more customer-focused. But Hite readily admits that if the department hadn't made the effort, the metric-savvy line managers would soon have forced the issue. "The more they would get into continuous improvement, the more they would ask these questions of us," he says.

At AT&T, too, it became clear that new measurements were needed to gauge the results of training. Executives who were getting more sophisticated measurements from the rest of the company expected more from the training department as well. "When you tell a vice president of a business unit that on a scale of 1 to 5, trainees rated the effectiveness of the instructor as 4.1, they look at you and kind of say, 'That's nice,' " Fawson says. "We were very proud to have those averages go up each year, but it wasn't meaningful information to the decision-makers."

Paradox or Not?

It might seem odd that training departments would fall under greater scrutiny while much of the business world chants the mantra that Training Is Good. At many companies, executives accept that training is not a cost but an investment — at least, that's what they claim. And yet, if the response to Fawson's seminar is any indication, trainers have suddenly become obsessed with proving training's effectiveness.

Jim Robinson, chairman of the Pittsburgh consulting firm Partners in Change, sees no paradox. Robinson, whose firm specializes in evaluation, says it is generally true that management recognizes that employees are assets whose performance must be monitored and improved. That leads directly to training. "But we're also in a period in which resources are limit-

ed in organizations," he says. The confluence of those two forces produces an emphasis on course evaluation, he contends. "Management says we really need to make sure we're getting satisfactory return on our dollars."

This pressures trainers to wade into the deeper water of Level 3 and Level 4 evaluation. But besides the obvious benefit — finding out whether training programs are, indeed, contributing to important goals — there are other advantages.

For one thing, evaluation can be a "value-added" service to internal customers, a benefit training departments can use to sell their services to line management. Rosenberg says it's persuasive to tell managers that a team of independent evaluators will check to make sure that the training did its job. That's one reason AT&T formed a separate evaluation unit.

In addition, Level 3 and Level 4 evaluations can be instruments for overhauling an entire curriculum. If an evaluation shows that a course isn't improving the performance of workers or producing more bottom-line benefit than it costs, the logical move is to kill it or change it.

Intel Corp. is on a campaign to do Level 3 and Level 4 evaluations for its entire curriculum at Intel University, says Eric Freitag, training, evaluation and improvement manager for the corporate university in Chandler, AZ. So far, he says, about 5 percent of all courses have been eliminated, roughly 20 percent have undergone major

---

THE 4 LEVELS OF EVALUATION

The most widely used model for evaluating training programs is one proposed in 1959 by Donald L. Kirkpatrick, now professor emeritus of the University of Wisconsin and a consultant in Elm Grove, WI. He recently wrote his first book on the topic, *Evaluating Training Programs: The Four Levels* (Berrett-Koehler, 1994). The model is so closely linked to him that it's usually called the Kirkpatrick model.

It is elegantly simple. Kirkpatrick maintains that there are four ways to measure the effectiveness of a training course.

LEVEL 1. At the most primitive level of evaluation, we find the battered and bloodied "smile sheets." Kirkpatrick, however, does not deride them as do many trainers who sniff that smile sheets are not an indicator of whether the training worked. It's true; they are not. But Level 1 evaluation, which seeks *trainee reactions* to a course, is not useless. Trainees who are put off by some aspect of the course design are unlikely to ingest the

learning points you've so carefully put in their trough.

LEVEL 2. Once you've determined whether they liked the course, it's useful to *test what trainees learned*. Sometimes this will take the form of a pencil-and-paper test; sometimes they'll be asked to demonstrate they can operate a piece of machinery. But the goal is to find out if they learned what you were trying to teach.

LEVEL 3. Here's where measurement gets tough to do. It's one thing to document that learners mastered the course content, but if they don't apply any of it when they return to the job, the course has wasted everyone's time. Level 3 evaluations try to measure *behavior change on the job*.

LEVEL 4. Most trainers profess that they want to tie training to the company's bottom line, and that's exactly what Level 4 evaluation attempts to measure. If a course achieved its objective by changing trainees' behavior on the job, did that change improve the company's *business results*?

modifications, and a substantial number have been changed slightly.

Another benefit of deeper evaluation is that it can uncover the barriers that prevent the training from being applied on the job, says Vickie Shoutz, a human resources planning representative with Hutchinson Technology in Hutchinson, MN, which makes computer components. When Shoutz and training specialist Julie Page did their first Level 3 evaluation nearly three years ago, their trainees were 150 workers in the company's tooling department. The employees were starting to work in teams and to interact more directly with customers; the department's manager thought their communication skills needed polishing.

Before the course, Shoutz and Page assessed the employees' skill levels by surveying customers, supervisors and coworkers on how frequently the employees displayed certain behaviors, such as handling conflict smoothly. An identical survey several months after the training showed that the workers used the appropriate skills about 75 percent of the time, compared with 50 percent of the time before the training.

That gave Shoutz and Page quantitative information, but they also wanted a "qualitative" component. So they conducted separate focus-group meetings with trainees and their customers, both before and after the training. That was when the two trainers heard about the kinds of barriers some workers faced on the job that might have prevented them from applying their new skills. For instance, one group of workers who had to work in a shadowy, cramped space told of how depressing it was to come to work and how much they envied their counterparts who worked in a bright, airy spot. Might that affect their ability to be model communicators on the job? No question. "We would never have learned that from a survey," Shoutz says.

Why Not Quick and Dirty?

Conducting a Level 3 or Level 4 evaluation seems daunting to most trainers. And it is, if it's done ex post facto. In other words, it's much easier to design evaluation into the scheme as you're designing the course itself. It's much more difficult to go looking for the right measurements that will tell accurately if an existing course is working.

"Evaluation and front-end analysis are two sides of the same coin," says AT&T's Rosenberg. "If you don't do the right front-end analysis, it's impossible to do Level 3 and Level 4 evaluation."

It's crucial to get the client involved in evaluation before the course is designed. The manager who requests training ought to be able to define the performance problem she's trying to solve (or the opportunity she's trying to grasp) and what kind of behavior she's looking for. If she can do that, she also ought to be able to suggest existing metrics that could help measure a change in behavior. Says Northern Telecom's Hite, "The key is to raise these issues early in the process so that the client will start thinking about how to measure the ultimate results. If that isn't raised immediately, then it may not come up until later, at which point you don't have any benchmark data."

HOW ARTHUR ANDERSEN CALCULATED ROI

You can do evaluation easy or you can do it hard. Actually, "easy" may be a misnomer if you're talking about measuring results at Level 3 or Level 4. But the path of least resistance is to plot evaluation while the training course is still a fresh idea. That was the approach taken by the Center for Professional Education in St. Charles, IL, the central training facility for the Arthur Andersen worldwide organization, in developing a Level 4 evaluation for a training course delivered to the big accounting and consulting firm's tax professionals.

Darryl Jinkerson, director of evaluation services for the center, says that planning for the evaluation started as soon as the center learned that a course would be launched to support a new area of business for the company. Until then, the company's tax professionals were trained only to help clients prepare their federal taxes. But many clients also wanted help in preparing their state and local taxes, which the tax accountants agreed to do in the interest of serving the client.

Eventually, however, the company decided that so much state and local tax preparation was going on that it was necessary to make sure the tax accountants understood thoroughly the laws of the jurisdictions in which they worked.

The training center developed a five-week course, which included two weeks of self-study and three of classroom work. Before the first group of 60 students could be immersed, they took a pretest to determine their knowledge of state and local tax affairs, as well as their confidence that they could prepare the tax returns accurately.

Evaluators also tracked the tax accountants' billable hours before the course began, determining how many of them were spent in calculating clients' state and local taxes, as well as how much revenue was generated by the activity.

After the 60 tax accountants completed the course, evaluators again tracked billable hours and found that the accountants were spending more of their billable hours doing state and local tax work.

Jinkerson and other evaluators also compared the billable hours of those 60 trainees against the hours of tax accountants who were doing state and local tax work but who hadn't yet had training. The trained group produced more revenue than the untrained accountants, undoubtedly because they were much further along the learning curve and confident of their skills, Jinkerson says.

That was borne out by one more measurement. The evaluators surveyed the 60 trainees and found a significant improvement in their confidence that they could prepare state and local taxes. And they were much more willing to promote that expertise to clients.

Jinkerson won't give specific figures for the evaluation's findings, but says that after 15 months, the amount of increased revenue gained by the company more than offset the cost of the training. On average, the increase in revenue for the trained tax accountants was more than 10 percent.

With all the effort that's involved, it would be impractical for most companies to do Level 3 and Level 4 evaluations on every single course. How do you make the cut?

Rosenberg recommends that trainers concentrate on the most expensive programs or the courses that are dear to top management. Fawson uses a decision tree analysis in deciding which ones will get a full-court press at AT&T. She gives heavy weight to factors such as the number of students involved (the more students, the higher the total cost) and the strategic value of the course.

A lot depends on the kinds of courses that are being evaluated. Technical and "hard skills" training have always been easier to track, simply because persuasive data are more readily available. If you ran a safety course, did accidents and workers' compensation claims decrease? If you trained secretaries to use new software for word processing, did they produce more letters faster? In contrast, getting good numbers on a soft-skills course is harder. It can be difficult — some say impossible — to get hard data on the effects of a diversity-awareness program, for instance.

Robinson recommends that a Level 1 evaluation be done for all courses. He recommends a Level 2 evaluation for any courses in which trainees need to retain a particular body of knowledge or apply a specific skill. An example might be a safety course, in which an employer may need to show that workers not only were taught safety procedures, but understood them.

A Level 3 evaluation is called for in cases in which the objective is to change behavior on the job and the client is particularly interested in the results, Robinson says. For instance, in the deregulated telecommunications industry, telephone repair technicians do more than string wire and install phones. As front-line customer service technicians, they also must deal effectively with customers, and maybe even woo them into buying upgraded products. Those behavior changes would directly affect the company's fortunes, so it might be prudent to make sure that skills learned in customer service courses are in fact being used on the job.

A Level 4 evaluation should be done in cases in which the results represent a top priority to the company and can be linked realistically to hard financial numbers. Empowerment may be important to the company, Robinson says, but it's almost impossible to measure the business results of any particular training course designed to support an empowerment strategy. "It's such a long-term payoff, and there are too many variables," Robinson says.

Level 4 evaluations need solid metrics, says Judith Hale, president of Hale Associates, a consulting firm in Western Springs, IL. Sometimes, she adds, those metrics are not that hard to locate. Suppose your accounting department averages receivables of $7 million a day. You could deliver a course teaching accountants better ways to track down money owed the company. Your Level 4 evaluation may require nothing more than checking to see if the daily receivables fell.

Workers Aren't Laboratory Rats

The Center for Professional Education, the central training location for the worldwide Arthur Andersen & Co. organization, is the acknowledged leader in training evaluation. Nearly 15 years ago, the center in St. Charles, IL, set up a formal evaluation group within its training function. Darryl Jinkerson, director of evaluation services, a 32-person unit, says evaluators look at the size and impact of a course before deciding how to evaluate it. Level 3 and Level 4 evaluations are reserved for large, high-profile initiatives or ones in which the stakeholders demand evidence of results.

At the center, all courses receive a Level 1 evaluation and about half get a Level 2 evaluation. Less than a third

Rx FOR GOOD PERFORMANCE

The most thorough way to gauge whether a trainee is applying new skills on the job after training is to have an independent, skilled observer take copious notes while watching the employee work. Nice, but usually impractical.

So Anne Marie Laures, corporate manager of training and development for Walgreen Co., in Deerfield, IL, chose the next best option in evaluating a course for technicians working in the company's drugstore pharmacy departments. She asked the pharmacists to do the observing and note-taking.

Pharmacy technicians are the people who do the support tasks in a pharmacy. They wait on customers. They take refill information over the phone from doctors. At Walgreen's stores, they're also expected to offer customers generic drugs in place of brand-name drugs when the two are identical and when state laws allow it.

Until recently, techs received only on-the-job training from the pharmacists who hired them. But three years ago, Laures' department established a course for new techs that involved 20 hours of classroom training and 20 hours of close supervision on the job. Since the company has about 2,000 stores, the initiative was bound to be expensive. Laures wanted to ensure that it was worth the money. She set out to evaluate the course at Level 3 and Level 4.

After some individuals went through the program, she identified a group of techs who were in their third month of service; some were trained on the job in the usual manner, and others had gone through the training course. She sent surveys to the pharmacists who supervised the techs, asking questions about the new employees' performance. For instance, how speedily did the tech enter information into a computer? How often did the tech interrupt the pharmacist's work to ask a question? How often did the techs offer a generic drug substitute to a customer?

In almost all cases, Laures found that the formally trained technicians were more efficient and wasted less of the pharmacist's time than those who received only on-the-job training.

She then ran the results through a regression analysis and discovered that sales in pharmacies with formally trained techs exceeded sales in pharmacies with on-the-job-trained techs by an average of $9,500 annually. Considering that the cost of training was $273 per trainee, Laures concluded the program was a bargain.

of courses receive a Level 3 evaluation and just 10 percent are evaluated at Level 4.

Taking the first steps toward a Level 3 evaluation can be frightening, and with good cause. Some experts believe that an evaluation at Level 3 is more difficult to accomplish than one at Level 4. The problem, says Donald Kirkpatrick, an Elm Grove, IL, consultant and author of the widely used four-level evaluation model, is that at Level 3, you're trying to measure human behavior; at Level 4, you're tracking some bottom-line figures that should already exist, such as productivity, quality, turnover, or the number of accidents. "But behavior is different," he says. "There are no existing figures on behavior."

And there are few how-to guides. The Kirkpatrick model, for instance, is descriptive, not prescriptive. This means that at Level 3, somebody has to invent methods of measurement for behavior.

It's a task that is hard, but not impossible, says Karen Neuhengen, senior training evaluation specialist at Motorola University in Schaumburg, IL. The key is to figure out the specific behaviors that represent a soft skill, such as leadership, and then track the changes in behavior that trainees exhibit. If you can reach consensus among the stakeholders on the set of behaviors — an arduous process for some courses — you're halfway there, Neuhengen says.

In the two years the evaluation unit has been operating at Motorola, about 20 Level 3 evaluations have been done or started, Neuhengen says. In one, involving a leadership training course for midlevel managers, the evaluators are using a 360-degree evaluation, a measurement method of choice for a Level 3 evaluation of soft skills. Motorola evaluators send a survey to the trainees, their bosses and their subordinates, which asks all three groups to rate the trainees on the frequency with which they display certain behaviors related to leadership. The survey is being done four times a year for two years.

Initially, says Neuhengen, evaluators will be looking for a decrease in variance between the three groups' perceptions as the hoped-for changes in behaviors become obvious to everyone. The surveys are supposed to serve as springboards to quarterly discussions between trainees and their bosses, in an effort to reinforce

the principles of the leadership course. Consequently, evaluators hope to see the scores rise over the two-year measurement period.

There are some in the training field who would sniff at such a "measurement," saying that even if the scores rise, it won't *prove* that training worked. There are far too many variables that affect performance to credit only training for some improvement.

Course evaluators agree completely, but they respond that what they're trying to present is *evidence*, not proof. It is quixotic to think one could control

---

Sometimes it's possible to show a direct link between training and results, but in most cases it's necessary only to show a relationship.

---

all variables in the real world to prove conclusively that a training course was the sole reason that performance improved. But if a course sought behavior change or bottom-line improvement and subsequent measurements showed that the goal was reached, that's evidence that training made a difference.

Anne Marie Laures, corporate manager of training and development for Walgreen Co. in Deerfield, IL, has undertaken several Level 3 and Level 4 evaluations in the past three years. Initially, she wrestled with the "proof" question and worried that other factors could muddy results. She finally decided that "there isn't a pure laboratory setting when you're dealing with the real world, and I don't know that you will find any organization where the executives are looking for pure data."

She recognizes there is a debate in the field about how valid some Level 3 and Level 4 measurements are, but adds, "maybe sometimes we're just too hard on ourselves."

No Level 4 at Motorola

Some trainers believe that success in a Level 3 evaluation simply *implies* success at Level 4. Motorola, for instance, does Level 3 evaluation in order to make sure that its individual courses are working. But, says Neuhengen, Motorola doesn't do any

Level 4 evaluation. Executives are willing to assume that if employees are exhibiting the desired behaviors, that will have a positive effect on the bottom line.

Arthur Andersen's Jinkerson says there's a difference between showing cause-and-effect and showing a relationship. Sometimes it's possible to show a fairly direct link between training and results. But in most cases, he says, it's necessary only to show a relationship.

Jinkerson and other Andersen evaluators are trying to link training to customer satisfaction, on the theory that if customers are completely satisfied with the work of Andersen consultants, they will stick with the company.

So Jinkerson gauges satisfaction by asking clients questions, such as: How satisfied are you with our particular skills? Our business acumen? Our knowledge of your industry? Jinkerson then examines the background of the Andersen employees who deal with the clients. He has found that the ones who had extensive training tend to have more satisfied clients. It may not be absolute proof, Jinkerson says, but "we don't think it's chance."

Andersen evaluators constantly troll for new ways to establish the relationship between training and results. In one recent case, the department used video cameras to do a Level 3 evaluation of a two-day course for executives on the essentials of giving good business presentations. First the executives were videotaped giving presentations before the course began. They were taped again at the conclusion of the course. Then six months later, they were videotaped as they gave presentations to clients.

In the meantime, evaluators had defined the elements of giving good presentations as quantitatively as possible. They checked to see how many times the executives used nonwords, such as "uh." They counted the number of times the executives made eye contact with people in the audience. The evaluators even defined the size and frequency of hand gestures that represented good performance. Given that list of factors, each of which was matched with a number to represent good performance, it was easy to measure improvement.

Bomb Threats in Barbados

Devising quantitative measures is crucial to a good Level 3 or Level 4 evaluation, but AT&T's Fawson says qualitative information can enhance the picture. AT&T trainers are encouraged to report any post-course phone calls they get from trainees who have used the principles on the job and are delighted with the results.

For instance, a course the company delivered on how to prevent violence and terrorism had a dramatic impact on a telephone company office in Barbados, where the local telephone company is viewed as a symbol of the disliked government. The island's lone office was getting frequent bomb threats, which disrupted communications to the entire island and made the employees call in sick nearly as often as they worked.

The course taught employees how to discern whether a telephone bomb threat might be fake, and how to quickly and efficiently search the building. Soon after the course was delivered, the manager called to report that his employees were coming to work regularly again and the number of bomb threats had dropped dramatically. Apparently, bomb threats lost their thrill when employees didn't always evacuate.

Fawson writes up one-page synopses of these case studies and includes a couple with each Level 3 or Level 4 report to executives. "There are some people who like to see the statistics, but others want to see dramatic examples. I really think we need both," she says. "The case histories just communicate better than statistics."

No one who does Level 3 or Level 4 evaluation pretends that it's free. But it helps reduce the cost if trainers can use measurements that are already collected. Northern Telecom's Hite recalls a Level 4 evaluation he did with the company's finance department, whose members were being taught to use a new computerized system to reduce the time it took to derive financial analyses. The measurements were already there; the evaluation added just 5 percent to the cost of the training, which the finance department bore.

But Hite says that the more experience trainers get with finding and choosing the right measurements among ones that are already available, the less expensive it will be.

Says consultant Hale, "There is a perception that evaluation costs money. I disagree. It only costs money if you don't design it well. You can design it so that your line managers do it for you."

What she means is that the responsibility for improving performance on the job belongs to managers. By setting up a Level 3 or Level 4 evaluation, the training department is simply giving those managers the means to determine whether performance actually is improving. And it's not just the training department that's interested in that.

Notes:

ROI of Soft-Skills Training

BY JUDITH PINE AND
JUDITH C. TINGLEY

You're sitting at the conference table with some production line managers. You say: "The problem-solving courses have reduced rework by 12 percent, resulting in a savings to the company of $500 a week. The cost of training your team was $5,000. That means you'll see a return on your training investment of 400 percent over one year."

Suddenly, the phone rings and snaps you out of your daydream. Reality returns. The fact is, the results of "soft-skills" training — in subjects such as problem solving, team building, communication, listening, stress management — are notoriously difficult to measure.

Soft-skills trainers seldom attempt evaluations designed to calculate return on investment (ROI). Trainers, as well as some line managers, generally prefer to think training is "good" whether it accomplishes anything measurable or not. Training goals are often stated in terms that make measurement difficult if not impossible: Become a better listener, improve quality, reduce stress. Maybe trainers fear that soft-skills training doesn't produce an outcome that can be tied to the bottom line. Perhaps some simply don't know how to conduct a results-oriented evaluation and calculate return on investment — though the training literature is full of models and cookbook formulas that explain how to do it.

So things have stood for many years. But the picture is changing. The recession, the epidemic of corporate downsizings, the flattening of organizational structures and the popularity of total quality management are sweeping away some of those old attitudes about the evaluation of training. Today, trainers are under increasing pressure to direct their efforts toward satisfying their internal customers — and many of those customers want to see a measurable, bottom-line impact from training. This translates into an effort to tie training directly to the business results that management is emphasizing — increased productivity, fewer errors, higher employee morale, a stronger bottom line.

Plenty of technical trainers already conduct return-on-investment evaluations. Now soft-skills trainers are beginning to ask the tough questions that link training programs to the operational results of the organization: "How do we know that training makes a difference on the bottom line?" "How can we measure the effects of training on attitudes, behavior and performance, and translate that effect into dollars saved or dollars gained?"

The Model

We set out to demonstrate that all four levels of Donald L. Kirkpatrick's classic evaluation model could be applied to soft-skills training. Furthermore, we wanted to prove that this is not an overpoweringly difficult undertaking, but something that a couple of ordinary trainers (namely, us) could do.

About 30 years ago, Kirkpatrick proposed that the efficiency and effectiveness of training can be evaluated or measured at four different "levels":

Level 1. Measurement of participants' reaction to the training at the time of the training.

Level 2. Measurement of participants' learning of the content of the training.

Level 3. Measurement of participants' use of their new skills and knowledge back on the job.

Level 4. Measurement of the company's return on the training investment.

Very rarely is a serious evaluation of a soft-skills program carried beyond Level 3. We wanted to apply all four levels of the model to soft-skills training in a contemporary setting.

The Study

We conducted this study at Garrett Engine Division, the Phoenix division of Allied Signal Corp. that manufactures jet engines. As part of a total quality manufacturing effort, we conducted a two-day course in team building with intact work groups, the maintenance teams that repair manufacturing machines.

Each team consisted of a first-line supervisor and hourly employees who represented all the trades commonly found in a maintenance department: electricians, mechanics and plumbers. All of the teams reported to the same manager and all were measured on the same performance criteria.

The team-building course included information and experiential exercises on communicating effectively, synergy in teams, stages of growth and change, characteristics of effective work teams and problem solving on specific work issues. In other words, the program was neck-deep in the sort of "soft" material that is usually considered too squishy to evaluate in terms of ROI.

We chose an experimental group that received this team-building course and a control group that did not. We felt this design would increase the probability that any change that occurred was a result of the training rather than an artifact of circumstances. To be more specific, we used a quasi-experimental design described by Campbell and Stanley in their classic text, *Experimental and Quasi-Experimental Designs for Research*.

We began with four similar maintenance teams. The primary function of each was to maintain equipment and machinery used in the manufacturing process. We randomly assigned two of these teams to the experimental group and two to the control group. The teams were similar, but not equal, so we gave pretests to both groups to create pretraining bench marks. Our thinking was straightforward: If the groups are similar prior to the training, and one group experiences training while the other doesn't, we can say with considerable confidence that any differences in performance that appear after the training are a result of the training.

Selecting and Measuring Outcomes

The key to determining a training program's return on investment lies in selecting the outcomes to be measured and linking the training to those outcomes. In the book *Training for Impact*, Dana Gaines Robinson and James Robinson emphasize the need to draw a clear, causal relationship between the skills and knowledge you're developing through training and the operational outcomes you want to measure. In other words, you need to be confident that if, after the training program, the costs of some business process go down or the revenues it generates go up, this is indeed because people have begun to do the things they were taught to do in the course.

In practice, this means that if you're designing a training program that you intend to evaluate at Level 4, you must start with Level 4 considerations and work backwards. First, what business outcomes do you want? Then, how should people behave in order to achieve those outcomes? Then, what do you have to teach them to enable and encourage them to behave that way? Then, how will you know if they learned the things you were trying to teach them? Finally, how should you go about teaching these things?

What kinds of operational results should you measure? An organization's mission and strategic plan determine the outcomes it considers valuable. Managers, employees and trainers should all be involved in deciding which specific outcomes to measure. Outcomes may be related to increased productivity, quality, internal or external customer satisfaction, or myriad other choices. But whatever the outcome, it must be measurable, it must be linked to the training, and you must be able to translate it into money saved or earned.

At Garrett, we chose decreased downtime of equipment as the desired outcome. We also measured job response time and completion time. Response time refers to the amount of time it takes the equipment maintenance people to respond to a call for service. Completion time is the time required to complete the job. The company already tracked this data routinely, so it was easy to acquire a measure of response and completion time two weeks before and two weeks after the team-building training.

Once we had determined the desired outcomes for Level 4, we moved back to Level 3. At Level 3 you're trying to link Level 4 outcomes to the behaviors the training was designed to elicit. For example, a Level 4 outcome for a soft skill like assertive communication might be increased productivity and savings resulting from shorter meetings. A Level 3 outcome would be that the trained people actually use assertive communication techniques in meetings.

In the Garrett study, we postulated that if a work group behaved in ways characteristic of a good team, they'd be likely to respond to and complete jobs more quickly. This is the link between behaviors at Level 3 and outcomes at Level 4. In particular, team members needed to improve their communication skills and share responsibility for tasks and team goals. We found a nationally normed team assessment instrument and used it before and after the training to determine how the members perceived their team's performance in these areas.

Once we determined the Level 3 behaviors we wanted, we decided what knowledge, skills and attitudes had to be learned in the training to develop these behaviors. This is a Level 2 outcome, a measure of the content taught. In the Garrett study, we gave team members a paper-and-pencil test after the training to evaluate their knowledge of effective team qualities, characteristics and behaviors.

Finally, we measured the participants' reaction to the training at Level 1 to find out if they considered the training useful, well-presented and informative. This involved the standard "smile sheet" that asks participants to evaluate the course, the delivery, the instructor and whether course objectives were achieved.

Evaluating the Results

A statistician who specializes in evaluating education helped us analyze the data. His task was to determine statistically whether differences on post-training measures could be considered a result of the training rather than the result of chance. He found that the program was effective at all four levels of evaluation.

Only the group that went through training was measured at Level 1. Trainees gave high ratings to the course and its instructor. They agreed that the objectives of the workshop were clear and had been achieved.

At Level 2, a posttest found that participants' knowledge of team-building concepts did improve, compared with both their pretest levels and with the scores of the group that didn't receive the training.

To measure Level 3 outcomes, skills and knowledge used on the job, we asked both the experimental and control groups to complete a team assessment instrument after the training. Training participants improved their pretraining scores in team communication, sharing responsibility for tasks, alignment on team goals and rapid response. In other words, people who participated in training considered their teams more effective after the training; they said behavior had changed in accordance with the workshop's teachings.

Was the training effective at Level

	Response Time	Completion Time	Total Down Time	Estimated Cost
Experimental Group				
Before Training	4.8 hours	13.6 hours	18.4 hours	$1,341
After Training	4.1 hours	11.7 hours	15.8 hours	$1,156
Control Group				
Before Training	4.4 hours	11.6 hours	16.0 hours	$1,165
After Training	4.4 hours	11.7 hours	16.1 hours	$1,211

Table 1.
CHANGES IN PERFORMANCE

4? Did this new behavior have an effect on the bottom line? Were costs reduced, profits increased or service improved?

We measured actual changes in performance on two variables: job response time and job completion time. Table 1 shows before and after figures for the experimental and control groups. Prior to the team-building course, the people in the experimental group were slower to respond to job requests than those in the control group. After the program, the experimental group responded more quickly. The control group stayed about the same.

A similar improvement occurred in job completion time. Prior to the team-building course, people in the experimental group uniformly took longer to complete jobs than those in the control group. Yet after the program, training participants were completing the average job 1.9 hours quicker than they were before. (Interestingly, the control group showed a slight increase in completion time, which resulted in an increase in cost per job for the control group. We attribute this increase to random factors that can affect any measurement process.)

The machines serviced by these maintenance teams are used 24 hours a day, seven days a week. The maintenance department had established a "burden rate," or the cost of machine downtime, prior to this study. This rate was the figure we used to evaluate the return on investment of the training. Clearly, if performance improved — i.e., the maintenance teams cut their response and completion times — then equipment would be down fewer hours and money would be saved.

We estimated the average response and completion times per job for the experimental and the control groups, both before and after training. Then we calculated the average total downtime per job. We used these estimates to figure the average cost of downtime per job, also shown in Table 1.

The average cost of equipment downtime per job for the experimental group after team-building training was $1,156. The average cost per job for the control group during the same period was $1,211. Thus, we can estimate the savings per job that resulted from the training is $55 ($1,211 minus $1,156).

The most conservative way to estimate the return on training investment is to compare the posttraining performance of the experimental group with the performance of the control group. Obviously, if both groups — or neither group — improve, we can't conclude that training made a difference. In this case, we can attribute the markedly improved performance of the experimental group to the training.

A less conservative way to estimate ROI is to measure the experimental group's performance before and after training.

Using the figures in Table 1, if you subtract cost per job before training from cost per job after training, you'll end up with a more impressive $185 saved per job.

How fast do these savings add up? We estimated the total cost of this team-building training at $5,355, which includes presentation time, materials, overhead and participants' time off the job. The average number of jobs per week per team was 55, with 40 jobs representing a light week and 70 a heavy week.

Figure 1 illustrates return on investment of the training over time. The horizontal line represents the fixed cost of the program ($5,355). Each sloping line represents estimated savings at the end of a given week. The steepest line represents savings given heavy workweeks, while the middle and lower lines represent average and light workweeks, respectively. When a sloped line crosses the horizontal line, savings have exceeded the cost of the program. If we assume average workweeks, program costs are recouped within two weeks.

You can also express ROI as a percentage. In the Garrett study, we calculated the ROI after four average workweeks:

$ 55 (average savings per job)
x 55 (jobs per week)
x 4 (number of weeks)
= $12,100 (benefits)
− $5,355 (cost of training)
= $6,745 ÷ $5,355 (cost of training)
= 1.25 x 100
= 125 percent ROI

What we don't know is how long the training effect will last. To project any long-term savings, we would need to continue to assess job-response and completion times of the trained group and the control group.

Just Do It

Soft-skills training can be tied to productivity measures — even by relative novices to the concept of ROI evaluation. We found Kirkpatrick's model a clear and useful guide to carrying out a systematic four-level evaluation.

Doing this kind of evaluation dramatically improved line management's perception of the training function, as well as our understanding of internal customer service.

Why feel threatened by the idea of determining ROI for a soft-skills program? Try it as a pilot project. Whether or not you can demonstrate a return on investment, the results will help you develop more effective training and improve your relationship with line management. Eventually, you will be able to demonstrate, indisputably, in bottom-line terms, training's value to the organization.

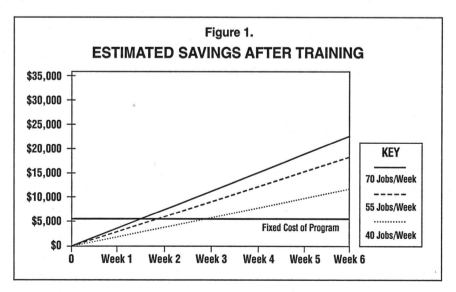

Figure 1.
ESTIMATED SAVINGS AFTER TRAINING

KEY

70 Jobs/Week

55 Jobs/Week

40 Jobs/Week

Fixed Cost of Program

Making Outdoor Experiential Training Work

BY GLENN MARTIN TARULLO

The national fascination with outdoor experiential training (OET) continues to grow. Premier companies such as IBM, General Electric and Du Pont take hundreds of employees out of their offices and into the woods in hopes of building teamwork, increasing communication skills or boosting self-esteem. Prestigious MBA programs at the Universities of Chicago and Pennsylvania use OET in hopes of making their students better managers.

Consequently, suppliers that offer OET programs are doing a booming business. In 1991, Larry Wilson's Pecos River Learning Center, the biggest for-profit outdoor training organization in the country, ran 4,000 managers through its home base in New Mexico while it trained another 16,000 at sites around the country. Outward Bound U.S.A., its nonprofit counterpart, challenged 6,000 managers that same year.

Given the popularity of OET (also known as executive challenge, outdoor management training, and so on), you'd assume there would be some reasonably compelling evidence to support its effectiveness. But while anecdotal reports are easy to come by, there is scarcely any hard data that can help trainers, organization development consultants or line managers put on effective OET programs.

There's a reason for that. It's all but impossible to study outdoor experiential training per se because the OET label is slapped on a tremendous variety of activities. It can apply to everything from a simple "trust walk" to a complex wilderness simulation. And OET programs are conducted by facilitators whose backgrounds run the gamut from ex-mountaineers to Harvard Business School professors who specialize in organization development.

The fact that participants do something outdoors — something often called an "initiative" — does not mean that OET programs have anything else in common. The truth is that too many different types of programs and experiences are categorized under this broad label to allow us to make any generalizations about OET's effectiveness.

If you are considering an OET program, how can you make sure it will work? There are no guarantees. But if you can give solid answers to these five questions, you can significantly boost the odds that your program will be effective.

1 What Do We Want To Accomplish?
As obvious as this sounds, many programs have only vague objectives. The reason is that clients often are vague themselves about what they want to accomplish. If your client — a group inside or outside your organization — proposes an OET goal that is no more specific than "improving communication," "increasing cooperation" or "encouraging creativity," you're in for trouble.

These objectives are so imprecise that you will have no way to measure whether or not your program succeeded or what difference it really made to your business. Since there is no hard data to help you judge the effectiveness of OET programs in general, and since you obviously shouldn't depend solely upon the supplier's word about the effectiveness of its program, you need to supervise the design of the program in a way that will allow you to measure its results.

Since building teamwork is probably the most frequently mentioned objective of OET programs, let's assume that your client wants to improve the level of teamwork within his group. Your first step is to try to diagnose exactly what factors are hurting the team. Questionnaires or preprogram discussions with team members can usually help you understand the issues. Using this diagnosis as a basis, you can determine the objectives of your program.

Try to frame these objectives in the form of a problem statement that is specific, measurable and relates to the performance of both the team and the overall mission of your organization. Then test these objectives against your client's sense of what he wants to accomplish. Designing a program that helps the client achieve these objectives becomes the basis for evaluating the success of your intervention.

For example, a senior manager may want to increase the amount of customer information that is shared among individual account managers to pump up the company's volume of product cross-selling. The measure of your program's success then becomes a quantifiable increase in cross-selling, not some vague feeling among account managers that they seem to work better together after the program. The key is to design a program that solves a real business problem in some measurable way.

It's particularly important to be clear about your objectives in OET because, unlike other types of training, outdoor initiatives are literally devoid of content. If you send managers to a course on presentation skills, you can be reasonably sure that the content of the program will focus on the skills and information they need to make better presentations. But if you send managers down a zip line or up a cliff or through a "spider web," you are not at all sure they will focus on the skills you want the program to develop — unless scaling cliffs or traversing rope courses are part of your company's strategic plan.

OET is driven by process, not content. Rather than information, OET gives participants an outdoor experience from which they can learn. We assume that adults can reflect on this experience, learn from it and use what they learn to improve on-the-job performance.

But unless you are absolutely clear

on the problems you want your program to address, you may not know which elements of the experience to process. Do you discuss how the group set its goals? Or do you focus on how willing people were to share information and resources? Being clear on the program's objectives allows you to focus on the particular learning points you want your program to make. It also allows you to choose outdoor initiatives that highlight specific behaviors. If the objective of your program is to increase participation in team goal setting, then choose outdoor initiatives that involve a participative goal-setting process.

2 Why Do We Want to Go Outdoors? The basic question here is: What do I hope to accomplish outdoors that I can't accomplish in a classroom? What is it about outdoor training that justifies the time and expense? Although there isn't much data to support this, I think the most effective types of OET programs have three unique characteristics that differentiate them from other training.

First, OET programs allow participants to interact on a very intimate level. Most of our interactions with coworkers are one-dimensional and governed by prescribed rules of business etiquette. We seldom let down our hair, shed our corporate masks, and deal with one another openly. Yet studies of high-performing teams consistently find that intimacy and honesty form the glue that both draws people into a team and holds the team together.

Outward Bound, for example, offers an OET program in which teams sail together in a 30-foot open boat. The intense experience of eating, sleeping and working together on such an intimate level can help team members develop a sense of trust, support and cooperation that simply cannot occur in a classroom.

Many types of outdoor training also allow participants to share a strong emotional experience. Helping your partner walk across a log suspended 60 feet in the air, rafting down a white-water river together or simply scaling a 10-foot wall can be an intense experience. It can quickly forge a group of individuals into a team.

Research on human growth and development supports the significance of such emotional events as catalysts for change. Most people in the training field realize that behavior is

difficult to change. In fact, when we look at the circumstances that seem to be associated with individual change, we often find some profound shock such as the death of a loved one, divorce or a serious economic setback. While none of these emotional events compel us to change in a particular direction, they do open us up psychologically. Because OET is itself out of the ordinary, and because it often involves some heightened level of emotional experience, it also can open up participants to the possibility of change in their work lives.

The final — and perhaps most important — characteristic of OET is its ability to become a metaphor for organizational behavior. The same behavioral patterns that limit a team's effectiveness in the office are repeated during outdoor initiatives. Groups often behave the same way whether they are building a wilderness shelter or developing a marketing plan. By analyzing what goes wrong during these outdoor initiatives, members of a team can get valuable insights into what is hurting them back at the office.

The most important characteristic of OET is its ability to become a metaphor for organizational behavior.

---

3 What Type of Facilitator Will We Need? Outdoor initiatives have no inherent "message." The message comes from our interpretation of the experience. And since it is the facilitator's job to help participants analyze, interpret and gain insight from these experiences, the competence of the facilitator is the single most important element affecting the success of your program.

This is another reason the research on outdoor programs is often contradictory. The power of these experiences comes from the insights drawn from them — not from the experience itself. Evaluations often wind up measuring a particular facilitator's competence in making an initiative meaningful, rather than the effectiveness of a particular program's design.

The facilitator is also responsible for introducing content into the program. Typically, a facilitator will end an initiative by asking the team members to generate a list of the things that they might have done to improve their performance. Debriefing an initiative this way can be a valuable experience, but it is limited by the quality of the recommendations on the list. Unless the participants are particularly insightful, the facilitator must offer additional suggestions on how the team might improve.

If the group is working on becoming more effective problem solvers, for example, the facilitator might introduce a model of effective problem-solving against which the team can evaluate its performance. The training model used in this case might be:

• Allow the team to experience an initiative that requires some type of complex problem-solving.

• Help the participants analyze the process they used to solve the problem.

• Introduce an "ideal" problem-solving method against which the team can evaluate its performance.

• Introduce a second initiative so that the team can practice its new problem-solving skills.

• Ask the team members to evaluate themselves again using the new model.

• Help the team transfer its new problem-solving skills to a current business problem.

4 What Role Should I Play During the Program? It's critical that you, the in-house trainer or consultant, clearly define your role in relation to both the outdoor facilitator and the program's participants. The worst possible approach to OET is one in which a) you have only a brief telephone conversation about the goals and logistics of the program with your outdoor facilitator; b) you bring participants to the outdoor site, where the facilitator takes over and delivers the "experience"; and c) then, once the facilitator has transformed your participants, they are given back to you for a safe return home.

Although it may seem natural or polite to let outdoor facilitators take over on their own turf, it's important that you assume responsibility in four areas.

First, be sure that you communicate your group's goals to the facilitator. Are they clear, measurable and related to the goals of the larger organization? Can they be explained in the form of a problem statement? Assuming you have done all the legwork with your client well in advance, you should be the person to open the program with a review of the goals and objectives. This ensures that all participants are clear about why they are going through the program.

Second, you need to decide whether these goals can be reached using the particular outdoor initiatives your facilitator has suggested. Do they support the types of issues the team needs to work on? Even if they do, will you need to introduce additional material? Is your facilitator capable of delivering this content? If not, this might be a place for you to jump in as a content expert.

Third, what will you do during the actual initiatives? Will you be part of them or just observe? Since you are probably not familiar enough with the initiatives to really help, the danger is that you may become neither fish nor fowl — neither facilitator nor participant. I suggest that since you are not part of the team, you do not take part in the actual initiatives. You should, though, take an active part in leading or participating in the analysis and debriefing following the initiatives.

Last, it is your responsibility to make sure that the learning derived from this outdoor experience gets transferred back to the job. Like it or not, your facilitator's involvement will probably end at the parking lot. It's up to you to see that the progress your group has made doesn't end there as well.

One way to do this is to make the issue of real-life application part of the debriefing process. For example, you might have a discussion about the specific things team members will do when they return to work. What procedures will they institute, which behaviors will they alter, or what norms will they establish back in the office? You might then prioritize the list they come up with and use it as a basis for an agreement of what will be done and who will be responsible for doing it. Your role then becomes one of monitoring how well members honor this contract, and helping them get back on track if they drift.

5 **Who Should Go?** In theory, this should be the easiest question to answer. If the goals of your program are to change individual characteristics such as self-esteem or risk taking, then who goes and when isn't particularly important.

I have found, however, that it's hard for these "personal transformation" programs to change elements of someone's personality or management style in a day or two. Remember, it has taken participants 30 or 40 years of dedicated practice to get them where they are when they show up for your program. Expecting transformation from a few days in the woods is asking a lot.

Nor is it clear how changing one individual at a time can improve the larger organization. Many organizational problems are caused by how team members interact with one another — how we plan, work and resolve conflicts together. So unless an entire team attends, teamwork can't be your program's focus.

Consider the ramifications for the manager of the team that attends OET. Often the manager will take the brunt of both the praise and criticism for a team's performance. And since many teams seek help only after things have gotten awfully bad, managers in such programs can expect a lot of the discussion to be focused on their failure — in the eyes of some team members — to manage the team better. Although this discussion may be essential for the long-term health of the team, it can put a great deal of pressure on the individual manager — and your relationship with that manager.

Like it or not, the manager may blame you and the program for putting him in this uncomfortable position. You should prepare the manager for such criticism, and help monitor the group process so that the manager does not become the whipping boy for the team's problems. Team members often ignore their own responsibility for their team's situation and zero in on the shortcomings of their manager.

By thinking seriously about these five questions, you can significantly improve the effectiveness of your outdoor experiential training. Since there is a lack of hard evidence on the effectiveness of outdoor programs in general, and because any research that does exist may not be directly applicable to your program, think of any outdoor training you do as an experiment. The goal of this experiment is to improve the performance of a work team in some significant and measurable way. Your responsibility is to manage the design of the experiment in a manner that increases its chances of success. If the training fails to meet your objectives, at least you can gather information that will help improve your next program.

Notes:

FEEDBACK

How to Get the Most Out of 360-Degree Feedback

BY GARY YUKL
AND RICHARD LEPSINGER

Feedback from multiple sources, alias "360-degree feedback," is something of a rage among training professionals. Consultants and practitioners alike tout it as the optimal tool for enhancing leadership and management capabilities, particularly when a company is trying to develop a more open, communicative culture.

More than many developmental tools, 360-degree feedback can prompt real, measurable changes in managers' behavior. The reason is simple: When people receive honest, specific feedback from their bosses, colleagues and subordinates, they often come to understand how their behaviors affect others — and the need for change in some of those behaviors.

Yet like other "magic bullets," multirater feedback often fails to bring about the advertised effects. Too often, 360-degree feedback is a one-time event that is forgotten as soon as managers return to the hectic world of work. When this occurs, the problem usually lies with the type of feedback that's being asked for, and how it is gathered, displayed, interpreted and acted upon.

Generally, the process works like this: Questionnaires are used to gather information about managers' behavior from those in a position to witness it daily: direct reports, colleagues, bosses, and sometimes suppliers and customers. Managers then receive feedback reports that summarize the responses given on these questionnaires. In most cases, participating managers also get the chance to discuss the feedback they've received during workshops conducted by a facilitator.

Many stumbling blocks can blunt the effectiveness of this process. Most fall into two categories: the design and administration of the questionnaire, and the design and facilitation of the follow-up activities. You can increase the likelihood that real behavior change will result from your 360-degree feedback intervention if you follow these recommendations.

The Questionnaire

In selecting a feedback questionnaire, look for the following qualities:

• *Well-researched:* Empirical research should show how each behavior itemized on the questionnaire is related to managerial effectiveness. Solid evidence that the behaviors are relevant for success increases managers' interest in getting and using the feedback. Providing feedback on behaviors that are not actually linked to effectiveness is a waste of time and money.

• *Behavioral:* The items on the questionnaire should describe specific, observable behaviors. People have difficulty giving accurate feedback when the descriptions of behavior are vague and general (such as "structures the work roles of direct reports"). The items should describe concrete behaviors: "Explains what results are expected when a task is assigned," or "Tells you when a task you are doing needs to be completed." Specific items like these provide the basis for feedback that is easier for managers to interpret and use for improvement.

• *Positive:* Behaviors should be described in positive rather than negative terms. Avoid questionnaires with items like, "Yells at you for making a mistake." Better wording would be, "Helps you understand the reasons for a mistake and how to avoid making similar mistakes in the future." Some direct reports will be leery about reporting that their boss does something that is ineffective (even if he does so only occasionally); they are more likely to say he does *not* use an effective behavior frequently. Moreover, a questionnaire full of negative items tends to make managers feel defensive and less likely to participate voluntarily in the feedback process. Finally, feedback about ineffective behavior does not tell people what they *should* be doing — only what not to do.

• *Personal:* Whenever feasible, behaviors should be described in terms related to the individual answering the questionnaire. It is better, for example, to ask for a response to "This manager praises *me* when I carry out a task effectively" than to "This manager praises *direct reports* who carry out a task effectively." Respondents shouldn't be expected to hazard guesses about a manager's behavior with others. This kind of wording also gives a more accurate picture when the manager behaves differently toward different people. Of course, such wording is not appropriate for behaviors that involve more than one person ("Holds a special celebration after the group successfully accomplishes a project") or for behaviors the manager performs alone ("Reviews performance reports for the organizational unit").

• *Multidirectional:* Managers tend to behave differently with people depending on their organizational relationship with them. For example, our research indicates that managers use different patterns of influence behavior when they are dealing with direct reports, with colleagues and with bosses. That's why feedback from different perspectives provides a more complete picture of a manager's behavior. But don't solicit 360-degree feedback about behaviors that are used exclusively in one type of relationship. Delegating, for example, is something managers do with direct reports. Colleagues and bosses generally will not have firsthand knowledge of a manager's delegating behaviors. Thus, you may need different versions of the questionnaire for respondents with different relationships to the manager. Each version should include only the behaviors that are relevant in that kind of relationship.

Administering the Questionnaire

A successful feedback system depends on enlisting the cooperation of a sufficient number of respondents who have knowledge about the manager's behavior. Managers need guidelines for how to identify appropriate respondents and gain their cooperation.

Some useful guidelines:

• *Select respondents carefully.* In most cases, the participating managers select respondents to fill out the questionnaires. This gives managers a greater sense of control over the process and increases the likelihood that they will accept the feedback. Some trainers worry that managers will distribute questionnaires only to their friends, but even friends will usually provide honest responses if they know their feedback will be held in confidence.

Still, advise managers to select a representative sample of people who are most critical to their effectiveness on the job. Also encourage them to identify people who are in a position to provide accurate feedback — ideally, those who have interacted with them on a regular basis for a year or more. Respondents should have had the opportunity to observe a manager's behavior for at least four months.

• *Ensure an adequate number of respondents.* The number of respondents should be large enough to ensure adequate sampling and to protect the confidentiality of the sources. You'll need at least three completed, usable questionnaires from subordinates, for example. Because some people invariably fail to return the questionnaire, the initial sample should be larger than the number of responses needed.

People asked to complete questionnaires also need guidance to help them provide accurate feedback:

• *Explain how the data will be used and ensure confidentiality.* People who are afraid of adverse consequences will be reluctant to fill out a behavior questionnaire, and, if they do complete it, they probably won't provide honest answers. This problem is especially acute when direct reports are asked to describe the behavior of a boss who is defensive or abusive.

To gain cooperation from potential respondents, explain the purpose of the survey, how the results will be used, and how confidentiality will be ensured. You might want to explain in a cover letter that the questionnaire results will be used to provide feedback, and emphasize that individual respondents' answers will remain anonymous. (One way to protect confidentiality is to ask respondents to mail their completed questionnaires directly to an external consultant who will analyze the results and prepare the feedback report.) Feedback should not be reported if there are too few respondents to protect individual confidentiality.

Action planning encourages managers to take control of their lives and decide for themselves how to become more effective.

The boss's feedback presents special problems if it is displayed separately from other feedback. Obviously, the boss's feedback won't be anonymous. Although the power relationship reduces the risk of adverse consequences, the boss may decline to participate in the process to avoid embarrassment or to avoid the perception that this is some kind of formal performance appraisal. It should be easy to get the boss to cooperate when the purpose of the feedback is purely developmental; the boss is able to provide relevant and unique information about the participant's behavior.

• *Help respondents avoid common problems in rating.* It's difficult to remember how much or how often a manager used a given type of behavior over the past several months. Instead, raters may base their responses on their general feeling about the manager. Thus, you may get a "halo effect" — that is, a manager who is well-liked may be given high ratings on all scales, regardless of her use of particular behaviors. Conversely, a manager who is strongly disliked may be rated negatively even on those behaviors that he performs often.

Another common bias ("attribution error") occurs when a manager who is known to be effective is rated highly on any scales the rater believes are relevant to effectiveness, regardless of the manager's actual behavior. For example, a manager may work well with individuals, but do little to build team spirit.

When raters fall victim to these biases, their feedback becomes less useful. Even managers who are very effective in general can benefit from identifying areas for improvement, but you'll have a tough time pinpointing their weaknesses if the feedback is biased.

You can alert raters to these biases, and urge them to rate each type of behavior independently. An even better solution is a short training session that teaches respondents to rate behavior more accurately. But rater training is costly and may not be feasible unless your organization plans to collect behavior ratings on a regular basis.

The Feedback Report

There are many ways to summarize respondents' feedback, some of which are more useful than others. In general, however, the feedback report should:

• *Clearly identify feedback from different perspectives.* Behavior descriptions obtained from different perspectives — direct reports, colleagues, bosses — should be presented separately. Aggregating feedback from different sources tends to make it more difficult to interpret. For example, if a manager tends to use consultation frequently with colleagues but seldom with direct reports, aggregate data will obscure the fact that the manager treats people differently based on their relationship and position in the organization.

• *Compare feedback from others with the manager's own perceptions.* Most feedback reports compare what others say about a manager's behavior with self-ratings by the manager on a parallel questionnaire. Just going through the process of rating themselves helps managers understand the behavior scales better. Comparing their own ratings with those of others also helps managers interpret the feedback. A high level of agreement among the various raters confirms that the manager's self-assessment is probably accurate; large discrepancies suggest that someone is not perceiving behavior accurately.

Managers often rate themselves higher than others rate them. For example, a manager may indicate that direct reports are frequently praised for their accomplishments, whereas the direct reports report that they receive little recognition from the manager. This is exactly the type of discrepancy that should get the manager's attention and probably indicates a weakness to be addressed.

However, it's important to explore the reason for a discrepancy rather than jump to conclusions about it. Self-ratings may be higher because the manager is biased, his behavior may not be visible to the other raters, or the other raters may have interpreted the items differently.

A discrepancy in the other direction may also occur, but this is less common. For example, a manager may rate himself lower than others do on inspiring subordinates to greater efforts, perhaps because the manager does not realize the extent of his positive influence as a leader.

• *Compare the manager's ratings to norms.* It is difficult for a manager to know whether her score on a specific behavior is high or low without some basis for comparison with other managers. For example, our research shows that managers, in general, use rational persuasion very frequently when they try to influence others. Yet a below-average score on this behavior will not be obvious without the use of norms. Ideally norms show where a manager falls in the distribution of scores for a large sample of managers. One good way to do this is to use a percentile score that indicates how many managers in the database got lower scores.

• *Display feedback for items as well as scales.* Most behavior scales or categories consist of several items. The behavior scale of "mentoring," for example, may consist of items such as: "Offers helpful advice on how to advance your career"; "Provides you with opportunities to develop your skills and demonstrate what you can do"; "Encourages you to attend relevant training programs, workshops or night courses to develop greater skill and expertise", and "Provides extra instruction or coaching to help you improve your job skills or learn new ones."

Some feedback reports provide feedback for the scales, but not for the separate items that comprise them. Both types of feedback are useful. Item feedback helps managers understand the behavior scales because the items provide specific examples for each category. Feedback on individual items also reduces problems caused by missing responses. Once the scale scores have been computed, the fact that different respondents skipped different items that make up the scale is camouflaged. Omitted responses may be counted as "never does" or not counted at all, but either way, blanks distort the overall scale score. Reporting results for individual items provides a more accurate picture of a manager's behavior and makes the feedback easier to interpret.

The best form of item feedback is a mean score for each item (the ratings from all respondents on the item are totaled and divided by the number of respondents). Some feedback reports also present the range of scores (highest and lowest), and even the distribution of answers from different respondents (how many people in each group selected each response). Again, the score distribution should not be shown unless there are enough respondents to protect the anonymity of individuals.

Gather information about managers' behavior from those in a position to witness it daily: direct reports, colleagues, bosses, and sometimes suppliers and customers.

• *Provide feedback on recommendations.* Feedback questionnaires typically ask respondents to describe what the manager does, not what the respondent would like the manager to do. We have found that asking respondents for recommendations provides a useful supplement to feedback about observed behavior. In particular, these recommendations should show how many respondents said the manager should use the behavior more frequently, the same amount or less. This information helps managers interpret their behavior feedback and identify their strengths and weaknesses.

For example, even though a manager has a moderately high score on a behavior such as delegating to direct reports, some people may prefer even more delegation. Without the recommendation it would be hard to discover this opportunity for improvement. Occasionally, respondents think the manager should use a behavior less, although this does not happen as often if the questionnaire describes only positive behaviors. Because of the extra time required to complete a questionnaire that includes a section on recommendations, these questions should focus on scales rather than individual items.

The Feedback Workshop

Sometimes managers receive only a written report on 360-degree feedback, but it's better to have a facilitator explain the feedback and help managers use it to the best advantage. A feedback workshop with 15 to 20 managers is an economical way to use a facilitator. A number of workshop activities can help participants understand the feedback, accept it, and use it to improve their effectiveness.

• *Explain the purpose and benefits of the feedback.* Both the managers themselves and the people completing the questionnaire are more likely to cooperate if they know the feedback is to be used only for developmental purposes and not for evaluation of current performance.

• *Explain the underlying model of leadership and management.* The behavior questionnaire should be based on a theory of effective leadership that identifies behaviors important for managerial effectiveness. This theory should be explained to managers early in the workshop so that they have a basis for interpreting the feedback and focusing on its most important aspects. A good theory also helps managers understand the need to modify their behavior, depending on the specific situation and their objectives and priorities. If developing subordinates is a high priority, for example, more delegation is appropriate. Obviously, managers should delegate assignments more frequently to someone who is competent and trustworthy than to a person who is inexperienced or irresponsible.

• *Involve managers in interpreting the feedback.* In some feedback systems, computer programs provide a narrative interpretation of the feedback and tell managers what they must do to improve. Managers who are responsible for making decisions about millions of dollars of company assets may understandably resent having a computer tell them to change their behavior. With some assistance from the workshop facilitator, most managers are quite capable of evaluating their feedback and determining its implications; they also know better than anyone else about special circumstances that have affected their results. Moreover, allowing managers some room to interpret their results increases the likelihood that they will accept the feedback.

- *Emphasize strengths as well as weaknesses.* Research shows that people are more likely to reject feedback if it is consistently negative. The workshop facilitator should help managers keep a balanced perspective by stressing positive as well as negative feedback. The facilitator should emphasize that the feedback is intended to give managers a sense of what behaviors they should continue, not just what they should be doing differently. The facilitator also should be prepared to provide advice, encouragement and support to managers who are concerned about correcting weaknesses.

- *Ask each manager to develop an improvement plan.* Feedback is more likely to result in behavior change if each manager develops a specific improvement plan. This action planning encourages managers to take control of their lives and decide for themselves how to become more effective. Moreover, in combination with a leadership theory to guide the process, the action planning will help managers learn how to analyze the specific needs of their leadership situation.

Follow-Up Activities

The benefits of a feedback workshop are more likely to be realized if supporting activities follow it. Useful follow-up activities include training, coaching and assessment of the feedback's effects.

- *Provide opportunities for skill training.* Skill training allows managers to learn *how* to improve their behavior, not just what behaviors need to be improved. You can tell a manager he needs to use influencing and inspiring behavior, but if he's not good at influencing and inspiring people, he's highly unlikely to get better at it without training that teaches him those skills. Training will also increase a manager's confidence about using the behaviors back on the job.

Just going through the process of rating themselves helps managers understand the behavior scales better.

The feedback workshop can be expanded to two days to include a day of skill-building, or training can be provided in separate sessions later. Considerations of time, logistics, participant needs, and the type of behaviors involved will determine the best approach. A combined feedback and training workshop takes longer to conduct, but the cost of travel, facilities and trainers may be lower for a combined workshop than for two separate ones.

- *Provide support and coaching.* Individual support and coaching for managers will help them apply what they have learned. One approach is to hold a follow-up session four to six weeks after the feedback workshop to review progress, discuss any difficulties the manager may be having, and provide encouragement and coaching. An alternative approach is to have managers meet with their bosses or with a human resource manager to

review progress on their improvement plans.

- *Assess the effects of the feedback workshop.* One way to assess behavior change is to hold review sessions to discuss how well the managers have implemented their improvement plans. Another approach is to conduct a follow-up survey among the people who responded to the questionnaire for a specific manager six months to a year after the feedback workshop to assess the amount of behavior change. This way, the company gets valuable information about the return on its investment in feedback workshops, the facilitators get information they can use to improve the workshops, and researchers get an opportunity to learn more about leadership and training.

With all these benefits, you'd think it would be common practice to conduct follow-up evaluations of feedback and training workshops. Unfortunately, systematic evaluation is the exception rather than the rule. This situation may improve, however, as companies become more interested in measuring the return on their investments in training and development.

Over the years, we have learned a lot about using feedback effectively, but we still have much more to learn. Thousands of feedback workshops are conducted every year, but few studies evaluate them. We need more research to discover what works well and what doesn't.

Companies that conduct feedback workshops have an unprecedented opportunity to evaluate the effect of variations in how feedback is collected, presented and used. Many academics would welcome the chance to collaborate with practitioners in this area. It is time to begin exploiting the opportunities we have to advance our knowledge about this increasingly popular form of management development.

An Interview with Joe Harless

The trouble with a training term that's on just about every tongue is: It's on just about every tongue. Used as a buzzword — "What this problem needs is a little front-end analysis" — the term can confuse as much as it enlightens. It sounds right, but is it really? This kind of question led us quite naturally to ask Joe Harless, coiner of the term front-end analysis, to join us in TRAINING's offices for an interview on the concept. Harless is president of Harless Performance Guild Inc. of Newman, GA, and author of the definitive book on the subject.

TRAINING: Joe, we want to begin by asking you straight out, is front-end analysis for real or is it just the Joe Harless *schtick*?

HARLESS: Front-end analysis is not anyone's *schtick*. It's not a *schtick*. It's very real — if you define real as having a definite set of procedures to follow, and data and case histories about its application along with a following of performance professionals who have embraced the procedures and are applying them in their work. If that is what "real" is, front-end analysis is as real a thing as anyone in the business of training could imagine.

TRAINING: Why front-end analysis? Why the name? Why the procedures?

HARLESS: It really began with training packages. We had been developing training packages and were very pleased with them — with their appearance, with the way they taught, with the test data we were getting on them. Our clients were pleased, too.

Despite all this — despite the fact that the trainees were mastering the skills and knowledge taught with our training packages and passed criterion referenced tests at the end — we wanted to see if they transferred those skills and that knowledge to the job. This led us to do follow-up evaluations which in those days we jokingly called rear-end analysis. And surprisingly, in spite of all our expertise in training technology, we found almost as many times as not that the skills were not in fact transferred to the job, that the trainees were not doing what our training packages had taught them to perform.

TRAINING: Why?

HARLESS: That, of course, is exactly the question we began asking and, being devotees of the scientific method, we advanced certain hypotheses. Perhaps the training objectives were not relevant to the trainee's real-world needs. Perhaps the training activities did not simulate the real world as closely as possible (we know that the closer the level of simulation to the real world, the greater the probability that those skills and knowledges will be exhibited).

Perhaps there was something in the environment that prevented the trainees from exhibiting the learned behavior on the job — a manager perhaps, or foreman who disagreed with our methods and would only reward our trainees for performance that was incompatible with what they had learned in training. Or perhaps the trainee had simply forgotten what we had trained him to do.

The scientific method demands that if you pose a hypothesis, you test it. So we began testing these hypotheses. In brief, we found that people don't do things on the job for one of three reasons: They don't know how to do them, they're prevented from doing them in some way or they lack the incentive to do them.

TRAINING: That seems simple enough.

HARLESS: It is. But its implications for the solution of performance problems are profound. That's where the concept of front-end analysis comes in. Rear-end analysis asks, Why didn't training produce a certain kind of performance? Front-end analysis asks, first, What are the symptoms and indicators that a problem exists? Second, What are the performance deficiencies indicated by those data — what is the performance problem? And, finally, What is the relative value of solving that problem?

TRAINING: Value? In terms of what?

HARLESS: In terms of money. Front-end analysis is about money first and foremost. So is training. If not, you're baby sitting or doing psychotherapy. But to continue, I was saying that with a problem identified, a significant front-end analysis question is, What is the potential value — that is, increased profits, reduced loss, etc. — of solving it? And is this potential value great enough to warrant our attention?

Assuming that the potential value is great enough to warrant an investigation, the next step is to ask ourselves, based on the data available, What are the possible causes — not probable causes, *possible* causes — of the problem? I have already indicated that our research indicated performance problems derive from one of three causes: a lack of skills and knowledge, a practical impediment or lack of proper motivation.

Hypothesizing one or more of these causes for a particular performance problem, we take the next step collecting evidence bearing on each hypothesis.

TRAINING: Can you give us an example?

HARLESS: Suppose a production line on which high-speed grinding wheels are used is having too many eye injuries. The workers are not wearing their goggles. We ask ourselves why — that's the basic front-end analysis question. And we hypothesize, first, that they are not wearing their goggles because they lack certain skills or knowledge — they don't know they should, they are not aware that their eye injuries can be prevented by the wearing of goggles. Or — our second hypothesis — they are not wearing their goggles because they don't *have* any goggles or don't have enough of them or they're locked up somewhere. Something is preventing them from performing as safe procedures would seem to require. Finally we wonder whether the goggles are uncomfortable or interfere in some way with their work. This would represent a motivation problem, our third hypothesis.

TRAINING: How do you test these hypotheses?

HARLESS: We ask for a demonstration. Generally if we want to know if a person can or can't do something, we have them do it — on the work site or under simulated conditions if necessary.

TRAINING: Can't you just go to the foreman and say, Hey, Tom, why aren't the men wearing their goggles?

HARLESS: You can. We do that — particularly when setting up a performance demonstration is difficult or terribly expensive. But we view this secondary evidence with some skepticism. The informant may have an ax to grind. He may be protecting his territory, covering his tracks, casting blame. So the data is suspect. We'd much rather look at the performance if we can.

All right. We've isolated a problem and we've come to some conclusion about what the contributing causes of the problem are. Now, before I go on to the next procedure, I've got to tell you about a bias, a rule we follow.

We believe that the nature of the cause of a performance problem dictates the type of solution. Now, that's a simple-minded rule. But it tells you something important. It tells you that if you have a training problem, you train. But if you have a motivation or incentive problem, you don't train. You do some other things. Or suppose you have something wrong with a performance environment — lack of feedback, bad equipment, not enough time. Then you re-engineer the way the job is done or re-engineer the performance environment. You do not

train. You don't motivate.

OK. Having decided what combination of causes is behind a performance problem, and following the rule that cause determines the solution (if it's lack of skills and knowledge, you do some kind of training; if it's environmental, you re-engineer the environment; if it's motivation, you give feedback or attach rewards to the correct performance), you next look at what solving the problem will cost.

Determining cost effectiveness in performance problem-solving involves questions like: How long would it take? How much will it cost? What are the relative probabilities of success? What are the political aspects? We make a detailed analysis of these questions before recommending any particular problem-solving activity or group of activities. And training is not necessarily the solution we come to — not even when we're dealing with skills and knowledge problems. In a remarkable number of cases we have found that you can avoid huge amounts of training with some kind of job aid. So what we're talking about in front-end analysis is not training problems and problem-solving through training, but better, more cost effective ways of producing human performance.

TRAINING: You're talking about a different kind of function for the training professional.

HARLESS: Absolutely. This kind of performance analysis has vast implications for trainers. You know, trainers are forever going around looking for respectability. They're always asking, How can we sell management on the idea of training? Well, the answer is you don't. You sell management on the benefits of solving *human performance problems.* You make it clear to management that you are there to *avoid* training when it's not cost-effective. That's how you get to be a hero. That's how you get to be respectable. That's how training directors become vice presidents of human performance or training. That's how you avoid being stuck off in some personnel department somewhere.

TRAINING: But practically speaking, how can a trainer transform himself into a performance manager?

HARLESS: You apply a little front-

end technology to your own situation. Suppose the boss comes to you and says, "I want you guys to produce me a 40-hour course on how to appreciate the beauty of the widget." OK? Devotees of the performance problem-solving approach apply a little front-end analysis saying, Yes, boss, that's terrific. But do you mind if I ask you some questions — to get some of your wise counsel, etc.? That's another way of saying what front-end analysis is — it's all the smart questions a trainer or manager or consultant asks before he writes training objectives or does anything.

Anyway, the smart question in this situation — and all similar situations — is: What is the performance problem? If it's a performance problem, is it a skills and knowledge problem, an environmental problem, a motivational problem, or some combination of those, and what's the most cost-effective means for solving them? Is the cost worth it? And now — and only now — are we ready to talk about training objectives and detailed goals.

That's how you apply front-end analysis techniques to an existing situation where a problem has developed. In its purest form, front-end analysis deals with new tasks that an organization intends to perform. It deals with anticipating and avoiding performance problems rather than dealing with them after the fact.

Some examples: Your organization is going to convert to a new accounting system. What are the performance implications? You are going to install a computerized management system. What are the performance implications? You're about to make and market widgets. What are the performance implications? Asking questions about performance requirements before you implement a new program of one kind or another can save you a lot of embarrassing — and expensive — problem-solving activities later.

TRAINING: Is that kind of planning and program-shaping activity legitimately a function of the training department?

HARLESS: You're assuming there should *be* a training department. But I say there should be a *performance* department that deals with the analysis of problems as well as their practical solution.

You ask, should there be a performance department *and* a training department? Perhaps so. But my experience is that training personnel — at least in industrial organizations — have the best chance of doing the kinds of things I'm talking about. The word training may be a barrier because the layman, when he thinks of training, thinks of things like writing audiovisual scripts or standing up and giving instructions and so forth. And maybe you need a training department within a performance department to do this sort of thing. But it would seem easier to expand the capabilities of existing training departments rather than to create whole new performance departments from scratch.

TRAINING: You'd expand the capabilities of the training department rather than, say, the personnel department?

HARLESS: Yes, because performance is already the legitimate province of the training department. Modern-day trainers are talking about ultimate performance when they insist on having instructional or training objectives. It's no giant step for them to say that these instructional objectives must be based on performance requirements based on thorough-going front-end analysis. The training department is the logical department to develop these performance analysis capabilities. In fact, that's happening. In one of the large hotel chains, a department of performance analysis has been established and the man who heads it up — the vice president of performance — was previously vice president, training.

TRAINING: So you're not against training?

HARLESS: Absolutely not. I'm a devotee of training. But *more relevant training, more cost-effective training . . . a lot less silly training.*

Notes:

The Hawthorne Effect: Orwell or Buscaglia?

BY BEVERLY GEBER

Chameleon words are those shifty-eyed little lizards of the language that assume multiple definitions over the years without ever straying too far from their roots. They come about as close as possible to being all things to all people without compromising themselves in the process.

The word "marriage" is a chameleon. (Remember "open marriage"? Remember "till death do us part"?) In the training world, the "Hawthorne Effect" is a chameleon. Ask several trainers and you'll probably get several definitions, most of them legitimate and all of them true to some aspect of the original experiments in Chicago that produced the term.

Jerome Peloquin, for instance, describes it as the rewards you reap when you pay attention to people. Peloquin, president of Performance Control Corp. of Westchester, PA, says that the mere act of showing people that you're concerned about them usually spurs them to better job performance. That's the Hawthorne Effect.

Suppose you've taken a management trainee and given her specialized training in management skills she doesn't possess. Without saying a word, you've given the trainee the feeling that she is so valuable to the organization that you'll spend time and money to develop her skills. She feels she's on a track to the top, and that motivates her to work harder and better. The motivation is independent of any particular skills or knowledge she may have gained from the training session. That's the Hawthorne Effect at work.

In a way, the Hawthorne Effect can be construed as an enemy of the modern trainer. Carrying the theory to the edges of cynicism, some would say it doesn't make any difference *what* you teach because the Hawthorne Effect will produce the positive outcome you want.

How do you respond to executives who denigrate training and credit the Hawthorne Effect when productivity rises? Peloquin recommends that you say, "So what?" Effective training performs a dual function: It educates people and it strokes them. And there's nothing wrong with using the Hawthorne Effect to reach this other training goal, Peloquin says. In fact, he contends that about 50% of any successful training session can be attributed to the Hawthorne Effect.

Scott Parry, president of Training House, in Princeton, NJ, calls the Hawthorne Effect the "Somebody Upstairs Cares" syndrome. It's not as simplistic as the idea — popular during the human relations craze 10 years ago — that you just have to be nice to workers. It's more than etiquette. When people spend a large portion of their time at work, they must have a sense of belonging, of being part of a team, Parry says. When they do, they produce better. That's the Hawthorne Effect.

Dana Gaines Robinson, president of Pittsburgh, PA-based Partners in Change, says she often hears a different interpretation of the Hawthorne Effect. George Orwell would understand this version; it has a Big Brother ring that's far less benign than other definitions. Robinson says people use it when they talk about workers under the eye of the supervisor.

She'll hear it when she suggests that someone should subtly observe workers on the job to see if they truly apply new procedures they've learned in a training course. Occasionally, managers object, saving that observation isn't a valid test. "Of course they'll do a good job if you're watching them," they tell her. "Isn't that the Hawthorne Effect?"

Well . . . not exactly.

The Hawthorne Studies (or Experiments) were conducted from 1927 to 1932 at the Western Electric Hawthorne Works in Chicago, where Harvard Business School professor Elton Mayo examined productivity and work conditions.

The studies grew out of preliminary experiments at the plant from 1924 to 1927 on the effect of light on productivity. Those experiments showed no clear connection between productivity and the amount of illumination but researchers began to wonder what kind of changes *would* influence output.

Specifically, Mayo wanted to find out what effect fatigue and monotony had on job productivity and how to control them through such variables as breaks, work hours, temperature and humidity. In the process, he stumbled upon a principle of human motivation that would help to revolutionize the theory and practice of management.

Mayo took five women from the assembly line, segregated them from the rest of the factory and put them under the eye of a supervisor who was more a friendly observer than disciplinarian. Mayo made frequent changes in their working conditions, always discussing and explaining the changes in advance.

He changed the hours in the workweek, the hours in the workday, the number of breaks, the time of the lunch hour. Occasionally, he would return the women to their original, harder working conditions. To his amazement, he discovered a general upward trend in production, completely independent of any of the changes he made.

His findings didn't mesh with the current theory of the worker as motivated solely by self-interest. It didn't make sense that productivity would continue to rise gradually when he cut out breaks and returned the women to longer working hours. Mayo began to look around and realized that the women, exercising a freedom they didn't have on the factory floor, had formed a social atmosphere that also included the observer who tracked their productivity. They talked, they joked, they began to meet socially outside of work.

Mayo had discovered a fundamental concept that seems obvious today: Workplaces are social environments and within them, people are motivated by much more than economic self-interest. He concluded that all aspects of that industrial environment carried social value. When the women were singled out from the rest of the factory workers, it raised their self-esteem. When they were allowed to have a friendly relationship with their supervisor, they felt happier at work. When he discussed changes in advance with them, they felt like part of the team. He had secured their cooperation and loyalty; it explained why productivity rose even when he took away their breaks.

The power of the social setting and peer group dynamics became even more obvious to Mayo in a later part of the Hawthorne Studies, when he saw the flip side of his original experiments. A group of 14 men who participated in a similar study *restricted* production because they were distrustful of the goals of the project.

The portion of the Hawthorne Studies that dwelt on the positive effects of benign supervision and concern for workers that made them feel like part of a team became known as the Hawthorne Effect; the studies themselves spawned the human relations school of management that is constantly being recycled in new forms today: witness quality circles, participative management, team building, et al.

Incidentally, the Hawthorne Works, the place where history was made, is history now itself. Western Electric closed it in 1983.

Notes:

INSTRUCTIONAL SYSTEMS DESIGN

(ISD) METHOD

ISD:
Technology for Everyone

BY TOM W. GOAD

It seems that trainers are constantly looking for better ways to do things. For quite a while a prime source of "better ideas" has been the U.S. military. Because of their enormous need for training and their foresight in budgeting for it, the military services often have been pacesetters in training technology.

A prime example is the Instructional Systems Development (ISD) model. Adopted officially by all the services a decade ago, ISD has been making believers out of nonmilitary training designers ever since. In effect, ISD is a system that already has been paid for and that can work for just about anybody who wants to train someone to do a job. Why not take advantage of it?

What is ISD? It is the model (or process) to which experienced trainers often refer when they speak of the "systems approach" to job training. A definition adapted from the military version might call it "a deliberate and orderly process for planning and developing training programs which assure that people acquire the knowledge and skills essential to perform jobs successfully."

The following statement from a military publication offers both a nice summary of the philosophy behind ISD and, by implication, a description of the sorts of training situations for which the model is most useful: "...instruction must equip people to do their jobs. More instruction than that is wasteful; less can cause big problems."

The five phases of the ISD process will sound familiar to trainers regardless of their familiarity with the model itself: analyze, design, develop, implement and control (evaluate). Basic stuff, right? Except that in ISD, the phases are interrelated, each feeding into the next and evaluation feeding into all of them, forming a closed-loop system.

Each of the five phases consists of several major steps. The development phase, for instance, includes these: specify learning activities; specify instruction-management plan and delivery system; review and select existing materials; develop instruction; validate instruction. In keeping with the military tradition of exhausting attention to detail, each of these steps is broken into several substeps. But ISD is not an all-or-nothing system. The trainer may use only those steps that apply in a given case, and may adapt when necessary.

ISD is a complete model of the training cycle. Virtually anything you might do in the name of training fits somewhere within its five phases (Figure 1 shows some examples). The model is research-based and field-tested, it uses front-end analysis to pro-

vide solid data, it considers alternatives, it's criterion-referenced (uses performance objectives), it's thorough — in short, it is an extremely comprehensive tool for designing instruction.

To get a complete picture of everything ISD stands for, you would almost have to go to the reference sources listed at the end of this article. But here are a few highlights of the system's "tools" and features.

Task analysis: One type of task analysis involves determining whether training is needed in the first place. The other type, a key feature of ISD and one for which worksheets are provided in the documentation, creates the basis for training and keeps it closely related to job performance. The designer's options extend to the point of detailing every subtask that must be performed to complete a single action of a given job.

Developing objectives: The name Robert Mager turns up repeatedly in ISD publications, and for good reason: The system is nothing if not "criterion-referenced." A number of tools and examples are offered to help instructional designers develop appropriate learning objectives.

Built-in learning principles: Concepts such as reinforcement, feedback, transfer of training to the job, and categorization of types of learning are integral to ISD technology. Figure 2 shows how the system breaks down four major learning categories into 11 subcategories. The illustration suggests a major advantage of the ISD model: You don't have to be a professional trainer or educator to make sense of it and use it.

Data-gathering tools: The "analyze" phase of ISD involves gathering data. The model provides structure for the process. One form, which can be filled out for each learning objective, includes slots for conditions, standards and test items. The form also

Figure 1. TRAINING ROLES COMPARED TO ISD PHASES	
Training Roles	**Related Phases**
Needs assessment	Analyze
Training planning	Analyze, design
Curriculum development	Design, develop
Media	Design, develop
Writing/producing	Develop, control
Conducting training	Implement, control
Measuring results	Control

requires the designer to specify the learning category involved, appropriate media relating to the objective, and lesson information. The entire ISD process lends itself to automation, and putting it on a computer is almost mandatory for large projects.

Developing and selecting materials: ISD sources are riddled with matrices, flowcharts, hierarchies and other tools to help trainers turn raw data and basic learning objectives into solid instruction. An example is shown in Figure 3. Once materials are organized, writing them also is a matter of following various guidelines. How-to formats are available for such tasks as writing learner workbooks and programmed-learning texts.

Preparation: The system stresses general preparation of the instructor and preparation of training material for the specific course.

Evaluation: ISD provides forms and methods for instructors, learners and outside observers to gather feedback and perform evaluations of two types: first during and immediately after the training course to evaluate the program itself; then after the fact, when trainees are back on the job, to determine the actual effects of the training on their performance.

As should be clear even from this brief sketch, the term ISD refers to an enormous load of training technology.

Figure 2. HOW ISD BREAKS DOWN LEARNING CATEGORIES	
Learning Category	**Sub-Category**
I. Mental skill	1. Learning and using rules 2. Classifying-recognizing patterns 3. Identifying symbols 4. Detecting 5. Making decisions
II. Information	6. Recalling bodies of knowledge
III. Physical skills	7. Performing gross motor skills 8. Steering and guiding; continuous movement 9. Positioning movement and recalling procedures 10. Voice communicating
IV. Attitude	11. Attitude learning

Source: Interservice Procedures for Instructional Systems Development.

Among its advantages, the model offers plenty of direction (you always know where to go next), it allows the designer to make effective use of subject-matter experts and it provides a high level of confidence in results.

There are some drawbacks and limitations to ISD as well. In the first place, most ISD applications to date have been for technical training. Although the system appears to have potential for nontechnical applications, it obviously applies primarily to straight skills-training.

Secondly, the designer must take care that the model's "cookbook" approach doesn't become trainer-oriented rather than learner-oriented.

Perhaps the biggest drawback is that ISD, because of its attention to every detail of the training process, can become extremely time-consuming. And time, of course, is the second major luxury (behind funding) that trainers lack. On the other hand, that same attention to detail — and the fact that the designer can choose to ignore sections that do not apply in a given case — can make the most out of the limited time available by ensuring that all critical areas are covered: If you use ISD correctly, you won't have to go back and do it over because you forgot something.

Figure 3. DESCRIPTION OF TRAINING TASK CATEGORIES				
Learning Category	**Sub-category**	**Action Verbs**	**Behavioral Attributes**	**Examples**
Mental skill	Rule learning and using	Apply Conclude Deduce Predict Propose Select Specify Solve Determine Repair	1. Choosing a course of action based on applying known rules. 2. Frequently involves "If . . . then" situations. 3. The rules are not questioned; the decision focuses on whether the correct rule is being applied.	1. Apply the "rules of the road." 2. Solve mathematical equations (both choosing correct equations and the mechanics of solving the equation). 3. Carry out military protocol. 4. Select proper fire extinguisher for different types of fires. 5. Use correct grammar in novel situations covered by rules.

Source: Interservice Procedures for Instructional Systems Development.

Training on Intranets: The Hope and the Hype

BY BOB FILIPCZAK

The next time an over-wired zealot corners you to crow that he's delivering training over his company's intranet, and you're behind the technology curve if you aren't, try a bit of cross-examination. Chances are you'll discover that this person isn't talking about training, precisely. That's not to say he isn't delivering *something;* it's just not training in the traditional sense of the word.

If your zealot persists, the discussion will almost certainly devolve into an argument about what *real* training is, what the elements of effective training are, and why you are such a technological ignoramus. It will behoove you to calm him down by discussing — reasonably, if possible — the following: What is an intranet? What's the difference between skills training and distributing information? Might an intranet be better used as a performance tool than as a training-delivery medium?

It's easy to divert these geeks into semantic battles. Start with easy stuff, like defining an intranet. For the record, it is an organization's internal computer network that uses the same software that runs on its larger cousin, the Internet, and is usually protected by a firewall, a form of security software that allows only authorized employees into the system. Most people use the World Wide Web system on the Internet, which they access with a Web browser. World Wide Web software also runs on most intranets, and employees surf them using browsers.

Intranets are hot for a variety of reasons, not the least of which is that they mimic the Internet in terms of accessi-bility to information, ease of use and platform independence. For those who don't work in the information systems (IS, a.k.a. the information technology or IT) department, that means: a) it's easy to surf intranets because browsers are so intuitive, b) almost anybody with a little Web know-how can create a home page, and c) you can access intranets with a Macintosh or an IBM-compatible computer.

How hot has the intranet concept become?

• Georgia Tech just released the results of what it calls the world's largest World Wide Web User Survey. Based on 11,700 responses to the survey sent to World Wide Web users via e-mail, Georgia Tech found that 34 percent of the respondents said their organizations have intranets; another 16 percent weren't sure. In Europe, 42 percent of respondents said their companies have intranets.

• *Fortune* magazine reported last November that Netscape, the company that created the most popular World Wide Web browser, made more than half of its $20.8 million in revenues in the third quarter of 1995 off sales to companies setting up intranets.

• Zona Research in Redwood City, CA, predicted earlier in 1996 that sales of software for intranets will increase from $476 million in 1995 to $4 billion in 1997, according to *Business Week.*

• According to research sponsored by Cognitive Communications Inc. and The Document Company Xerox, 85 percent of the 162 respondents from *Fortune* 500 companies are either implementing or planning to implement an intranet in their organizations. Most respondents (73 percent) were either directors or managers of their companies' communication department.

Potential vs. Performance

Defining training should be easy, but it rarely is. If "training" refers to any means of delivering information to people so they can do their jobs better, then intranets can be fantastic vehicles for disseminating training. But if you want the word to denote a skill-building process in which employees receive information, are taught skills and allowed time to practice them, then intranets still offer only the *promise* of delivering training.

Moreover, many people envision training provided over an intranet as similar to interactive multimedia training: The participant interacts with the machine in real time, makes choices, branches off in different directions, takes tests, gets feedback, and is beset by text, graphics, animation, audio, and sometimes video stimuli. So far, intranets can deliver just a few of those options.

Brandon Hall, editor of "Multimedia Training Newsletter" in Sunnyvale, CA, is excited about intranets' potential as a training medium. But, he admits, "for people who are used to the incredible instructional-design capabilities of full-blown multimedia training, yeah, we're not nearly there yet."

Elliott Masie echoes Hall. "I haven't seen any overwhelming examples of using the intranet itself as a training-delivery system," says Masie, president of the Masie Institute, a consulting firm in Saratoga Springs, NY, and a true believer in electronically delivered training.

"We're not there yet," agrees Michael Gallagher, director of Advanced Engineering and Research Associates, a consulting company in Arlington, VA, that held a series of conferences on using intranets for training and documentation this summer. "There are many examples of what some people have claimed is training on the open Internet, and it's pretty lame," he says.

Even companies that have a vested interest in seeing intranet-based training come to fruition confess that it's not quite ready for prime time. That's because the tools — authoring systems and ways to deliver large files seamlessly across networks in real time — aren't yet available, says Pardner Wynn, president of Stanford Testing Systems, a software developer in Spokane, WA. His company aims to remedy that situation with an Internet-based authoring tool called IBTauthor. In midsummer 1996, the authoring program had been in beta-testing for about two weeks, but Wynn didn't expect to see any examples of Internet/intranet training for a couple of months.

"If the Web offered the interaction and multimedia capabilities of CBT, it would be perfect," says Jim Moore, director of Sun U, the educational wing of Sun Microsystems, the computer manufacturer in Mountain View, CA. But it doesn't. According to Moore, Sun's new programming language, Java, is the answer to that deficiency. Java, one of the first Web-compatible programming languages, allows users to access and execute software programs live on the Net.

Employees using Java for training would click on an "applet" icon on a Web page, and the software would download to their hard disks and automatically activate itself. Because these applets are so small and will download so fast, the user will perceive that the program is running live on an intranet.

For example, let's say you're taking some training on the company intranet. When you get to the point where you're supposed to put the right circuit board in the right slot, you would click on an icon, and a simulation of that exercise would be transferred to your hard disk. As the training went "live," you wouldn't even realize that you were interacting with a program on your hard disk instead of some Web server in Peoria.

All this sounds swell, but Eric Peterson, manager of research and development for Sun U technology, admits that those training applets are still under construction.

Nevertheless, excitement about training over intranets rages on. In a survey sponsored by OmniTech Consulting Group and TRAINING Magazine, more than one-third of respondents (36 percent) said they were currently using intranets to distribute multimedia-based learning. Hall offers one explanation for that high percentage: Respondents are

continued on page 122

'CHUNKING CBT' FOR INTRANET DELIVERY

If downloading computer-based training (CBT) is one way to get your intranet to deliver interactive multimedia training, you might want to think about chunking. No, that's not a strategy for consuming large amounts of chocolate; it's a way to chop CBT into its smallest parts and send them through the network. This has two advantages: It gives learners just the instruction they need when they need it and it conserves bandwidth.

Karen Maillaird, vice president of human resources development at Sprint Corp. in Westwood, KS, chunks CBT on the corporate intranet, but is a little concerned that her company may be the first on the block to try it. "We've made all the calls trying to see who's doing this. We can't find anybody, which has me worried," quips Maillaird.

Right now, the training delivery scheme at Sprint consists of a series of home pages that use hypertext links to grab one of the 1,000 chunks of CBT on the server. Some of it is for newly recruited salespeople who are learning, as Maillaird describes it, to "get by the dragon at the door." The training is designed to help them learn effective ways to get appointments with clients. The system, explains Maillaird, will even do remediation, sending a chunk of instruction to students based on their responses to questions on a home page, essentially customizing the course on the fly.

Currently Sprint has nine courses for IBM-compatible computers and eight for Macintosh computers, all chunked for delivery on the intranet. (Internal Web-style networks don't care what kind of computer users have, but the chunks that land in their hard disks do.) In addition to the instruction, the training is linked to chat rooms where trainees can network with each other and where a "cybercoach," one of Maillaird's trainers, can help students with questions.

Before Sprint chunked this instruction for the intranet, explains Maillaird, the company would download whole CBT courses over the local area network. But new product material would be obsolete in 30 days. To bring it up to date, her department would have to change the whole course; using the current strategy, only small pieces need to be updated. Moreover, participants often had to send in the results of their CBT courses via snail mail. Maillaird, clearly accustomed to a more automated environment, says "I mean, people mailed their diskettes in, and that's insane."

Instructional designers must approach courses with a different mind-set to chunk training for network delivery, says Maillaird. Most CBT is developed in a sequential, linear fashion. But when chunks are linked by the hypertext built into home pages, she says, you have to think in a mind-mapping mode. Instructional designers must be able to anticipate all the different ways in which employees might wend their way through a course, and plan the course accordingly. Making sure the material is covered when you can't control the learner can be difficult. Hypertext movement through the courses is the jewel of the system, says Maillaird, but it also adds a level of complexity that can be staggering.

She says she had to pull a couple of her most creative developers off projects because they couldn't master this more chaotic environment. Michael Gallagher, director of Advanced Engineering and Research Associates in Arlington, VA, agrees that instructional designers will have to change the way they think about designing intranet-based training. "It'll walk and talk and quack like computer-based training, but it will be developed differently and it will be accessed differently," says Gallagher.

Maillaird says Sprint is still in its infancy in delivering training over the intranet, but it is clearly ahead of the rest of the pack. What she describes is what Sun is still only promising with Java. Consultant Elliott Masie sees the chunking of training — or granularization, as he calls it — as one element important to making training available over intranets. "Multimedia Training Newsletter" editor Brandon Hall agrees, saying that chunking will be partially driven by the movement toward electronic performance support systems that allow people to get only the training they need when they need it. — B.F.

INTRANETS AS PERFORMANCE SUPPORT TOOLS

Many of the "training" stories you hear about intranets describe how employees access information over a company's internal network — information that wasn't easily found or available before — and then use that information in their work. Pardon us for splitting hairs but, technically, that isn't training. That kind of information retrieval falls more accurately into the category of performance support and, since it's digitally based, it's a form of electronic performance support (EPS).

Many companies are already using such networks as performance tools. Because almost anybody can put information on an internal intranet, it's relatively easy to turn it into a very accessible collection of corporate knowledge, says Elliott Masie, president of Masie Institute, Saratoga Springs, NY. Add a good search engine, a software program that searches for key words among all the home pages, says Masie, and you've created an EPS system employees can use to get the information they need when they need it.

For example, Masie says, a receptionist with access to an intranet full of information about the company can suddenly be transformed into a customer service representative. Instead of transferring the phone call to someone else, the receptionist can access information and give it directly to a customer.

Consultant Diane Gayeski has helped companies use their intranets as performance tools. One notable case is Raymond Corp., a forklift manufacturer in Greene, NY. Like many industries, the forklift business has shifted from supplying simple mechanical workhorses to making and servicing computer-controlled vehicles. Raymond's field technicians, the people who repair these new forklifts, were having trouble dealing with the change, says Gayeski.

The company needed a better way to get information out to technicians, who were carting around a library of repair manuals that weighed — we're not making this up — 1,200 pounds. In fact, says Gayeski, many Raymond dealerships had to buy its field people bigger trucks to carry all the manuals. Even then, technicians didn't have room for the parts they needed to carry along with the manuals. Welcome to the Information Age.

And when the manuals needed to be changed? "You can imagine the updating of 1,200 pounds of manuals for technicians in the field wasn't exactly a precise activity," says Gayeski. As a preliminary step, Raymond opened CompuServe accounts for all of its dealerships and put updated information on line so technicians will be able to access the most accurate information, eventually getting in through their laptops. Raymond will shift all of its documentation to an intranet once it has one set up, says Gayeski.

Significantly, this solution allowed information to flow both ways. Before Raymond put documentation on line, technicians called in when they were having problems, but not when they figured out a good way to fix something. The CompuServe forums give the company a way to collect that corporate knowledge and send it out to other technicians, says Gayeski.

Even something as simple as a comprehensive catalog of training courses can be difficult to assemble if your company is large and widely dispersed. At 3M, the St. Paul, MN-based manufacturer, it was all but impossible to put together a catalog of courses offered by all the different training units. John Humphrey, senior technical development administrator, describes 3M as radically decentralized, almost like 60 companies wrapped into one. The company's intranet, however, provided the means to assemble the entire course catalog for the dispersed training functions. "The intranet gave us a wonderful vehicle for putting together a single catalog. That's something that's never happened before," says Humphrey.

Catherine Maxey, a communications manager for Dow Chemical in Midland, MI, has been working with the HR department to decide what information it's going to put up on Dow's intranet. She discovered early on that clumping data onto a network is all well and good, but organizing that information for the poor employee new to browsing takes more doing.

Maxey decided to organize the main home page into three sections: compensation, benefits and policies/programs. She tried to structure the information to respond to the way employees asked questions, rather than according to HR function. In some cases, that meant using English instead of HR jargon. "Employees don't call up and say, 'I have a question for the strategic center that focuses on work force planning,' " says Maxey. They simply have a question about career planning.

Next year Dow plans to create a global job-posting database with information about openings up to the midmanagement level. Maxey is also looking at some of the tracking possibilities of the intranet with an eye to using it to do work-flow management.

Work-flow management, a term that frequently comes up in discussions about intranets, is also a concern of Elizabeth Davidson, a project manager for the *Los Angeles Times'* intranet. She's working with some new software, still a bit rough, that's supposed to be able to track purchase orders across departmentss and find more efficient ways to get work done.

Already up and running on the *Times'* intranet is a variety of HR information, says Davidson. She helped HR put the company phone book up on a home page, as well as a corporate communications information map, employee forums, and a page where employees can check on their 401(k) accounts. This last bit is a more interactive section of the intranet because it presents a 401(k) model that employees can actually play with. If the employee wants to see what would happen if she changed her 401(k) distribution, the program calculates the effect of the change over time and shows her how those choices would alter her retirement income. — **B.F.**

publishing content on home pages that includes both text and graphics, a very loose definition of multimedia.

Where's the Beef?

If training via intranets is more bun than beef, why do we hear so much about it? Probably because many technologies are poised to deliver real-time skills training over intranets in the very near future. Most agree that Java *will* do what it promises. Wynn's authoring program grew out of an SAT prep course he built for college-bound students that ran live on the Web. It's been cited by *Newsweek* as a hot spot on the Internet.

And there is one apparent exception to the current rule: Shockwave. This is a software program from Macromedia, the San Francisco-based maker of authoring systems Authorware and Director, that has proven it can deliver interactive multimedia over both the Internet and corporate intranets. According to Carlos Sanchez, product manager for Shockwave, the program can translate any course developed in Authorware or Director for the Web. That means if you built a multimedia course using Authorware, you can run it right now on your company intranet.

A few companies are already doing it, says Sanchez. You can see examples of that training in the Vanguard Gallery at Macromedia's home page provided you've got the Shockwave player plugged into your browser. Almost everyone we contacted who was interested in delivering training over an intranet is looking at Shockwave.

The problem with pumping multimedia through intranets is bandwidth. The cables that carry your data from computer to computer often have limited space: The more data you send, the slower it goes through the pipes. And multimedia is very data-intensive, consisting of big files that demand a lot of bandwidth. Many companies don't have the capacity or are unwilling to dedicate the cable space to multimedia training. Shockwave, Sanchez explains, is actually two programs, one called Afterburner that compresses the multimedia so it gobbles less bandwidth, and a translator that runs inside your Web browser and decompresses what's coming through the cables.

Diane Gayeski, a partner with OmniCom Associates, a consulting firm in Ithaca, NY, has tried Shock-wave and says she is impressed by the amount of interactivity it allows a multimedia program to deliver. Her only concern is how fast the whole thing will run, especially if a user is getting it via a modem instead of a direct connection to an intranet.

If training via intranets is more bun than beef, why do we hear so much about it?

So it all boils down to this: While delivering training on intranets is currently more a goal than a reality, we can see tantalizing glimpses of the future. The economic and logistical sense of intranet-based training has already sold most progressive trainers on the concept, says Hall, who notes it took at least three years for trainers to buy into using CD-ROMs to deliver multimedia training, while training via intranets has reached the top of many trainers' wish lists in one-third the time. CD-ROMs, says Hall, had to be pushed into peoples' faces many times before they believed in the technology. They seem to be buying into intranet-delivered training sight unseen.

What Have We Got?

So we can agree that interactive multimedia training via intranet is not yet a widespread phenomenon? Afraid not. Some trainers insist that our definition is simply too narrow. Effective instruction, they contend, can take many forms.

Sue Koopman is a loud dissenter to the conclusion that "we're not there yet." A technical trainer and engineer for Lawrence Livermore National Labs (LLNL) in Livermore, CA, Koopman insists that her intranet-based instruction is as valid a form of training as any classroom instruction. And more than 200 satisfied employees say they like it better than classroom courses.

The training courses she's put up on both the Internet and LLNL's intranet consist of reference materials, registration forms, a chat area where students can direct questions to subject matter experts who often respond in real time, and a test at the end of the course. That test at the end is the linchpin, says Koopman, the thing that makes this real training and not just static information. Web technology has been using interactive forms — pages that you fill out to receive immediate, automated feedback — for some time. Her tests give similar feedback, telling trainees whether they passed the course and offering hints on the items they missed. Courses consist of training LLNL employees have to take, like pressure safety orientation, because of federal regulations. That course, for example, includes diagrams, text and questions that hyperlink to answers. After you're through figuring out how cryogenic chemicals can freeze your hand to metal, you can proceed through other modules and then take the test.

This intranet testing allows Koopman to track participants while they take the tests or to check results after they are done. If everyone starts missing the same question, she can quickly fix either the question or the course material.

Since these courses include testing, she contends that intranet-based training is alive and well and living on her server. "To me, it seems like [intranet-based training] is 'there,' and it's just ready to get better," says Koopman. You don't have to take Koopman's word for it. She's made her courses available to the general public over the Internet to demonstrate your tax dollars at work: *"http://www-Training.llnl.gov/wbt/"*

Pat Alvarado, an information-products consultant at NCR's El Segundo, CA, operation, has also put a couple of self-study courses on the company's intranet. They consist mostly of technical-training materials for field engineers but, like Koopman's courses, the training includes interactive testing that gives trainees immediate feedback. Alvarado, too, can track the progress of trainees taking the course, and send them congratulations and certificates when they pass the test at the end.

These self-study courses supplement the classroom training that NCR field engineers get whenever a new product is introduced. Alvarado still sends out paper-based courses to engineers who want them, but now most of the training he slates for self-study is developed simultaneously for paper and NCR's internal intranet.

Testing at the end of the courses provides for Level 2 evaluation of the training, meaning that it determines whether trainees learned the material.

Alvarado is considering a Level 3 evaluation, a six-month follow-up survey that will be e-mailed to participants to see if they are using the new skills on the job. But distributing these courses on the intranet is so new to NCR that Alvarado hadn't reached the six-month point when we talked to him.

Lack of interactivity is one drawback to these self-study courses, says Alvarado. He is currently looking at using Shockwave to deliver multimedia training. He also considered using NCR's intranet to download computer-based training to people's computers — which was possible before intranets were around — but decided against it. "It's something we might look into, but right now I just don't see it as a practical way of distributing CBT," says Alvarado. Whole CBT courses tend to be large files, so they take a long time to copy from the server. And it's more difficult to track participants or update courseware using this method of distribution. So for now, he continues to distribute CBT on disks.

The Promise of WBT

Even if fully interactive multimedia training on intranets is not yet a reality, people are excited about the possibilities it offers. We've already mentioned the chat rooms and forums that some companies have built into intranet training. That's something you never got with the disk you threw into a CD-ROM drive.

LLNL's Koopman argues that this is what true interactivity is about. Consultant Gayeski agrees that intranet training will be much better than the best CBT if it connects trainees to one another and to subject matter experts. Karen Maillaird, vice president of human resources development at Westwood, KS-based Sprint Corp., describes a forum called "Opening Lines," in which new salespeople can discuss different ways to get a foot in the door of prospective clients. Other more risqué names for the forum were jettisoned, laughs Maillaird (see "Chunking CBT," page 120).

The ability to update courses in one central location is another advantage of "Web-based training," a term Hall is trying to establish to describe any training that exists on the Internet or even on private intranets. Stanford Testing's Wynn claims that ease of updating is the only sales pitch he

needs when it comes to convincing a client of the merits of IBTauthor. Of course, if your training remains unchanged for two years or more, then intranet-based training probably doesn't make sense; timeless material should be pressed into a CD-ROM. On the other hand, if your content changes quickly and needs to be updated often, says Wynn, then consider intranet training.

Does it sound as if intranet-based training could eventually replace computer-based training at your company? Don't throw away those old CD-ROMs. For one thing, they make excellent coasters or pretty mobiles for your kids, jokes editor Hall.

Many people envision training provided over an intranet as similar to multimedia training. So far, it's not.

Some companies use CD-ROMs in conjunction with intranet content, says Sue Weiner, a partner with Cognitive Communications, an intranet consulting firm in Stamford, CT. A disk at the trainee's desktop contains a lot of the multimedia and static information, while an intranet connection provides updated information or corrections to the program that proofers may have missed.

Central updating of training is an important consideration for John Cochran, director of interactive communications and visual identity for Honeywell, the Minneapolis-based manufacturer of electronic controls. Honeywell locations are scattered across more than 90 countries, and its employees speak 80 languages. If Cochran had to press and distribute CD-ROMs every time someone found a translation error or product specifications were changed, he'd have time to do little else.

More important, however, is the tracking potential the intranet will provide. It hasn't been practical to maintain records of individual performance with classroom training, Cochran points out. When this type of training becomes a reality, you will not only be able to track how employees did on each question or exercise,

you'll be able to figure out how long it took them to finish each module. Such live tracking may give trainers insight into how people learn the material, not just whether they learned it. Live tracking of participants, says Cochran, will allow for "the kinds of feedback we don't have today. And if your sample size gets to be large — for example, if you're delivering this to several thousand people — my guess is that the kinds of profiling capabilities the intranet gives us might rewrite some of the books on how we do training."

The intranet also allows for rapid-fire delivery of training. With CBT, trainers often waited until a whole course was finished, then pressed it on a CD and sent it out. With intranet-delivered training, points out Sun's Moore, modules can be made available as soon as they're completed. Getting training out fast is particularly important at Sun because 100 percent of revenues come from products that are no more than 18 months old. "So if you took a year to develop a course about a new product, by the time you got it out there and found the people to take it, it would have been replaced by some other product," says Moore. If your company is currently caught in the maelstrom of "change," he says, "a learning technology that isn't reflective of the pace of change isn't going to fit."

Corporate Knowledge

One of the main forces driving increased intranet interest and activity is the amount of information people can access on the Internet. "The ability to surf the world at large has created enormous interest in searching internally," says consultant Masie. Employees who are used to having access to lots of information are asking, "Why don't we apply what's cool about the Internet to our own corporate organization?"

And that appears to be what's happening, sometimes as a planned activity, sometimes in pockets and obscure corners of companies. Intranets are not always centrally planned. Executives who propose a corporate intranet may be surprised to find that the company already has four or five of them running on different network servers.

At Dow Chemical in Midland, MI, communications manager Catherine Maxey says her company's intranet started as a skunkworks in the research department, where employees were already accustomed to surfing the Internet. It really took off this year, she says, when employees got new computer workstations on their desks equipped with Netscape.

Phil Gibson, director of interactive marketing for National Semiconductor, the Santa Clara, CA-based computer chip manufacturer, has seen what corporate knowledge can do for salespeople. Currently his department runs an intranet alongside the popular groupware product Lotus Notes to make sure his field salespeople have access to the information they need.

His combination of Notes and the company intranet — which he says will converge in 18 to 24 months — allows salespeople to find information in a fraction of the time they previously invested. For his sales force, Gibson says, the right information is just as effective as training because it helps his people get the same results: more sales.

How to Win Friends and Influence Intranets

The lines between just-in-time information and just-in-time training begin to blur when the result is the same: increased productivity. Masie argues that, in the bigger picture, intranets are about corporate knowledge and employees' access to that intellectual capital. "If there's an arena that is knowledge-centric, it ought to be on the radar screen of the training department," he says.

So what should you do first?

Even if you're not ready to do anything else, says editor Hall, start building a strategy. Trainers should be looking two years out at what they want to do, he says, "because every other department in the company is going to be doing it, their competitors are going to be doing it, their customers are going to be demanding it, [and] their internal users are going to be demanding it. They need to be ready with a response."

Many training departments start slowly; they simply put up a home page that is a comprehensive course catalog. Others put up training mate-

---

Intranet training will be much better than the best CBT if it connects trainees to one another and to subject matter experts.

---

rials, PowerPoint presentations and handouts that can be referenced after classroom training is completed. Still others, like Sprint's Maillaird, suggest going straight for the gold ring of intranet-based training as soon as it's available. "You might as well jump into the training delivery because that's where your payoff is," she says.

The next step is to start hanging out with the gatekeepers of your intranet, likely the IS or IT department. "This is the age where every trainer has to go make a friend in the IT department. Take your ITer to lunch," suggests Hall.

Corporate intranets are a perfect place for trainers and IS people to collaborate, says Elizabeth Davidson, a project manager for the *Los Angeles Times'* intranet. Originally from the IS department, Davidson was sent to a recent conference at the training department's expense and sat next to someone from training. "That was a first time for both of us, and I was really excited," she says. Now she works closely with both training and organization development.

If you want an intranet and haven't got one, Davidson recommends finding a champion among your executives. Her target was the vice president to whom she reported. She took him to Silicon Graphics Inc., a high-tech company in Mountain View, CA, with a reputation for having a very advanced intranet. "He had been kind of sitting on the fence up to that point," says Davidson. "After the demo he said, 'It's not if but when,'" and proceeded to fund her project. Others describe similar scenarios; once an executive has a home page of her very own, she quickly signs on as corporate intranet champion.

It's not as hard to get invited to the table as you might imagine. John Humphrey, senior technical development administrator at 3M, St. Paul, MN, belongs to an intranet special interest group and says that's a great way to get involved at the ground level. Consultant Weiner points out that because intranets are so new, there aren't a lot of entrenched ideas about who should do what. Although the IS or communications department often gets the ball rolling, the technoids in engineering and research may have had one for years without telling anyone.

It's as simple as getting on the phone with IS or communications and asking to be included early in the development process, says Weiner. "The training community has an awful lot of knowledge about learning and about interactivity and about all of the things the intranet is actually trying to achieve," she says. "And I think training professionals will bring an awful lot to the table."

ISO 9000

What You Should Know About ISO 9000

BY SUZAN L. JACKSON

You've probably come across the term ISO 9000 in recent months. You may be puzzled by it or unfamiliar with its implications. But chances are good you'll be hearing much more about it soon.

In the near future, this set of five international quality system standards will be implemented by most U.S. companies that wish to do business internationally. Preparing an organization to meet the standards for ISO 9000 certification (yes, this *is* a certification system) poses a significant training challenge. Everyone from top management on down needs to understand the implications of these standards. Employees who are directly involved in the internal auditing process required by ISO 9000 will need specialized training to fulfill their responsibilities.

First, a little background. ISO 9000 standards were developed during the 1980s by the International Organization for Standardization to establish basic, uniform requirements for quality assurance systems. After their release in 1987, the standards achieved international significance because they were adopted by the European Community (EC) and by the individual EC nations. The EC is using them to provide a universal framework for quality assurance. As trade barriers are torn down by the EC1992 agreement, and Europe becomes economically unified, ISO 9000 has become a tool to ensure the quality of commercial goods and services across borders.

To guarantee that the standards are consistently applied from business to business, a third-party audit system has evolved. An independent, accredited registrar assesses whether your organization's quality system works as stated and documented. If the system meets ISO 9000 requirements, it is certified. Regular surveillance audits ensure that your quality system doesn't atrophy. If your system fails to pass one of these audits, it can be decertified.

In addition to the EC, NATO and the U.S. Department of Defense, at least 51 countries around the world have accepted the standards. The United States has adopted ISO 9000 as the American Society for Quality Control and American National Standards Institute Q90 series of standards.

Competitive Wallop

The competitive impact of these developments is considerable, especially in Europe. The EC requires companies that produce regulated products, such as medical devices, to be registered to the standards. Although the lion's share of products are not regulated, producers of unregulated products are "encouraged" to become registered voluntarily.

So far about 20,000 European companies have been registered. By the end of 1992, when economic unification is to be completed, many more European companies will have met ISO 9000 requirements.

Thus, even for companies whose products are unregulated, ISO 9000 is becoming a de facto market requirement for doing business with the European Community. If two suppliers are trying to land the same contract, the one that registered its quality system to ISO 9000 has a clear edge. Many people believe that within five years ISO 9000 registration will be necessary to stay in business. The whole world is moving toward the standards. The Japanese, for example,

have adopted the standards and have recently mounted a national effort to get their companies registered.

The Payoff

ISO 9000 is not just a set of hoops to jump through to keep the Europeans happy. Although it is not an awards program, meeting the requirements of the standards will yield a basic competitive quality system that will cover all key business and manufacturing functions. It will also result in significant cost savings.

The British Standards Institute, a leading British registrar, estimates that registered firms reduce operating costs 10 percent on average. Of course, the average savings will depend on where you start. But our experience at Du Pont suggests you can expect significant returns.

The 105 Du Pont plants or sites that have been registered here and abroad report substantial benefits. At one plant, on-time delivery increased from 70 percent to 90 percent. At another site, cycle time went from 15 days to 1½ days. At another, a product line went from a 72 percent to a 92 percent first-pass yield. At a warehouse, errors decreased by 95 percent. Still another site reduced test procedures from over 3,000 methods to 1,100. And the list goes on.

The Scope

ISO 9000 requirements do not refer to products and services, but to the systems that produce them. The standards are designed to give buyers confidence that registered companies will consistently deliver the quality buyers expect. The standards are generic: They apply to all products and industries, and are meant to complement industry-specific product standards for quality assurance.

The standards cover everything that affects quality. To pass an audit, the quality system must work as stated and documented. The unwritten quality concept for an ISO 9000 audit is: If all personnel were suddenly replaced, the new people could use the quality system to continue making the product or providing the service as before.

Some of the quality system elements for which ISO 9000 establishes requirements are: management responsibility, contract review, document control, purchasing, process control, design control, control of nonconforming product, corrective action, handling, storage, packaging, delivery, quality records, internal quality audits, training and servicing.

ISO 9000 was designed to be inclusive, not exclusive. It does not mandate that you use one approach rather than another. As long as you can say what you do and do what you say, you can get your system registered. Here, for example, are the kinds of questions ISO 9000 auditors might ask about "process control," one of the key elements in all quality systems:

Is the control scheme (whichever one you've established for use and designated in your documentation) adequate for your needs? Is it understood by those who run the process? Are they properly trained? Is the documentation up to date? Do you have an audit system that regularly assesses whether the control system is functioning as it should be?

Implementing ISO 9000

The cost of implementation varies a good deal from company to company. Much depends on your starting point. If you just won the Malcolm Baldrige National Quality Award, you'll have little trouble getting your system registered. But if you have no formal quality system at all, or if your system has atrophied, registering a plant or business will take much more time and money.

A Du Pont site in Europe with roughly 300 employees estimated that bringing its quality system up to snuff required 50 "people-months" of effort over nine calendar months. This is a fairly representative estimate. Similar Du Pont plants in the United States have taken from nine months to more than a year to establish a quality system. However, Du Pont has a long-standing commitment to quality improvement, so these plants had a foundation on which to build. If they had started from scratch, the effort would have required even more time and energy.

The process necessary to implement ISO 9000 in a given company varies as well. But all organizations go through the same basic stages and must provide similar training.

ISO 9000 changes the way an organization does business. Thus, management must commit to ISO 9000 and the change process. The first step is to educate corporate leaders. They must understand what registration will require and decide whether or not they want to pursue it.

To register a 300-person manufacturing plant, for example, requires a time commitment from a management representative (who will dedicate between 50 percent and 100 percent of his time, at least temporarily, to getting the company registered), and a lesser time commitment from a steering group of upper-level managers and a group of coordinators for each area of the company affected by the pursuit of standards. All employees at every level must decide the best way to do their jobs and then document it.

A substantial training investment is necessary as well. Expect to spend two days training steering committee members and area coordinators, three days training internal auditors, five days training the management representative and the lead auditors, and one day training those who write the quality manual.

You may need to train as many as 10 percent of your employees as internal ISO auditors.

Next, management should develop a strategic plan. Many companies work with consultants on the plan, but the process should take no more than a day or two. In any case, the strategic plan should map out:

• The scope of the business to be registered. Will you register a particular manufacturing process and related facilities, a geographical site or a whole corporation?

• The status of the current quality system. Where are we now?

• What must be done. How do we improve the quality system to meet ISO 9000 requirements?

• The costs in money, time and resources to achieve registration.

• The action steps.

Where the Buck Stops

Although ISO 9000 demands a companywide commitment, particular individuals must be assigned responsibility and authority for implementing the standards. Most employees will work part time on ISO 9000. But in many companies the leader of the effort, the management representative, works full time on the project until the company is registered.

The management representative has "official standing." ISO 9000 requires companies to designate a management representative to lead the implementation effort. But companies are allowed a good deal of flexibility in whom they select as management representative. It might be a quality manager, engineer or operator. Regardless of who is chosen, that individual must have the ability and be given the authority to carry the effort through to a successful conclusion.

The management representative needs a good deal of support. Most companies appoint a steering group of upper-level managers to represent the cross section of functions — manufacturing, purchasing, sales, laboratory, maintenance, and so on — affected by ISO 9000. This team should lead and guide the organization's efforts and ensure that adequate resources are available.

Each area affected by the pursuit of ISO 9000 registration should have a coordinator who acts on the strategic direction provided by the steering group.

ISO 9000 requires the organization to conduct an extensive program of internal audits using trained auditors. These internal auditors must be independent of the area they audit, which means that a number of people from various levels and functions act as auditors. You may need to train as many as 10 percent of your employees as internal auditors.

Training for steering group members, area coordinators and internal auditors should:

• Explain how the standards should be implemented in your organization. These requirements apply to quality elements such as corrective action, training, contract review, process control and purchasing. They are written in such generic language, however, that trainees may not understand the implications of the standards for *your* organization without detailed explanations.

• Provide a thorough introduction to auditing.

• Provide an overview of how the quality system will be documented to meet ISO 9000 requirements.

The Internal Quality Audit

As your quality system implementation moves forward, it's critical to measure progress. The primary measuring technique is the internal audit. Regular audits must be scheduled to identify problems and check the effectiveness of corrective actions.

ISO 9000 requires a system of internal audits, but it doesn't specify the level of training necessary for auditors. In addition to training internal auditors on the requirements of the standards, expect to spend about two or three days training them on auditing techniques.

The management representative and the leader of the auditing program should take a more intensive five-day "lead assessor" course, the same training that licensed ISO 9000 registrars complete. The leaders of the effort will be more effective if they have auditing expertise.

The Quality Manual

ISO 9000 requires you to document everything you do that affects the quality of goods and services.

To meet these rigorous demands, most companies use a multitiered approach to documentation. The top level is the "quality manual," which describes the quality system and serves as a road map for those who use it. Subsequent tiers include general procedures, work instructions and forms.

The quality manual provides an overview of the entire system. It guides the auditors through the system during assessments, and acts as an internal reference and training document. Given the manual's importance, many companies train their employees in how to prepare an ISO 9000 quality manual. Typically, such a course presents different approaches to documenting each section of ISO 9000. The technical, quality assurance, manufacturing and support people responsible for writing the manual should attend.

Assessment and Registration

As the quality system is put in place, companies audit and reaudit various areas of operations to benchmark their progress. When an organization feels that its quality system is at least 75 percent complete, it may ask an accredited registrar or other third-party audit team for a pre-assessment. This external evaluation gives the company an authoritative estimate of its readiness for a final audit. It also allows for midcourse corrections.

Although an organization may choose to have a pre-assessment conducted by any qualified third party, it's important that a properly accredited registrar conducts the final assessment. Accrediting bodies have been set up in numerous countries to approve qualified registrars. Many of the registrars active in the United States, such as the British Standards Institute, have been accredited by their national accrediting agencies. In this country, the American National Standards Institute (the U.S. representative to the International Organization for Standardization) and the Registrar Accreditation Board (an affiliate of the American Society for Quality Control) have established the American National Accreditation Program for Registrars of Quality Systems to accredit domestic registrars.

The final audit begins with a review of the company's quality manual, which the auditors typically use as their guide. Depending on the size of the operation, audits are usually conducted by two or more auditors and take two to three days. The auditors check to see that the documented quality system meets the requirements of ISO 9000 and that the organization is practicing what is documented.

ISO 9000 provides a foundation for an effective quality system. It requires a discipline and consistency that must be followed shift in and shift out, day after day. Some organizations feel that many of their practices already go beyond the requirements of ISO 9000. But ensuring that these very basic quality system elements are firmly in place guarantees that future quality efforts are built on a strong foundation. ISO 9000 is a way of doing business, not a fad. It locks quality into individual enterprises and whole economies.

Notes:

Performance Aids: How to Make the Most of Them

BY JOEL RAKOW

What do you do when paper jams in your friendly photo-copy machine? Stomp and curse? Call the repair service? Or read the instructions mounted on the inside? If you choose the latter you must rely on a performance aid — the words and pictures developed to walk you through the quick-fix process. But the aid you see inside the copier is only one of many types of performance aids (this one's called a *proceduralized aid*) that trainers use to convey information.

Most training professionals know performance aids can substitute for formal training in some instances. Aids also are effective memory joggers for infrequently performed tasks — like fixing the copier.

Less obvious, though, is the fact that there are several different types of performance aids, each with various formats and each with specific training applications. How can a performance aid work for training problem X? What type of aid is appropriate? What format should it have — a checklist, a chart, a sample form? And, how will it be used? Answers to these questions will help you select and use performance aids more imaginatively and effectively.

There are five basic kinds of performance aids, as shown in Figure 1. This "Aid to Performance Aids" identifies the common types of performance aids and describes the attributes of each. Typical formats for each type of aid are listed along with guidelines for selecting when to use each type.

It is important to recognize the difference between an aid's format and its type. Different formats determine how an aid is used on the job, even for an identical task. For example, a checklist of the necessary steps for a task could be used either before or after completing the job as a refresher or a reminder. By contrast you'd rarely use a computational worksheet at any time other than while performing the task. Nonetheless both formats fall into the cueing category; they signal specific action without providing step-by-step instructions.

On the other hand, the difference between types of aids is crucial to job performance. Each type of aid functions in only one way during training.

The type of performance aid determines what information is provided for the trainee while the format determines how the trainee will use the aid on the job. In either case, which type you choose and, perhaps to a lesser extent which format, greatly affects the success of your training program.

Example-style performance aids are common in many areas of everyday life. They can be found in the appendices of many dictionaries, and in brochures from banks, insurance companies and other businesses that require customers to complete information forms. A straightforward form letter serves as an example aid for the sales representatives of a major computer firm. It not only illustrates the format and general tone of an introductory letter, it also uses a number indexing system to describe several key objectives of such a letter and to locate where the objectives are satisfied.

Figure 1. AN AID TO PERFORMANCE AIDS

TYPE	ATTRIBUTES	TYPICAL FORMATS	WHEN TO USE
Example	Illustrates responses required to complete a task	Forms filled in with correct information or sample of document (letter, etc.)	When format or location of information is important
Cueing	Signals a specific action without providing step-by-step directions. Also, directs attention to specific characteristics of objects, procedures, situations or information	Checklists, worksheets; using photo-diagrams, arrows, underlining or circles; task lists	When each step in a several-step procedure is relatively simple, but an error will result if a step is out of sequence. Also, with lengthy or seldom-used procedures
Association	Relates unknown information to existing or already known conditions or information	Conversion tables, graphs, code books, reference documents	When information must be transformed for use in predictably different environments or when the conversion process is not important
Proceduralized	Provides pictures and text in a programmed sequence that both illustrates and describes each step in a procedure	Do-it-yourself repair books for cars, bikes, appliances and so on	When training for skills in the manipulation of objects, materials or equipment
Analog	Provides information that cannot be presented directly	Schematic drawings, organization charts, flowcharts, formulas, equations and symbolic logic	When correct job performance requires conceptual knowledge of organization, structure, relationship or flow

Cueing aids are also fairly common. In their least-developed form they can be shopping lists, "to do" lists or any simple checklist. Figure 2 shows a cueing aid designed to lead sales representatives of a major soft drink company through a fairly complex pricing computation. The form was designed because the sales representatives needed to evaluate the figures of different retailers who independently set their own prices. To use this form they simply filled in the blanks and performed the calculations.

Association aids are great if you must organize large quantities of information such that specific information can be isolated. Examples of association aids include metric conversion tables and mileage charts that list the distance between several cities. Figure 3 is a similar association aid that helps a major communications firm market its products to the hospital industry. It identifies several communication activities that exist in a hospital admissions department. For each activity the sales representative can find opportunities for improvement, specific communication needs, possible solutions, the impact of the solution and suggestions for calculating that impact. Aids like this not only help train new sales representatives, they make it easier for experienced reps to develop sales strategies.

Proceduralized aids are becoming increasingly popular, especially in do-it-yourself repair manuals. In many cases, such aids can completely replace the need for training. Although expensive and time-consuming to develop, they can have long-term cost benefits. Many manufacturers supply such aids to reduce

their customers' demands for education and support.

Some companies modify this format by producing audiocassettes that contain a large part of the instructional content. Used in this way, the instruction manual stands alone as a cueing aid, simply signaling each step in the operating procedure. This design eliminates extraneous information when the trained operator needs only reference and not instruction.

Analog aids are familiar to most of us in the form of organizational and flowcharts or schematic drawings. These aids represent large quantities of verbal or conceptual information that's difficult to communicate effec-

tively. Although it is possible to communicate verbally everything such a chart represents, it would be extremely difficult. Using this kind of diagramming both to plan and communicate has led to many technological advances. For trainers, analog aids are excellent in both front-end analysis and instruction.

Each type of performance aid provides special advantages over others. It makes good sense to spend plenty of time choosing the best one for your application. Think about what kind of information you need to present and how it will be used. The aid you pick will have a substantial impact on job performance.

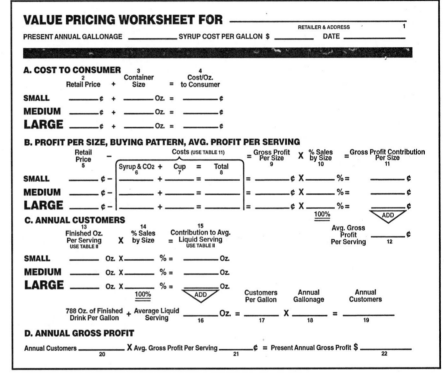

Figure 2. *This worksheet exemplifies a cueing aid. It signals the calculation of each component in a seven-step process.*

Figure 3. *This association aid relates information about the primary communication activities of the admissions department in large hospitals to the sales needs and resources of sales representatives for a major communications firm.*

Department Operation Analysis Chart: ADMISSIONS

PRIMARY ACTIVITIES	IDENTIFY RESPONSIBLE PERSONNEL	PROBLEMS OR OPPORTUNITIES FOR IMPROVEMENT	COMMUNICATIONS NEEDS	POSSIBLE SOLUTIONS	POTENTIAL IMPACTS	RELEVANT COST/REVENUE FACTORS NECESSARY TO COMPUTE TANGIBLE BENEFITS
• Receive admission requests from doctors' offices and information requests from patients.		• Doctors (patients) encounter difficulty reaching Admissions through hospital switchboard or due to busy indication from admissions.	• Ability to receive and originate calls from (to) patients, doctors' offices for Admissions	• Direct Inward Dialing • Hands-free Headsets • Directory Listing • Additional Lines	• Improves public image.	• Do not quantify.
					• Easier access to doctor/patient relieves switchboard.	• Quantify by conducting a Traffic Study Analysis.
• Fill out admissions forms for patients prior to admissions.		• Admissions clerks spend time unnecessarily in correcting errors on patient's admissions forms created when patients fill out forms and return them by mail.	• Communicate directly with patients to reduce errors and administrative time involved in check-in procedures.	• Pre-admission telephone procedures	• Improves efficiency of the Admissions department.	• Do not quantify.
		• Admissions personnel are delayed in contacting patients due to difficulty in dialing outside calls, both local and long distance.	• Ability to receive and originate calls from (to) patients, doctors' offices for admissions and P.A.T. information.	• D.O.D. • Additional Lines • Touch-tone®	• Easier access to doctor/patient relieves administrative time.	• Do not quantify.
			• Foreign Exchange Lines			• Examine account records.

Improve Communications with the Johari Window

BY WILL LOREY

"Improved communications" is high on every needs analysis survey, whether the participant be worker, boss or top executive. Too often, however, the worker says it's his boss's problem; the boss, in turn, sees the problem as below or above his position (or both); and the top executive is positive that it's the lower-echelon personnel who don't communicate.

Many communication difficulties arise because we're all different, in terms of education, background and experience, and our terms of reference and description are not always similar. For example, when the boss says, "Get that report out first thing tomorrow," does he mean that the report gets first priority tomorrow, or that the report must be finished tonight so it can go out in the first mail tomorrow morning?

The "Johari Window" is an excellent model for demonstrating that improved communications must start with the individual. Whatever his or her place in the organization, everyone must take a personal ownership in communications and stop thinking — and saying — it's the other person who needs to work at better communicating. One way to improve communications is through the frank, honest authentic process of giving and receiving feedback. In this instance, feedback means providing *others* with information on how their behavior is affecting *you* and also providing others with the opportunity to let you know how *your* behavior is affecting *them.*

The word Johari is a combination of the first letters of the first names of two brilliant psychologists, Joseph Luft and Harry Ingham, who found that their feedback model had high impact upon groups and individuals. Their model is a communications process through which you give and receive information. Because its four "panes" resemble those in windows, the model is known as the Johari Window.

The trainer appreciates the Johari Window concept because it can be explained easily and quickly and nearly everyone relates in personal terms, building the ownership necessary for change to happen. Because the individual must assume the responsibility for initiating action to give information and receive feedback necessary for self-improvement, the Window has two dimensions. One dimension is for myself, and the other is for any specific individual (or group) with whom I wish to broaden or open communications. This is represented as:

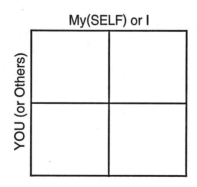

As the individual examines the self, he realizes that there are many aspects about his present self that are known to him and others. Conversely, there are also things about himself that he's not aware of and things about himself that others definitely don't know.

The vertical panes of the Window represent, on the left, "things I know about myself" and the right side contains "things that I do not know about myself." The horizontal panes represent "you" (or the specific name of another individual or group), with the upper level containing "things you know about me" and the lower level containing "things you do not know about me." Thus, the four panes can be identified:

Open arena

The first pane, called the Open Arena, consists of information that is available to both me and you, in that "I know it about myself" and "you know it about me." This is shared exchange of data or information readily apparent/available to the other. Physical aspects — weight, height, sex, race, color of eyes and hair — are examples of information in the Open Arena. The fact that I wear glasses is known to both of us. As we get to know each other better, we both will know that I am very susceptible to winter colds. The Open Arena will increase in size as we share personally relevant information. The better we know each other, the more we understand the what that is being communicated.

Blind spot

Pane two, the Blind Spot, contains information that I don't know about myself but which you know. This can range from mannerisms, irritating and otherwise, to my biases and prejudices. For example, I may say that I fully support the company's EEO programs but I use the word "gals" when speaking to women employees. One of the best ways to eliminate my insensitive behavior is to solicit feedback from you or the group. This feedback should: 1) be work oriented, 2) refer to behavior I can change if I so wish and 3) not be ego destructive. If I offer you the opportunity to provide feedback information on my blind areas, it is to improve communications; it is not an open invitation for you to vent your pent-up frustrations and emotions.

Facade

The third pane, the Facade, is filled with information that I have withheld from you. This may consist of my feelings about certain issues, my past background and experiences, my weaknesses and any strong reactions to people, places and things. If I reveal these to you or the group, you will see me as I really am, and you may judge me negatively. But I must provide you with some of this information so you know where I stand and how I feel and so you won't be forced to guess about or misinterpret what my behavior means.

Unknown

Pane four, the Unknown, represents all those things that neither you nor I know about me. Some may be buried so deeply that I may never be aware of them. Others, such as untapped resources or ways of dealing with stress, may be recognized either through personal effort to learn more about myself or through feedback. One part of this area contains the "future" and that will always remain uncharted terrain.

The basic purpose in using this model is to increase the size of the Open Arena and, at the same time, to reduce the other areas. On the one hand, I must take the initiative to *give* feedback (or information) to you, and, on the other, I must ask you to *provide* feedback to me about how my behavior affects our relationship. While this will not be an easy task for everyone, small, nonthreatening steps can be taken in both directions.

As each individual assumes the responsibility for working at more effective communications, both personal and organizational, the Johari Window should begin to look like this:

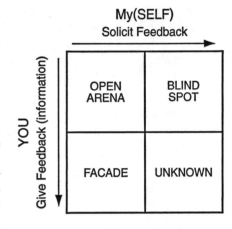

Notes:

Different Strokes: Learning Styles in the Classroom

BY BOB FILIPCZAK

As you learn to paint, you slowly develop a sense of color, dimension and texture. As you get better, your paintings show more depth, added dimension and a wider range of color. Adapting to others' learning styles is a similar exercise: With practice, you bring additional elements to your training that paint a more complete picture....

No? That's not quite right? Let's start again.

Think of the next training course you teach as a musical score. You've got lots of notes, you can change the rhythm, add instruments and alter the volume. So why play your participants a one-note song, a 90-minute lecture....

That's not right either? Start again.

Adapting to people's learning styles is like running an obstacle course. You jump, you climb, you crawl and you give it all you've got to react to a constantly changing environment and reach the finish line. If you do it right, the learning sticks and you finish exhausted. If you don't....

Still no cigar? Once more, from the top.

A good trainer has to be able to juggle some very diverse elements if she wants to hit all the learning styles of the people in a training session. And the more elements she can juggle, without dropping any, the more of an impression she can make....

OK, so none of these works for all of you, mostly because each paragraph attempts to account for the different learning styles among all of you readers. The foregoing is also a demonstration of how difficult it is to accommodate the different ways people learn. The first paragraph, for example, was designed to appeal to visual learners, those for whom a picture paints a thousand words. The second description attempts to engage auditory learners, people who learn best by listening. The third description was for kinesthetic learners, those who need to get their whole body involved to get the most from a learning experience. The last description was aimed at the tactual learners, people who can sit in a chair in a classroom but who need to get their hands involved in the learning.

In a nutshell, those are the four most widely recognized learning styles, though kinesthetic and tactual learners are sometimes grouped together under the former label.

When we talk about learning style, what, exactly, are we talking about? Rita Dunn, director of the St. John's University Center for the Study of Learning and Teaching Styles in Jamaica, NY, has been studying learning styles for more than 25 years. "Learning style," she says, "is the way individual people begin to concentrate, process, internalize and remember new and difficult material." Actually, says Dunn, the term "learning styles" is not very accurate. The four styles are perceptual strengths, our preferred way of interacting with information.

And limiting our understanding of learning styles to just four areas is also a mistake, says Dunn. She and a team of faculty and students from St. John's have developed the Productivity Environmental Preference Survey (PEPS), an assessment for determining adults' learning styles that identifies 21 variables in the way we learn.

Discussions limited to the four commonly recognized learning styles, argues Dunn, contradict her research and a 34-page bibliography of studies conducted by universities all over the world based on her model. In the interest of brevity, however, we're going to concentrate on the four perceptual styles — plus a pair of "processing" styles.

Think Globally, Learn Analytically

An important learning-style distinction that few trainers take into consideration is an individual's processing style, says Barbara Waggoner, a training consultant in Stamford, CT, who has collaborated on research with Dunn. Along with the four styles of perception, two styles describe how information is processed once it's inside a learner's head: global and analytic.

Global processors, explains Dunn, want an overview of the subject first. Once they've got the big picture, they assimilate the particular facts that create the larger view. Analytic processors, on the other hand, like to be presented with the individual facts first and the bigger picture after the facts have been delivered. Joe "Just the Facts, Ma'am" Friday from the TV series "Dragnet" was clearly an analytic learner. According to Waggoner, an analytic learner may prefer a more structured course in a formal classroom setting, while a global learner doesn't mind if the subject matter is less organized and might prefer to sit on a couch with his feet up rather than at a desk.

According to Dunn, 55 percent of adults are global learners, while 28 percent are analytic. The rest can process information comfortably either way and adjust according to circumstances. The traditional education system is designed to teach analytic learners; Dunn and Waggoner agree that most training ignores the needs of the global learner.

They also contend that splitting up a training class and segregating participants according to processing style is the ideal solution. If you already have enough headaches getting programs scheduled, this may not strike you as particularly practical. Still, Dunn says, she wouldn't put globals and analytics together because it would be "adding confusion and slowing down the tempo of learning. I really would have separate classes."

If perceptual and processing preferences aren't enough to worry about, Dunn has researched another one: the time of day that is best for learning.

We've all used the phrases, "Oh, he's a morning person" or "She's a night owl," but Dunn's research seems to substantiate that different people learn information, especially difficult material, more readily at different times of day. This is one learning preference that changes as you age. According to Dunn, only 28 percent of young children are at their brightest in the morning, while 55 percent of adults learn better in the morning.

So what's the ideal method for teaching difficult material? Dunn recommends giving learners information in their primary perceptive style — visual, auditory, kinesthetic or tactual — and then reinforcing the information with a secondary preference. If, for example, an individual has a visual preference, show him a flip chart of the information and reinforce it with something kinesthetic like a role-play.

The final ingredient in the recipe for making teaching or training as effective as possible is to have learners do something creative with the material. Dunn claims remarkable results with learners writing poems or songs about the information they've studied. They performed better on tests and got better grades.

Waggoner, who's worked with the likes of American Cyanamid and Anheuser-Busch, concurs with Dunn's formula and says that encouraging trainees to write a poem, compose a song, draw a picture, or per-form a skit using the material they've learned is tremendously effective.

Waggoner contends that asking participants to use new ideas or skills creatively is more effective in solidifying learning than a test. Simply regurgitating material only engages the left side of the brain, says Waggoner, and that limits retention.

Not in Our Company, You Don't

One warning about asking your employees to do an interpretive dance of Deming's 14 points comes from Richard McBride, principal of Richard A. McBride Associates, a consulting firm in Sumas, WA, that specializes in instructional development. He argues that corporate culture actually dictates the learning styles used in a training program. "Cultural relevance is probably more important than individual learning style," says McBride.

For example, the training he designs for one of his clients, a Wall Street brokerage firm, contains a lot of lecturing. "Although we know they would do well if they could break through their cultural block," he says, "their learning style is much more academic." Consequently, he doesn't include a lot of stories, activities or games in that company's training. The corporate culture spoke loudly, saying: "Tell me. Don't show me. I'm smart enough to figure it out for myself," says McBride.

Are You Still Out There?

About this time, the kinesthetic learners reading this are fidgeting and saying to themselves, "This is a great head trip with all this learning-style theory, but what am I supposed to do with it?" The tactual learners are looking for some concrete suggestions about how to change what they are currently doing. The auditory learners may be mumbling, "I wish they had just sent an audiocassette of this thing."

Well back off, all of you! I'm a visual learner with a global processing style, so you're going to get this article in words and pictures. Got it? And if you don't like it, you can go do jumping jacks or fix a carburetor or go to a Grateful Dead concert for all I care. I'm sticking with my strength and you can just adapt to it.

Of course, no trainer worth his flip chart would throw such a tirade. But he might be tempted to if he doesn't understand his own learning style. Understanding your own style is as important as understanding your audience's. It influences how you present material and may even blind you to the perceptual and processing preferences of those you train. So your first step in accommodating diverse learning styles is understanding your own.

Next, you need to determine your participants' learning styles. You can do that either by giving them a self-scoring test and collecting the results, or by using norms to estimate the mix in your audience. According to Dunn, the learning-style distribution in an "average" group is: 30 to 40 percent visual, 20 to 30 percent auditory, and 30 to 50 percent kinesthetic/tactual.

But you probably don't have a statistically average sample of people showing up in your classes. That's why McBride takes corporate culture into account: Companies tend to hire similar people with similar learning styles.

And you may face a group of ringers. Joanne Ingham, associate dean of students at Polytechnic University in Brooklyn, NY, recently conducted a study with several collaborators, including Dunn, of the learning styles of a group of employees. Ingham tested employees who drove delivery trucks for a bakery. Instead of a normal distribution, she found the group was 80 percent kinesthetic and tactual, about 19 percent had auditory preferences and only 1 percent showed a visual preference.

HOW TO READ THIS ARTICLE

Even a basic knowledge of learning styles allows you to recognize that a magazine article (like this one) usually engages only one perceptual preference. So you visual learners are in luck; we've supplied text and graphics to appeal to your preference and deliver this information directly to your unguarded cerebrum. The rest of you, however, have to get creative. Here are some ideas to help you overcome the restrictions of this medium.

- **Auditory learners.** Try reading this article aloud to yourself or get your kids to read it to you. Hey, how many times have you helped them with their homework? It's payback time.
- **Kinesthetic learners.** Pick up this magazine and start pacing back and forth in your office while reading. Your coworkers will assume you are intense, driven and smart. They'll run to their offices and try to look like they're working, too. Healthy alternatives: If you've got a stationary exercise machine, read this article during your workout. If you enjoy making people get out of your way, read this while walking through a crowded mall.
- **Tactual learners.** Get out your highlighters, folks, because you can interact with this text in a number of ways. Highlighting phrases with wild abandon is one way, but it still might be too passive for you. Make notes on the article to really get your hands involved or use scissors to cut out relevant information (don't try this if you've had too much coffee).

According to Dunn, the company felt the drivers were having too many traffic accidents. When Dunn, Ingham, et al. went back to look at the safety training, they discovered that the material was delivered primarily by lecture, supported by handouts and manuals the drivers were supposed to read. With a group composed largely of kinesthetic and tactual learners, it's little wonder the original training was less than effective.

Most trainers assume an average group, however, and design programs that draw on a mix of media, exercises and structured discussions. It's a shotgun approach, but many argue it's all they have time for. Dunn, on the other hand, insists, "You can't just guess. You have to know what you're doing."

Testing people before the training is particularly helpful if you have a group with a strong preference in one area, like the truck drivers. If the test confirms that the group is "normal," you probably can just mix up the presentation styles according to the above formula.

Does testing sound like a lot of work? Many learning-style assessments take 20 minutes or less to administer.

Twist and Shout

So you've decided against a straight lecture with a couple of overhead transparencies. You've bravely chosen to include a mix of presentation styles that will appeal to all the learning preferences in the class. What's next? What do you actually do?

Some of the obvious stuff has already become part of most trainers' tool kits: slides, flip charts, role-plays, small-group discussions, exercises, videos, hands-on demonstrations and so on. What else is there?

Bob Pike, president of Creative Training Techniques, a consulting firm in Minneapolis, and editor of "Creative Training Techniques" newsletter, is well-known for his ability to mix a variety of methods into his presenta-

tions. He specializes in teaching other trainers how to make their instruction more effective.

Pike keeps his workshops moving at a fast pace so that he can include techniques that appeal to a variety of learning styles. "If a [method] is being used right now that does not particularly fit you, it's OK because in 10 minutes we're going to be doing something else," says Pike. His train-the-trainer workshops are designed to teach trainers to "flex" their instructional styles, he says, which enables them to meet the needs of a variety of learners.

This "style-shifting" is difficult to visualize, but easy to recognize when you see it.

Laurence Martel, president of the National Academy of Integrative Learning, a nonprofit research organization in Hilton Head, SC, tells the story of a scientist at the Massachusetts Institute of Technology who attended one of his training sessions. This participant was very bright and

---

LEARNING STYLES ESCAPE CLASSROOM! CITY IN PANIC! DETAILS AT 11

It would be downright foolish to assume that learning style is something you encounter only in the classroom. Substitute terms like "perceptual" or "processing" for "learning," and you'll recognize that these differences bleed into most of our waking existence.

But with all the talk about lifelong learning, knowing your own learning preferences will probably become more important to your job, in and out of the classroom. Because the line between learning and working is quickly disappearing, the world is your classroom.

One of the first, and most important, steps in the lifelong learning scenario is making learners aware of their preferences. Almost every expert we spoke with agreed that awareness alone can improve a person's ability to learn, inside and outside the classroom. And it makes sense. Learners can adjust, if they know what they are adjusting for.

Laurence Martel, president of the National Academy of Integrative Learning, a nonprofit research organization in Hilton Head, SC, tells of helping 10 medical students who were about to flunk out of school. He discovered that eight of them had a strong learning preference for the afternoon, while most of their difficult courses were in the morning. By recognizing that they were handicapped in the morning, the students adjusted their attitudes and realized that they had to pay particular attention in their morning classes. "They stopped blaming themselves for being inadequate," says Martel.

Aside from style identification, Martel contends that just letting employees know they *are* learners is an important step in the right direction. "An awful lot of

employees out there think they're stupid," says Martel. "It's our job, both in and out of the classroom, to tell them otherwise."

Martel also thinks there are a lot of "wounded learners" in our work force. He says eight out of 10 people he talks to identify with the term because "it rings at the gut level with most people that they've had a lot of bad experiences in being tested, in being judged, and in being told, 'You're worker bees and don't have the moxie to be in management,' " says Martel.

He also puts learning styles at the heart of the diversity movement. Companies have to come to grips with the relevant differences in the internal wiring of employees, he says, not the irrelevant differences of gender, race or ethnicity. Trainers can immediately make diversity part of their daily activities by adjusting to and respecting people's learning styles.

Barbara Waggoner, a training consultant in Stamford, CT, agrees that the impact of learning styles is not confined to the classroom. In fact, she says, popular management trends such as empowerment and teamwork fail to take into account the learning styles of employees.

Companies that hope to empower employees by pushing decision-making to the lowest levels may be more successful if they put employees in the right environment (including ergonomic factors such as light, background noise, temperature and office layout), and let employees empower themselves. Likewise, plopping everyone onto a team ignores the learning preference of those who work best alone or with just one other person, says Waggoner. — B.F.

outspoken, constantly asking questions — and interrupting the class. Martel suggested to the trainees that they weren't restricted to their chairs and desks while they concentrated on the material. In fact, he said, they could walk around the room or pace back and forth. The scientist got up immediately and started pacing.

After about 15 minutes, the scientist told Martel: "This is the first time I've ever been liberated in my life. I didn't realize that a lot of my ability to process information requires me to move around. And when I'm forced to sit in these chairs, I manifest it as being kind of a pain in the rear end."

Martel, in this situation, was able to accommodate the participant's preferred learning style, to "style-shift."

Everett Robinson, vice president for Consulting Resource Group International of Abbotsford, British Columbia, is collaborating with Pike on some learning-style research. He says that style-shifting is a three-step process: It requires trainers to identify and understand participants' learning styles, recognize and suspend their own style preferences, and adapt their training methods to the styles learners exhibit. If you don't test learners ahead of time, says Robinson, you style-shift "on the fly," much as a talented improvisational actor would.

Pike and Robinson have found that some training techniques are almost universally well-received. Among them: demonstrations, field trips, discussion groups, storytelling and games (as long as the games make sense in the context of the course, adds Pike).

Striking a Balance

Trainers aren't the only ones who have to learn to style-shift. Learners themselves have to realize that they must pay more attention to information presented in a style they don't like. In other words, style-shifting is the responsibility of both trainer and learner.

Dave Williams, a partner with OmniCom, a communications consulting firm in Ithaca, NY, suggests that knowing your learning style is great, but not if you use it as an excuse

---

"This is the first time I've ever been liberated in my life. I didn't realize that a lot of my ability to process information requires me to move around."

---

to ignore information because it's not presented the way you'd prefer. "Fine, I've got a style," says Williams, but it should not become an obstacle to learning via other methods.

Learners need to strike a balance between relying on their learning strengths and striving to strengthen styles with which they are less comfortable. Style should become less important as you stretch yourself as a learner, Williams says. And, indeed, Waggoner's research verifies that learning-style flexibility increases with maturity.

Is there ever an advantage to employing methods that run contrary to the learning styles of the audience? Some say yes, but others advise caution. Throwing a bunch of analytic executives into a white-water rafting exercise, for example, challenges them to stretch as learners. But using a teaching method outside of participants' comfort zone is not a good way to introduce new and difficult material, warns Dunn.

So where does all this leave us? Have the educational system and the training community missed the boat by failing to accommodate people's learning styles?

Traditional childhood education uses an auditory model, with visual reinforcement, and ignores both kinesthetic and tactual learners, Dunn points out. It also appeals to analytic processors, though only 12 percent of school-age children are analytic. Do companies make the same mistakes? "Absolutely," says Dunn, "because what do they do? They bring in high-priced consultants who speak." This is absurd, she adds, because "at most, I mean really the outermost, you don't have more than maybe 30 percent auditory people."

As learning becomes a more important part of our jobs, understanding our own learning preferences, as well as the styles of our coworkers, is going to become an imperative. The best way to help people learn is to create an environment where they *can* learn, says Martel. "It isn't building learning organizations. It's understanding the fundamental nature of the human capacity to learn."

Notes:

Second Thoughts About the Myers-Briggs Type Indicator

BY RON ZEMKE

Business and industry make up a nice-sized chunk of the market for psychological tests. By one estimate, sales of tests and inventories for selection, team building, and career and management development weigh in at about $100 million a year.

Hottest of the lot is the Myers-Briggs Type Indicator, or MBTI as insiders call it. Every year, between 1.5 million and 2 million people in the United States take the MBTI. Developed by the mother-daughter team of Katharine Briggs and Isabel Briggs Myers, and refined over a 40-year period dating to World War II, the test is based on the theories of Swiss psychiatrist Carl Jung. The MBTI divides people into 16 distinguishable personality types, based on high and low scores on four "scales." According to the theory, these scales are measures of four independent, intrinsic predispositions (see box on page 140).

Though often given during career and marriage counseling, the Myers-Briggs is most commonly used in the corporate world. Trainers and organization development specialists frequently use the MBTI in team building and communications training. For example, members of a department or task team who must work closely or intensively on the same project are given copies of the instrument to fill out. Then, as a group, they are led through exercises and explanations that impress upon them how the panoply of psychological types on the team can be both a barrier and an asset to working together effectively.

As a communications-style analyzer, the MBTI is touted as helpful to sales-people and executives learning to become more effective in both one-on-one and group situations. The ability to cater to a customer's — or boss's — style or type, it is held, makes you more effective. What could be more leader-like than a speech to the troops that has a little something in it for all 16 of the MBTI personality configurations?

The Critics

As the MBTI has grown in popularity, it has attracted increasing critical scrutiny.

G. Stephen Taylor, a management professor at Mississippi State University, is typical of one class of skeptic. He worries about the tendency of managers to see any personality test as an easy answer to organizational problems. (MBTI aficionados object to the word "test," demanding that the instrument be called a "type indicator," but Taylor's point still applies.)

"I ask managers whether they are planning to pay people to be likable or to do a good job," he says. "They get the point." According to Taylor, the best research available shows a very weak relationship between personality and performance: "On average, personality accounts for about 10 percent of the variance between success and failure in group performance. That means there are a lot more important factors to be concerned with."

Even if an organization does want to delve into its employees' personalities, the fact that the MBTI is a "manipulable" test can make its readings questionable. As Taylor puts it, "I've taken it a number of times, and I pretty much have been able to get the profile I want." More on this later.

Another common objection targets the claim that the MBTI is useful in helping individuals "value differences." More often, critics say, the instrument becomes a way of pigeon-holing people and even giving them type-based excuses for substandard performance. ("You know how we N's are; we never like to spell a word the same way twice.")

A corporate trainer in the Atlanta area, who asked not to be identified, worries that her organization has gone "type happy." "Around here," she says, "everyone knows that it's important to be an 'E' [extrovert] and troublesome to be an 'I' [introvert]. So people work real hard at looking like 'E's,' whether that's comfortable or not, and getting into one of the right types on the test. It's like making sure you drink the same single-malt scotch the CEO drinks and that you work out at the right health club."

The vogue in this organization is brown-bag lunches and MBTI. "It's a little like a mass horoscope reading or something," she says. In other words, it's quick and easy. "First you call Domino's, then you call the training department. We both deliver in 30 minutes or less."

The almost giddy zeal that surrounds the MBTI in this Atlanta organization isn't unique. It also surfaces in published reports about the instrument. A recent opinion piece in *The Wall Street Journal* by Ernest Auerbach, former president and chief operating officer of New York Life Worldwide Holding Inc., demonstrated the evangelical spirit that can seize adherents. "Insights provided by the MBTI are so extraordinarily useful," Auerbach wrote, "that the test should be routinely administered to adults as they enter the workplace, to parents raising children and to young adults thinking about getting married."

Typemania also leads to stories like one that showed up last year in *USA Today.* Editors of the paper called upon Otto Kroeger, author of *Type Talk: The 16 Personality Types That Determine How We Live, Love and Work,* to assess George Bush's MBTI style — based on "key words White House watchers used to describe him" — and interpret Bush's management strengths. Kroeger pronounced Bush an INFP. This means, he said, that the president "has high ideals, and he's a gracious, gentle person with a low need to be hard-charging, macho."

Kroeger runs one of the four groups in the United States that are authorized by the Center for Applications of Psychological Type (CAPT) in Gainesville, FL, to train and qualify professionals to administer the MBTI. Nevertheless, such horoscope-like use of the MBTI concepts does not necessarily sit well with CAPT. Comments Jerry Macdaid, the center's director of research: "Speculation of that kind in [a public forum] undermines our seriousness about the integrity of psychological assessments. It runs the danger of trivializing what's very complex."

But what is it about the MBTI that engenders such enthusiasm in the first place? According to Paul Thayer, head of the psychology department at North Carolina State University, the test's popularity is not hard to understand. "It is an interesting instrument. The logic and descriptions [of Jung's types] are straightforward and nonthreatening. The [feedback] makes you feel good about yourself. It encourages you to feel you can be successful. It leads you to think you know more about yourself and that you can kind of read others. There's something very appealing to all of us in that."

In addition, Thayer observes, the MBTI is well-packaged and marketed, and it's easy to use. "The training manuals by [organizational behavior consultant Sandra] Hirsch and others have everything you need to make very professional presentations. You can become a very successful presenter fairly quickly."

Still, as a research psychologist, Thayer is concerned about the popularity and widespread use of MBTI. "I am not down on the instrument per se," he says. "I'd just like to see a hell of a lot of good research done. As it stands, all the things claimed for it — well, it sounds more like a panacea than a psychological instrument."

Among the things that trouble Thayer are claims that the MBTI can be used to put together more effective teams. "The evidence is very spotty," he says. "The research that has been done is not very good." That applies to team building in general, as well as to the ancillary use of personality instruments, he says. Enthusiasts talk about putting together "complementary" teams, meaning teams composed of people whose various thinking styles or communication styles or Jungian types complement one another in such a way as to make the team optimally effective. "There are one or two studies that are quite supportive of that," Thayer says. "But other studies clearly show that the definitions of 'com-

plementary' are highly unreliable. People don't even agree as to what these are."

Another concern involves the training that frequently accompanies MBTI feedback. Says Thayer: "It is very doubtful whether a couple of hours of insight training accompanied by the instrumented feedback can change much behavior. Even in behavior modeling training, which we know changes behavior, there has to be a lot of opportunity for trainees to practice. You don't get sufficient practice in a couple of hours."

Research

Because of the many claims made for the MBTI, the National Research Council, a subgroup of the National Academy of Sciences, included the MBTI in a 1991 examination of several training techniques alleged to have exceptional impact on human performance. The examination, conducted by a panel of 14 psychologists, covered both the published, refereed literature and a special evaluation of the use of MBTI and five other instruments in four advanced training programs for U.S. Army officers.

In its report, the National Research Council Committee on Techniques for

THE 16 DIFFERENT PERSONALITY TYPES				
		SENSING TYPES (S)		INTUITIVE TYPES (N)	
		THINKING (T)	FEELING (F)	FEELING (F)	THINKING (T)
INTROVERTS (I)	JUDGING (J)	**ISTJ** Serious, quiet, earn success by concentration and thoroughness. Practical, orderly, matter-of-fact, logical, realistic and dependable. Take responsibility.	**ISFJ** Quiet, friendly, responsible and conscientious. Work devotedly to meet their obligations. Thorough, painstaking, accurate. Loyal, considerate.	**INFJ** Succeed by perseverance, originality and desire to do whatever is needed or wanted. Quietly forceful, conscientious, concerned for others. Respected for their firm principles.	**INTJ** Usually have original minds and great drive for their own ideas and purposes. Skeptical, critical, independent, determined, often stubborn.
	PERCEIVING (P)	**ISTP** Cool onlookers—quiet, reserved and analytical. Usually interested in impersonal principles, how and why mechanical things work. Flashes of original humor.	**ISFP** Retiring, quietly friendly, sensitive, kind, modest about their abilities. Shun disagreements. Loyal followers. Often relaxed about getting things done.	**INFP** Care about learning, ideas, language and independent projects of their own. Tend to undertake too much, then somehow get it done. Friendly, but often too absorbed.	**INTP** Quiet, reserved, impersonal. Enjoy theoretical or scientific subjects. Usually interested mainly in ideas, little liking for parties or small talk. Sharply defined interests.
EXTROVERTS (E)	PERCEIVING (P)	**ESTP** Matter-of-fact, do not worry or hurry, enjoy whatever comes along. May be a bit blunt or insensitive. Best with real things that can be taken apart or put together.	**ESFP** Outgoing, easygoing, accepting, friendly, make things more fun for others by their enjoyment. Like sports and making things. Find remembering facts easier than mastering theories.	**ENFP** Warmly enthusiastic, high-spirited, ingenious, imaginative. Able to do almost anything that interests them. Quick with a solution and to help with a problem.	**ENTP** Quick, ingenious, good at many things. May argue either side of a question for fun. Resourceful in solving challenging problems, but may neglect routine assignments.
	JUDGING (J)	**ESTJ** Practical, realistic, matter-of-fact, with a natural head for business or mechanics. Not interested in subjects they see no use for. Like to organize and run activities.	**ESFJ** Warm-hearted, talkative, popular, conscientious, born cooperators. Need harmony. Work best with encouragement. Little interest in abstract thinking or technical subjects.	**ENFJ** Responsive and responsible. Generally feel real concern for what others think or want. Sociable, popular. Sensitive to praise and criticism.	**ENTJ** Hearty, frank, decisive, leaders. Usually good in anything that requires reasoning and intelligent talk. May sometimes be more positive than their experience in an area warrants.

Adapted from Isabel Briggs Myers, *Introduction to Type.* Palo Alto, CA: Consulting Psychologists Press Inc., ©1987.

the Enhancement of Human Performance announced four conclusions about the MBTI:

1. **The types are "memorable."** Of the five instruments used in the Army programs, MBTI was far and away the best *remembered* by trainees who had been exposed to it. Specifically, the committee found that trainees remembered filling out the MBTI and receiving feedback on it better than they remembered doing so with any other instrument (97 percent recall vs. 68 percent for the second-highest-scoring instrument).

Particularly impressive was the recall of specific styles. Eighty-seven percent of trainees remembered their MBTI style designation—and what the letter abbreviations meant — compared to 26 percent recall of "similar" details for the next-best-remembered instrument.

2. **Trainees see their MBTI results as "true" and valuable.** Eighty-four percent of the Army officers said the MBTI confirmed what they already knew about themselves (compared to 55 percent for the second-place instrument) and that the results confirmed what supervisors and/or peers had said about them. A significant percentage believed they would find this confirming feedback valuable in their work relationships.

3. **The instrument has a high self-perceived impact.** Eighty percent of respondents indicated that MBTI had either "very much" or "some" impact on their behavior. This compares to 39 percent for the second-highest-scoring instrument. Seventy-four percent said the MBTI caused them to change the way they related to others — though they did not or could not indicate exactly how their behavior had changed. Few respondents attributed any such change to the other instruments used in the programs.

4. **The MBTI is often the highlight of a training program.** Sixty-one percent of the Army trainees rated the MBTI as the most powerful part or element of the program they had attended. Equally interesting, 26 percent rated the MBTI as the most uncomfortable part of the program. Sixty-one percent of respondents said that they would change their behavior based on MBTI feedback. Again, however, few could specify what they would change.

These obviously impressive results led the NRC committee to conclude: "The MBTI had a very different effect on respondents than all the other instruments — on memory, on self-insights, and on short- and long-term planning and actions."

In addition, the reviewers were impressed that, compared to the MBTI, none of the other instruments in these programs were well-remembered. Also, none of them prompted much intent to change or seemed to provide much personal insight.

Critics see the instrument as a way of pigeonholing people and even giving them type-based excuses for substandard performance.

The committee concluded that the MBTI is probably the most popular instrument in use today for developing self-insight and insight into others' behavior.

That certainly sounds like a glowing endorsement. In fact, however, the National Research Council's report is much less positive about the MBTI than the foregoing suggests. "Unfortunately," the report continues, "the popularity of the instrument is not coincident with research results."

Specifically, the NRC's researchers—and other investigators — point to three areas of concern: The instrument's reliability, its validity and its effectiveness in some of the situations for which it is recommended.

Reliability. An instrument is reliable if it yields the same scores every time you take it. Just as you would be suspicious of a thermometer that gave you three radically different readings within a five-minute period, you have to question the reliability of a personality test that can assign you a different personality each time you take it.

The NRC report cites a review of 11 studies of MBTI test-retest outcomes that showed that type stability ranged from 24 percent to 61 percent; that is, as few as 24 percent of respondents — and no more than 61 percent — were assigned the same type when they took the test a second time. A change in at least one of the four categories occurred for 27 percent to 44 percent of test takers. The median of test takers changing on at least one factor was 37 percent.

This question of basic reliability has been further sharpened by studies of purposive faking or manipulation of type scores. A recent study done at the University of London, for example, found that MBTI was one of the most easily manipulable instruments among those scrutinized. In other words, you can make the MBTI describe you pretty much as whatever type you like.

MBTI advocates object that the instrument is not intended to place people in rigid categories. They even suggest that changes in MBTI results can depend upon current assignments and pressures, and that work and nonwork situations may evoke different responses to the same questions.

But this sort of transience is frowned upon by psychometricians, particularly those involved with tests used to guide hiring decisions. They suggest that assessment instruments that can be influenced so easily do not, in fact, deliver useful information.

When it comes to hiring, many MBTI supporters do not argue the point. The Center for Applications of Psychological Type says that while the MBTI is useful for placement and counseling, it is not *intended* to be used as a selection instrument. CAPT's Macdaid doesn't dispute that the instrument's type scores can be swayed. "It is quite possible that a person wanting to make a good impression can influence the scores on the scales," he says.

Allen L. Hammer is a researcher with Consulting Psychologists Press Inc. of Palo Alto, CA, the publisher of the MBTI, and editor-in-chief of the company's interpretation manuals. He contends that the MBTI is being held to psychometric standards different from other career development instruments. "The underlying concept for the use of instruments in career counseling since the 1930s is matching people with a job that is congruent with their interests and preferences. The MBTI does that as well or better than any instrument on the market," Hammer says.

Validity. An instrument's validity hinges upon whether it measures anything "real." For the MBTI, validity includes at least three touchstones: a) Does the instrument give the same readings that skilled Jungian psychologist/therapists give? b) Does the instrument agree with other instruments that measure similar attributes? c) Do the instrument's results agree with the "self-typing" of people knowledgeable about MBTI or Jungian personality theory?

How well does the MBTI stack up against these criteria? According to the National Research Council, the answer is, so-so. In general, the Introversion/Extroversion scale of MBTI receives high marks from researchers on all three major tests of validity. But the Sensing/Intuition and Thinking/Feeling scales show generally weak validity.

CPPI's Hammer argues that the NRC's report missed some solid evidence for the validity of MBTI's scales. But he agrees that the validity of the 16 individual types, as opposed to that of the four broad scales, is open to question. "The validity of the types as types needs work," he says.

A just-published book titled *Portraits of Type*, by Harrison Goth and Avril Thorne, two of the best-known personality researchers in the world, reviews five decades of research on MBTI types and makes a more positive assessment about their validity than did the NRC, according to Hammer. "But you can't fault [NRC] for not referencing the book," he adds. "It wasn't published when they did their review."

Effectiveness. For businesses, and especially for trainers, a critical issue is whether or not the MBTI is useful in team building, communications and other applications. Evidence comes in two forms: anecdotal and sketchy.

North Carolina State's Thayer, who did a background paper for the NRC on the Myers-Briggs, concludes that the research on applications in the education, training and development, and team-building areas is incomplete, inconsistent and flawed.

He adds, however, that the body of research is growing in quantity and quality. Because of the popularity of MBTI in team building, for example,

---

The zeal that some practitioners bring to their use and advocacy of the MBTI can be off-putting to the nonbeliever.

---

considerable work is in process. "There is a study going here at NC State between my department and chemical engineering looking at type and teaching success," he says.

CPPI's Hammer shrugs at skepticism about the usefulness of MBTI in team building. "Organizational development people have been using the MBTI for team building for 20 years, and they repeatedly see the same patterns and successes. That is pretty

powerful to me," he says.

And there's more evidence to come. Consultant Sandra Hirsh, author of *Introduction to Type in Organizations*, has a book in press that explores team building with the MBTI.

Bottom Line

Where does all this leave us? To some extent, MBTI undoubtedly has become a victim of its own success. Its very popularity makes it a target of criticism. The zeal that some practitioners bring to their use and advocacy of the MBTI can be off-putting to the nonbeliever. T-shirts, coffee mugs and wall placards declaring "ENTJ Spoken Here" and "INFPs Do It Better," lead to skepticism, particularly on the part of academics unaccustomed to such fervent endorsement of a psychological instrument. "It ain't natural," one of the critics told us.

Yet according to the accumulating evidence, the instrument does *something* for those who buy into it. Just what that something is is an open question, depending upon whom you ask.

Perhaps the best advice is to keep your eyes — and your options — open, and see how the current spate of claims, counterclaims, criticisms and new research initiatives play out. As Thayer put it, "It would be nice if the MBTI turns out to be half as useful as some of the claims."

Notes:

MENTORING

The Democratic Version of Mentoring

BY ERIK GUNN

In a telephone company with a reputation for complacent conservatism, the new hire was a shot of adrenaline.

Actually, more like a spine-stiffening jolt. The employee, recruited from the cable television industry, was "totally market-driven — a very aggressive person who brought some really assertive characteristics," recalls Nancy Teutsch, a vice president for human resources at Ameritech, the Chicago-based five-state Baby Bell. But the same hard-charging drive that had helped him get the job in the first place was almost his undoing.

"This person came in and almost instantly alienated people by talking about 'Bell-heads' and criticizing our old culture," Teutsch says. True, Ameritech itself was trying desperately to change many attributes of that culture, but the new hotshot broadcast his scorn "in such a way that it appeared he was criticizing his team members. People viewed that as so obnoxious they didn't hear the wisdom he was bringing about fast cycle time and market responsiveness."

Managers intervened and the man shaped up, Teutsch says. But the experience was typical of problems that led to a program at Ameritech for new hires, especially those from other industries. The telephone company teams newcomers with more seasoned types for 60 to 90 days. The relationship is aimed at helping newcomers ease into the company without squelching the ideas, attitudes or skills for which they were hired in the first place.

Ameritech doesn't call the program "mentoring." The official term for staffers who fill the mentor role is "rec-

iprocal guide"; Teutsch uses the nickname "coaching buddy." But despite its short-term time frame, the reciprocal-guide program reflects much of what's happening in formal mentoring programs around the nation.

In what Tom Peters likes to call "the nanosecond '90s," corporate mentoring programs haven't gone away. But today's versions tend to be more tightly focused and shorter in duration. At the same time, many are more open, at least on paper, to a broader range of employees within a company. And while a wave of popularity for mentoring programs in the mid-1980s was sparked in part by efforts to improve the promotion and retention of women and minorities, today's programs often reflect a wider variety of corporate agendas. Even where the explicit aim is to improve a company's cultural diversity, the consensus is growing that white men, not just women and nonwhites, should be provided with mentors if they want.

They're Back

Formal mentoring programs blossomed in the decade after management theorist Rosabeth Moss Kanter concluded in 1977 that having a mentor was critical to career success. Employers wanting to improve the representation of women and minorities in the executive ranks created specialized mentoring programs to help achieve that goal. In 1993, more than one in five respondents to a joint survey for the Society for Human Resource Management and the publishing firm Commerce Clearing House said their workplaces had mentoring programs geared for minorities; twice as many rated such programs as necessary.

Affirmative action for women and

minorities wasn't the only aim, of course. Many firms either established structured mentoring programs or simply encouraged managers to create informal mentoring relationships as an additional tool for succession-planning, making sure future leaders were constantly in the pipeline.

Now, after a few years of quiescence, mentoring programs are back. No source could cite numbers, but many observers see a definite resurgence of interest. "Every time I turn around people are talking about developing a mentoring program," says Marquette University management professor Belle Rose Ragins, who studies women's issues in business.

"Employers and organizations are not offering the kind of security and caretaking that they used to," adds Kathleen Kram, who teaches organizational behavior at the Boston University School of Management and consults with private companies on mentoring. Whether formal or informal, says Kram, "mentoring is seen as an alternative to that."

Indeed, far from being cast off as expensive frills in the endless rounds of corporate restructuring and downsizing of the early 1990s, some mentoring programs actually have been fueled by the changes. That's the case with Ameritech's "coaching buddy" program. Even as the company has been selectively hiring experienced managers and professionals from other industries, Ameritech has shed thousands of white-collar employees in the last several years to gird for emerging competition in local and long-distance telephone service.

The same is happening elsewhere. "As organizations downsize, the people who are kept in an organization tend to have deeper skills in a specific area," says Margo Murray, president of MMHA, an Oakland, CA, consulting firm, and author of the book *Beyond the Myths and Magic of Mentoring*. Downsizing companies may turn to mentors to teach additional skills to workers who remain, in hopes of creating a more flexible work force. "We're seeing more pairing for specific skills rather than pairing [in the sense of], 'I'll tuck you under my wing and take you along for the rest of your life,'" Murray says.

In addition, firms "are hiring external expertise at higher levels than they did before," Murray says. A bank, for instance, may turn to someone from the securities industry to manage a branch office as its financial products expand. The new manager needs coaching in the bank's culture, but also needs an opportunity to share knowledge that may be new to his banking colleagues. "We're creating more mentoring partnerships, so it's a two-way transfer of skills and experience," Murray adds.

This more democratic approach to mentoring appears increasingly popular. Traditionally, "the mentor is someone who provides wise counsel," says William Gray, who operates The Mentoring Institute Inc., a Vancouver, British Columbia, consulting firm. "There's still a place for that. But it is only half the concept of mentoring that we use. The other half is that the mentor acknowledges that today's protégés are better-educated and know more than the protégés of yesterday. They bring with them ideas, creativity, initiative, responsibility, a passion to do something. The mentor needs to empower protégés as well as to equip them with what the mentor already knows."

A Sense of Inclusion

In much the same spirit, companies are moving away from mentoring programs that focus only on minorities and women. "Organizations, in a variety of ways, are trying to figure out how to make mentoring more available to a wider group of employees," says Boston University's Kram.

Take General Electric Co. The Fairfield, CT-based conglomerate's mentoring program grew out of earlier efforts often tailored primarily for minorities and women at GE subsidiaries. And the goal of the program remains creating "an environment that is inclusive," says Gene Andrews, the parent company's manager of work force diversity.

"We are investing quite a bit in recruiting the best that we can," Andrews says. "We want people as they join this organization to as quickly as possible feel a real sense of inclusion so that there's no question that they're part of the team."

Orientation programs and a "buddy system" for new employees help, he continues, but if women and minorities get left out of the informal loop — sharing lunch or getting a drink after work with some of the older white men who continue to dominate the managerial ranks, for instance — then they feel excluded. Their growth is stifled, their productivity and innovation suffers, and in the long run they may go elsewhere, forcing the company to replace them at a cost of as much as $100,000 per person, Andrews estimates.

But the very value of inclusiveness quickly led GE to make its mentoring program available to everyone. One reason was to avoid backlash of the sort dogging affirmative action programs — the notion that a program exclusively for minorities and women constitutes a form of preferential treatment. But another seemingly contradictory concern was even more important: making sure everyone in the organization takes mentoring seriously. "If it's seen as a program just for women and minorities, in the eyes of the majority it loses its value," Andrews says.

Kram, who worked with GE in establishing its program, says that approach reflects a general movement in corporate America to go beyond narrowly drawn affirmative action goals to the more sweeping objective of managing diversity: "There's a shift in orientation from helping women and people of color to creating a culture that empowers all people of whatever background to succeed."

Moreover, not all white men have benefited from mentoring, either. When consultant Gray gives workshops, he asks everyone — including the men — if they can recall a time "when they needed mentoring and no one stepped forward to provide it," Gray says. "Almost every hand goes up."

Today GE, with 157,000 U.S. employees, boasts more than 1,000 pairs of mentors and protégés around the corporation. Mentoring is most heavily entrenched at the company's appliance-manufacturing unit in Louisville, KY. There GE has matched 300 pairs of mentors and protégés. Among them are 12-year GE veteran Doug King, 34, operations manager for laundry manufacturing, and Lance Harrington, 28, a process engineer who has been at the company for five years. King has mentored Harrington for more than two years, and also has had a mentor of his own.

"The mentoring is very informal," King says. "Sometimes we might see each other five times a week; other times, not for two months."

For Harrington, the program proved its value when he joined a team that was working on a problem involving the use of new plastic-molding equipment. What he lacked in experience Harrington made up for in enthusiasm, sparked by classes he was taking on the subject of injection molding plastic. Harrington's studies suggested to him a solution to the problem.

Persuading his more seasoned teammates proved difficult, however.

MENTORING DO'S AND DON'TS

BY ERIK GUNN

Not everyone agrees on all the details, but companies with mentoring programs usually subscribe to similar rules. Among them:

• Do make a business case for a program, and get top management commitment for it.

• Don't limit the program to certain groups — minorities and women, for instance. Otherwise, you may stigmatize the beneficiaries and inspire backlash among the excluded.

• Tell mentors and protégés about what to expect from the relationship and what not to expect. If there are cross-cultural mentor-protégé pairs, train the partners as well in sensitivity to those issues.

• Don't portray the program as a guaranteed path to promotion — and communicate clearly to dispel that impression.

• Do clarify and communicate your selection criteria for mentors. And recognize that not every good employee has the right style to be a successful mentor.

Experts differ on how easy it ought to be for mentors and protégés in formal programs to opt out of "arranged marriages." In some companies, like General Electric Co., that's easy to do early on if the relationship isn't working. Others encourage protégés to stick with the partnership even if things get rocky, urging them to use the opportunity to learn from and get along with people different from themselves.

He kept talking, but they weren't listening, King recalls. It turned out that Harrington's analysis was the correct one. The experience left Harrington feeling a bit like Wesley Crusher — the brilliant teenage ensign on television's "Star Trek: The Next Generation" who forever must overcome the patronizing skepticism of the adult crew. Harrington went to King for advice on "how I could have gotten those team members to listen to me quicker." He credits King with helping him develop a facilitator's style: drawing out everyone's ideas, then taking the group through them methodically. As a result, he says, "Now I'm one of the team."

CSX Transportation in Jacksonville, FL, a unit of CSX Corp., designed its mentoring program to include hourly, unionized employees, not just managers and professionals. Protégés are matched with more senior-level mentors, not necessarily from the same departments, for a period of one year. The railroad's mentoring program grew out of concerns in the late 1980s about the lack of advancement among women and minorities, though it has always been open to white males as well, says Derrick Smith, assistant vice president for minerals marketing at the rail carrier.

Up to now the opportunity to be assigned a mentor has been offered only to employees in nonoperating departments such as sales and marketing, finance and the like — about 20 percent of the company's 29,000 employees. (About 130 people have actually been paired up with mentors in five years.) This year CSX began a pilot project to introduce mentoring to its operations employees, the bulk of its work force.

Grass Roots

While some mentoring programs are highly structured, both GE and CSX keep theirs very informal. GE outlines some broad objectives to make sure each of its 12 member companies develops a mentoring program, but leaves many of the details up to individual business units. The CSX program is not administered by the company's human resources department, although department representatives join those from other areas in the team that runs it.

"This is an employee-driven, grassroots effort, run by a committee of employees," says CSX's Smith. With this committee matching mentors and protégés, the program has more credibility, adds Doug Klippel, manager of organizational development at the corporation: "We aren't seen so much as a flavor-of-the-month from human resources."

By contrast, Douglas Aircraft Co. in Long Beach, CA, a unit of McDonnell Douglas Corp. of St. Louis, has a much more structured mentoring program in which protégés are hand-

---

"We don't put a gun to anybody's head. You're talking about people who are there because they want to be."

---

picked based on their promotion potential. However, enrollment in the program is neither a guarantee nor a requirement for future promotion, says Susan Boyle, a senior human resources specialist at Douglas.

Boyle acknowledges that because the program is open only to a select few, it runs the risk of being resented as elitist. But side by side with the formal program is a corporate expectation that "every employee should have a mentor and be a mentor," Boyle says. Using guidelines laid out in a Douglas handbook that goes to all salaried employees, "every employee here can have a mentor if they want one," she adds.

If every employee, no matter how inexperienced, can also *be* a "mentor," the term obviously is used very loosely. This is the case with many of the informal, "democratic" relationships currently being described under the rubric of mentoring. They often are a far cry from what most people would still think of as the real thing.

Perhaps the most dramatic example of the new, more democratic approach to mentoring is group mentoring. Beverly Kaye, a Sherman Oaks, CA, consultant who has promoted mentoring groups with colleague Betsy Jacobson, sees a group approach as the logical extension of efforts to flatten hierarchies and encourage teamwork. "The group process says we can learn from each other as peers," Kaye says. "If it's one on one, you hear only the advice of the person on high."

In Kaye's scheme, a senior staffer still plays the role of mentor, but "the agenda is in the hands of the 'mentees,' not the mentor," she says. "The mentor comes in and responds to the kinds of things that the mentees want. It empowers the group to really think about what they want. It supports the notion of teams in organizations, and it supports the idea of diversity in action."

Compare that approach — or Douglas Aircraft's "everyone can be a mentor" campaign — with Douglas' formal mentoring effort for high-potential employees. The elite program is closely monitored, with written surveys of participants and a steering committee that revises the program periodically. Mentors and protégés also set goals and objectives for the protégé to meet during the yearlong period the relationship is to operate, and evaluate progress toward achieving them.

GE, meanwhile, relies mainly on focus groups of employees to gauge results and fine-tune its program. At CSX, where pairings last at least a year, the company evaluates its program by surveying participants halfway through and again two months after the 12-month period ends. Those surveys, says Klippel, are aimed at helping CSX "build a profile of what a successful relationship looks like."

Consultant Murray says that evaluation of mentoring programs has never been more important: "I really believe that in today's economic environment, unless you measure and show results, no new systems or programs stay in place." Murray's firm uses a test to measure improvement among protégés in skills such as time management, communication and decision-making.

Ideally, Murray says, a mentoring program is integrated into the organization's overall systems for grooming and developing its work force. "If an organization maintains it and supports it, it becomes a way of life."

Flameouts

But some programs don't last. At the Internal Revenue Service in Kansas City, MO, a mandatory mentoring program for new managers begun about five years ago has been phased out, says Phyllis Kitchen, an employee-development specialist. With the advent of government reengineering a couple of years ago, "our managerial ranks thinned," Kitchen says. "We don't have enough people to make it meaningful or workable right now."

And like many other human resources initiatives, some programs fade when their champions move on. That's what appears to have happened at the *Norfolk Virginian-Pilot* and *Ledger-Star* newspapers, where newsroom employees for a while were getting cross-training from colleagues in a short-term, one-on-one program. When Connie Sage, the newsroom editor in charge of staff development, moved into a corporate position with parent company Landmark Communications Inc., the program largely disappeared, Sage says.

Formal mentoring programs continue to face skepticism in some quarters, dismissed as little more than "arranged marriages." At Ameritech, the same company that has begun providing new hires with short-term

"coaching buddies," Neal Kulick, another human resources vice president, remains wary of longer-term, more formalized arrangements. "I don't think you can prearrange matches between people that will sustain themselves over time," Kulick says.

But Kulick's own unit of the company doesn't rely entirely on chance to create mentoring relationships. Senior managers meet regularly to review the names of newly promoted and talented junior managers, and quietly assign themselves the job of getting to know them individually. "It's something we can do to accelerate the development of high-potential people," Kulick says. "We set up additional relationships to broaden people's knowledge of who the talent is. It's informal, there are no rules, and nobody's writing reports."

At the same time, he adds, the company is trying to create an atmosphere of self-reliance in which junior

employees and senior ones alike form mentor-protégé relationships on their own. "When people come into the business, we explain to them that nothing's going to get handed to you," Kulick says. "We try to motivate the parties to be out there looking for matches, if you will, but [we don't] try to arrange them. Some people network well and some people don't."

Of course, it's for that very reason that advocates say formal mentoring programs are needed — to help those who don't excel at networking. And companies that have mentoring programs, along with the consultants who help establish them, say the idea can work. As for the "arranged marriage" criticism, "this is a voluntary thing," says CSX's Klippel. "We don't put a gun to anybody's head. You're talking about people who are there because they want to be, and people who want to be involved in these programs tend to make things work."

Notes:

MIND MAPPING

Brainstorming on Paper

BY CHRIS LEE

I've never been quite certain if I'm right-brained or left-brained. Sure, I'm a writer, which might tip the scales toward such right-brain specialties as imagery, wholistic vision and analogous conceptualizing. But on the other hand (or brain), I'm a journalist, not a poet. Most magazine articles depend more on research — fact gathering, interviewing and the like — than on personal interpretation of archetypal symbolism. Once all the facts are collected, the actual process of journalistic writing demands as much sorting, organization and clear expression as creativity. It's a very linear activity.

And if you want to know the truth, I've never been convinced that right-brain/left-brain/whole-brain devotees have discovered any earth-shattering truths about the mind. Granted, brain researchers have pegged certain functions to specific parts of the brain. But a cottage industry of zealots seems to have taken that ball and run with it a hell of a lot further than scientific findings justify.

That bias notwithstanding, I approached the job of researching the definition and practice of mind mapping with what I hoped were equal parts of skepticism and objectivity. I had only the vaguest idea of what it was ("Isn't it what people are doing when they claim to be taking notes, except it looks like they're just doodling?"), so I called Anne Durrum Robinson, a human resource development consultant in Austin, TX. I knew she could give me the basics as well as suggestions for further reading.

She characterized mind mapping — also known as clustering, thought trails and hurricane writing — as "brainstorming on paper. The basic principle is to get information down the way your mind handles it, not in a

rigid outline. You're tapping into all your mind's resources before you begin to organize the information. You can use it for any kind of writing — creative, business or professional — or to take notes on reading or lectures."

Robinson says the rules are simple: print (otherwise you may write too much), use key words and create your own symbols for decision points or central ideas.

Mind mapping is fruitful, she says, because it helps you record all your random thoughts without judging them. The idea is to indulge in divergent (nonlinear) thinking until you get a sense of a "felt shift," a direction or trend around which your thoughts are coalescing. Then your judgmental, or convergent, thinking comes into play to refine your ideas. It's a particularly helpful technique for people who are right-brain dominant, she says. "Some right-brained children can't do outlining, but they can do mind mapping."

Now, I was intrigued. As a kid, I was always stymied by outlining. I completed grade-school writing assignments backwards: First I'd write the report and then I'd oblige the teacher with a "bogus" outline completed after the fact. Robinson suggested a couple of books, adding that because they championed something as nontraditional and messy looking as mind mapping, they "curled English teachers' hair." It was a good enough recommendation for me.

The first, Tony Buzan's *Use Both Sides of Your Brain* (E.P. Dutton, Inc., 1974), posits that list-like methods of organization, such as traditional outlining and note-taking, operate "against the way in which the brain works." The linear nature of speech and print notwithstanding, the brain actually deals with "key concepts in an interlinked and integrated man-

ner," he says. Similarly, mind mapping starts with a central concept and branches out to related ideas, enabling the brain to recall, add and review information more easily.

Buzan advocates mind mapping for note-taking, problem solving, writing — "any activity where thought, recall, planning or creativity are involved." Most people will feel some apprehension about developing a "messy" page of scrawled boxes, circles and arrows. But, he concludes, "notes which look 'neat' are, in informational terms, messy.... The key information is disguised, disconnected and cluttered with many informationally irrelevant words. The notes which look 'messy' are informationally far neater. They show immediately the important concepts [and] the connections...."

Buzan made sense to me, so I checked out Robinson's other recommendation: *Writing the Natural Way: Using Right-Brain Techniques to Release Your Expressive Powers* (J.P. Tarcher, Inc., 1983), by Gabriele Lusser Rico. Drawing on the work of brain and creativity researchers, Rico developed what she calls "clustering" as a method of teaching creative writing to college students.

She did it by translating psychiatrist Anton Ehrenzweig's conceptualization of the creative search to paper. She explains the discovery process: "I circled [the word] maze in the center of a blank page and clustered, electrified by the connections in my head that spilled and radiated outward from its center.... As I continued to cluster, I suddenly experienced a shift from a sense of randomness to a sense of direction in all this welter, and I began to write." As soon as she introduced the "nonlinear brainstorming process of clustering" to a freshman composition class, she says, "... my students' writing made a dramatic turnabout, and it has been my approach to teaching writing ever since."

Rico leans heavily on the idea that clustering releases the creative potential of the right brain before the logical left brain gets into the act. She terms the two hemispheres "sign mind" and "design mind" and defines them as follows: "Sign mind is largely occupied with the rational, logical representation of reality and with parts and logical sequences.... By contrast... the design mind constantly thinks in complex images; it patterns to make designs of whatever it encounters, including language. . . ."

The clustering technique allows you to tap the patterns and associations of your design mind, she says. Then the corpus callosum, a sort of traffic light between the two sides of the brain, "shifts from *stop* to *go*, making right-brain associations accessible to the left brain, which in turn can give them sequential, communicable form."

The second step in using clustering for creative writing is what Rico calls "the trial-web shift." She explains: "You are clustering, seemingly randomly, when suddenly you experience a sense of direction. The moment between randomness and sense of direction is the moment of shift." She likens this "aha!" to the experience of looking through the lens of a camera at a blur that suddenly comes into focus when you adjust the focusing mechanism correctly.

The differences between Rico's clustering and Buzan's mind mapping seem to be more of application and design, rather than mechanics or rationale. (In clustering, the key concepts and associations are circled and linked by connecting lines; in mind mapping, the radiating structure may include arrows, colors, idiosyncratic codes or geometrical shapes that indicate relationships.) Rico uses her technique for creative writing applications; Buzan employs mapping to solve problems, plan, take notes or "outline" writing of any kind. And that's where it suits the business purposes of mind-mapping fans in the training field.

"I use mind maps to write books, plan projects and develop courses," says Dudley Lynch, president of Brain Technologies Corp. of Fort Collins, CO, and editor of the "Brain & Strategy" newsletter. "[The technique] gives you permission to be

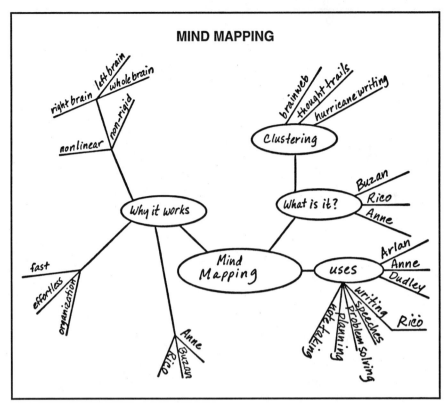

MIND MAPPING

open, to consider anything in the whole wide world. I call mind maps 'brain webs.' I like that term. I think it's descriptive of how the brain works."

Arlan Tietel, division training manager at 3M's magnetic media division in St. Paul, MN, uses mind mapping and has taught it to employees. "I use it to take notes for myself, I've advocated it in workshops as a method to take notes, and I've used it to construct a leader's guide of the information to be communicated in a workshop," he says. "I'm not a good note-taker in a linear style, but I used mind mapping at a conference [recently], and I got everything [said] for the day on one page. It's also the only time anyone ever asked me for a copy of my notes."

Why mind mapping instead of an A-B-C outline? "I use it to force myself into a more creative mode — more right-brained than left-brained," Tietel says. "It helps me to capture and recall information."

I constructed the mind map reproduced here after completing the research for this story. It was a first attempt — actually a sort of hybrid mind map and cluster — but most of its branches eventually found their way into this piece. It worked just fine as a substitute for traditional outlining. But so does my own method of jotting key words and phrases on the tail end of my computer file. I add and subtract as I write.

So am I right-brained or left-brained? I still don't know. Maybe I just have an aversion to outlines.

MULTIMEDIA-BASED TRAINING

On the Trail of Better Multimedia

BY BOB FILIPCZAK

Michael Allen was in trouble. As the director of Control Data's Plato project in the 1970s, he had a team of people building the pioneering computer-based training courseware to the tune of $10 million a year—as high as $20 million in some years. Most of it, admits Allen, wasn't very good. Some was downright horrible.

In March 1979, Bill Norris, then chairman and CEO of Control Data, told Allen that something had to give. He changed Allen's mandate from building training courses to coming up with a program that would allow "mere mortals" to make their own computer-based training. The challenge Norris put in front of Allen was to reduce the time it took to assemble a CBT course by a factor of 40-to-1. That is, the courseware it took his team 40 hours to build should take only one hour to create using this new software.

Thus began work on the first authoring software, or at least the first thing to be called an "authoring" program. Allen himself traces the origins of authoring to very early work by computer programmers who built small routines and tools that allowed them to create and change their programs more efficiently. But the "routine" Allen built was a complete system, a set of tools that allowed average trainers or educators to build their own computer-based training. He met and even exceeded Norris' 40-to-1 target, an achievement that surprised no one more than Allen himself.

In the early 1980s, Allen took his program and started his own business. He called his product "authoring software" to distance it from the perception that it might be just another form of computer programming. Later revisions gave birth to one of the more popular authoring systems, Authorware. Allen's business then merged with a firm called Macromind and became Macromedia, a San Francisco company that now sells both Authorware and a program called Director. Allen himself went on to launch another company in Minneapolis, Allen Interactions, to help companies develop better multimedia-training courseware.

Fast-forward to the present. According to the 1995 *Computer-Based Training Report*, published by the Boston-based Patricia Seybold Group, today's top five authoring programs, in order of popularity, are Authorware, Quest, IconAuthor, Toolbook and Phoenix (see box page 150 for supplier information).

In the intervening years, CBT has changed its name to multimedia, reflecting the fact that it no longer consists strictly of text and graphics. The bar has been raised. Trainees no longer must endure CBT that amounts to a lot of text, a few crude graphics, and a "press enter to continue" message at the bottom of the screen. Multimedia courses offer sound, video, animation, simulations and sophisticated graphics. (Indeed, the term "multimedia" seems to function as a kind of tossed gauntlet, a challenge to developers to see how many effects they can cram into their products.)

But while all of the authoring programs have different strengths, their mission is still true to Allen's mandate back in 1979: Make computer-based training easier to build.

So Is It Easy Yet?

Let's put it this way. Most everyone agrees that authoring systems are much easier to use now than they were 10 years ago. There is also a consensus that authoring will continue to get simpler—if "simpler" means that it will be easier for a beginner to use a system to create *something* that runs on a computer and purports to be a training course. (Don't lose that thought. We'll come back to it.)

Paradoxically, as authoring programs become easier to use, they are also becoming increasingly complex. Greg Koorhan, associate creative director for Eagle River Communications, an interactive marketing company in Vail, CO, explains that developers of authoring programs are catering to both experienced users, who continually push the envelope on interactivity and creative multimedia, and to new users. "The simpler stuff is becoming simpler and the harder stuff is becoming available," he says.

Nevertheless, learning to use an authoring program isn't a no-brainer quite yet. Among the most common criteria experts cite for choosing an authoring system are good technical support and good training. And learning the authoring software itself is just one of the issues developers face, says Ron Ashmun, vice president and manager of multimedia productions for Seafirst Bank, a Bank of America subsidiary in Seattle.

Ashmun says that most of the work in developing a multimedia training course involves what he calls "asset creation." That means shooting and digitizing the video, recording and digitizing sound, creating the animation, and converting all the bells and whistles into a form the authoring program can assemble. "I think a lot of beginners in this business think that they just have to learn an authoring language," says Ashmun. "Well, surprise, surprise! That's the end piece."

Tom King, a partner with Solis, a multimedia consulting firm in San Mateo, CA, compares multimedia development to a wheel. The authoring system, he explains, is the hub of the wheel. The spokes consist of audio editing, video editing, graphics software, animation tools and administrative databases. King says that one of the most important things to look for in an authoring program is how well it communicates with all of these disparate computer packages.

What To Look For

There is far more to creating an effective computer-based training course than just mastering one of these authoring systems. It involves lots of skills and, in some cases, lots of people. As Ashmun puts it: "This is hard. Don't let them kid you, this is really hard."

Still, you have to choose an authoring system. What should you look for? We can start by saying that almost all of the major authoring systems can accomplish similar results. "You can probably code anything you want in any of these packages," says Laura Keiles, a project manager at AT&T's network wireless systems division in Whippany, NJ. "It all depends on how much time you have."

What she means is that it might take more work to force a program to do what you want if the task in question isn't a particular strength of the software. Replacing one video clip with another, for example, may be easy or difficult depending on which authoring program you use.

We already mentioned that the authoring program should be able to communicate with other software, and that the supplier should have training and technical support available. Brandon Hall, editor of "Multimedia Training," a newsletter based in Sunnyvale, CA, also stresses the importance of good tutorials. These self-directed training programs, he says, often leave a lot to be desired, so choose carefully.

According to the *1995 Computer-Based Training Report*, the top four features of an authoring program valued by survey respondents were, in order of importance: flexibility, ease of use, graphics, and ease of maintenance.

How do you judge those factors? Neil Silverstein, training manager for multimedia-based training for Duracell, the Danbury, CT, battery manufacturer, says that authoring companies should be able to provide references of clients who use the software. Talk to these users about your specific concerns, Silverstein suggests.

Better still, he adds, get demos of the software from the suppliers. Most of these demos aren't just dog and pony shows; they have limited authoring capabilities so you can actually build a small "dummy" training program. That, says Hall, is the only real way to find out how easy any given program is.

If that sounds like a lot of work, it is. But authoring systems aren't particularly cheap. Most fully functional authoring systems cost between $1,300 and $5,000. According to the *1995 Computer-Based Training Report*, the median amount spent on authoring systems over the last 12 months was $4,400.

Then there is the issue of run-time fees. A run-time fee is like a royalty payment that you send to the authoring company if you use the company's system to create a computer-based training program that you sell to another party. Only about 25 percent of the respondents to the *CBT Report* paid any run-time fees in the last 12 months. Writes the report's editor, Floyd Kemske: "We view this as indicative of a trend toward the reduction of royalties and run-time fees in this market. Marginal comments on many of the questionnaires reflected a deep-seated philosophical opposition to such fees."

Finally, Hall suggests that you consider whether the authoring software is popular enough to have created a plentiful supply of consultants and contractors who "know" the program. After all, you may not be building every piece of your multimedia training in-house, especially if deadlines start to loom large. Make sure help is available if you decide to outsource some of the work.

WHERE TO FIND THEM

Want to find out more about the authoring systems mentioned in this article? Here's where to call.

Authorware — From Macromedia, 600 Townsend St., #310 West, San Francisco, CA 94103, (800) 288-4797. This is the system that Michael Allen, chairman and CEO of Allen Interactions, a Minneapolis consulting firm, helped develop while he was working on the Plato project for Control Data. Another program from Macromedia, Director, is made for more advanced users who want to put together sophisticated animation.

Quest — From Allen Communication, 5 Triad Center, 5th Floor, Salt Lake City, UT 84180, (800) 325-7850.

IconAuthor — From AimTech Corp., 20 Trafalgar Square, Nashua, NH 03063, (800) 289-2884. This company also has a product called CBT Express that is designed to give the authoring novice a break. This user-friendly authoring environment consists of templates that you can reuse while you develop the training program.

Toolbook — From Asymetrix, 110-110th Ave. N.E., Ste. 700, Bellevue, WA 98004, (800) 448-6543. This was the software company started by Microsoft co-founder Paul Allen.

Phoenix — From Computer Associates, 7965 N. High St., Columbus, OH 43235, (800) 829-9000.

One new product bears mentioning, mostly because of the attention it's been getting in the training industry: *Designer's Edge* from Allen Communication. Gloria Gery, president of Gery Associates, a consulting firm in Tolland, MA, calls Designer's Edge an electronic performance support system for instructional designers. Brandon Hall, editor of "Multimedia Training," a newsletter out of Sunnyvale, CA, agrees that this program is like nothing else out there. It's not just a computer-based training program to teach authoring novices how to do instructional design, it actually helps you assemble your training course as it teaches you how to do it.

Click and Twitch

If you're concerned with creating good multimedia courses, there's one little problem. Knowing how to use an authoring system doesn't make you a good training developer any more than knowing how to type makes you a good writer. An awful lot of boring, poorly designed and downright ghastly CBT is circulating out there. And adding multimedia elements hasn't always been a blessing. The question arises: So now we can bore people using more of their senses?

Bad CBT acquired the moniker "page turner," meaning that what's happening on the screen is emulating nothing more sophisticated than a book. Adding multimedia made it less like a book, but Allen still calls these linear, non-branching, boring courses "click and twitch" programs, meaning you can now use a mouse to go forward and backward, and that's it. Some are comparing these multimedia titles to watching a videotape. A videotape may be somewhat better than a book, but it's still a far cry from multimedia's full capabilities.

When fonts first became available on word processing programs, the flurry of typefaces that exploded onto documents was exciting, diverse and impossible to read. Likewise, multimedia has introduced all kinds of bells and whistles beginner's can add, and unfortunately, they sometimes do. "They just throw on these pretty pictures and throw on these movies, and it's a hodge-podge of information coming at you without any type of rhyme or reason. In training ... you better have a good design," says Silverstein.

Multimedia pioneer Allen agrees. About three years ago, he started delivering a little speech to developers who bought his Authorware program. On the one hand, he wanted to thank them for buying his product. On the other hand, he told them: "The stuff you people are producing just really makes my heart drop. I thought that if we made it so much easier to do, we would open the door for so many different creative and talented people." Instead, Allen mourned: "What seems to have happened, in large part, is that we have a lot more of the same old junk. You can [just] produce it less expensively now."

So what constitutes good multimedia training? Some argue that it's the same thing that has always made any training effective: clear objectives and solid instructional design. Others say that multimedia is so new that we have to completely rethink how we are going to use it to train people, that we are just beginning to understand concepts like interactivity and nonlinear learning.

So are trainers just a bunch of slack-jawed yokels gawking at a brave new world, or do they perhaps have some skills that can translate from the classroom to the computer screen?

The Right Stuff

Randy Jurgensen is the unit manager for computer-based training for a division of McDonnell Douglas in St. Louis. He designs multimedia training for military customers of the San Diego-based aircraft manufacturer. Currently he is working on a course to teach pilots of Finland's air force how to fly F-18s. Call him a high-end developer.

"The thing that kills most CBT products early on," Jurgensen says, "is the lack of a firm product definition." He proposes that good training is good training, no matter what the medium. Thus, good product definition, good design and solid content is the basis for good multimedia training. "A lot of people look at the whizbang of getting it on the screen," he says, and then don't look any further. When people trade content for glitz, the product suffers, he suggests.

Knowing how to use an authoring system doesn't make you a good training developer.

Shirley Borella is a learning-product specialist for Hewlett Packard in Andover, MA. She designs training for customers of HP's medical-imaging systems. "The secret to good development of computer-based training is design, design, design," says Borella. She says the worst products she has seen have failed because no instructional designers were involved.

Allen is not so sure that classic instructional-design skills are the answer. He says he has seen multimedia programs designed by talented, creative people who understood instructional design quite well and created very good-*looking* products. But the courseware was, in his word, flat. He took the packages and re-authored them to include a lot more interactivity. The resulting improvement in the courses amazed his clients, he says.

"I really don't think [interactivity] is a matter of limitations in the technology or in the authoring tools. I think the limitation is that we all seem to be in a rut," says Allen. We don't use this new medium to unlock our creativity and create really riveting training courses that are unlike anything we've ever seen before, he says. His answer is to include so much interactivity that the training functions more as a simulation in which people interact with something on the screen and they see the consequences immediately.

The best computer-based training helps people *build* skills, not just read about skills, Allen says. That's what interactivity is all about. But understanding interactivity just might be a special talent, and a rare one at that, Allen opines.

Nevertheless, a truly outstanding teacher might be a good model to start with, he suggests. We all remember the teacher who somehow knew how to get us involved in the learning. It was a combination of insight, excitement, and an ability to re-create the teacher's own learning experiences. A good facilitator, one who really knows how to open up a dialogue with trainees, is also an example of the kind of interactivity Allen says is necessary to make multimedia training sing.

But can you really have that kind of dialogue with a computer? Jurgensen of McDonnell Douglas says yes — but creating such an environment is hard work. "A lot of it has to do with [designers'] fundamental understanding of how they deal with students in a class," he says.

Like an in-depth task analysis, it starts with getting an excellent classroom instructor to document what she does in the classroom. You have to try to rebuild every kind of interaction the instructor initiates. The designers "actually go through and almost build a knowledge model of what the instructor would do in each case and plan for it," explains Jurgensen. This is a long and arduous process, he says, but once it's done it's awesome: It seems to the students that the program is almost reading their minds. That is essentially what you're trying to do, says Jurgensen.

Seafirst's Ashmun agrees. "You've got to think all those questions through ahead of time. You've got to think of how many ways the learners can screw up," he says.

Because of the complexity, and because multimedia development requires several different skill sets — computer skills, video skills, instructional design skills and more — many multimedia training projects incorporate a whole team of people into the development process. Consultant King is an advocate of the team approach, but he concedes that it does call for still another crucial skill set: management ability. The manager of a multimedia project team has to be very good, he says, because the people involved probably aren't used to working together. Most instructional designers, for example, don't work with video editors or technical-authoring experts in the normal course of putting together a training program.

Not everyone agrees, however, that a team of developers is necessary when assembling a multimedia-training project. Says Allen: "One can immediately assume that you need a large team to develop a product. If you find talented, inspired people, those teams can be pretty small. And in many cases an individual can do it."

Allen worries that if the project involves too many people, a management-by-committee mentality will prevent the project from breaking out of traditional courseware-design paradigms. AT&T's Keiles works in a team to develop multimedia training, but she, too, concedes that even with all the technical expertise she could ask for, the core of a multimedia team is still one person with one good idea.

There is, however, a camp that suggests that questions of team vs. individual development or instructional design skills vs. computer skills are almost beside the point. According to this school of thought, multimedia is so new, so revolutionary, and so unlike anything we've ever known that we are all, quite frankly, in over our heads.

"This stuff with interactive multimedia is really new for humans," says Ron Sauers, a member of the technical staff at AT&T's Bell Laboratories in Murray Hill, NJ. It's not something that can be "studied" in the usual sense, he suggests. Developing it is like wandering into a new frontier. He draws an analogy to writing: The only way to get good at writing is to keep writing; with any luck, you'll improve along the way.

So too with multimedia, Sauers says. Grab it, learn it, build it, and you

might learn something about the medium as you go. "What do we really know how to do," he asks, "in this godlike arena where we get to control other humans' perception of reality?"

Keiles, too, waxes philosophical about what multimedia really is: "Multimedia is not art. It's more than art. It's art that is perceived as knowledge."

"Grab it, learn it, build it, and you might learn something about the medium as you go."

Did We Forget to Mention?

Why would you bother with learning authoring systems and developing multimedia courseware in the first place? We saved the question for last only because the case histories and research over the years have proven again and again that interactive, self-paced training *can* save money, save trainees' time away from the job, increase retention of the material learned, and promote world peace. Well, maybe not that last one.

Nevertheless, when it's done right, multimedia training can be a very cost-effective way to go. A quick look at this month's cover story may suggest the primary reason we are seeing a groundswell of interest in the idea of delivering training via computer.

"You almost can't afford not to do this," says Seafirst's Ashmun. "You can put a lot of education on a desktop at a very attractive price. To not do it means you're spending a ton of extra money. I mean, you better have a good reason why you're not doing it."

Ashmun admits he is a booster of multimedia; he *likes* the stuff. "But quite honestly," he says, "this is a bank

and I had to sell the dollar side of this. It was a big issue in cutting out travel expenses."

Then there is the future to think about. It's generally agreed that somewhere down the line, authoring software will converge with object-oriented programming (OOP), a current hot button in the computer industry. The idea behind OOP is to bring the realm of computer programming down to the average user, so anyone who can use a computer can begin to assemble his own programs. Instead of learning chains of cryptic computer code, you will be able to build a computer program by connecting a series of icons or pictures, each of which represents a programming subroutine. Assemble the pictures, and Eureka! You've built a computer program. Microsoft's Visual Basic is one of the first stabs at object-oriented programming to hit the mass market.

Some argue that authoring software is the nearest thing we have to a current example of what OOP will someday accomplish. If so, trainers who already know how to author may actually be out on the frontier of computer software advances.

Be that as it may, those who already know how to use authoring systems universally agree that the rest of the training world will be forced to follow their lead. Says editor Hall, "I can't think of any trainers who, in terms of their own career planning, would not want to get up to speed on an authoring program and be familiar with the technology."

The argument most often advanced is that even if you don't have to sit down and do the actual assembly of your department's multimedia training, you must be able to communicate with those who do in terms they can understand. Learning an authoring package is a first step toward that kind of communication.

NEEDS ANALYSIS

Concept in Search of Content

BY RON ZEMKE

The concept of training needs analysis is being subjected to new scrutiny these days. In the textbooks and journals of the late 1950s and early 1960s, trainers were routinely advised that a needs analysis was simply a finding out of what is going on now and a matching of this against what should go on, both now and in the future. The gap between the two gave clues to the amount and kind of training needed.

In a very simple work world, one where jobs are completely and accurately defined and described, where they remain stable for long periods of time, and where job performance is carefully and frequently measured, such guidance may be sufficient. Write when you find that sort of world. For most trainers, reality is jobs so undefined or ill-defined only a personnel rep could love them. It's a world where job details and procedures, indeed whole jobs, transmogrify overnight; where job performance, if evaluated at all, is evaluated in terms so behaviorally coarse as to shed scarce light on the idealized kinds of data the ancient definitions request.

In addition to the problems of finding actual and ideal performances to compare for "gaps," today's trainer is acutely aware of the problems of causation a needs analysis must be prepared to deal with. Work by the likes of Thomas F. Gilbert, Geary A. Rummler and Robert F. Mager has caused the scales to fall from most trainers' eyes. The "gaps" between actual and desired job performance can come from a myriad of potential causes. Lack of skill and knowledge are but two.

Today's trainers know that at the very least they must look at such diverse factors as organizational climate, job design, performance feedback, performance consequences and work group politics if they are to avoid misprescribing training as a remedy. What most contemporary trainers picture when they hear the term *training needs analysis* is, at the very least, what Rummler calls a *performance audit:* "A framework for viewing human performance problems and a set of procedures for systematically determining the worth of correcting the problem, finding the causes of the problem, and designing solutions to the problem."

The key word here is *framework*, which is close in contextual meaning to words like *model* and *theory*. It has become increasingly apparent that a needs analysis is less a common-sense problem analysis exercise and more a form of applied research; a structured investigation aimed at finding the significant human-factors components of important organizational performance problems and determining the primary cause or causes of those human performance problems. By definition, the needs analyst has become an individual with a model or theory of how and why people behave as they do who mucks about looking at real-world problems through the prism of that model or theory. The needs analyst or performance auditor is both an impartial and biased observer — a change agent concerned at once with competence, performance, worth and value. The needs analyst is simultaneously concerned with the organization and with people, as well as the dynamic tension of both constituencies' needs.

Needs Analysis Tools

As the philosophy of needs analysis has deepened and broadened, the tools and tactics have been refined. The practice today is less that of common sense and more of applied research, the tools a growing interdisciplinary amalgam. In the past, a survey asking managers to guess how many of their people could use a time management course was considered pretty state of the art. Today it is considered quaint. Survey technology has become a computer-based science and few would ever again rely on any single measurement technique as the basis for making a training investment. The stakes are too high.

Dr. John W. Gunkler has noted that there are an amazing number of needs analysis procedures and techniques cited in the literature today. He sees a taxonomy of three distinct types:

- **Type 0** – Pseudo needs assessment procedures
- **Type I** – Primary data source procedures
- **Type II** – Secondary data source procedures

Under **Type 0** he places market research, consumer demand analysis and educational goal setting. **Type-I** techniques are of two subtypes: those procedures that collect data about and from the target population, and those procedures that collect data about the target population from another population. In the former subtype we would find behavioral observations of and interviews with performers in the target population. Procedures in the second subtype would be surveys of and interviews with supervisors or managers of the target population.

Type-II procedures are composed of analysis and interpretation of data *about* the population, and analysis and interpretation of data about previous "treatments." An example of the former would be a Yankelovich-type public opinion study of today's worker. The latter might be an analysis of the courses and grades of people like those for whom we are going to be designing training. Gunkler points out that none of these tools and procedures are unconditionally the best way to do a needs analysis. The trick, he says, is to apply the right tool to the right problem at the right time in the right way.

Dr. John J. Leach points out that the added care and precision being brought to bear on the conduct of training needs assessment is really to help us avoid the common errors of the past, among them:

- failing to distinguish between wants and needs.
- uncritical acceptance of management statement of needs.
- failing to correlate needs with organizational plans and objectives.
- assuming all needs can be met through training.
- underutilizing needs in program selection and development.
- depending on intuition and the literature to explain the meaning of expressed or demonstrated need.
- the tendency of needs assessment to be reactive rather than future-oriented.

Dr. Michael Scriven, an education evaluation specialist, has pointed out that as resources become scarce, it becomes more and more important to be sure that those resources are going where they are most needed and are being used in the best possible manner. By turning more of our attention to the matter of careful needs analysis — in essence the evaluation of what needs to be done — we increase the chances that we will not only be doing good training, but that we will be doing training for good and justifiable reasons.

Notes:

NEUROLINGUISTIC PROGRAMMING

A Second Look at NLP

BY MARILYN DARLING

Just when you thought you'd heard the end of the subject, one more seemingly normal acquaintance becomes enamored with Neuro-Linguistic Programming — NLP as it is known to those who love and hate it. Some of its adherents can remind you of cult worshippers. As soon as you mention those three magic letters, their eyes brighten, color flows into their cheeks and you know that if you stick around, it could turn into a very long evening.

NLP. It's been associated with everything from fixing a jury to fire-walking. What is it that gets otherwise normal people so excited? If you ask believers about it, you're likely to get odd descriptions of how people's faces change color several times a minute, or baffling claims about how you can divine a person's thoughts from the way she moves her eyes. You may hear stories, told with a sense of mystic awe, about Richard Bandler and John Grinder, who developed NLP in their mountain hideaways in Santa Cruz, CA: how they can cure a phobia in 10 minutes just by touching people at exactly the right moment.

Or, worse, the NLP enthusiast may ask you a ridiculous question like, "How do you *know* how to spell your name?"

And then he'll *watch* you.

NLP has been evolving since the mid-1970s. Unfortunately, practitioners and fans sometimes get so wrapped up in the tricks and techniques — eye movements, hypnosis, gaining rapport and such — that they communicate (and maybe understand) fewer and fewer of the underlying theories and discoveries that lend NLP its potential value. This leaves most of us without a frame of reference to understand and evaluate it. With NLP, it's tough to become an intelligent critic, let alone an informed consumer.

What, if anything, does NLP have to offer to the training and development field? This article does not include any illustrations of how to read eye movements. It won't teach you how to put anyone in a trance or how to walk over burning coals. I will try to describe how NLP came about, and how it is used — and misused — in the business context.

Modeling

Bandler and Grinder's early work was done strictly in therapeutic settings. But the communication issues and processes they uncovered often are encountered in the business setting.

While studying math and computers at Stanford University in the mid-70s, Richard Bandler became fascinated by the gestalt therapy concepts of psychologist Fritz Perls and family therapist Virginia Satir. He studied their techniques and began to hold gestalt sessions. He invited John Grinder, a professor of linguistics at the University of California, Santa Cruz, to attend some of them.

They made a deal. If Bandler could teach Grinder how to do what he did, Grinder would try to describe what Bandler was doing linguistically. From that beginning, they began to "model" communication and behavioral-change techniques using linguistics. Among the people they modeled at work were Satir, Perls and medical hypnotist Milton Erickson.

Why was modeling necessary? For the same reason that a skilled trainer who has studied an expert is often more successful at teaching the expert's skills to others. When skilled people try to explain or teach what they do, they discover that many of their skills are completely unconscious. Or they find it difficult to put into words some of the nuances that make them successful. Or they try to teach others in the way they learned, assuming that if it worked for them, it can work for everyone.

For any combination of reasons, exceptionally skilled people may be unsuccessful at passing on their gifts. Bandler and Grinder believed it possible to break down everything that makes up a "talent" into observable, describable relationships and bits of information, making it easier for others to learn the talent.

They discovered that the gifted therapists they studied were successful not so much because of any one technique that worked magically over and over, but because they had learned how to observe and listen to their clients very closely. Bandler and Grinder concluded that gifted communicators are masters at living in other people's worlds and at learning how to use people's own experiences and resources to help them change.

What sort of information were they picking up? Modern linguistics starts from the premise that "the map is not the territory." In other words, any particular way of looking at the world does not tell us everything there is to know. Because we are not the thing we observe, our "maps" have gaps in them — gaps that we often fill in ourselves in order to make sense of things by generalizing from our past experiences. This *distorts* our maps of the world.

For example, for many years we used a standard IQ test as *the map* for intelligence. We observed that minorities in the United States tended to score lower on those tests than members of the majority population. It was logical to conclude that the minority population was less intelligent, as a whole, than the white majority. Because of this faulty map, "genetic differences" were used for years to justify separate and unequal treatment.

Bandler and Grinder used a series of linguistic rules to develop a process they called the Meta-Model, a technique that could be used to listen for the "gaps" clients revealed in their attitudes and perceptions, and to generate a series of questions that could be asked to fill in those gaps. This technique exposed distortions and generalizations in people's attitudes and behavior — distortions that had been maintained unconsciously but were no longer useful, or were being applied in the wrong contexts.

For example, the Meta-Model could be used as follows to break a misperception. Note the focus on the specific words and phrases the "client" is using:

"My boss hates me."

"How do you know he hates you?"

"Because every time I make a suggestion, he looks at the ground and mumbles something."

"Every time?"

"Well, at least recently."

"How recently?"

"Oh, say the past two weeks."

"Did you know that he's been under the gun for the past couple of weeks to submit next year's budget?"

"No, I didn't."

"When you look down at the ground and mumble when someone makes a suggestion to you, does it always mean you hate them?"

"No, I guess not."

"The next time that happens, why don't you ask him if it would be better to talk about your idea at a different time and see if he takes you up on it."

As they refined their ability to codify client experiences more precisely using spoken language, Bandler and Grinder began to look for other sources of information based on non-verbal behavior, including visual clues (eye movements, changes in skin color, breathing, muscle tension) and auditory clues (pitch, volume, pace). They claimed that these techniques, pulled together, helped explain how expert therapists were able to gather a staggering amount of information about clients.

Knowing what their experts saw and heard helped Bandler and Grinder establish a framework — which could be taught — for how interventions were selected or modified for each client.

Many, if not most, of the information techniques that make up NLP are not unique to NLP, and have not been billed as such — at least not by Bandler and Grinder. Because a number of techniques have been modeled directly from Erickson, Satir, Perls and many others, experienced therapists, trainers and consultants may recognize the ideas of their favorite schools of thought being described within the NLP context. Other techniques are not discouraged in NLP, they are valued. What NLP *tries* to do is test and remove any inappropriate limitations, so that the core ideas can be applied in any situations where they would be useful.

Quick Change Artists

The possibilities sound wonderful: a clearer understanding of goals, a deeper, more complete perception of the people around us, and the ability to teach "unteachable" skills.

So what's the problem? Because I've observed NLP from a distance for several years, it strikes me that for a system of thought that appears useful to so many fields in so many ways, NLP hasn't lived up to its claims. There should be no phobias left. Everyone should have perfect pitch. Most, if not all, of the world's ills should have been vanquished by now.

I think one of NLP's biggest weaknesses is that Bandler and Grinder — as well as many of their students — show an unnerving tendency to overstate their case. They have made bold and sometimes unsubstantiated claims — phobia cures in 10 minutes,

---

A MINI GLOSSARY

BY MARILYN DARLING

NLP has "stolen" many ideas from the fields of linguistics and cybernetics. Some examples:

Nominalized experience. "Nominalization" is a linguistic term that refers to turning a process into a name or an event. Once a process is named, it can be bound and categorized. Saying, "I have a *fear* of high places," serves to bundle together a group of sensations that result from certain perceptions and memories into a thing that exists on its own. "Attitude," "talent," "intention" and "phobia" are all words we use to compartmentalize our experience into a sort of shorthand as a way to understand and talk about it.

Unfortunately, two things happen when we name or "nominalize" our experiences. First, listeners understand the words we use based not on our experience, but on theirs. Second, once the experience "exists" on its own, it is seen as somehow separate from us and inaccessible to change. NLP practitioners try to bring nominalizations back into direct experience so that the original experiences or processes can be examined more closely and, if a conflict exists, modified or eliminated.

Ecology and well-formed outcomes. Within the context of NLP, human beings are viewed as "ecological systems." The concept of ecology is integral to the field of cybernetics — the study of systems. When a change happens in one part of the system, it affects other parts as well. This is what people mean when they caution, "Be careful what you wish for because your wish may come true."

Changes produce side effects. People quit smoking and gain 20 pounds. I know a man who attended a poorly run assertiveness training seminar only to find that the result of his "new" self was increased tension headaches and the loss of several close friends. He had no contextual cues as to when *not* to be assertive.

Ideally, NLP practitioners can accurately predict what side effects a change might precipitate because they gather more specific information about how a client's internal systems function now, and because they help the client define a very specific objective or outcome. They can actually observe, test for and mitigate unintended changes.

The law of requisite variety. This law of the field of cybernetics states that the element in a system that exhibits the greatest variety of behavior is the controlling factor in the system. In the realm of human communication, the law holds that the person who demonstrates the most flexibility — the largest repertoire of options in response to a given situation — is the person likely to control or be successful in that situation.

As Bandler and Grinder put it, "When what you're doing isn't working, try almost anything else until you get the outcome you're looking for." This could be called the Golden Rule of NLP. The point is that when speaking English to someone who doesn't understand the language, yelling the same thing louder will not get your point across. There are a few implications in that one for training, aren't there?

---

lifelong perfect pitch, etc. And they repeat mythic tales of power and wonder. I remember Bandler and Grinder announcing at one point that they were learning how to walk through walls — or at least how to make large groups of people believe they saw them do it.

If such claims were true, NLP should be universally acknowledged as one of the century's greatest discoveries. In fact, it languishes in relative obscurity, largely ignored by the academic and business worlds.

The real crime here is against one of NLP's own guiding principles: "Know thine audience." Outrageous claims drive people away in hordes (Tony Robbins' trendy NLP-based fire-walking seminars seem to be an exception, at least so far). Concentrating on building a reputation through example and keeping NLP's basic premises in mind would do a lot to give the techniques the hearing they deserve.

The philosophy espoused by NLP is a challenge. Not all "certified practitioners" have been able to "get it." It is relatively easy to memorize techniques, even to become skilled enough at a particular "trick" to impress people. But it takes time, effort and dedication to test and break deeply ingrained limitations. The limitations and ulterior motives of some practitioners have been translated into the NLP message.

Take rigidity, for example. It's possible for NLP to become as rigid as any other tool because of a trainer's need to be "right." In fact, as NLP gets passed down through the generations, as it were, its techniques are becoming compartmentalized — treated rather like a cookbook of change, which on a creativity scale of one to 10 would rate somewhere below zero. The techniques become inflexible and unadaptable as a result.

There is now a prescribed "phobia cure" which is different in some concrete way from the "insomnia cure." The methods often are taught in a step-by-step process without the framework that allows them to be used creatively in other situations.

Bandler and Grinder warned their students not to let any technique take on a life of its own. Each one should always be evaluated for its usefulness in effecting a desired change. Yet novices can stumble into a cookbook course in NLP and end up learning some particular set of techniques that

may or may not be applicable to their needs. They are likely to walk away slightly bewildered and totally unimpressed.

Compounding the problem is a jargon jungle that gets darker and denser with each new technique. "Four-tuples," "Meta-Model," "swish patterns," "submodalities" and, indeed, "Neuro-Linguistic Programming" itself, are terms that trip lightly off the tongues of NLP practitioners. While some of them serve as useful shorthand, they also create a Berlin Wall between the learned and the curious.

Gifted communicators are masters at living in other people's worlds.

For these reasons (and because of people who promote NLP as a weapon to use in clawing your way to the top), NLP has moved at a snail's pace in the training and development world.

If all this doesn't scare you away, if you're still intrigued by the possibility that beneath the manure there lies a pony, then we should answer the question, "How might I use NLP in training and development?"

Change

Two of the most obvious uses to which NLP can be put in business are: 1) creating personal and group change and, 2) discovering and teaching the skills of various experts.

Although NLP grew from therapeutic soil, advocates argue that its change process is equally applicable to evaluating and facilitating group dynamics, to training (especially when an organizational change is involved) or to self-development. Here is a bare-bones outline of an NLP approach to the task of creating change in a group environment.

1. *What exactly is the change desired?* Define precisely the goal a group or business wants to reach. Define it in terms of how it will look and feel. Define the goal so that its soundness can be tested, so group members will be motivated to reach it, and so they'll know when and if they've arrived.

2. *What's stopping them?* Determine exactly when the group members' internal limits (defined as infor-

mation, actions or beliefs that demonstrate discrepancies between their "map" and the actual territory) get in the way of their desired actions, objectives or growth.

3. *What purpose do these limits serve and how are they applied?* Find out why the limits are there and what decisions and actions they affect.

4. *What works and when?* What should be tossed out? Break down the limitations into valid and invalid discriminations, based on their value in facilitating action or growth in particular contexts.

5. *What would work better, and when should it be used?* For information, actions or beliefs that you find to be invalid, substitute (using any of a variety of techniques) different information, a different viewpoint or a different way of getting something done.

6. *On the whole, does the group function better as a result of this change effort?* Test the group's new information, actions or beliefs to make sure they are working to the group's benefit in the proper situations, and that no unanticipated changes have been made that might harm the group's ability to function in other areas (referred to as an "ecological check").

The NLP change process focuses on getting to a desired objective by removing all obstacles, including limiting perceptions.

But while this may look like a fairly straightforward procedure — easy to talk about, if not easy to *do* — there is no right way to get from step one to step six. Bandler and Grinder would say, "If it works (and it doesn't upset the ecology of the system) use it." NLP techniques add value to the process by fine-tuning the group members' observation skills and by teaching them how to respond with flexibility to the situation.

Skills

The process of discovering and teaching unique skills offers some of the most exciting potential for using NLP in business. The best teachers a company could ever hire, in terms of passing on skills that are uniquely suited to its business objectives and environment, are on the company's payroll already.

Unfortunately, top performers seldom have the time or the ability to teach others what they know; at least, they rarely seem to make efficient and effective teachers. NLP's claim is that a skilled practitioner can work with (or "model") top performers to understand the conscious and unconscious elements of the skills that make them successful — and can teach those skills to others.

NLP practitioners are using these modeling skills across the country to teach such talents as singing, composing, speed-reading, creative writing and leadership. By using NLP skills, they say, people inside your company can teach things like project management, public speaking or sales and customer service — and do it as well as, or better than, an outside consultant.

The basic NLP skills that are fundamental to understanding individual and group learning processes also can be applied to any training process. These skills simply ensure that the "message sent" is the "message received" and that the style trainers use to present the material meets the learning needs of the audience. Obviously neither of those objectives is by any means unique to NLP. NLP just offers a certain approach to achieving them.

Is It Manipulative?

Can NLP techniques be used to manipulate people to do something against their best interests? Sure. More than once? Less likely. Can the same be said of a great many other psychological techniques? Of course.

We are all persuasive to some degree. Ministers are some of the most persuasive people I know. And as the Jim and Tammy Bakker debacle demonstrated, their persuasiveness can be used for all sorts of ends. But as subsequent events also demonstrated, what goes around comes around.

The concept of a person's or a group's *ecology* — its integrity as a system — is considered by ethical NLP practitioners to be a critical aspect of any change or training effort. If the ecology is not honored, the change won't stick. It's like sales: The most successful salespeople, over the long run, are those who understand and satisfy *all* of their customers' needs.

What it comes down to is that like so many skills and tools, NLP can be used for many different purposes — some helpful, others limiting and manipulative. Should we throw out NLP because it can be used for the latter? NLP's basic philosophy is both sound and exciting in what it can offer us as a basis for learning and change.

But buyer beware. NLP certification, though conceived with good intentions, does not guarantee a thing. When you go shopping for an NLP expert, you'll have to rely on your own judgment.

Notes:

Training and OD: Separated at Birth?

BY ALLISON ROSSETT

On an airplane somewhere between Denver and San Diego, an executive mused about why his training people and his organization development people couldn't seem to work together. He thought he was encouraging collaboration, but what he saw instead was foot-dragging.

"Is it something about our organization?" he wondered. "Is it something I'm doing? Is it the individuals involved? Or is this typical?" His questions forced me to admit that I think a gulf indeed exists between training and organization development (OD), at least more typically than not.

I first noticed the chasm more than a decade ago. During a consulting project at a manufacturing company, the training staff complained at length about a manager they considered unreasonable. Without exception, they attributed her faults to her background in OD.

Not long after, I suggested to a group of colleagues that we all attend an American Society for Training and Development (ASTD) luncheon presentation on the topic of organization development. Several of my training associates chose to pass, observing that OD wasn't particularly relevant to training.

Yet another example presented itself about five years later. I was teaching a class on needs assessment for some training professionals in a computer company. One of the messages was that the data one gathers in assessing a performance problem will often point to solutions other than training — solutions like team-building, culture change, strategy align-ment or feedback systems. One gentleman objected, arguing pretty much as follows: "I have a problem with this because we don't know about all those approaches. We aren't the people who handle any of that. We don't work with them. They aren't even located anywhere near us." There were nods all around. In a room with about 30 managers, nobody disagreed.

Such has been my experience of the relationship between the training world and the OD world. So the phone call from Sandy Quesada not long ago came as a surprise. Quesada was then a training manager at Amoco Corp. in Houston. She remembered that I'd been tracking the peculiarities between training and organization development, and wanted to know if I'd play a role in getting Amoco's training and OD units to work together more closely. (Didn't I think that their shared commitment to analysis might be a good place to start?) Within the month, someone at another company, this time in financial services, called to chat about a similar initiative.

Suddenly people are interested in collaboration between training and organization development. Why now? Maybe it's the quality movement with its belief in cross-functionality. Maybe there's growing recognition that what counts is results, and that business results depend upon alignment between what people are taught and what organizations actually practice and applaud. Maybe it's a newfound inclination to use systematic assessments to define solutions to performance problems. Maybe it's renewed customer focus. Maybe "performance technology" is finally shifting from idea to reality. Or maybe it's the collective impact of years of wasted opportunities. Whatever the causes, there is growing enthusiasm for aligning OD and training.

How might we go about that?

What They Do

Just what is organization development? Plenty of definitions can be found among practitioners and in the literature. (Lee Bolman and Terrence Deal's *Reframing Organizations* and Michael Harrison's *Diagnosing Organizations* are two favorite sources.) But the only way to achieve much agreement on a single definition is to sketch very broadly and, consequently, not very usefully: OD involves attention to diagnosis, strategy, roles, systems, processes and measurements that enable organizations and people to achieve their goals.

A more useful question is: What do OD professionals do? Here we can draw a more robust picture. Some create high-commitment work teams, an effort that often involves rethinking leadership and power relationships. Others participate in projects that transform organizational structures, beliefs, values, cultures and systems. OD people use a wide array of interventions, including leadership development, team-building, organizational design, culture change, strategic planning, facilitation of meetings and groups, conflict resolution, enhanced participation programs and performance management.

What, then, is training? *Webster's* defines it this way: ". . . to make a person or animal efficient in some activity by instruction and repeated practice . . . ." Somehow that fails to capture the richness of the field I know and love.

So what do trainers do? Most analyze needs. Some build training courses. Others deliver courses. Some coordinate people and facilities. Many create instructor-led programs; some create self-study programs in print and technology-based formats. Trainers conduct evaluations, create job aids and electronic performance support systems, build multimedia products, serve as performance consultants, select and coordinate training vendors, coach employees in the workplace, establish on-the-job development programs and more.

Siblings . . .

Trouble is, every time I assign an activity to training or to organization development, I can think of an example that contradicts the classification — a training manager whose life is devoted to team-building or an OD person who is a skilled course developer or instructor. In many ways, training and OD professionals are siblings:

Both traffic in change. Training and OD practitioners agree that they have responsibility for growing their people and organizations, for playing significant roles in transformation. Amoco has now established an entity called the Organizational Capability Group (OCG), charged with coordinating efforts to bring about corporate change. Training and organization development are but two of many specialized units formally linked to enhance initiatives aimed at performance improvement. Says Katie Smith, practice area leader for instructional systems development (ISD) at Amoco: "When it first happened, I didn't have a clue about how it could work. Since OCG, many of our OD consultants are now in long-term productive relationships with a single client, and they are right there and positioned to leverage training and the other OCG service units."

Both are driven by clients' needs for improved performance. Whether the request is for a course on Lotus Notes or a curriculum to update the skills of auditors or assistance with strategic planning, training and OD professionals perceive themselves as responding to and serving their customers' articulated requirements.

Both acknowledge responsibility for customer education and business partnership. While being responsive to the needs that customers express, most trainers and OD people agree to some responsibility for developing the customer's understanding of performance improvement and, therefore, the accuracy of customers' perceptions of their own needs. In other words, professionals in both fields believe that the customer is not always right. More, they believe that ethical practice often forbids giving customers exactly what they ask for. Instead, the professional is supposed to probe and study the nature of the performance problem, and sometimes to disagree with the customer's proposed solution. ("Yes, I know you want a team-building course, but the problem here seems to be fuzzy goals, not poor teamwork.") As Jeff Lickson of The Consortium, a Houston consulting firm, puts it, both trainers and OD specialists are supposed to "Just say whoa" to hasty requests.

Both are committed to assessment and measurement. OD and training professionals espouse allegiance to searching analyses, continuous measurement, and basing their recommendations on solid data. Most trainers and OD people would hesitate to admit that they based an intervention on a hunch, or on a personal preference (for multimedia or visioning or whatever), or because the boss likes it. Practitioners in both groups take pride in diagnosis. There are, of course, cases that demonstrate that this is sometimes more a goal than a description of actual practice.

> "We don't know about all those approaches. We aren't the people who handle any of that. We don't work with them."

Both are committed to systematic approaches. Embedded in the literature and customs of both groups is a demand that practitioners go about their business systematically instead of "winging it." They are supposed to use defined processes and orderly approaches. They should have clearly articulated goals. Their activity should be data-driven.

In addition, another mantra is enjoying rekindled allegiance — systems thinking. The systems paradigm commits the practitioner to analyzing causes, using these root causes to define strategies, and establishing cross-functional and wholistic approaches to improve performance. In the training world, systems thinking has roots in classic books and teachings by people like Robert Mager and Joe Harless. Today, readers in both the training and OD camps are embracing works such as Peter Senge's *The Fifth Discipline: The Art and Practice of the Learning Organization* and Geary Rummler's *Improving Performance: How to Manage the White Space on the Organization Chart.*

... But Not Twins

Though there are many similarities between them, OD and training professionals tend to be keenly aware of their differences. The distinctions that follow are generalizations, valuable for the discussion they encourage, not for their application to any one setting or person:

Focus of attention. Historically, trainers have prided themselves on what they can do for individuals, while OD specialists have looked more toward the entire organization. More recently, members of both groups have been talking about the need to expand their views to encompass the work, the worker and the workplace. Though alliterative and appealing, this enlargement of perspective is far from a done deal and is complicated by the emerging importance of teams. Who serves teams? While the obvious answer is that we all do, teams present opportunities for both collaboration *and* conflict between trainers and ODers.

Nature of the customer. There is a perception that the customers associated with organization development tend to reside at higher levels in the organization. In a mixed group of training and OD professionals, one OD specialist pointed to what she saw as a difference between them: "We work with the executives and I don't think you do." While the number of exceptions to this statement is probably growing, the trainers in the room didn't disagree.

This perception doesn't encourage trust, according to Cora Pendergast, a San Diego consultant with master's degrees in both educational technology and organization development. She notes that trainers are sometimes reticent with OD people, who tend to earn more money than trainers and whose role is to assess the organization and share information with an executive.

Perception of role and power. Another perception is that OD professionals are more typically found in strategic roles while trainers labor in tactical arenas. When pressed on this, both sides do some breast-beating, with trainers acknowledging the need to be more strategic, and OD people admiring the trainers' tangible tactical successes and the customer appreciation that comes from them.

An incident during a class on how to conduct a needs assessment illustrated how the differences in perspectives can play out. The group was working on a case in which an executive sought help with what was initially described as "messed up performance appraisals." We talked for 15 minutes or so about diagnostic strategies to ferret out the nature of the problems with the appraisals, and how to determine a good solution. We were, I thought, appropriately skeptical about training as the sole solution to this appraisal problem. But then an OD specialist in the class challenged our complacency: "I think we're jumping into fixing the appraisals too quickly. Before we look at randomly pulled appraisals and model appraisals, and before we interview supervisors and so on, shouldn't we be talking to management about whether the organization ought to reconsider its approaches to hierarchy, appraisal and performance review? You're assuming the leadership knows what it's doing with its performance management strategy." And we were. Few trainers are naturally inclined to challenge the basic assumptions underlying organizational practices, to push hard at the wisdom of a request, or to provide leadership in discussions of strategy and alignment. OD people are more likely to describe that as their role.

Where we live. At Amoco and elsewhere, most organization development consultants are entrenched in long-term relationships with clients, while training professionals tend to be peripatetic, engaging in more and shorter interventions for several corporate units. One effect of this is that trainers may spend more of their time on project management and documentation, since unfamiliar clients are more likely to demand a formal rationale for any intervention and to insist on seeing some concrete evidence of success. The positive side is that these demands encourage the kind of analysis and measurement that trainers say they want to do anyway.

Areas of comfort. Suppose a needs assessment reveals that the main cause of a department's performance problem is that its manager is inconsistent and capricious. How comfortable are you about going where that data wants to take you? If you're a trainer, the answer probably is, not very. This is a rather sweeping generalization, but more OD professionals than trainers are at ease in the realm of conflict, climate and feelings.

Computer-training manager Dawn Hall of Hunter Industries in San Marcos, CA, is forthright about it. "I didn't know what organization devel-

opers did," she says, "so I couldn't figure out how to coordinate with them. Now I'm getting them involved in conflict resolution and team facilitation. They're better at it than I am." Consultant Pendergast agrees, noting that OD specialists "take more interest in personal change and attitude, while trainers tend to focus more between the ears, more on skills acquisition."

Event vs. process orientation. While both training and OD professionals get tagged with reputations for analysis paralysis, OD people suffer much more from that image. Valid or not, the perception is that ODers love process and resist closure. Trainers, on the other hand, get credit for consummating their projects. But here's the rub: These trainers are then charged with being satisfied with educational events instead of pursuing the more elusive but higher-value systems fixes.

Some Marriages

The executive on the airplane isn't the only leader interested in improving the relationship between training and organization development. Now, finally, some companies are moving to blur conventional distinctions between the two. Like Amoco, they see it as a strategy for performance improvement.

Both trainers and OD specialists are supposed to "Just say whoa" to hasty requests.

Andersen Consulting Education. This St. Charles, IL-based group has received national awards for its commitment to training. But where once Andersen Consulting hired primarily instructional designers and technologists, the company now makes sure to select some people with formal training and experience in organizational design and strategic planning. It's a business decision, says Larry Silvey, a partner and managing director at Andersen; the firm isn't doing education for education's sake. The purposes are change, performance improvement and business outcomes. For that, Andersen needs a bigger and more cross-functional tool kit.

AT&T Universal Card Service. Linda

Swanson, vice president of human resources at this 1992 Baldrige Award-winning company, says her unit is shifting to a more consultative role, where OD people, human resources people and trainers perceive themselves first and foremost as business partners to each other and their customers. Bob O'Neal, director of training at Jacksonville, FL-based UCS, puts it like this: "In the past, training would do performance analyses and come up with training and nontraining solutions. Then we'd beg to put solution systems in place. The new organization formalizes all this."

The new collaborative goals are reinforced by the measurements the HR unit now uses to gauge its success. Instead of counting bodies in classes or the number of team-facilitation gigs it runs, the new organization will be judged by its ability to contribute to business results. O'Neal is laboring to link services to real problems in the organization and then to measure the improvements that occur.

The United States Coast Guard. The Coast Guard has been moving in this direction for several years, as indicated by the "Training Division's" name change to the Training and Performance Improvement Division. According to Lt. Cmdr. Terry Bickham, commanding officer of the Pacific Area Training Team, this is much more than a change in the letterhead. In July 1994, the Coast Guard commandant issued the equivalent of an executive order (COMDTINST 1500.23) articulating a new philosophy of training, education and development. The document recognizes the limitations of training without root-cause analysis and presses the organization toward systemic solutions. An attachment to the actual Coast Guard document demonstrates a much broader philosophy of performance, referring to a wide array of "job performance influences," like job aids, achievable criteria, policy, feedback, worthy tasks, confidence, strong leadership, timely training, coaching and more. The order ensures that trainers and OD specialists will cooperate in the effort, no matter their place in the organizational hierarchy.

Bickham cites the topic of leadership as a recent success. Historically, the Coast Guard offered formal leadership training in several locations and formats, each associated with the rank or enlistment status of trainees. Henceforth, all offerings, including those provided to midlevel enlisted people, will occur at the Coast Guard Academy in New London, CT. The idea of bringing together many levels of Coast Guard people at the academy represents a significant cultural change, says Bickham. "It says very strong things about the importance of leadership in our organization, top to bottom. It was the right thing to do, and it wouldn't have happened without the big-picture collaboration of trainers and organizational developers."

Aligning Training and OD

The relationship between training and organization development may be evolving, but it's certainly not happening everywhere. When pressed to describe the connection between training and OD in his company, a training executive at a large technology firm dropped his voice and admitted to managing it so that he and his people "didn't bump into the organizational development group." This executive is a strong advocate of shifting training's focus away from educational events and toward systemic solutions based on good needs assessments, and he was slightly embarrassed about the gulf between his people and the OD unit. He acknowledged the oddity of the rift, given his belief in cross-functional performance support, but he hadn't done anything about moving toward either acquaintance or alliance.

Situations like that serve neither the professionals nor their companies. Here are some suggested strategies for enhancing collaboration between OD and training:

• *Capitalize on high-level sponsorship.* This article began with an executive — not a trainer or an OD person but a client of both functions — who sat on an airplane and wondered why the two didn't collaborate. It was the Coast Guard commandant, not someone from training or OD, who could employ a directive to make collaboration the rule rather than an exception.

• *Develop high-level sponsorship.* If it doesn't exist, try to create it. If your organization's leaders are unaware of the possibilities, educate them. Cite examples of the cynicism generated when employees are trotted off to classes that have nothing to do with the key behaviors the organization really desires or rewards. Nearly every company has examples of unsupported training events. You'll likely have to look no further than mandated sessions in telephone skills, continuous process improvement, diversity or teamwork.

• *Demonstrate the fit with existing and emerging initiatives.* Is a quality-improvement drive under way at your company? That's a natural. So is the recent interest in "the learning organization." Peter Senge in *The Fifth Discipline* and David Garvin in a 1993 article on organizational learning in the *Harvard Business Review* both lament the cost of organizational boundaries and cheer the benefits derived from more permeable membranes. General Electric CEO Jack Welch identifies "boundarylessness" as a key tenet of GE's corporate strategy.

• *Create pilot collaborations.* Before enacting anything resembling formal reorganization, try some pilot projects. Measure their impact. Publicize the business results they achieve. Establish teams that include OD and training people, and assign them to help key clients solve performance problems. Create ad hoc and visiting relationships so that familiarity can encourage alliances.

• *Encourage people in each specialty to learn more about the other.* Focus on the commonalities as well as the differences. Use sample requests for training or OD assistance as the basis for discussion about similar and distinct perspectives and approaches. Together, read and discuss the work of Edgar Schein, Chris Argyris, Rosabeth Moss Kanter, M. David Merrill and Roger Schank.

• *Analyze what hinders collaboration.* There are often incentives that create distance and even competition between the two service units. Recognize the rivalry that can emerge in bill-able contexts, when both groups are trying to achieve their target percentages or recover their costs. Examine the history of the relationship. Work with the leadership of the two specializations to address these obstacles and transcend turf battles.

Drawing Pictures

The fact that it is hard to make any case at all *against* building alliances between training and organization development doesn't mean that those alliances are easy to bring about. Many trainers are genuinely sold on the idea of broader analyses and examining nontraining solutions to performance problems, but that doesn't necessarily inspire them to reach out to OD specialists. The Coast Guard, Amoco, AT&T's UCS unit and Andersen, large organizations all, have chosen to bring specialized people together in structured and ad hoc ways. In other places, the trend is toward expanding the individual training professional's repertoire. One friend in government suggests that this individual-development strategy occurs because partnerships are perceived as too hard to effect.

OD and training are professions in transition, buffeted by shifts in priorities regarding empowerment, organizational structure, and specialization vs. generalization. The only certainty is management's desire for higher quality, lower costs, faster cycle times, and overall performance improvement. Eventually, these critical goals will precipitate more leveraging of training and OD through means narrow and grand, formal and informal.

At a training conference last year in Atlanta, Amoco's Quesada and I asked about 100 people to draw a graphic picture of the relationship between training and OD in their organizations. We got circles. We got squares. We got smiley faces and frowning faces. We got lots of white space. What we didn't get much of was overlap, proximity and arrows. What kind of picture would you draw?

Can You Outsource Your Brain?

BY MARC HEQUET

Can you outsource your brain? If training departments constitute the gray matter of the corporate organism, that's the question some face as companies downsize and outsource more and more of the functions that once were regarded as in-house musts.

In 1988, Corning Inc. cut a deal with College Center of the Finger Lakes (CCFL) under which CCFL delivers and administers a large share of the company's training, freeing Corning's internal training staff to focus on areas of particular strategic importance.

And in 1993, chemical giant E. I. du Pont de Nemours and Co. of Wilmington, DE, and The Forum Corp., the big Boston-based consulting firm, joined in a training partnership in which Forum acts as DuPont's corporate training function. Forum said it was talking to more prospective partners for similar pairings, hoping to sign up "one or two" in the subsequent 12 months and up to 20 in the next five years.

Why outsource the training function? The argument goes like this: A training department is permanent, embedded overhead that costs a company every minute of every day. Ideally, an outsourced function costs only when you use it. Such an arrangement is supposed to leave a company with a lower unit cost on its product and with more cash available to deploy quickly elsewhere as needed.

Companies have long turned to outside suppliers for selected training needs — bringing in an outsider to lead management-development workshops, for example. Observers suspect that this kind of thing is happening more and more. But DuPont and Corning arguably have relationships with training suppliers that are different in kind, not just in degree.

In the DuPont-Forum deal, Forum will develop and deliver courses for its partner. Twenty former DuPont trainers who now work for Forum, teaming up with other Forum consultants, will scour DuPont for business needs; develop or buy curricula not already in hand; schedule DuPont, Forum or outside instructors to teach courses; and measure the effectiveness of their training for DuPont. In short, says Forum Chairman John Humphrey, "We are their training department."

Forum won't disclose its fees or DuPont-related revenue, but says DuPont pays either on a per-day or more often on a per-project basis. In comparison, Corning pays CCFL on a per-enrollee basis, with about 7,000 employees per year attending courses that cost between $65 and $300 per person.

Forum says its DuPont deal helped boost its 1995 revenues to about $50 million. The consulting company, with 260 full-time employees and another 190 part-time, is growing at a rate of about 25 percent per year.

Corning's partnership allowed it to double its training volume and meet an ambitious corporate goal of 5 percent of employee time spent in training, without increasing staff. Outsourcing to CCFL, moreover, let it focus on courses it wanted to keep internal for their strategic leverage — including training in quality, diversity, union-management relations, partnership-building, and new employee orientation. Corning Inc. turned over 60 courses it considered less strategic to CCFL, including effective presentations, accounting, selling skills, and statistical process control.

Fear and Outsourcing

Outsourcing most certainly focuses trainers' attention. Indeed, the very word has unnerving connotations. DuPont and Forum call their arrangement "insourcing." "When you use the word 'outsourcing,' " says a training director at another company who declined to be interviewed on the record, "it strikes fear in people."

Some observers say the DuPont-Forum deal does indeed hail a new age of utilitarian pairing between business and training firms. Others predict it will prove to be merely a new wrinkle in a familiar cycle: staff up, lay off, outsource, staff up.

Clearly, many training departments have become intermediaries for outside suppliers. "Today's training organization has turned more into a brokering function," says Bill Jackson, selection and assessment services vice president with Development Dimensions International Inc. of Pittsburgh. "Forum is taking that to its next logical step."

An Ill-Tended Garden

DuPont says its partnership with Forum is about core competencies — and DuPont has decided human resources development is not a DuPont core competency.

In 1991 DuPont, deep in a period of self-examination and restructuring, found that its training organization had gotten to be like an ill-tended garden. In the Wilmington area alone, DuPont uncovered about 500 employees spending more than half their time on training and development.

Many were specialists seeking a chance to teach their specialty. "They were running around like ministers in search of a congregation," says Ty Alexander, DuPont human development, staffing and personnel relations director. Adds Steve Crawley, senior engineer and training manager for DuPont's Chambers Works specialty chemicals site in Deepwater, NJ: "It used to be, 'Here's what we offer. Take it or leave it.' "

Over a two-year period DuPont cut trainer numbers from 500 to 100 by centralizing the training function, reassigning some trainers, and giving severance packages to others. But one more step was in order. "We needed something dramatic," says Ed Trolley,

DuPont training and education manager. "It wasn't just about incremental change."

DuPont started talking with Forum in 1992, while it was shopping other training firms as well. DuPont settled on the Boston-based firm in May 1993, and signed a contract in August 1993 that took effect Jan. 1, 1994.

'Window' Shopping

Under the contract, Forum delivers all DuPont's training and development services worldwide except training for chemical plant operator mechanics (which is provided by community colleges and technical schools), and safety and diversity training, both of which DuPont has kept in-house as a part of its corporate "heritage," says Gerald Jones, Forum executive vice president and general manager of the DuPont/Forum partnership.

On the human resource development side, Forum takes over. It provides assessments for DuPont and schedules classroom instructors from Forum or from other suppliers. Buying from outside through "one window" — Forum — DuPont hopes for better-managed purchases and volume discounts. Forum promises cost savings from reduced travel and less worker downtime.

Forum has drastically cut back DuPont's curriculum, slashing its client's course catalog from 1,000 offerings to about 150. Little-attended courses went. So did courses that scored low on trainee evaluations, like one on coaching for new managers. Evaluations said the course raised awareness but provided no skills. DuPont once had 54 time-management courses. Now it has two. Once it had more than 20 writing courses. Forum kept the best two and axed the rest.

Formerly, managers were each allocated a certain amount of training for their department, and used it as they saw fit, whether they needed it or not. Now managers pay for their department's training out of their business-unit budget as an inducement to target training more carefully. "They're making an investment decision about something that's connected to their business success," says DuPont's Trolley.

Forum runs 50 or more courses per month for its big client's 23 business units. What's to keep Forum from using materials it developed for DuPont elsewhere — or even leaking DuPont proprietaries? The partners' contract spells out restrictions on what Forum can and cannot do with its curricula developed for DuPont.

The partnership keeps office in a DuPont facility in Wilmington — eating lunch with DuPonters, running into them in the hall, learning their acronym-laced language and the subtleties of their culture.

How much internal resistance have DuPonters mustered? "A fair amount," admits DuPont's Trolley. "At every tactical level, there were objections from the original training organization. It meant that organization was no longer going to do that work."

Bold Alliances?

The new arrangement places a premium on the partnership's performance. For Forum, "it says you're not going to be able to differentiate yourself on the basis of your latest leadership research," says Humphrey. "We're going to have to differentiate ourselves on the basis of, 'Can you make a difference in the client?' "

What if a big vendor made a pitch for the whole corporate training function? "We would listen to them," says US West. "It makes sense."

It may be an auspicious moment for bold alliances. Big companies are looking at every aspect of their operations. Continued downsizing may mean more outsourcing of departments, training included. More companies downsized in 1994 than the previous year, though the average reduction was smaller and came with job creation as well, according to the American Management Association's eighth annual survey of corporate downsizing. And one in four responding companies planned to downsize before the end of June 1995 — the most ever in the survey's eight-year history.

Is Internal Better?

US West, in the midst of a 9,000-job cut, says its training staff has been centralized and reduced by 40 percent. Nevertheless the conviction persists at US West that internal trainers are better for assessing, designing and delivering courses. "We believe that internal people who have been here and know the nuances of the organization are better and can get at it quicker," says Maryanne Johnson, who directs leadership and professional development centers for US West.

And yet US West has discussed major outsourcing of training. What if a supplier made a pitch for the whole corporate training function? "We would listen to them," says Johnson. "I believe vendors are undoubtedly at the beginning of a wave of strategic alliances and partnerships. It makes sense to me. I'm keeping my ear to the ground on this one."

At Northern Telecom Ltd. in Canada, an effort to make training offerings more uniform nationally began in 1989. The goal was to eliminate redundancies and ensure equity — for example, the company wanted workers in Calgary, Alberta, to get the same training opportunities as those in Ottawa. Uniformity achieved, it means that a supplier could step in and provide training nationwide without missing a stride.

Indeed, Northern Telecom says it has already heard such pitches — and declined because the supplier didn't quite measure up and didn't cover all the bases. Geographically, at least, some supplier somewhere no doubt qualifies. "It's only a matter of time before one big firm comes to us and says, 'We've got partners based wherever you do business,' " says Rod Brandvold, senior manager for executive development in Ottawa.

Too Close to the Heart?

Some trainers welcome the prospect of a major partnering, seeing it as a chance to shed grunt work and focus on corporate priorities. "I have friends who have been in the field 20 or 25 years. Their heart and soul is in this profession," says Barry Arnett, education and training strategy director at IBM in Atlanta. "A lot of them see this as by and large good, because it lets them focus on higher-order skills, the more strategic part of the job."

But many trainers are of two minds. Arnett balks at the idea of outsourcing anything as close to a company's heart as the training function. "The training arm of a company is a major change agent and is one of the key ways you can get improved human performance," he says.

Whether companies are indeed outsourcing more is hard to document. TRAINING Magazine's annual *Industry Report* shows spending for outside products and services hewing stubbornly to about 20 percent of total training budgets. Spending for off-the-shelf training packages has risen slowly but steadily since 1990, however, and spending for custom packages and outside services has shown more recent upticks.

Nearly everybody outsources some training already. A 1994 Society for Human Resource Management survey of 913 companies found that 92 percent have used an outside training source sometime in the last five years, with suppliers including private firms, industry groups, colleges and universities, and vendors of off-the-shelf packages or books.

Typically, organizations rely on a combination of inside and outside suppliers. Outsiders are more likely to be exclusive providers of training for certain types of employees. According to 1994 *Industry Report* respondents, outside suppliers are the sole source for 31 percent of training for executives, 20 percent for senior managers, and 18 percent for professionals. Those numbers have remained stable for the past five years, which argues against any broad-based outsourcing trend.

Why Not Outsource?

First Interstate Bancorp, a Los Angeles-based 13-state bank holding company, is in the midst of a 3,000-worker downsizing. The training function, however, has been relatively untouched. Indeed, says Sara White, vice president and manager of corporate training, her own staff increased by two to 14 from internal transfers.

She's wary of outsourcing too much of the training function and relying on what could be ham-handed off-the-shelf efforts by suppliers trying to solve intricate internal problems. "I would question whether it would be more cost-effective in the long run," White says.

Outside suppliers don't know the corporate culture or language, don't understand the nuances, don't know the hot buttons. Then there are the inevitable pockets of resistance. Even if a training effort seems fully supported from the top of the organization, consultants often encounter guerrilla defiance. When your responsibility is the entirety of a giant corporation, as is Forum's at DuPont, the potential for such heel-dragging multiplies enormously.

Another concern: What if an outsourced training function gradually loses its freshness, its independent judgment? What if it takes on the bureaucratic cadence of its host? "I could see it — being treated like and acting like overhead," muses DDI's Jackson. "You would have to remain intensely customer-focused."

Any training department will find a multitude of reasons not to enter such an arrangement. Some organizations use trainers for more than just training — running focus groups, for example. If you let those people go or reassign them, some internal scrambling is inevitable.

Any supplier who could deliver consistently good courses across a broad geographic area would deserve a look, acknowledges Northern Telecom's Brandvold. But it would be a long, hard look. "Personally, I suppose my reservations are the same as anyone who doesn't want to be dependent upon one supplier," Brandvold says. "I also believe there are pockets of innovation happening in training firms all over, and fear that if we line up with just one vendor they might not be as innovative as we want them to be."

Brandvold has one more concern. "We find that when we've teamed up with external designers, we are dragging them to catch up to where we are," he gripes. "If the vendors would get ahead of us, we'd use them. But it's hard for vendors to understand what's going on in a corporation unless they're living there."

Trend or Cycle?

Nevertheless, some suspect a fundamental change is afoot. That conclusion depends on whether you believe downsizing is a trend or a cycle, says IBM's Arnett. "It looks like there's some permanent downsizing going on, and if that's true then the pressure will be everywhere on corporations to keep looking for opportunities to do more with less."

But outsourcing your training department? Heaven forfend! Isn't that like outsourcing your brain? Is that any way to be a learning organization? "Learning doesn't take place in the training and development department," retorts Forum's Humphrey. "The training and development department facilitates a learning organization."

So does the DuPont story herald a relentless trend that will transform the business landscape? Or is it just another swing in a cycle of insource-outsource-insource?

Time will tell. Either way, every training manager faces a difficult decision about what learning should be kept close to the corporate heart, and how much can be turned over to a partner in a strange new mating dance.

PARETO PRINCIPLE

Why Things Aren't Fair

BY RON ZEMKE

All things being equal — they aren't. That, at least, is one way to interpret the theories of Vilfredo Pareto (1848-1923), a French-born economist and sociologist whose Italian parents fled their native country in search of political freedom. That familial backdrop presumably was what led Pareto to study the distribution of wealth in Italy instead of France, which led in turn to his listing in many references as an Italian economist and sociologist instead of a French one. So spare us the letters.

In the course of that study, he discovered, not surprisingly, that a small percentage of Italy's population controlled most of the country's wealth. Or to be absolutely precise — and exceedingly obtuse — Pareto discovered that "there is frequently an inverse relationship between the percentage of items in each of a set of subclasses and the importance of the subclasses."

Had he stopped with the simple observation that "some got it and some don't," there wouldn't be much reason to remember Pareto or his work. But as it happens, his studies of the distribution of wealth led to the development of intricate mathematical models to quantify and account for uneven distributions of all sorts of stuff.

From his studies comes Pareto's Law. In English — as opposed to math, Italian or French — Pareto's Law says that in any series of elements or variables, a small fraction of the elements account for most of the effect; you can get a lot of outcome from very little effort *if* you know where to concentrate your effort. In the workaday world, Pareto's Law — later rephrased as "the law of the vital few and the trivial many," and called

Pareto's Principle by statistical-quality-control guru Joseph M. Juran — is known colloquially as the 80/20 Rule.

It has become a popular rule of thumb that suggests such delightful clichés as: Eighty percent of the money deposited in a bank comes from 20% of the customers; 80% of the profit comes from 20% of the products; 80% of the griping comes from 20% of the employees; 80% of the value of your work comes from 20% of your activities, etc.

The trouble comes in figuring out *which* 20% gives you the 80%. Fortunately, Juran and other SQC types have taken the modeling and math

out of Pareto's Principle and made it useful to normal folks in the form of the Pareto Diagram.

Pareto Diagrams are simple bar charts (or other graphics) that can be used to log inventory vs. shipments, activities vs. time, or outcome against effort in order to see where the best payoff for problem-solving or productivity efforts is likely to come from.

Suppose we want to reduce rejects from an assembly operation. Where would we begin? According to the Pareto Principle, we would start by breaking the problem down into *types* of rejects. If a true Pareto distribution appears, one or two types of errors will dominate our count. It then makes sense to start the attack on the sort of rejects that occur most frequently.

The Pareto Diagram for the hypothetical Alachula Pot Works in the accompanying figure suggests that if we want to make a big impact on the reject problem, we should start by looking for causes of cracked pots, since cracked pots account for 50% of all rejects. Focusing on squatty pots, a much less common cause of rejects, would do much less in terms of reducing the reject rate.

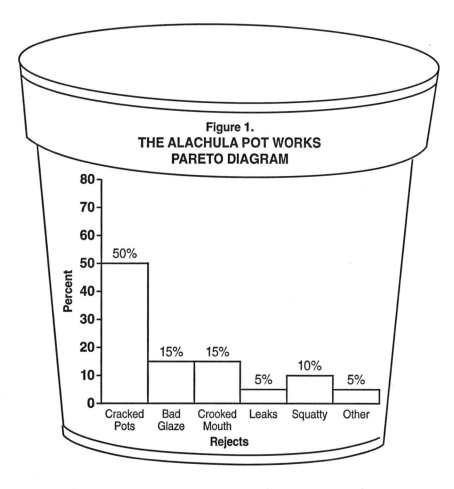

Figure 1.
THE ALACHULA POT WORKS
PARETO DIAGRAM

Looking at types of errors is only one way to break down the reject problem. It might be just as reasonable to collect the data for the Pareto Diagram by shift or team or by individual, especially if there is some reason to suspect that the errors are out of proportion by person, team or shift.

While the Pareto Diagram is no great shakes as a model of high-tech wizardry, it is certainly a straightforward way to sort the "vital few from the trivial many."

A historical footnote: Pareto's studies of the distribution of wealth in Italy led him to (or perhaps excused) a great disdain for democracy and democratic principles. His economic and sociological tracts, particularly *The Mind and Society*, became the philosophical underpinning (or perhaps an excuse for) the rise of Italian Fascism under Mussolini. Of Pareto's seven major books, at least one (that's 14.3%) contributed to a heck of a lot of trouble for about 80% of the world.

Notes:

PARTICIPATORY LEARNING

Getting Them to Open Up

BY DUGAN LAIRD
AND FORREST BELCHER

Dear Know-It-Alls:

I keep reading that it's important for trainers to get people to "open up" in the classroom. Once and for all, why? I'm a modern person, and I can accept nudity on TV and the movie screens if it's appropriate and tasteful, but this insistence on emotional immodesty in a training session strikes me as embarrassing and unnecessary. People are in a classroom to add to their knowledge or skills, not to strip themselves bare. Sometimes trainers act like amateur psychologists. What do you say to that?

A Skeptic

Dear Skeptic:

We agree with some of your points. There are indeed faddists and unqualified "psychologists" whose zeal for open expression of emotions in classrooms has been totally inappropriate. We don't like this any more than you do.

On the other hand (Do you feel we're getting ready to zap you?), under some circumstances, openness is critical. For one thing, learning means making a change — and for most adults change is awkward, stressful, threatening. Feelings and emotions are real factors in the learning dynamic. If those emotions are bottled up, the experience might more accurately be called a "learning static." We need openness as a release mechanism for the inherent tension of a learning environment. Maybe that's why Carl Rogers makes such a strong point about the need for instructors to inquire about and respond to the *feelings* as well as the *thoughts* of students.

Secondly, suppose you're working in an organization where emotions run rampant in three directions: high, deep and widespread. The lack of openness in some companies is so serious a problem that training specialists are asked to conduct workshops in which people learn to express and hear and accept and adjust to the emotions of the workplace as well as to the tasks themselves. Thus, the very objective of the training is to learn and practice openness and to develop mechanisms for maintaining it on the job.

Do these explanations clarify? Confuse? Convince?

The Know-It-Alls

Dear Know-It-Alls:

Oh, your answer was clear all right, if a bit glib. But it raised two more questions in my mind. One, shouldn't deep feelings be controlled as a sign of maturity? Two, can't we protect the anonymity of people who raise emotionally loaded issues through something like a classroom "suggestion box"?

Skeptic

Dear Skeptic:

You raise two good points, which we'll answer in reverse order. First, is anonymity necessary? Certainly people are entitled to protection from reprisals for things they say in the classroom. But one of the goals of any organizational team should be, we feel, open sharing of those feelings that accelerate and those that impede the achievement of group results. In a classroom workshop, as a way to help people feel comfortable about opening up, you might *guarantee* that nothing said in the session will get back to the workplace. By the end of the training, people should be comfortable sharing feelings as well as

ideas. Suggestion boxes strike us as a bit immature — an artificial way to hide from ourselves. We like an environment in which each member of the "society" is honestly and openly responsible for his or her own ideas and feelings. This doesn't mean that you drop your defenses completely and run around babbling everything you know and feel. But you can enrich relationships and accelerate learning by mature and genuine openness.

That brings us to the second point: We feel emotions to be natural, inevitable and totally adult. Emotions aren't a burden, they're just there. By being open, we often can convert potential conflict into synergistic joint effort. Finally, we believe there is no such thing as "too much" or "inappropriate" emotion — only the need to make the inevitable emotion manageable and constructive.

The Know-It-Alls

Dear Know-It-Alls:

I've been following your correspondence with "Skeptic" and it makes me inquisitive. You talk as if feelings centered mostly on relationships and process. I am concerned with such classroom issues as asking questions, responding, willingly sharing ideas and workplace problems. Don't people have emotions about things like these? And what about policies, procedures and people in the workplace? Aren't we emotional about these things, and don't these emotions have to come out in class? I am, as I say,

Inquisitive

Dear Inquisitive:

You're absolutely right. Thanks so much for pointing this out. The fact is that asking questions, sharing workplace problems — almost any sort of talking — involves a lot of feeling and emotion.

The Know-It-Alls

Dear Know-It-Alls:

Your stuff about "openness" is all well and good, but I become frustrated and angry when I read theory without any practical advice attached. You've told me *why* to be open; what about *how*? How do I achieve openness in classes and workshops? Get down out of the clouds and into the real world!

A Realist

TIPS FOR HANDLING TROUBLEMAKERS

Maintaining effectiveness in the classroom isn't only a matter of enforcing civilized deportment — keeping the humor out of the toilet, banning spit wads, encouraging the postponement of knitting projects until break time, and so forth.

Rosemary Lambie, an assistant professor at Virginia Commonwealth University's School of Education in Richmond, reminds us — and the trainers she teaches under a federal grant — that being a stand-up trainer often demands quick-witted parrying of irrelevant, rambling, distracting or otherwise unproductive discussion arising from the subject matter.

Feel you need some help in this area? Lambie is glad to oblige.

- To counter demands for off-the-cuff solutions to specific (and often esoteric) problems, simply refuse to offer suggestions or opinions outside your own field of expertise. "Let trainees know from the beginning that you do not have all the answers," says Lambie. Save problem-solving specifics and cases for discussion at the end of the session.

- Maintaining focus on the subject at hand is easier if trainers "define the reservation" for themselves with notes and an outline, and define it for trainees by presenting an overview in perspective before plunging into detail.

- Prepare "several surprise activities that can be pulled out at any point at which there is a lull or problem with attention." The purpose of this recommendation, Lambie says, "is to have plans for getting trainees moving and talking." Announce and stick to a schedule of breaks, and don't allow your own break time to be taken up with questions and requests for documents, articles and so on.

- Confront troublemakers by asking what their objections are and giving them a chance to air their feelings. Prepare a pretest and use it to spot those who already know the course content. Draft the know-it-alls into the work of presentation.

- Realize that "10% of any population is negative," says Lambie. "Out there in that sea of faces there will be some who will not respond." Dealing with cynicism, a related problem, is easier if you avoid preaching or arguing, Lambie adds. Just say, "You might be right," or "I see your point," and move on.

Dear Realist:

OK. Here are some preliminary steps for helping people open up in the learning environment.

First, be open yourself. Identify your feelings as they occur, and describe them to your class in "here and now" terms. It is appropriate (even productive) to say things like, "I'm getting nervous about the time we're spending on this subtopic, Bill," or "I am really pleased when you demonstrate your willingness to look at both sides of a hot issue like this, Clare." Open instructors can express anger and sadness, as well as pleasure. The really important thing is to lower your own defenses and take risks — that's what you're asking your participants to do. You might even break down and admit to being wrong about something.

Second, use "open questions," which, as their name implies, invite sharing and analysis (nonjudgmental analysis, please) of feelings. "How do you feel about this?" "What are you feeling right now?" "What feelings and emotions are affecting us in this activity?" Even the more direct and confrontive question, "Why are you here?" can encourage an open expression of feelings. Note that open questions never have "correct" (externally verifiable) answers; whatever the respondent says is presumed to be an accurate statement. You can't disagree with a person's feelings, and it certainly doesn't help much to tell the person who answers an open question, "Well, you shouldn't feel that way."

Third, select low-risk open questions and model low-risk openness. Why embarrass people with questions like, "Are you really being honest with yourself about this?" or, "Let's face it, none of us really wants to change this procedure, so let's get rid of our hatred for the managers who forced it upon us. How do you feel about that, Charlie?" No. Simply state very early in the proceedings that this is a classroom and therefore a workshop where everybody has an opportunity to try out, test and experiment with new behaviors. One new behavior involves the right to express opinions and feelings that are subject to sudden amendment. That right is backed by a guarantee that no negative consequences whatsoever will follow any such expressions.

Fourth, give gentle, positive reinforcement to every early sample of openness on the part of participants. Phrases such as "Thanks for sharing that with us," or "I see," or "I feel good about knowing your feelings on this issue, Jane," make good reinforcers.

Well, Mr. Realist, there are four ways to secure openness. How do you feel about using them in your next workshop?

The Know-It-Alls

Dear Know-It-Alls:

How do I feel about using the ABCs of openness in my next workshop? Talked down to, that's how I feel. Doesn't everybody do the things you've been talking about? Surely you can come up with some more advanced tips. Just call me your

Experienced Realist

Dear Experienced Realist:

It's always a bit embarrassing to cover material that seems extremely basic. Sometimes we fear we start sounding "preachy." But we'll defend that discussion because we think less-experienced trainers might not stop to think about these extremely important behaviors. And more experienced trainers often verbalize these points while failing to practice them. Their egos, along with their needs for control and authority, sometimes get in the way.

Once you have established an open environment — or if these simple methods don't seem to be doing much good — there are some structured activities that encourage openness.

Present models for openness. The Johari Window is a good example — and it's easy to draw one on a flip chart (see illustration).

You can discuss what each of the four "window panes" means and why we are reluctant to open up the side of ourselves that is "unknown to others."

A HIERARCHY OF VALUE

If the main objective of most training programs is to change behavior, improve skills and impart job-related knowledge, it seems indisputable that trainers should use a consistent method and a common vocabulary to set goals and conduct evaluations of training needs and trainee accomplishments.

So argues training consultant Margery L. Pabst of Development Dimensions International's Houston, TX office. She says her behavior-oriented hierarchy of learning stages (see chart) can serve instructional designers as "benchmark" indicators — the closer a training program comes to enabling the learner to *use* information and skills on the job, the higher its value and prospect of success.

"The focus is on the process of learning and the accomplishments of the learner rather than on the content and materials of each individual training program," says Pabst. Although any such list should reflect "increasing levels of skills sophistication," she allows that the choice of terms is arbitrary: "It is the principle of consistency that is advocated here."

LEARNING STAGES FROM SIMPLE TO COMPLEX	
Level, Stage	**What the Learner Does . . .**
Imitation	The learner . . . imitates, matches, recites, retells, copies
Selection	The learner . . . locates, selects, seriates, orders
Classification	The learner . . . groups, classifies, compares, contrasts
Definition	The learner . . . names, states, supplies, labels, describes
Construction	The learner . . . builds, writes, changes, draws, modifies
Application	The learner . . . uses

Often, just by talking about the *processes* of openness, we move toward open behavior.

JOHARI WINDOW

	WHAT INSTRUCTOR KNOWS	WHAT INSTRUCTOR DOESN'T KNOW
What Participants Know		
What Participants Don't Know		

The Johari Window is only one example. You also might want to consider the Dalton Change Model or even Lewin's Force Field Analysis. Such abstract models may lack any real payoff, however, if not accompanied by some instrument trainees can use to gather data about themselves (their views and feelings) and probably to share that data with others. The instrument might be a simple agree/disagree scale. Here's a sample from a communication course:

	Strongly Agree	Tend To Agree	No Real Opinion	Tend To Disagree	Strongly Disagree
1. Managers should always tell employees everything they want to hear.					
2. Managers should always have an open-door policy when communications break down.					
3. When communications break down, it's usually the sender's fault.					
4. And so on.					

Or, you might use a forced-ranking exercise:

Here are five qualities that are important to effective management. Rank them in the order (1 for most important) you give each quality. You may not allow any ties.

	RANK
PATIENCE	_____
HONESTY	_____
SENSITIVITY	_____
RESPONSIVENESS	_____
CONSCIENTIOUSNESS	_____

By answering such questions, learners gain certain insights about themselves. That in itself helps promote personal openness. Sharing the collected data with the group contributes to greater social openness. If the environment needs to be protective, let the revelations be posted so there is no possible way for individual respondents to be identified. Or begin the sharing process in very small groups (two people), then proceed to foursomes and so on until you achieve an "open society."

Even if you don't use this expanding method, you'll find it helpful to let the sharing begin in small groups. This permits people to participate in groups with different constituencies, and they get practice in being open with ever-shifting populations. This matters because it's one thing to be open with a specific group of people and quite another experience to be open with several different groups. Do these techniques make sense to you Experienced Realists?

The Know-It-Alls

Dear Know-It-Alls:

Yes, you make sense. l understand the devices you are using and how they are administered. But doesn't all of this take a lot of time?

Another Experienced Realist

Dear Experienced Realist:

Yes, gathering and sharing this sort of data does take time. But remember, being open can be pretty uncomfortable — even threatening — which makes it a difficult lesson to learn. Like all difficult learnings, openness takes time. If we believe in teaching it, we must be prepared to *invest* the necessary time.

One way to accelerate things is to clarify norms and expectations. Make a contract with the class at the earliest possible moment. As trainer, you might say: "Here's what I'm willing to do as an instructor. I'm willing to start on time, to answer your questions, to listen to how you feel about our processes, to give you all my energy. In return, here's what I'd like from you: I'd like you to be here on time, to express your feelings about what's happening as well as your ideas about the content, to share your experiences and to participate willingly. Do we have a contract?"

In such contracting you are, of course, "modeling openness." This is the first step, and you must take it very early. You can also probe the participants' feelings about this contracting process and reinforce their expressions of those feelings. Thus, the dynamics of openness begin immediately — openness is seen subtly as a natural part of this learning experience. If the responses are sluggish, of course, you'll need extra time for data gathering.

We're getting the feeling that we may have told you more about the "Why and How of Openness" than you really care to know. We'd like to close by quoting Sidney Jourard's testimony from *The Transparent Self*: "People become clients of psychotherapists because they have not disclosed themselves in some optimum degree to the people in their life." And again, also from Jourard, "Self-disclosure is a symptom of personality health."

We believe that at the end of any learning experience, people ought to feel better about themselves, about the tasks they're asked to perform and about the organization for which they perform those tasks. That's our honest opinion, and we feel good about having expressed it. See how open we are?

That's why they call us . . .

The Know-It-Alls

Notes:

Frick Teaches Frack

BY BOB FILIPCZAK

It probably began with Zog teaching Thag how to field-dress a mastodon. If Zog was a particularly talented instructor, he may even have outlined some specific learning objectives before the session and asked for an evaluation — or demanded a skill demonstration — at the end. But working life has become too complicated to depend on Zog to be a naturally gifted teacher. Unstructured on-the-job training (OJT) may have gotten Thag through a mastodon autopsy, but it's unlikely to teach him to run a computerized cash register anytime soon.

More recently, OJT has often meant having a new employee "go sit by Nellie" or follow Sam around the factory floor for a few days playing monkey-see, monkey-do. Sam probably doesn't know much about training, which means the new guy may pick up as much by trial and error as he does from trying to decipher Sam's instructions.

This is not a very good way to train somebody. It doesn't enforce common work standards. It doesn't ensure that the trainee will actually do things the way Sam says they should be done. It allows the trainee to pick up Sam's bad habits along with his good ones. It can be downright dangerous.

Furthermore, unstructured OJT generally doesn't do much for the trainee's confidence. Says HRD Hall of Fame member Martin Broadwell, president of the Center for Management Services, a consulting firm in Decatur, GA: "Ninety-five percent of the training that's done on the job is done so poorly that the job suffers measurably. And both the trainer and the trainee agree that it's the trainee's fault, but it isn't."

So whose fault is it? Blaming Sam,

who's never been within 10 miles of a train-the-trainer course, is pointless and unfair. The culprit is the organization that tells Sam to train somebody without giving him any tools to do so.

Note that we didn't say it's a mistake to use Sam as a trainer; as a peer and coworker of the new employee, he may be the ideal person for the role. That's why some companies have turned to an approach in which Sam is taught a thing or two about adult learning theory and training techniques before being turned loose on a novice worker.

Let's call this approach "structured peer training," mostly to differentiate it from the haphazard attempts at on-the-job training that have become the lamentable standard in many organizations. (We recently overheard a young woman on a city bus telling her companion about training in a new hire at a fast-food restaurant. She herself was a relative newcomer, and she confessed that she didn't even know how to do most of the things she was supposed to teach the new person to do. Her supervisor told her not to help the trainee with a task, but just to stand back against the wall and watch. Presumably, the novice would learn by trial and error.)

Structured peer training is essentially OJT — at least, it rarely takes place in classrooms and is not the same thing as using a manager or subject-matter expert as an instructor in formal training courses. Like classic OJT, most structured peer training involves one trainer with only one or two trainees. The difference that makes a difference is that this approach reinforces the learning process with some thought and planning. To begin with, the people doing the instructing are deliberately chosen, trained and supported.

Any Volunteers?

To make this strategy work, the organization has to start by paying attention to the people it selects to teach job skills to their coworkers. Among companies that do some form of structured peer training, there is a degree of consensus about the kind of candidates to look for. Good communication skills are often mentioned, particularly listening skills. Another crucial characteristic is patience. This is important because peer trainers, like all trainers, field the same questions over and over again. Aspects of a job that are obvious to someone who has been doing it for years are far from obvious to the new worker, and the trainer must recognize that. Says Dave Venables, general manager of human-resources development for parks at Walt Disney World Co. in Lake Buena Vista, FL, "There are no dumb questions" when you're dealing with new hires.

Exemplary job performance is another characteristic to look for in a good peer trainer, but it shouldn't be first on the list. It's tempting to recruit your best performer as a trainer on the theory that new employees will be trained to the highest standards. But those who can *do* can't always teach; the most skillful performer is not necessarily good at translating what she does to the uninitiated.

Whatever you do, however, don't choose a poor performer. "I've seen people do that," says Ken McClung, senior partner for the Instructional Design Group of Morristown, NJ, who has helped set up structured peer-training systems for Morgan Guaranty Trust Co. and Merrill Lynch. "You have a person you can't figure out what to do with, so you have [him] train the new person." That road leads invariably to disaster, he says.

There are various ways to select peer trainers. Some organizations tell managers what to look for and let them identify likely candidates. Others ask for volunteers, thinking that those who volunteer will have an interest in training, which will come in handy as they try to balance their regular job with their new training responsibilities. Even so, says McClung, the company should help by easing the peer trainer's regular work load.

Naturally, some workers will eschew extra work, especially if it doesn't mean extra pay. Others welcome the added responsibility, however, because it feels like a promotion — and at some companies, it is. At Disney's parks, for instance, almost all supervisors were once peer trainers, Venables says.

Once you've chosen peer trainers, you must help them develop some training skills. Does that mean turning them into full-fledged, card-carrying trainers? No, but it does mean introducing them to basic concepts such as adult learning theory. Indeed, adjusting to the different learning styles of trainees is one of the toughest challenges of the role, says Penny Foldy, a peer trainer who teaches new hires how to run food attractions at Disney World.

At T.J. Maxx, the national retail chain based in Framingham, MA, peer trainers receive five days of training at national headquarters. To prepare them for field assignments, they study adult learning theory, questioning skills, facilitation skills, and the technical skills involved in running cash registers and keeping inventory. According to Marg Balcom, assistant vice president for training and development, the company identifies line workers who are particularly high performers, and sends them out on four-week assignments to train new employees before the opening of a new store.

An obvious question arises: How much train-the-trainer training does a peer trainer need? Carolyn Nilson, a consultant in Sandisfield, MA, and author of *Training for Non-Trainers*, suggests that, minimally, peer trainers should be able to design a lesson and to recognize whether the trainees are "getting it." The primary concern, she says, is to "make sure that lessons are taught, not just information dumped."

Even though you probably won't be turning your peer trainers into certified instructional technologists, McClung suggests giving them a briefing on job analysis. Too often, he says, an inexperienced peer trainer will try to explain a job by starting in the wrong place or leaving out critical steps along the way. Doing a job analysis will give the peer trainer a logical way to look at the tasks involved in a job.

Broadwell introduced an innovative concept when he was teaching British Petroleum workers to train their coworkers to operate an oil refinery. He conducted "train the learner" training for new employees; that is, he taught the trainees what kind of instruction they should expect from peer trainers. Broadwell told them that they ought to be able to explain to the trainer exactly what they intend to do before they touch a machine they will operate. Then the trainee should recite it again, before he touches the equipment. This communication does two things: It tells the trainer if the novice knows the correct procedures, and it helps reinforce the learning.

Learners at British Petroleum were told they ought to be able to explain to the trainer exactly what they intend to do before they even touch a machine.

Training By the Book

One word that comes up in the conversations of almost everyone who has set up a structured peer-training system is "checklist." Peer trainers use checklists of job procedures to stay on track during training. Supervisors use them to check the work of newly trained employees. Trainees use them as job aids. These checklists can be time-consuming to develop, says McClung, but they will save your peer trainers a lot of hassle later.

Broadwell is another proponent of developing checklists or manuals and sticking to them during training. First, he says, it keeps the training consistent and standardized. Second, if the trainee has a question and there's no peer trainer in sight, he can turn to the manual.

Finally, Broadwell says that using the procedures standardized in a manual helps prevent a common hazard of OJT. As he puts it, "The whole point of peer training — the whole point of any structured training — is to keep people from learning all the bad habits from sitting next to someone." Checklists can ward off the problems that arise when Sam tells his trainees about the shortcut he has discovered that works *nearly* every time.

Peers may be good trainers, but they ought not be in charge of evaluating the performance of their trainees, experts agree. Once the peer trainer evaluates the employee, the two are no longer peers. Formal evaluation is a supervisory responsibility and ought to remain one, McClung says; peer trainers are usually uncomfortable with it.

At Disney World, says Venables, supervisors use checklists to evaluate new employees after training. Then the supervisor discusses the novice's performance with the peer trainer to nail down areas where the training "took" and areas where it didn't.

Rewards

Organizations promote the peer-trainer role as an honor in itself, but most understand that such honors are more attractive when accompanied by a tangible reward or recognition. At Disney's parks, peer trainers are paid extra while they're instructing. They also have a trainer designation on their name badges as they work around the park.

One of the enticing aspects of peer training at T.J. Maxx is the opportunity for employees to take a break from their regular jobs for a month or so. It's exciting for many of them to go through training, then train others amid the hype and executive attention given to a new store opening. Balcom says this kind of responsibility and exposure is highly motivating for employees in the retail environment, where wages generally are low and turnover is high.

Recognition can be another motivator. Consultant Nilson recommends congratulatory dinners or lunches for peer trainers at least once a year. But recognition can come in many forms. At Golden Corral, a chain of family restaurants based in Raleigh, NC, peer training works much as it does at T.J. Maxx, with exemplary workers being asked to train employees of new restaurants as they are launched. But additional prestige is lent to the job by the fact that peer trainers sometimes act as instructors for supervisory-level people in the organization, according to corporate training director Doug Higdin.

Sylvester Garcia, a crew trainer at the Golden Corral in Amarillo, TX, teaches his coworkers the art of meat cutting. But Garcia's restaurant is one of the company's certified training sites, so supervisors from other restaurants also come to learn. Garcia teaches them how to cut meat, and he learns how their restaurants operate.

Transfer of Training

Structured peer training offers some clear advantages not just over casual OJT but also compared with many formal training courses. In the latter area, the big advantage lies in the area of "transfer." Proving that the skills taught to an individual in a classroom actually show up later on the job is a perennial challenge for most full-time trainers. Peer trainers can watch trainees closely on the job to make sure they're doing what they've been taught to do. And if the trainee has a question a month later, his trainer is probably within shouting distance. As Disney World's Foldy points out, the questions keep coming all year-round. Disney World even lists locations of peer trainers in each area of the park. Consequently, Foldy says, "you're always training."

What's more, peer trainers can be excellent resources for full-time training professionals. Peer trainers see almost instantly what works and what doesn't, and they can feed that information to the people who design the organization's training courses. At Disney World, peer trainers came up with a list of customer questions that get asked most often. The list was later incorporated into the company's training plan, Venables says.

Another advantage of peer training is credibility. Venables was a peer trainer himself 20 years ago — teaching employees to drive a ferryboat between the parking lot and the park. But now, he says, "If I went out to a ferryboat this morning and tried to train someone, I'd have no credibility." Peer trainers who do the job every day and deal with all manner of customers have a claim to knowledge and authority that a full-time classroom trainer simply can't match.

Other reasons to consider structured peer training? How about speed and cost savings? International Flavors and Fragrances (IFF), a New York-based manufacturer of food additives, saved time and money by using peer training in connection with a companywide total-quality-management initiative. At first, says Drew Von Tish, a quality-process facilitator for IFF, the company hired consultants to spread the TQM message. But it soon became evident that the outside experts didn't have enough feel for the corporate culture to make the training effective.

IFF switched to peer trainers, who now teach subjects including leadership, group facilitation, statistical process control, computer skills and chemistry. According to Von Tish, the instruction now is more customized to the needs of the company and its individual units. The training is also more effective, its costs are lower and employees are gaining new skills.

Consultant Marc Dorio, president of Dorio Associates in Titusville, NJ, helped IFF set up its training program. Speed, he says, is often an important advantage of peer training. If you want to change a company's culture quickly, peer trainers can disseminate large amounts of information throughout the work force. With a staff of deputized trainers out in the field, you can spread the word about, say, new purchasing procedures in a matter of hours rather than the weeks it might take if your five-person HRD staff had to do it.

Obviously, the peer trainer is no substitute for a professional instructor running a full-scale formal training program — when such a program is really called for. For many organizations, however, structured peer training is not an alternative to formal courses, it's an alternative to no training at all — or to the slapdash hazards of unstructured OJT. If that's your choice, it's not exactly a tough call.

Notes:

Blueprint For the Learning Organization?

BY JACK GORDON

There is a traditional scenario that serves to introduce the concept of "performance technology." It goes something like this:

Training director Sheila is sitting in her office at the Acme Widget Corp. In walks a line manager. We'll make him someone with a nice hyphen in his title. Let's see...Bob, the vice president-sales.

"I need a training program for my salespeople," says Bob.

"Oh?" says Sheila.

"They aren't following through on our new consultative selling policy," Bob complains. "They don't probe to uncover the customer's real needs. They don't try to find the best solution for the customer. And they're never honest if it looks like our widget won't be the right answer to the customer's problem. They're doing nothing but the same old hard sell they always did. They need another training program on consultative selling."

How should Sheila respond? The answer hinges on the way she perceives her job. Is "training director" a title she takes literally? Does she see herself as a provider of instructional programs? Does she measure her contribution to the organization — her success — by the number of courses the organization allows her to run, and the number of people who pass through those courses? If so, she will leap at the chance to provide Bob's reps with another training program on consultative selling.

And chances are excellent that the program's effect on the sales reps' approach to selling widgets will be approximately zero. They'll attend the course, they'll learn the material, they'll pass any test that Sheila or Bob might devise to demonstrate that they know how to do consultative selling the way Bob says he wants it done. Then they'll go back to the job and try to stuff widgets down the customers' throats.

On the other hand, suppose that as far as Sheila is concerned, "training director" means "person in charge of helping this organization succeed by improving the performance of its people." Suppose she understands that there are many reasons why people don't behave the way their bosses want them to (or in the manner most likely to achieve the organization's goals, which is not necessarily the same thing). One possibility is that Bob's sales reps don't know how to perform correctly, in which case training them would be a good idea. But why does Bob assume that lack of know-how is the problem?

What if they *do* know how to do consultative selling? Training them again would be a waste of time and money. So instead of whipping up a program, Sheila begins to investigate. Maybe she questions Bob. Maybe she questions some of Acme's customers. Maybe she digs through some company documents. Maybe she observes some sales reps as they interact with customers.

What kind of information is she looking for? She might start with the reasoning behind the new consultative selling policy. What is its goal? That is, what desirable result is "consultative selling" supposed to achieve for the organization? Is it "increased customer satisfaction"? If so, how are "satisfied customers" defined and measured? Are we talking about fewer people who return their widgets, demand their money back, and then bad-mouth Acme on the street as a venal purveyor of useless products? Well, then:

Q: What pain befalls a sales rep when a disappointed customer returns a widget and demands her money back?

A: None. Returns are handled by the service department. There is no mechanism for tracing a returned widget back to the rep who sold it.

Q: How are reps rewarded?

A: They're paid on commission. They make money only when they close a sale.

Q: What happens when a rep takes the time to ask probing questions and to seek the best solution for the customer?

A: It takes longer to make each sale. So the rep makes less money.

Q: If a rep endears Acme to a customer by being honest about the widget's lack of utility for solving the problem in question, what's in it for the rep? For instance, what are the chances that this rep will see this customer when the customer returns to Acme next month to buy a widget she really does need?

A: Slim to none.

Q: How does a rep win his supervisor's approval? What does he get praised for? How does he get promoted into management?

A: He who sells the most widgets gets praised and promoted.

Q: So we're exhorting the reps to do consultative selling, but they make more money, they get more strokes and they feel no pain when they give customers the old hard sell?

A: Yep.

Something has to change around here, all right, Sheila figures. But the answer is not a training course — at least, not a course aimed at the sales reps.

Sheila is thinking of job performance as something that occurs within a *system* of goals, measurements, incentives, skills, consequences, feedback and more. She's thinking that if she wants to change the way somebody behaves, she has to pull the right levers in the system. She is thinking like a performance technologist.

But here a few questions arise. First, won't Sheila run into a political hailstorm when she tells vice president Bob that he is, in so many words, an idiot? The answer is yes, and trainers have argued for years about how to handle that dilemma.

Second, isn't "technology" a rather odd word to apply to what Sheila is doing here? A bit grand? A trifle high-falutin?

"I was surprised when all the fuss started [in the 1970s] over the term 'performance technology,'" says Allison Rossett, a professor of educational technology at San Diego State University. "It's always seemed more like 'intelligent practice' to me."

A third question arises as well. This one has attracted far less attention than the others, but it may be the most interesting. Here it is:

Who says Sheila has to work in the training department?

For that matter, why would the analytical process she's demonstrating have to start with somebody's request for a training program?

Marc Rosenberg, project manager of training quality for AT&T in Morristown, NJ, can define performance technology in several ways, but one definition he likes is, "a quality process for human resources." Indeed, PT's perspective dovetails in so many ways with the "quality" perspective that Rosenberg considers it likely the term "performance technology" will fade from the lexicon within the next 10 years, subsumed by the quality movement.

Just as quality techniques need not and should not be confined to a "quality department," there is no obvious reason why all sorts of people couldn't learn to think about job performance the way Sheila does.

As much as anything else, Rosenberg says, performance technology is a mind-set. "It's a perspective. It's a systematic framework by which anyone — managers, salespeople, technicians, workers — can look at organizational problems from the standpoint of human performance."

Systems

The concept of performance technology — also known as *human* performance technology and performance engineering — is a creature of the training world. PT was born out of the frustration of corporate training specialists. It evolved from the realization — all too apparent to the cleverest of these specialists — that a training program, no matter how well-designed, is simply not a very good answer to a lot of the job-related performance problems that training programs commonly are asked to solve.

Comparatively speaking, the concept of the "learning organization" was born with a silver spoon in its mouth. Thomas Kramlinger, a consultant with Wilson Learning Corp. of Eden Prairie, MN, sees the learning organization as having been "conceived in discussions between high-level corporate executives and the Sloan School of Management at the Massachusetts Institute of Technology (MIT)."

Regarding the seminal role of the Sloan School, Kramlinger might get an argument from companies such as Johnsonville Foods of Sheboygan, WI, and from organizational behavior experts such as Harvard's Chris Argyris. But his basic point is valid: The learning organization (albeit to a lesser extent than the "total quality organization") is a vision that seems to capture the fancy of top managers in a way that performance technology never has.

> ## "In America we've got 10,000 prima donnas marching around whose work supposedly is too complex to be described behaviorally."

In an April 1991 TRAINING article, Linda Honold, a former manager at Johnsonville Foods, defined a learning organization as: "... one whose members are continuously, deliberately learning new things. They apply what they learn to improve the product or service quality, the processes involved in making the product or providing the service, the quality of the environment in which employees work, and the performance of members of the organization."

The most popular (and most elaborate) description to date of how a learning organization might operate is contained in *The Fifth Discipline: The Art and Practice of the Learning Organization*, by Peter M. Senge, director of the systems thinking and organizational learning program at MIT's Sloan School.

Here's how Senge defines a learning organization: "... an organization that is continually expanding its capacity to create its future ... [one where] people continually expand their capacity to create the results they truly desire ...."

Here's how Joe Harless, head of the Harless Performance Guild of Newnan, GA, and a member of TRAINING Magazine's Human Resources Development (HRD) Hall of Fame, defines the purpose of performance technology: "... to assist humans to do and accomplish things that are compatible with worthy societal, business and personal goals."

According to Senge, the road to the learning organization is paved with systems thinking. Systems thinking is "the fifth discipline." It's the cornerstone, the driving force, the sine qua non of the learning organization.

Another of PT's aliases is "the systems approach" to improving human performance.

Systems thinking can be a hard pill to swallow, Senge writes. "Some have called systems thinking the 'new dismal science,' because it teaches that most obvious solutions don't work — at best, they improve matters in the short run, only to make things worse in the long run."

In at least one key sense, PT is the dismal science of the corporate training world. It teaches that the most obvious thing trainers *do*, the most visible reason for their presence on the payroll, the area of their special expertise — that is, designing and conducting training courses — represents only a small slice of the real pie. Furthermore, PT teaches that if the intention is to improve the *performance* of an individual or a group or an entire organization, training quite often is the *wrong* piece of the pie.

According to Senge, systems thinkers develop a keen appreciation for the principle of "compensating feedback." This is the phenomenon whereby "well-intentioned interventions call forth responses from the system that offset the benefits of the intervention."

That is the very idea expressed by Rossett when she states an elementary principle of performance technology: "Training in a vacuum produces only cynicism. Nothing changes just because somebody goes to a course."

In a keynote address at the "Best of America" human resources conference in Tampa, FL, Senge warned the assembled training professionals that they might not like what he had to say. "Training may or may not be important to the learning organization," he declared. "We've lost our sense of what learning is. Learning is not about taking in information ...

Learning is about the enhancement of our capacity to take action. It's always connected to action."

PT measures the success of any "intervention" — be it a training program, a new incentive system, or whatever — by the action it produces. To the performance technologist, the ultimate question to ask about a training program, for instance, is not whether the trainees "learned" the material, but whether their behavior has changed since they returned to the job — and whether this new behavior produces *accomplishments* that benefit the organization.

"Performance technology," says Harless, "is a systematic process for influencing the actions of people to produce valuable outputs for an organization's purposes. And one would hope the organization's purpose is valuable to society's purpose."

None of this is meant to suggest that Senge is merely rehashing the teachings of performance technology. He writes of several different kinds of "systems" (they bear names like "shifting the burden" and "limits to growth"), some of which have more to do with market forces than with human performance per se. His prescription for improving performance relies heavily on exercises designed to uncover the hidden or unconscious assumptions that underlie decision making and communication; this is not an area with which PT has been concerned. Senge's book is targeted primarily at high-level managers.

As Kramlinger sees it, Senge writes about the learning organization in a fascinating but rather esoteric manner. By contrast, Kramlinger says, "Performance technology is more about, 'Here's a horsey, here's a ducky.' It talks about practical, everyday kinds of things you can do to change what's going on in an organization."

Just the same, Kramlinger suggests, if what we want is a learning organization, PT may very well provide the how-to manual that enables us to build its foundations.

Here's A Horsey, Here's A Ducky (Part I)

Although PT's roots arguably stretch back to Frederick Taylor's studies of factory workers at the dawn of the 20th century, the term performance technology didn't come into vogue until the 1970s. Yet PT has been attacked recently by some training professionals as a dinosaur whose time already has passed. Its perspective is too simplistic and too mechanistic, the critics say, for the brave new world we have entered. In a nutshell, the argument lays out like this:

PT places its focus on the individual performer: Witness the lonely stick figure in the classic "performance system" diagram on this page. Increasingly, however, the basic "unit of performance" in organizations is not the individual but the team. Furthermore, PT has a distinct behavioristic bias. It demands that desirable ("mastery") performance be defined in terms of observable, measurable actions and outcomes. That's fine if you're talking about repetitive, manual, assembly-line sorts of jobs like the ones Taylor studied, but those kinds of jobs are disappearing.

Today's workers are being asked to *think*. Today's companies are full of "knowledge workers," much of whose most important "behavior" goes on inside their heads. In other words, knowledge work is largely covert instead of overt. Knowledge work cannot be "prefigured" by some outside analyst who first identifies the three or six or 10 key things a "master performer" does, and then gets everybody to do those same things, just as the master does them. What with technology and working relationships changing so fast these days, people often are confronted with new tasks — and if the task is new, there is no master performer to study. In knowledge work, the performer faces a wide

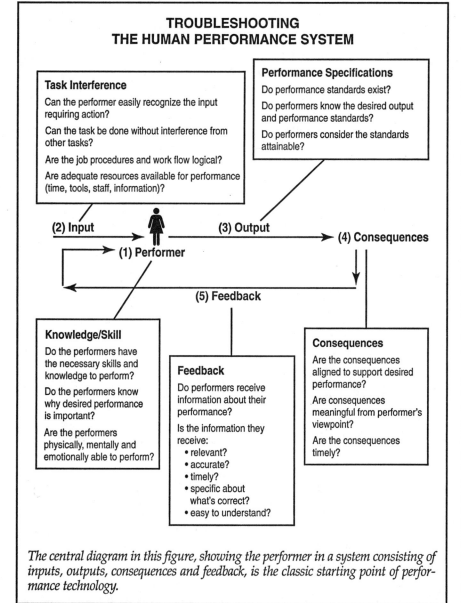

TROUBLESHOOTING THE HUMAN PERFORMANCE SYSTEM

Task Interference

Can the performer easily recognize the input requiring action?

Can the task be done without interference from other tasks?

Are the job procedures and work flow logical?

Are adequate resources available for performance (time, tools, staff, information)?

Performance Specifications

Do performance standards exist?

Do performers know the desired output and performance standards?

Do performers consider the standards attainable?

(2) Input　　**(3) Output**　　**(4) Consequences**

(1) Performer

(5) Feedback

Knowledge/Skill

Do the performers have the necessary skills and knowledge to perform?

Do the performers know why desired performance is important?

Are the performers physically, mentally and emotionally able to perform?

Feedback

Do performers receive information about their performance?

Is the information they receive:
- relevant?
- accurate?
- timely?
- specific about what's correct?
- easy to understand?

Consequences

Are the consequences aligned to support desired performance?

Are consequences meaningful from performer's viewpoint?

Are the consequences timely?

The central diagram in this figure, showing the performer in a system consisting of inputs, outputs, consequences and feedback, is the classic starting point of performance technology.

Reproduced from "The Systems View of Human Performance," by Geary A. Rummler and Alan P. Brache, TRAINING, September 1988. ©The Rummler-Brache Group, 1988.

variety of challenges. She has to figure out what to do as she goes along. She must "configure" her performance somewhat differently every day.

In short, a paradigm shift has occurred in the working world. More often than not, the ideal employee today — the closest thing you've got to a master performer — can be best described as a "learner-problem solver." And PT doesn't have much to say about how to build one of those.

It is commonly observed that a lot of people in the training business talk about performance technology, but only a handful actually practice it as a career. The trouble with the case against PT as outlined above is that when you call up a few of those premier practitioners and confront them with the dinosaur argument, they kick it to rags without breaking a sweat.

Harless is one such A-list practitioner. Performance technology focuses on individuals, not teams? "Nowadays," he answers, "our whole approach to performance technology is done by forming teams at various levels of the organization."

Another premier PT consultant is HRD Hall of Famer Geary Rummler, of the Rummler-Brache Group in Warren, NJ. The system diagram with the stick figure in it? That's Rummler's. You're troubled by the little fellow's singularity? "Draw several figures in the diagram and call them a team," he suggests. "Nothing changes."

Kramlinger observes that the principal change for a performance technologist working in a team-based organization might be that the team becomes a client, rather than just a group of "subjects" the PT expert is studying at the behest of management. (Harless believes the team members ought to become performance technologists, more or less — systems thinking! — but that's getting ahead of our story.)

PT has precious little to say about creating learner-problem solvers? On the contrary, argues Harless, PT has a subset called instructional technology, which suggests the single most useful way to go about that very task. "If [somebody] can't teach problem solving successfully," Harless insists, "it's probably because he started out thinking of 'problem solving' as a generic competency. He started with a subject-matter base, instead of a performance base."

That is, the unsuccessful teacher of problem solving will take a content-free approach to the topic, proceeding as if "problem solving" means the same thing to a medical diagnostician as it does to a vice president-sales or to somebody who repairs television sets.

Want to teach problem solving in a

In at least one key sense, performance technology is the dismal science of the corporate training world.

---

way that really makes a difference? Harless asks. Or decision making? Or critical thinking? Or leadership? Or any other "covert" skill that is dark and mysterious and not at all like an "overt" skill? He suggests you start by clarifying the performance outcomes you're really after: "Solve problems involving what? Make decisions about what? Think critically about what? Lead whom to do what?"

Let your instruction follow from those kinds of questions, Harless maintains, and you can achieve performance improvements in the neighborhood of 85 percent. Teach any of those skills as generic topics, and you'll be lucky to see a 15 percent improvement in job performance.

And that's looking only at *training* interventions designed to improve problem solving or other "covert" performances. Start by defining the accomplishments you're actually looking for when you say you want employees who are better at solving problems, and a performance technologist might point you away from training altogether and toward some solution with even higher leverage.

"The only thing that changes when you move from overt to covert behavior is that it puts more pressure on the analyst to describe, capture and make overt what that covert behavior is," Harless says. "But it's the only thing really worth doing.... Adults want to know what's successful. Why don't we tell them?"

The PT approach doesn't apply to knowledge workers? Pick a plump, juicy, esoteric knowledge worker, Rummler offers, licking his chops. How about a computer-software designer?

"Like a lot of jobs in a primitive state of technology, software design looks more like magic than craft," he says. Managers will say they can't describe the key behaviors or even the crucial outputs of a "master" software designer.

"Bull," Rummler says. "It's the same old thing. [Software designers] have outputs they've got to deliver, just like everyone else. If I say, 'Of your four design centers, which is the best?' they can always tell me immediately: 'It's Hong Kong,' or whatever."

" 'Why?' "

" 'Well, they produce software with fewer bugs, there's a faster turnaround....' "

Where's the big problem identifying a master performer? Rummler demands. "Here's a whole design center that's a master performer." For that matter, the quality movement's love affair with "benchmarking" is about nothing other than identifying and studying mastery performance. Benchmarking simply applies the idea to analyzing exemplary work processes in organizations other than one's own.

Furthermore, Rummler fails to see why anyone would find it impossible to isolate the key behaviors of the best individual software designers: "A supervisor eventually can give you six key things that the best performers do. True, you can't describe the actions of a master software designer down to a gnat's eyebrow, but you don't have to."

Right now, Rummler says, the Japanese are eyeing the computer software market. And they're thinking of software design in a different way than we do. "In America," he says, "we've got 10,000 prima donnas marching around whose work supposedly is too complex to be described behaviorally. The Japanese are saying, 'Bullshit, that's an industry.' They'll use existing code, they'll [have designers] share what they do, and they'll make software twice as fast as we do."

Here's A Horsey, Here's A Ducky (Part II)

The people in a learning organization must master five "disciplines," Senge says. Systems thinking — the fifth — is, again, the bedrock that underlies them all. The other four are called team learning, shared vision, personal mastery and mental models. Performance technology connects with most of them.

The discipline of "mental models"

has to do with exposing and, if necessary, changing the unconscious assumptions that underlie our actions and our interpretations of reality. Senge points to Chris Argyris' concept of separating "espoused theories" from "theories-in-use" as the primary mechanism that allows us to tackle the challenge. This seems to be the discipline about which PT would have the least to say.

"Personal mastery" asks that every member of the organization continually clarify what is truly important to him, and learn to perceive more clearly the gap between where he is and where he wants to go. In part, Senge's demand is that we stop thinking in terms of abstract labels and define our goals in clear, operational terms.

This sounds a great deal like performance technologist Bob Mager's longtime crusade against "fuzzies." Mager, who heads a consulting firm called Mager & Associates of Carefree, AZ, is another HRD Hall of Famer. Tell him you want to improve "teamwork" or "leadership," or that you wish your employees to become "empowered," and his first question is likely to be: "What behaviors will you accept as evidence that the condition you're looking for exists?"

"Shared vision," in Senge's terms, has to do with "alignment." Everyone in the organization should be pulling in the same direction toward a common, overriding purpose, and the purpose must be something other than simply "to make a lot of money." The vision must come from top management. And again, its clarity and concreteness are paramount.

Performance technology commonly speaks of goals and purposes rather than "visions," but . . . well, at this point we're simply going to hand the ball to Harless. This is how he outlines the PT approach to building an effective human performance system:

There are thousands of things you can do to try to influence performance. But all of these myriad "interventions" can be classifed into one of only four categories:

• *Selection/assignment.* You can hire people with particular skills, knowledge or characteristics, and assign or reassign them to particular kinds of jobs.

• *Information.* You can give people information bearing upon the challenges they face. This information can come in the form of performance feedback, training, job aids, on-the-job

coaching, specifying what "successful performance" is, allowing access to relevant data about the company and its competitors, and so on.

• *Environmental.* You can change something about the work, as opposed to something about the worker: Redesign the job, redesign working relationships (for example, form cross-functional teams), provide different tools, remove hazards, eliminate constraints to good performance, and so on.

• *Motivation/incentives.* You can give people reasons to want to do a good job: Pay them well, provide opportunities for advancement, change the kind of feedback you give them, let them choose which tasks or projects to work on, explain to them why it's important that they do something in a certain way.

Want to take your organization in a new direction? Want to pursue a new vision? Harless suggests a process he calls "new performance planning front-end analysis."

First, he says, sounding a lot like Senge, specify the new goal or new direction in as much detail as possible. "That's best done by the leadership of the organization."

"Your only alternative is to try all possible combinations of interventions and hope something works."

Next, ask what new things people will have to produce — what accomplishments will be necessary — to achieve the new goals.

Third, what actions — what behaviors — are most likely to produce those accomplishments? "We speculate," he says. "We say, 'OK, if we're going to produce this new output, what are the probable successful and efficient actions people should take in order to do that?'" Teams, he says, are a very good mechanism for asking and answering these questions.

Finally, he adds, "Given those new directions, given those new outputs, given those probable new successful behaviors, what new things can we do to positively influence those actions?"

The result of all this is a road map

that tells us, with at least some specificity, what kinds of performance interventions to use. "This tells us whom we should hire to do these new things. It tells us where in the organization we should assign people to do these new things. Critically, as it relates to training, it tells us what new information they should be given in training courses, job aids and so forth to support that new performance. It gives us a handle on how to structure the environment — work processes, work relationships, tools, equipment, desks, chairs — in order to foster that new performance. And last but by no means least, it tells us how we can try to influence people's 'affect': What do we do to make them *want* to do these new things?"

There is nothing particularly mysterious going on here, Harless points out. "What's your alternative to this?" he demands. "Your only alternative is to try all possible combinations [of interventions] and hope something works. That's the most expensive thing I know of."

As it applies to training, in particular, the try-something-and-hope-it-works approach is known as "spray and pray." The company sprays training on its managers and workers, then sends them back into an unchanged environment and prays that something good happens. As Rossett puts it, "PT is supposed to provide a supporting structure that transcends prayer."

"The central theme of performance technology," says Harless, "is to describe successful outputs and the behaviors, overt and covert, that will produce those outputs. That's the common skill to us. That's also the common skill to running an organization. It's the common skill to developing a learning organization. And damn it, it's the key to quality, too."

Teams

"How can a team of committed managers with individual IQs above 120 have a collective IQ of 63?" writes Senge. "The discipline of team learning confronts this paradox . . . . [T]eam learning starts with 'dialogue,' the capacity of members of a team to suspend assumptions and enter into a genuine 'thinking together.'"

Once again, we slip the old pigskin to Harless.

"The basic theory behind team approaches is that something called synergy will happen," he says. "In other words, if we take a group of people and give them common inputs, they will produce more together than they would separately."

The question becomes, what can we do to increase the likelihood that synergy will, indeed, occur?

"I believe synergy is heightened if certain things happen," Harless says. First, the team must have a common purpose: to increase sales, to improve service, or whatever. "The whole point is, synergy for *what*? It has to be a focused thing."

Second, team members must have a common language by which to discuss whatever it is they're investigating or planning or doing. "You can't use layman's language, because there ain't no layman's language," he says. So why not the language of performance technology, with its specific meanings for terms like "accomplishments," and its convenient classifications for different types of performance "interventions"?

Third, "team members must follow at some level of specificity or generality a common process for their work."

Maybe it's a problem-solving structure from the quality movement's bag of techniques. Maybe it's a common way of identifying problems that need to be solved. Or maybe it's the systematic approach offered by performance technology. "The point is, they don't just behave randomly. They agree on some kind of structure."

Fourth, they have access to the resources they need — time, money, information, tools, and so on.

Fifth, the team operates in a supportive environment. It has the authority to make decisions and to act upon them. There are appropriate incentives, there are no barriers to effective performance (for instance, team members are not "punished" for performing in the desired way, as was the case with vice president Bob's widget sales reps, who lost money whenever they engaged in consultative selling), and so on.

Finally, team members must have ways to evaluate and measure their output. They need a way to gauge their progress and their performance.

That recipe for synergy relies heavily, of course, on the principles of PT.

You say you'd like your employees to start behaving in ways that will transform your company into a learning organization? One that can "continually expand its capacity to create its future"?

"Question one," says Harless, "is *not*, how do we influence people's thoughts or feelings? Question one is, what are this organization's goals? *Then* what do we want people to produce in order to meet those goals? *Then* what do people need to do to produce those things? *Then* what kind of people do we need, where do we assign them, what kind of information do we give them, what environment do we put them in, and how do we [get them to want to perform]?"

Go at the question of organizational change from this perspective, he says, "and you have a way to behave at any point in time. If a 'learning organization' doesn't do that, it's barking up the wrong tree. It's just behaving randomly."

Notes:

What Exactly Are We Talking About?

BY CHRIS LEE

Productivity, or more precisely the lack thereof, has been the premiere business issue for more than 20 years. The lag in the U.S. productivity rate began to alarm economists, managers and politicians in the early '70s. For a while there, you couldn't open a newspaper, magazine or business book without encountering: 1) a comparison of our productivity rate with another country's, 2) the reasons behind the U.S. productivity decline, 3) who deserved the blame, 4) the author's prescription for fixing things, or 5) all of the above.

As a result, most of us have suffered productivity overkill. The word is so ubiquitous in business discussions, it ceases to register in any meaningful way. We all know — intuitively — what we mean when we use the term, and probably we all could agree on a vague definition for our own particular jobs: It's what we get done in a day, a week or a month. Because many of us produce something that can't be counted as physical units, however, we might feel that this doesn't quite cover the whole idea. We want the concept of productivity, at least as it might be applied to us, to include a qualitative, as well as quantitative, connotation.

At the bare-bones level, productivity is defined simply as the ratio of inputs to outputs. You calculate the productivity of Acme Widget Corp. by dividing its widget output by the inputs it used to produce them. This straightforward concept is rather quickly complicated by considerable practical and theoretical debate among economists as to which inputs and outputs should be part of the calculation.

Most of us assume — incorrectly — that the input side of the equation refers to labor, the number of hours worked to produce an output. This is a natural enough assumption, considering that the most widely cited productivity figure from the U.S. Bureau of Labor Statistics is the rate of labor productivity. BLS arrives at this figure by dividing the real gross domestic product (the gross national product adjusted for inflation) by the number of hours worked. But this is only part of the picture. Inputs include all the *resources* a company uses to manufacture its product, i.e., materials, capital and energy as well as labor.

Nor is quantifying output as simple as counting widgets. Few companies produce a single, homogeneous commodity. Most must combine their outputs on some common basis to arrive at their productivity rates — measures such as the labor required to produce each unit or each unit's dollar value, adjusted for price changes.

Another complication: Output often measures *efficiency* (the number of units produced), without telling you anything about *effectiveness* (defective or useless units). The question of outputs becomes even stickier when you consider service industries. "The ratio of output over input is a useful measure in a manufacturing environment, but it falls down in the white-collar and service areas," says John Belcher, vice president of the American Productivity Center in Houston. "You have to refine the terms because the outputs for white-collar workers are intangible, undefined."

The outputs produced by managers, for example, are the services they provide to the organization. Traditional measures of productivity inevitably focus on efficiency, not a very useful gauge of managerial productivity. "You can be efficient at providing things of little value to the organization," Belcher explains. "Effectiveness is more important. What you want to get at is value and quality of service. You need to reorient [output] to measure the effectiveness of the service provided."

Belcher recommends using an aggregate of several measurements to monitor white-collar productivity. He suggests asking employees themselves to help select the measures by using Nominal Group Technique, a structured brainstorming process, to agree upon a "family of measures" that indicate value and quality of service. In a monograph, *The Productivity Management Process*, he illustrates this approach using the services provided by a computer center. In this case, an appropriate "family of measures" might be: downtime, percent of time user deadlines are met, rerun time, number of user complaints and on-line response time.

What family of measures might a human resources development department use? Jac Fitz-enz, author of *How to Measure Human Resources Management* (McGraw-Hill, 1984), suggests three basic measures: cost (per trainee and per training hour), change (knowledge, skill and/or attitude improvement and performance change), and impact (evaluation). Fitz-enz contends that this type of measurement system "promotes productivity by focusing attention on the important issues, tasks and objectives" of a staff function. "The ultimate measurement," he adds, "is not efficiency, but effectiveness."

Regardless of how you decide to measure productivity, however, the great debate of the past decades has revolved around a single premise: the need to improve it. According to the American Productivity Center, the labor productivity rate of the United States increased at an average annual rate of 3.2% from 1948 to 1965, when the rate of increase began to fall. The BLS pegs 1973 as the year that the productivity slowdown appeared in the general business economy; the rate actually declined from 1978 to 1980.

While the growth in the U.S. productivity rate has rebounded (since the third quarter of 1981, manufacturing output per hour has grown at an average annual rate of 3.8%, according to *The Wall Street Journal*), it still compares unfavorably with that of other industrialized countries.

Why? Blame has been tossed about like a hot potato: declining capital investment, interfering government regulations, the more labor-intensive service-based economy, a younger and less experienced work force — you name it. Belcher contends that one major cause remains unquantified, perhaps because it is unquantifiable: "American managers took their eye off the ball. The productivity rate grew steadily from the end of World War II until the late '60s. We were successful, we had no competition. It wasn't a difficult economy to manage."

Many pundits — and some American managers themselves — agree with him. Senior managers of 195 companies, surveyed for a study published in the *Harvard Business Review*

("The Awkward Truth About Productivity," September-October 1982), shouldered much of the responsibility. When asked to select the single most important reason for America's declining productivity, the top two choices were "management's ineffectiveness in addressing this problem within separate organizations" and "management's excessive concern with short-term results."

When these same managers were asked why their companies' productivity-improvement efforts were "disappointing," they also indicted themselves, affixing blame to: a piecemeal, unplanned approach to running the business; inadequate coordination among departments; insufficient investment in training and developing lower-level managers; and lukewarm commitment and involvement by top management. On the other

hand, those who felt they had successfully improved productivity credited capital investment in plant, equipment and processes, top management commitment and involvement, good financial controls and information systems, and good employee relations. The first mention of training's contribution was 10th on a list of 16.

What's the lesson here for trainers? Good intentions won't get you far. Productivity, as Belcher points out, "doesn't increase on its own." It must be managed. So while productivity improvement is an intrinsic ingredient of every training program that aims at improving the efficiency or effectiveness of human performance, ultimate responsibility lies at management's door. If top management waves the productivity flag but lacks a coherent strategy, well-intended piecemeal efforts are bound to fail.

Notes:

Self-Fulfilling Prophecy: Better Management by Magic

BY LEN SANDLER

In 1911 two researchers with the unlikely names of Stumpt and Pfungst began an investigation of an even more unlikely horse named Clever Hans. The unlikely thing about Hans was that he could add, subtract, multiply, divide, spell and solve problems involving musical harmony.

Any number of animals had been taught to perform such tricks before, but they all had to be cued by their trainers. The really clever thing about Clever Hans was that he could run through his repertoire even when his owner, a German mathematician named Von Osten, was not present. The horse would answer questions for anyone. Von Osten swore he was mystified by the whole thing,

In *Teachers and the Learning Process* (Prentice-Hall, 1971), Robert Strom describes what Stumpt and Pfungst learned:

"Among the first discoveries made was that if the horse could not see the questioner, Hans was not clever at all. Similarly, if the questioner did not himself know the answer to the question, Hans could not answer it either. . . . A forward inclination of the head of the questioner would start Hans tapping, Pfungst observed . . . as the experimenter straightened up, Hans would stop tapping . . . he found that even the raising of his eyebrows was sufficient. Even the dilation of the questioner's nostrils was a cue for Hans to stop tapping."

In other words, unwittingly, people were giving the horse the correct answers by communicating their expectations to him via physical signals. Hans was able to pick up on those signals — even subtle ones. He

was clever only when people expected him to be.

As it is known and taught today in management and education circles, the notion of the self-fulfilling prophecy was conceptualized by Robert Merton, a professor of sociology at Columbia University. In a 1957 work called *Social Theory and Social Structure*, Merton said the phenomenon occurs when "a false definition of the situation evokes a new behavior which makes the original false conception come true."

In other words, once an expectation is set, even if it isn't accurate, we tend to act in ways that are consistent with that expectation. Surprisingly often, the result is that the expectation, as if by magic, comes true.

Magic certainly was involved in the ancient myth from which the idea of the self-fulfilling prophecy takes its other common name. As Ovid told the story in the tenth book of *Metamorphoses*, the sculptor Pygmalion, a prince of Cyprus, sought to create an ivory statue of the ideal woman. The result, which he named Galatea, was so beautiful that Pygmalion fell desperately in love with his own creation. He prayed to the goddess Venus to bring Galatea to life. Venus granted his prayer, and the couple lived happily ever after.

That's where the name originated, but a better illustration of the "Pygmalion Effect" is George Bernard Shaw's play *Pygmalion*, in which Professor Henry Higgins insists that he can take a Cockney flower girl and, with some rigorous training, pass her off as a duchess. He succeeds. But a key point lies in a comment by the trainee, Eliza Doolittle, to Higgins' friend Pickering:

"*You see, really and truly, apart from*

the things anyone can pick up (the dressing and the proper way of speaking and so on), the difference between a lady and a flower girl is not how she behaves, but how she's treated. I shall always be a flower girl to Professor Higgins, because he always treats me as a flower girl, and always will; but I know I can be a lady to you because you always treat me as a lady, and always will."

It boils down to this: Consciously or not, we tip people off as to what our expectations are. We exhibit thousands of cues, some as subtle as the tilting of heads, the raising of eyebrows or the dilation of nostrils, but most are much more obvious. And people pick up on those cues. The concept of the self-fulfilling prophecy can be summarized in five key principles:

• We form certain expectations of people or events.
• We communicate those expectations with various cues.
• People tend to respond to these cues by adjusting their behavior to match them.
• The result is that the original expectation becomes true.
• This creates a circle of self-fulfilling prophecies.

Does It Really Work?

A convincing body of behavioral research says it does. In 1971 Robert Rosenthal, a professor of social psychology at Harvard, described an experiment in which he told a group of students that he had developed a strain of super-intelligent rats that could run mazes quickly. He then passed out perfectly normal rats at random, telling half of the students that they had the new "maze-bright" rats and the other half that they got "maze-dull" rats.

The rats believed to be bright improved daily in running the maze — they ran faster and more accurately. The "dull" rats refused to budge from the starting point 29% of the time, while the "bright" rats refused only 11% of the time.

This experiment illustrates the first of a number of corollaries to our five basic principles:

Corollary #1: High expectations lead to higher performance; low expectations lead to lower performance.

Rosenthal concluded that some students unknowingly communicated high expectations to the supposedly bright rats. The other students communicated low expectations to the supposedly dull ones. But this study went a step further. According to Rosenthal, "Those who believed they were working with intelligent animals *liked* them better and found them more pleasant. Such students said they felt more relaxed with the animals, they treated them more gently and were more enthusiastic about the experiment than the students who thought they had dull rats to work with."

Corollary #2: Better performance resulting from high expectations leads us to like someone more; lower performance resulting from low expectations leads us to like someone less.

Rats aren't good enough for you? In another classic experiment, Rosenthal and Lenore Jacobson worked with elementary school children from 18 classrooms. They randomly chose 20% of the children from each room and told the teachers they were "intellectual bloomers." They explained that these children could be expected to show remarkable gains during the year. The experimental children showed average IQ gains of two points in verbal ability, seven points in reasoning and four points in overall IQ. The "intellectual bloomers" really did bloom!

How can this possibly work? In *Pygmalion in the Classroom* (Holt, Rinehart and Winston, 1968), Rosenthal replies:

"To summarize our speculations, we may say that by what she said, by how and when she said it, by her actual facial expressions, postures and perhaps by her touch, the teacher may have communicated to the children of the experimental group that she expected improved intellectual performance. Such communication together with possible changes in teaching techniques may have helped the child learn by changing his self-concept, his expectations of his own behavior, and his motivation, as well as his cognitive style and skills."

There was no difference in the amount of time the teachers spent with the students. Evidently there was a difference in the quality of the interactions.

The teachers also found the "bloomers" to be more appealing, more affectionate and better adjusted. Some students gained in IQ even though they had not been designated as "bloomers," but they were not regarded to be as appealing, affectionate or well-adjusted. Apparently, the bloomers had done what was expected of them and the teachers were comfortable with them. The other students who did well surprised the teachers; they did the unexpected and the teachers were not as comfortable with them. It may be that they were thought of as overstepping their bounds or labeled as troublemakers.

Corollary #3: We tend to be comfortable with people who meet our expectations, whether they're high or low; we tend *not* to be comfortable with people who don't meet our expectations, whether they're high or low.

As for our expectations of what will happen or how someone will behave, we form them in a thousand ways, many preconceived. We all are prejudiced in the literal sense of the word; we "prejudge" either positively or negatively. We like to think we know what's going to happen before it happens, and we don't like to be proven wrong. We want to feel that we can control things. The impulse has given rise to religion, which says we can influence the gods with prayer; magic, which says we can manipulate events with secret powers; and science, which says we can understand the logic behind events and use it to predict similar events.

Figure 1.
HOW TEACHERS COMMUNICATE EXPECTATIONS

- Seating low-expectation students far from the teacher and/or seating them in a group.
- Paying less attention to "lows" in academic situations (smiling less often, maintaining less eye contact, etc.).
- Calling on lows less often to answer questions or to make public demonstrations.
- Waiting less time for lows to answer questions.
- Not staying with lows in failure situations (e.g., providing fewer clues, asking fewer follow-up questions).
- Criticizing lows more frequently than highs for incorrect responses.
- Praising lows less frequently than highs after successful responses.
- Praising lows more frequently than highs for marginal or inadequate responses.
- Providing lows with less accurate and less detailed feedback than highs.
- Failing to provide lows with feedback about their responses as often as highs.
- Demanding less work and effort from lows than from highs.
- Interrupting lows more frequently than highs.

From *Educational Sociology: A Realistic Approach*, T. Good and J. Brophy, Holt, Rinehart and Winston, New York, 1980.

Figure 2.
HOW MANAGERS COMMUNICATE EXPECTATIONS

- Seating low-expectation employees in low-prestige office areas far from the manager.
- Paying less attention to lows in business situations (smiling less often and maintaining less eye contact). Giving them less information about what's going on in the department.
- Calling on lows less often to work on special projects, state their opinions, or give presentations.
- Waiting less time for lows to state their opinions.
- Not staying with lows in failure situations (i.e., providing less help or giving less advice when subordinates really need it).
- Criticizing lows more frequently than highs for making mistakes.
- Praising lows less frequently than highs after successful efforts.
- Praising lows more frequently than highs for marginal or inadequate efforts.
- Providing lows with less accurate and less detailed feedback on job performance than highs.
- Failing to provide lows with feedback about their job performance as often as highs.
- Demanding less work and effort from lows than from highs.
- Interrupting lows more frequently than highs.

Corollary #4: Forming expectations is natural and unavoidable.

And the simple truth is that almost all of us behave pretty much according to the way we're treated. If you keep telling a teenager, for example, that he's worthless, has no sense of right or wrong and isn't going to amount to anything, he'll probably respond accordingly. If you keep telling him (sincerely) that he's important to you, that you have every confidence in his judgment as to what's right or wrong and that you're sure he's going to be successful in whatever he decides to do, he'll also tend to respond accordingly. You transmit those expectations to him and he'll begin to reflect the image you've created for him.

Corollary #5: Once formed, expectations about ourselves tend to be self-sustaining.

Exactly how do we communicate the expectations responsible for the Pygmalion Effect? The process works in very similar ways with people as it did with Clever Hans. In *Educational Sociology: A Realistic Approach* (Holt, Rinehart and Winston, 1980), Thomas Good and J. Brophy list a dozen ways in which teachers may behave differently toward students. Figure 1 shows their list.

Does It Work at Work?

It doesn't take much of a leap to see how Good and Brophy's list of teacher behaviors might apply to managers and subordinates in the business world, let alone to adult education and training. Figure 2 shows some obvious parallels. And research into the impact of self-fulfilling prophecies has not been limited to the classroom.

In one study a group of female applicants for a machine operator position was tested for intelligence and finger dexterity. Their supervisors were told that some of the women (actually chosen at random) had scored high on the tests. The results? The foremen gave more favorable evaluations to those workers whom they had been led to believe had higher test scores. And there's more: The actual production records of these women were substantially better.

Another example is the work of Albert King, a professor of business administration at Kansas State University. King randomly picked some novice welders, mechanics, presser machine operators and assembler trainees, and told their supervisors that these workers showed special potential for their jobs. Trainees from whom supervisors expected better job performance delivered just that. They were rated higher by their peers, scored better on objective tests and had lower absence rates. The average performance rankings for the high-expectation group were substantially higher than for the control group.

Expectations, as if by magic, come true.

One dramatic illustration of the Pygmalion Effect achieved notoriety in the 1960s when it was reported in *Look* magazine as "Sweeney's Miracle." Jim Sweeney taught at Tulane University and was responsible for the biomedical computer center. He insisted that he could teach a janitor named Johnson to become a computer operator. The University required a certain score on an IQ test to qualify a person to become an operator trainee. Johnson failed the test miserably. Sweeney threatened to quit unless the administration allowed him to give Johnson a chance. After much work, Johnson not only became an operator but wound up running the main computer room and being responsible for the training of new operators.

Sweeney's story brings up an important point. The Pygmalion Effect really begins with a belief in your own ability to manage yourself and others. The best managers share this belief.

Warren Bennis, a professor of management at the University of Southern California who has written extensively on the subject of leadership, recently interviewed 90 successful business leaders and their subordinates to determine what traits the leaders had in common. One of the characteristics that came through loud and clear was a positive self-image.

Why are the best managers able to create high performance expectations while weaker managers cannot? For decades theorists have pointed to the manager's self-confidence. In a 1969 *Harvard Business Review* article called "Pygmalion in Management," J. Sterling Livingston, a professor of business administration at Harvard and president of the Sterling Institute, put it like this:

"If he has confidence in his ability to develop and stimulate them to high levels of performance, he will expect much of them and will treat them with confidence that his expectations will be met. But if he has doubts about his ability to stimulate them, he will expect less of them and will treat them with less confidence."

Why is it that subordinates whose managers have low expectations of them tend to produce lower performance? Livingston uses the example of salespeople to make the point.

"Unsuccessful salesmen have great difficulty maintaining their self-image and self-esteem. In response to low managerial expectations, they typically attempt to prevent additional damage to their egos by avoiding situations that might lead to greater failure. They either reduce the number of sales calls they make or avoid trying to 'close' sales when that might result in further painful rejection, or both. Low expectations and damaged egos lead them to behave in a manner that increases the probability of failure, thereby fulfilling their managers' expectations."

Corollary #6: Good managers produce employees who perform well and feel good about themselves; bad managers produce employees who perform poorly and feel badly about themselves.

Pygmalion in Action

One of the critical tools a manager uses to influence employees is the performance review. Most managers underestimate its importance. Certainly the review is used as a report card, as a means of calculating the size of raises, as a way to introduce areas needing improvement and as a permanent record of what someone has accomplished. Much more importantly, though, reviews influence future performance. They offer a good example of how self-fulfilling prophecies work, for good or ill.

Take the case of a bright, young, aggressive employee. Let's assume she is abrasive, disruptive and disrespectful at times. However, she can also be creative, hard-working and full of enthusiasm. Given proper channeling, she can produce excellent results.

Some managers, required to assign her to a performance category, would call her "excellent." They're impressed by her strengths. Others, focusing on her weaknesses, would call her "poor." Still others, weighing the pluses and minuses, would call her "average."

Even with the scant information you have, you can see that any of these ratings could be justified. But what these managers are doing, probably unknowingly, is helping to determine the young woman's future performance. If she's rated "excellent," what will happen? She'll tend to be even more abrasive, disruptive and disrespectful. She'll also probably be more creative, enthusiastic and hard-working. She will do more of what she believes her manager wants.

What if she's rated "poor?" She'll likely be less abrasive, but she'll also be less creative and enthusiastic.

Suppose she's rated "average?" Depending on what her manager says about the rating and why she got it, she may adjust her behavior slightly.

The variable here is the manager's rating. It is based on the manager's values, prejudices and feelings. Most employees will take the cues and alter their future behavior accordingly.

Corollary #7: Performance ratings don't just summarize the past, they help determine future performance.

Communication

A manager cannot avoid communicating low expectations because the messages are often nonverbal and unintentional. As with observers communicating to Clever Hans and teachers communicating to students, managers nod their heads, prolong or shorten eye contact, express themselves in a certain tone of voice, etc.

Some managers refuse to admit they communicate negative expectations: "I never said anything negative to him. I hardly spoke to him at all." (As if that doesn't send a powerful message.) The key is not what managers say, but the way they behave.

Corollary #8: The best managers have confidence in themselves and in their ability to hire, develop and motivate people; largely because of that self-confidence, they communicate high expectations to others.

A manager increases or decreases initiative by the frequent or infrequent use of praise, criticism, feedback, information, etc. The manager, therefore, plays a highly significant role in the success or failure of an employee.

Robert Rosenthal breaks down the various ways in which teachers communicate expectations to students into four general categories. The same categories suggest ways by which managers can influence the success of subordinates.

• *Climate.* Managers create a warmer social and emotional mood for high-expectation employees. They smile more, nod their heads approvingly and look into subordinates' eyes more often. They are generally more supportive, friendly, accepting and encouraging.

• *Input.* More assignments and projects are given to high-expectation employees. In addition, these assignments are more challenging and afford higher visibility.

• *Output.* Managers give high-expectation employees more opportunities to speak at meetings, to offer their opinions or to disagree with the manager's opinions. They pay closer attention to their responses, and give them more assistance or encouragement in generating solutions to problems.

• *Feedback.* Managers give more positive reinforcement to high-expectation employees. They praise them more for good work and criticize them less for making mistakes. Consequently, confidence grows.

Like the teacher with the student and the trainer with the trainee, the manager has a profound impact on the success or failure of the subordinate. To quote Livingston once more, "If he is unskilled, he leaves scars on the careers of the young men (and women), cuts deeply into their self-esteem and distorts their image of themselves as human beings. But if he is skillful and has high expectations of his subordinates, their self-confidence will grow, their capabilities will develop and their productivity will be high. More often than he realizes, the manager is Pygmalion."

ROLE-PLAYS

How to Turn Bystanders into Role-Players

BY DUGAN LAIRD
AND RUTH SIZEMORE HOUSE

If you're training people to change their behavior in some way, sooner or later you'll probably be getting down to cases — to the case methods, that is.

By offering learners the chance to address specific examples of a principle or a theory, the case method tends to allow more meaningful learning than is possible through discussion alone.

When learners simply analyze a prepared "case," however, they remain outside the experience, "looking in on life." To give trainees a deeper level of experience, instructors often use role-plays. In a role-play, of course, learners enact the situation rather than merely talk about it. In a significant way, role-plays let learners escape the environment of the classroom to behave as they would in another place and at another time — for example, on the job, tomorrow morning.

Thus case studies lead naturally to role-plays, especially in situations where learners need to:

• Try out new behaviors the trainer is recommending.

• Try out behaviors they themselves see as potentially useful.

• Practice new behaviors to make them habitual.

• Experience difficult situations from the viewpoints of other people.

• Test a theory in a practical "behavioral laboratory."

Let's examine that last point. For example, in a discussion during a case study, a trainee might say, "Well, I'd just let Edith know who's boss around here." That may be an excellent idea under the circumstances set up by the case, but announcing what one would do does not mean one actually knows how to do it, nor that one *could* do it in an actual situation. The role-play provides a chance to illustrate that fact.

As the instructor, you might simply say, "That's an interesting approach. Let's try it out. I'll be Edith, and you say what you would say to let me know who is the boss around here."

Nobody has moved "on stage," no lights were dimmed, no curtains were raised — but all the same, a role-play has begun.

That's an important point: Role-playing can be spontaneous and very informal. In fact, the most effective role-plays usually are informal and untheatrical. The more students use their imagination and the less they depend upon props, the greater the learning. And the less sound and fury with which you introduce the idea of role-playing, the less resistance you'll run into.

A number of trainers prefer to use the term "reality practice" rather than "role-playing," feeling that the former term better explains what role-plays are about. They also feel that calling it reality practice helps them deal with the fact that a lot of people don't like to role-play.

Why wouldn't trainees like to role-play? There are a number of reasons. But there also are a number of things the instructor can do to overcome them. Here are 13 tips on how to use role-plays effectively.

1 Use the multiple format. This means simply that instead of asking one set of players to move to the front of the room and do the enactment, you give roles (and/or observer sheets) to everyone in the class. As soon as they have had time to read their respective roles, they can complete a number of simultaneous enactments in small groups. By wandering around the room, you can gather data to lead a profitable feedback analysis — and you'll know when to stop the role-plays.

Multiple plays serve a dual purpose in that they put *everyone* into the action and, at the same time, eliminate the intimidating effect of "spotlighting" one group of players at the front of the room. Even if you intend to introduce "spotlight" plays later, multiples are an excellent way to begin.

2 Give specific checkpoints to all observers. These probably should be listed on printed "observer sheets," which are useful regardless of whether you use the multiple or the "one-scene-in-front-of-the-class" format.

Sample questions for a sales-training session might look like these: How did the customer handle the initial complaint? (Quote specific words.) What did the salesperson's nonverbal behavior say to the customer? (Cite specific postures, gestures, facial expressions.) What was the first verbal response to the salesperson? How did the customer react to these words? At what point, if any, did the customer's behavior begin to change? Would you describe the customer as more irate, less irate or totally satisfied at the end of the conversation?

Observer sheets for a supervisory-training session would include similar questions: What words did the supervisor use to put the employee at ease? How did the supervisor word the denial of the employee's request? How did the employee respond? (Note both verbal and nonverbal behaviors.) What vague phrases on the part of either player inhibited understanding? Did you note any cases where one person interrupted the other? (Jot down words to remind you of these occasions.)

3 Keep the number of characters to a minimum. Two or three is best; five is probably too many. Other learners can be given an active role through observer sheets. Since the role-play needs to focus on the details of specific behavior, neither you nor the observers should be trying to analyze what every single person does in a "mob scene" — leave that to Cecil B. De Mille. If there are too many characters, too many people will try out too many things and nobody will get meaningful feedback. The amount of data generated by the role-play will be unmanageable and the learners will be lost.

4 **In writing role-plays, be sure the characters have distinct and conflicting objectives or ideas about how to solve a problem.** Reality practice must involve the opportunity to "'work things out." If all of the characters are in harmony, there can be no confrontation. This is especially important in interpersonal-skills training: Differences of opinion or values are necessary to stimulate true interaction.

This variety of viewpoints is something like the "ambiguity" sought in case studies. Further ambiguity is inherent in the role-play because the differences can be resolved in as many different ways as there are players for any role. The fun of the interaction (as well as of the learning) comes when those differences are evaluated in the analysis that must follow every enactment.

When using role-plays to "imprint" a procedure or to provide practice, give the players a "job aid" — a list of specific steps they should take. Here, ambiguity lies in the way they execute the separate steps, not in the steps they select to solve the problem.

5 **During the enactments, wait for the "second lull."** That strange-sounding advice refers to the fact that when people role-play they typically will start off slowly, then build in intensity until they have passed a crisis in the interaction. Then things will "fall off" in what amounts to the "first lull" — a period of introspection, analysis . . . and learning.

After the lull they will reenter the role-play with some new insights and new plans; noise levels will rise along with the intensity of the role-playing. Then there will be a second lull. Wait for this second lull before you halt the enactments and begin to analyze the results.

6 **Always follow a role-play with an analysis.** Players deserve feedback on how others perceived their solutions and the way they executed those solutions. Everyone in the group is interested in how other people handled the situation, and all want ideas on how they could improve their own performance.

7 **When possible, let players repeat the enactments.** This allows them to polish behaviors that gave them problems the first time and/or to try out behaviors they didn't think about until the feedback session.

Nobody has moved "on stage" and no curtains were raised — but all the same, a role-play has begun.

---

8 **Change responsibilities so observers become characters.** Everyone gets a chance, if not in the same situation, at least in parallel situations.

9 **In emotionally charged confrontations, let the characters reverse roles.** This does not require a new case or an elaborate new set of instructions. Just step into the role-play and tell the players to "switch." By shifting suddenly from the "boss" role to the subordinate role, for instance, a trainee can gain new insight and develop some empathy about what it's like to be on the receiving end of the orders and conditions he himself just finished laying down.

10 **Let learners write up their own role-plays.** This allows them to describe roles in conflicting situations they face in their own work. It tends to make the role-playing more

realistic, more relevant and, therefore, more credible.

11 **Introduce the role-play by relating it to a specific learning objective.**

12 **Reinforce the way role-players solved the problem, not the way they played the roles.** This above all is the key to administering role-plays effectively.

You aren't running a community theater here, so beware of comments like, "Charlton Heston better watch out." Far better to say, "Did you notice how well Barry controlled his desire to interrupt?" or "What were some of those excellent open questions Sharon used to get the applicant to reveal his past prison record?"

There should be no Oscars for role-playing — only reinforcement for the best execution of appropriate behaviors.

13 **"Rotation" and "doubling"** are two optional methods you might want to try to increase participation in your role-plays.

In rotation, any observer who wants to try a different approach may replace any player during the enactment — just walk up, tap the player on the shoulder or whatever, and step into that player's role. The action continues. In doubling, added players may enter the action, standing or sitting beside or behind the original player so that several people simultaneously are enacting one or both of the roles in the situation.

Using these techniques, you can eliminate the bystanders to a classroom interaction. And "learner participation" won't amount simply to busy work: It will be part of a purposeful and responsible learning process.

5 Ways To Sink Self-Managed Teams

BY LAWRENCE HOLPP

The scene: A seminar on self-managing teams (SMTs).

The players: Clients from the public sector, from manufacturing, service and health-care industries, and a consultant who is the seminar leader.

Public-sector client: This empowerment stuff sounds great, but there are just too many decisions that truly need to be made by management. If we let the teams have real responsibility for decision making, we could get into trouble.

Manufacturing client: Our team-empowerment program worked well at first, but then the teams wanted to do too much. They wanted input into decisions they weren't ready for.

Consultant: How did you know they weren't ready?

Manufacturing client: They messed up and we had to go in and change their decision.

Consultant: I see.

Service client: Empowering our teams has been no more than a qualified success. We found we had to pull back on our empowerment goals.

Consultant: What do you mean by your empowerment goals?

Service client: Oh well, you know, letting the teams do their own hiring, budgeting, planning and day-to-day scheduling. The teams started meeting all the time and their work suffered. The first thing they suggested was an office reorganization.

Consultant: I can see how that could be tricky.

Health-care client: Our teams program started out great. We gave our teams all the empowerment they wanted.

Consultant: What do you mean by all the empowerment they wanted?

Health-care client: Well, we let them do everything: make their own schedules, hire new people, work with the suppliers, deal with patient relations and insurance companies. Everything.

Consultant: All at once?

Health-care client: Sure, isn't that what empowerment is?

Consultant: Let's talk.

If you recognize yourself or your organization in the comments of the imaginary clients above, don't be alarmed. You're not alone. I've found that for every success with self-managed teams, there are up to five failures or highly *qualified* successes.

The problems organizations encounter while empowering teams range from the mundane and predictable ("Management didn't really want teams and didn't support them.") to the more subtle ("Our work structure tends to reward individual effort rather than team accomplishment."). I've run across five major ways in which organizations unthinkingly undermine the process of creating self-managing teams (SMTs). If any of them sounds familiar, it might be a clue about how to make your teams more effective.

The Dump

The most common act of thoughtless sabotage is what I call the Dump. The Dump occurs when management decides to give teams a try, holds a short meeting to work out the details, decides that the process is a "no-brainer" and delegates to teams 27 key duties that were formerly the province of management.

The result is usually open rebellion. While predictable from the vantage point of an objective, outside observer, this reaction invariably provokes astonishment from management. But the only mystery here is why managers are so surprised. How would *they* react if their bosses decided to triple their duties? Problems associated with the Dump arise from several flawed assumptions.

Assumption #1: Everyone wants to manage and be in charge. This is an understandable error for managers to make, since they obviously like their jobs and consider them prestigious. Why else would they put up with all the nonsense that comes with the position?

Fact: Many employees are leery of the manager role. They see managers coming in early, leaving late and trapped in interminable meetings. Somehow they're not motivated by this vision.

Assumption #2: The kinds of assignments that are delegated to the team — maintaining its own time cards, staffing the shift, scheduling routine maintenance, planning the vacation schedule and so forth — are simple, easily assumed tasks.

Fact: When the formal power of the supervisor is removed, even the simplest jobs, like monitoring the use of safety glasses, are fraught with complexity. The problem is not the task, but the social issues of who is in charge, who gives orders to peers, who deals with conflict, who handles frequent transgressors, and how discipline is handled.

Assumption #3: When workers can take responsibility for the whole job, they will be able to produce better-quality products and services.

Fact: While that's probably true in the long run, it's also true that most workers already feel they're doing a quality job. Adding more work, including self-managing work, interferes with the job they are doing right now. In their minds, this reduces, rather than enhances, quality.

Assumption #4: Team members are people with homes, mortgages, kids to raise, lawns to mow and taxes to pay. Thus, in their private lives, they already know how to "manage" a great many affairs. They can easily take on new work duties, such as budgets, staffing, housekeeping and resource planning.

Fact: First of all, not everyone gets those private chores done on time and with the degree of quality demanded in a business environment. Second, there are systems, procedures, people and forms at work that are demanding and sometimes not very cooperative. Learning and adopting new behaviors requires both technical and interpersonal training. Third, learning should go from the simple to the complex. Handing a team a lot of jobs at once will only create havoc.

The Bait and Switch

A second problem comes when management offers more than it is actually willing to part with. The Bait and Switch begins like this: Management holds a meeting to explain the vision and values — laboriously developed with the help of a consultant — that will drive the new SMTs. Since managers are very proud of their vision, they expect team members to get excited, too. In the festive, energetic mood they're in, managers may say a few things they later regret.

Here's an excerpt from a talk given by a very enlightened plant manager in a greenfield start-up operation that is committed to self-managing teams. His quotes are followed by some common interpretations of his message.

What the manager says: We want to have the highest-quality product in the industry produced at the lowest cost.

What team members think: Sounds good. That means they'll have extra money to give us raises and bonuses.

Manager: We want everyone to share ideas and participate in the decision-making process.

Team members: It's about time. I'm going to tell management exactly what I think about the way this place is organized.

Manager: We expect teams to take the initiative in planning and organizing their own work with little direct supervision.

Team members: Great. We won't have to listen to our supervisor; we can do our own thing.

Manager: We want teams to hold their own meetings and solve production and quality problems on their own, working directly with customers and suppliers to achieve the highest levels of quality possible.

Team members: Good. We'll keep meetings off-limits to managers and supervisors. Not only that, but we can bypass purchasing and accounting and cut our own deals with suppliers.

The result of this kind of misunderstanding is that management, well-meaning but imprecise in its communication, gets cast as the bad guy when teams start blasting away in all directions. While it's great to have a vision, the communication of that vision must be accompanied by specifics. Empowerment is a sliding scale of structured "hand-offs" of responsibility. Management must develop a detailed implementation plan that complements its vision and carefully regulates what teams do and how they do it on their journey to self-management.

All too often management doesn't have a clear idea of what it wants teams to do in the first place.

Read My Mind

Very often management doesn't know what it wants the teams to do in the first place. Various executives may have done some easy reading on empowerment and, since they want to downsize anyway, see teams as the natural vehicle. If empowerment has suffered the same whips and scorn that greet most quick-fix business philosophies, it may be because management is somewhat befuddled about the whole process of how to "empower." Management loves the results, but the method of achieving them is somewhat elusive. Often with the best intentions, management will announce its plan for teams, provide for some "teamwork" training, then hope the whole thing somehow catches fire. Even when it does, the fire quickly rages out of control.

Here's what the "Read-My-Mind" empowerment process sounds like from the point of view of the team members listening to a kickoff speech from an enthusiastic executive. What team members think appears in parentheses.

"Thank you all for joining us for our first empowerment (*What's that?*) meeting today (*We had to come.*). We are embarking on a new method of management (*What's wrong with the old one?*) and seek your input on how to improve our quality and service (*So that's why they fired the old boss.*). From now on, we want you to take a more active role in helping to manage our business (*Somebody's getting promoted?*), while continuing your excellent work as members of teams (*No promotions, just more work.*). We expect teams to begin to take on more responsibility (*What does that mean?*) and have a say in day-to-day decisions (*What decisions?*) that affect the running of the business.

"We want our supervisors to take on a whole new role (*Who's going to cover for us when we're sick, then?*) and team members to take on many traditional supervisory duties (*We'll have to fire ourselves?*). In the meantime, management will work collaboratively with teams by becoming more visible and accessible (*Great. They'll be on our backs all the time now.*). We look forward to working hand in hand with team members (*You're going to work the cash registers and welding machines?*) and to team participation in management meetings (*We'll go on the golf outing from now on?*). In the future, we hope to run a leaner, flatter organization (*Layoffs — I knew it.*) where quality comes first (*So we can stop reworking all those junk components we get?*) and respect for people (*Finally they'll get rid of the time clock.*) is practiced daily."

In the Read-My-Mind approach, that's pretty much the end of the message. Management may provide a little training in how "empowered" employees talk to each other, run meetings, solve problems and so forth, but as far as actual concrete tasks and assignments, team members haven't a clue what they'll now be expected or allowed to do.

This practice may be, in part, an unintended result of visioning exercises in which management is told that visioning is a cerebral, poetic activity that teeters on a delicate balance beam between imagination and action. While visioning does require a short detour through the right hemisphere of the brain, it can only be communicated through words and actions. A vision without a clearly articulated action plan is nothing more than a hallucination. Management that falls prey to the Read-My-Mind error finds itself with teams that go off willy-nilly in their own directions.

Yes, But

Sometimes management delegates a set of duties to the team but then has second thoughts. This doesn't necessarily happen when the team makes a mistake; often it develops in the middle of the night when the manager has a "what if?" nightmare. The next day, the "what if?" becomes a "yes, but." The underlying causes of the "Yes, But" phenomenon generally can be found in three areas.

• **Lack of home-office or corporate support.** Perhaps the teams program is the brainchild of someone at the site or plant level, and it hasn't been entirely sold to the approvers at the corporate level. This results in timid local-management members who feel guilty and are waiting to get caught. They're afraid to let the teams take on any responsibility since they don't feel empowered themselves.

• **Lack of supervisory support.** Sometimes senior executives interpret participation as something that happens between line workers and themselves. They like nothing better than going down to the plant floor to sit in on meetings or listen to team presentations. Unfortunately, they often forget to let middle managers and supervisors in on the fun. The result is balky supervisors who revel in pointing out problems from morning to night. The executives, thus upbraided, grow shy and fearful, and begin to withdraw support.

• **Overidentification with the team's success.** The manager behaves like the Little League dad who hovers over junior during batting practice to the point where the kid is afraid to swing at anything. Some plant managers get so involved with the teams that they become overprotective, fearful that the slightest misstep foreshadows a colossal failure. The result is that the teams never learn by doing. Instead, they fall back on management and never learn to take responsibility.

The solutions to the first two problems are fairly straightforward: Get support from all stakeholders before embarking on the team journey. Handling the third is a more personal endeavor. Managers may honestly fear that a team will make a catastrophic mistake, but the fear can be minimized if team actions are supervised at first. Allow small mistakes on small tasks. The teams will learn the value of anticipating potential problems and breaking big projects into smaller strategies for action. They will also learn invaluable emotional lessons that can only come from failure.

Try It; You'll Like It

This pitfall is a variation on an older axiom, "Do as I say, not as I do." The image here is of management reassuring teams that the water is fine without having set foot in it itself. Management knows the team process is good, but doesn't really want to spend the time and effort it takes to become a team itself.

This is not an uncommon phenomenon. In fact, I've found that management is seldom willing to put itself through the same paces it requires of the teams. Managers rarely attend training programs in team skills. Their meetings go on too long, are unplanned and result in more meetings. They fail to empower each other. What's more, they deal obliquely with conflict and avoid quality tools and techniques. Not surprisingly, teams see this behavior and lose enthusiasm for the whole process.

In all fairness to management, it often sees its role as defender of the team. Its sacrifice of pieces of its power provides teams with breathing space to experiment and grow. Meanwhile, management is reacting and responding in a more traditional way to requests from above, assaults from outside and politics as usual. If you, as a member of management, find yourself in this position, hemmed in and unable to practice what you preach, here are some tips to keep the troops loyal and orderly.

First, tell them the truth. People will understand if you are short-staffed, under pressure to get production going, or are dealing with senior managers who don't share your team-oriented leanings.

Second, go slowly. Proceed with your empowering delegations at a pace that allows you to avoid reversing directions. When you delegate too much too quickly, you are more likely to find yourself having to change course or risk being perceived as wavering in your support.

Third, pick one commitment action and stick to it. A commitment action is an activity that shows you are acting on what you profess. If using quality tools is critical, use them in management meetings. If safety is a top priority, never walk onto the shop floor without full protective gear. If you are espousing the use of respectful interpersonal skills, don't slip into the role of Attila the Hun even when production is slipping or people are straggling in late.

The Perfect Recipe

Now that we've reviewed several ways to sabotage self-managed teams, we're left with one question: How do we *avoid* sabotaging them? If it is easier to diagnose the flaws of programs that don't work than to describe the ideal program that will work, it may be because there is no perfect recipe. It takes knowledge and creativity to design a process that reflects the organization's business needs, personalities and history.

When developing SMTs, it's important to stay loose, avoid blaming, roll with the punches, take things a day at a time, and every other cliché you can think of. That's because common sense is at least as valuable as expertise.

Here are a few guidelines you should follow in the early stages to boost the chances of success.

1. Develop crystal-clear business reasons for SMTs. I have never worked with a client who didn't have an ironclad business plan. I have also never worked with a client who had much more than a few ideas written down about the SMT plan. SMTs require just as much planning and goal setting as the engineering for a plant start-up. In some cases they require even more, since the engineers at a plant start-up usually know what they are doing while the design team for SMTs does not.

It's prudent to put together a business plan for teams. In it, explain why you want teams, what you expect them to contribute and which goals or milestones you plan to use to evaluate their success.

2. Get the resources before you develop the vision. There is nothing worse than starting on the journey to SMTs and running out of gas within the first few miles. There's a lot of literature that says teams will save money, improve quality and productivity, and help eliminate layers of management, but most of the literature fails to mention the enormous cost of an SMT program. Most of these costs occur up front, so don't expect to get any benefits right away. Do expect to spend a lot in the form of training, overtime, administrative time, higher staffing to accommodate both production and team activities, and necessary team facilities such as meeting rooms, flip charts and so forth.

Plan to devote the equivalent of 15 percent of your operating budget to team activities. A conservative estimate assumes that for each 40 hours of labor, four to six hours will be taken up in team training, meetings, action planning and related self-development. If you don't have the stomach or pocketbook for this, forget SMTs.

3. Do not assume that everyone has religion. Belief in real participatory management is a little like the gift of faith. You either have it or you don't. The single greatest cause of failed teams is sabotage by managers and supervisors — not because they're bad people, but because they don't really believe in the idea and don't want to go along with what seems like a crazy, impractical philosophy. And yet, it may be hard to divine their resistance, since it's easy to fake a belief in participatory management.

Be aware that no visioning sessions or heart-to-heart team building will change a long-held set of values and beliefs about management's role. Instead, try spending time with managers to clearly define their new roles in the SMT process. Put these roles in writing and throw out the old job descriptions and performance-appraisal forms. Write new ones that reflect what managers are supposed to do, such as coaching, supporting, facilitating and praising.

4. Tell the teams what they are supposed to do, and tell yourself what you expect from them. When teams are not given a road map showing which responsibilities they can take on, they will frequently overreach themselves and get into trouble. This prompts management to snatch back responsibilities and authority. A fuzzy empowerment timetable brings both SMTs and management much grief, since vague expectations produce muddy results.

To preclude this, try using a "boundary diagram." It's a bull's eye in which each of the circles indicates a period of three to six months. Negotiate exactly which activities you expect from the team during the first few months and write them in the center of the bull's eye. Go to the next circle, which represents the second or third quarter (depending on how long you expect them to take to complete the activities in the center) and add some additional activities. Continue this process until you have several concentric circles that add up to a year or more and encompass a wide range of new responsibilities. The team can use this diagram to clarify its present position and its progress as it takes on self-management responsibilities.

Equally important is to identify activities that are outside the team's boundaries. If you don't want the teams getting involved in sales and marketing, finance, personnel matters, materials ordering or workstation redesign, say so and indicate out-of-bounds responsibilities by placing them outside the bull's eye entirely.

Through careful planning, you can navigate your self-managed teams to success and not end up with just another promising program that was tried and found wanting.

Notes:

10 Secrets Of Successful Simulations

BY R. GARRY SHIRTS

The most satisfying experience in training or education, no matter what the subject, is the so-called "Aha!" moment, that instant when sudden, spontaneous insight cuts through the tangle of loose ends in a learner's mind to reveal a simple, memorable truth.

Having spent nearly 30 years designing experiential simulations, I am convinced that this form of training is uncommonly capable of producing "Aha!" moments. In a simulation called "Star Power," the moment occurs when trainees, who might be police officers or corporate managers, unexpectedly realize that the only way to keep power over others is *not* to use it. In "Bafá Bafá," the moment comes when trainees suddenly grasp the idea that good intentions can actually worsen cultural misunderstandings. In a team-building simulation called "Pumping the Colors," it happens when trainees abruptly comprehend that the rules a team operates under are actually the *team's* responsibility.

When combined with other unique strengths of simulations — their ability to simplify systems, to demonstrate other people's perspectives, to develop "battlefront" skills in safety and to solve problems from the inside out — these eye-opening moments can endow trainees with a vivid, often deeply personal understanding of even the most abstract training concepts.

Simulations, however, are widely misunderstood. The most experienced trainers, called upon to design a simulation, often create a workaday version of the board game "Monopoly." These are sometimes successful as play but rarely effective as training.

Here are 10 secrets for creating successful training simulations. They represent lessons learned from my own hard-fought struggles to understand the elusive, often perverse human dynamics at work in simulation training. Taken in sequence, they can supply relatively safe passage through the tricky terrain of simulation design.

1 Don't confuse replication with simulation. The temptation in designing a simulation is to make a small-scale replica of some full-blown reality. It seems logical that the closer the simulation comes to reality, the more valid and memorable the experience will be. If you're designing a flight simulator for airline pilots, this may be so. But in "soft skills" training, the opposite is usually true. The job of the designer is to look past the details to the *essence* of a reality.

Two Navy projects taught me that lesson.

A sailor on shore leave in Athens, after buying a memento in a bazaar, discovered a shipmate had bought the same memento from the same merchant for a lot less money. Unaware of the Greek custom of bargaining, the sailor returned to the bazaar and flattened the hapless merchant.

The Navy asked me to devise a simulation that would teach sailors to respect — and expect — unfamiliar customs and relationships in foreign cultures. Since the Greek culture was only one of many the sailors would encounter, my associates and I created a simulation that postulated two abstract cultures defined in broad strokes: One was patriarchal and relationship-driven, the other individualistic and task-oriented. In neither cul-

ture did we attempt to simulate language, religion or attitudes toward time, work, leisure or whatever.

Trainees were divided into two groups. Each learned the rules of its own culture. Then representatives from one culture had to visit the other and attempt to function. Despite my initial fears that the simulation might be too abstract, it was an immediate hit. Its simplicity captured the sailors' imaginations so quickly that they experienced culture shock when visiting the "foreigners." By concentrating on a few key elements of the cross-cultural reality — its essence — we allowed the simulation to heighten and clarify the experience. "Bafá Bafá" has since been used extensively by the Peace Corps and a number of corporations.

The Navy then asked us to design a simulation to help newly arrived American sailors learn to live in Japan. One objective was to show trainees how complex a foreign culture can appear when you don't understand the language, so we replicated the Japanese experience in considerable detail. We set the exercise in a model of a Japanese railroad station and hired Japanese housewives to staff shops and ticket windows. The sailors were to face a series of real-life quandaries: asking directions, ordering train tickets, buying gifts and so forth.

When the simulation got under way, however, all this authenticity quickly buried our good intentions. The trainees were lost in detail. We had exaggerated the problem and overwhelmed the point of it all. The simulation collapsed of its own weight.

2 Choose the right subject to simulate. Some subjects lend themselves better to simulation training than others. I don't claim to have discovered any ironclad rules to determine likely subjects, but I believe a topic is more apt to be suitable for simulation if it embodies at least one of the following characteristics:

Seeing the world through other people's eyes. A pharmaceutical company wanted a training program that would awaken its complacent marketing department to the competition threatening its principal product line. We designed a simulation that divided the marketing staff into five competing teams — one represented our client company and the others its principal competitors. Each team designed an aggressive marketing plan to increase its "company's" share of the threatened product's market segment. The unqualified success of the competitors' marketing plans revealed just how vulnerable the client company's product was. The marketing staff was shocked into action.

Performing tasks simultaneously. Traditional training methods teach skills in a linear fashion, one by one. In the real world, skills are often needed in clumps: A manager may find herself simultaneously negotiating with a vendor, listening to a customer complaint and planning the response to a memo from her boss. A simulation can create an environment in which she learns to do all three — and more — at once.

Performing under pressure. Some people are skillful negotiators, excellent listeners, clear direction givers — but only when they don't have to perform under pressure. Simulations can create environments full of genuine but nonthreatening pressure, affording such people opportunities to practice their skills under duress.

Developing systems thinking. Many people find it difficult to grasp the concept of how systems operate. They know the parts of a system are related, but they resist understanding the relationships because they think they are impossibly complicated. A simulation can put people inside a system. As part of the system, they see firsthand how change to one component affects the others.

Recognizing cognitive dissonance. People often hold contradictory attitudes or beliefs without being aware of the contradiction. This is known as cognitive dissonance. For instance, if a manager sincerely believes he is nonsexist yet behaves in a sexist manner, chances are he suffers from cognitive dissonance. Many of the "Aha!" moments created in simulations come when such a person suddenly realizes that he or she has been living a contradiction.

3 **Develop a design plan.** In preparing to design a simulation, you must make two key planning decisions. First, will you design it alone or use a design team? Second, will you employ a structured creative process or fly by the seat of your pants?

Whether you go it alone or put together a team, you need to fill the following roles: *principal designer*, who

has firsthand knowledge of training simulations (and, for a team, the commitment to lead); *subject matter expert*, who has a thorough understanding of the subject to be simulated; *administrator*, who sets and maintains the design schedule, oversees acquisition or production of materials, and schedules alpha and beta tests (more on these later); and *client or representative*, who provides a reality check as the project develops (in an oversight capacity only).

While some feel the most productive creative process is no explicit process at all, I believe a simple but well-defined creative program can counteract the pressures that often cause designers to settle for second-rate ideas. I have tried most of the creative techniques espoused by experts, and I've found that their best advice can be distilled into three suggestions:

1. *Avoid premature closure of ideas.* Don't stop searching for ideas after the first workable one appears. Often the best idea comes second, third . . . or 10th. Think of ideas as stepping stones to other ideas rather than as destinations in themselves.

2. *Get outside a problem and look at it from different angles.* For example, try approaching a problem in a marketing simulation from the point of view of a customer, a salesperson, a distributor, a person who's never seen the product before, someone who doesn't speak English — you get the idea.

3. *Give your subconscious a chance to work on the problem.* The solution to an especially intransigent problem will often pop into your head when you least expect it — on the freeway, in the shower, at the beach. Give it the opportunity.

4 **Design the simulation so trainees take responsibility for their actions.** Most simulations are divided into two sections, the simulation proper and a session analyzing the results. Conscious learning occurs primarily during the analysis session. Learning is sidetracked, however, whenever trainees disavow responsibility for their behavior during the simulation. If they can claim they did what they did only because the simulation suggested or encouraged that action, their motivation to learn from the experience evaporates.

When you design your simulation, watch out for these guaranteed responsibility avoiders:

Pretending. If the rules even imply that trainees should "pretend" to be someone or do something, then at the end of the simulation they will exclaim, "That's how I thought such a person would act!" When you allow trainees to become actors playing roles, you compromise their stake in the outcome. Instead of telling someone to act like the president of a company, for example, assign him the authority and responsibilities of the president. Design all "roles" in a simulation so that trainees must be themselves.

Using competition for its own sake. Employing competition between trainees to increase interest in a simulation can, and often does, backfire. Trainees can then justify all kinds of inappropriate behavior in their quest to win. If competition is not a factor in the real-world situation you are simulating, leave it out.

Giving inappropriate importance to chance. Stymied simulation designers often fall back on the trusty old device of a deck of cards, with outcome-altering directions like, "The company is being sued" or "The workers are on strike." Such cards invite trainees to escape responsibility later by insisting, "We made the right decisions, we were just unlucky." Limit chance to events that actually occur randomly in the real world.

5 **Use symbols to deal with emotionally charged ideas.** Occasionally a simulation focuses on an emotionally charged issue that threatens to overpower the learning experience. For example, in the early '70s a teachers' association asked me to design a simulation to teach campus conflict resolution. My scenario proposed that a trivial misunderstanding between a white and black student had escalated into a riot. I tested it with a group of college professors from a state university. They were divided into four groups — a black militant group, a white right-wing group, a moderate black group and a moderate white group — and were given the task of resolving the conflict.

Seconds after our first test began, the black militant group (all white, middle-class males) leapt onto a table and began shouting obscenities. The right-wing group responded with threats of violence. The moderate groups attempted to mediate but were buried in the verbal mayhem. After an hour, we stopped the simulation and discussed the experience. The professors loved it. I hated it. I felt that instead of responding honestly, the participants had merely stepped into stereotypical roles — the opposite of my mandate. I canceled further tests and went back to the drawing board.

I realized that by incorporating such emotionally charged and guilt-laden themes — "black," "white," "race riot" — I had subtly threatened the participants, making it difficult for them to respond genuinely. In hiding behind stereotypes, they were taking advantage of a convenient escape hatch. This made it impossible to get at the essence of racism: power or the lack thereof.

I changed the name of the simulation from "The Race Game" to "Star Power." Instead of blacks and whites, I named the groups Circles, Squares and Triangles, and gave the Squares power over the other groups. At the next test, I worried that trainees would not identify with such abstract groups, thus weakening the simulation's emotional impact. I stopped worrying when I noticed a Triangle questioning a Square's right to order him around. The Square drew himself up. "You want to know why I can tell you what to do?" he growled, shoving his badge in the Triangle's face. "Because I'm a *Square*, that's why!"

6 Don't play games with trainees.
When we first tested "Star Power," we instructed the facilitator to stack the odds, in secret, in favor of the first group of trainees to begin acquiring power (on the theory "the rich get richer"). This tactic served our purpose well — until it was revealed during the analysis session. The trainees were so angry to discover the deception that their fury overpowered all discussion.

We changed the rules, but only slightly. We told the facilitator to explain at the start that whichever group did best in the early going would gain an advantage in later stages. We still stacked the odds, but without secrecy. It worked. The trainees, no longer feeling manipulated, now accepted the concept "the rich get richer" without complaint.

Another kind of game playing can backfire by trivializing the whole experience. I refer to the use of cute proper names, like the "Yell and Holler Telephone Company" or "Caught in the Act Security Services."

No matter how clever such names seem to the designer, they undermine the authority and effectiveness of the simulation by signaling trainees not to take it seriously.

7 Use non-trainees to add realism.
Non-trainees, people who have no stake in the outcome of the simulation, can add an exciting, even crucial sense of realism.

In "Pumping the Colors," a team-building simulation, trainees build a water transfer system that is tested near the end of the simulation by a non-trainee "customer." The team has to provide this untutored stranger with written instructions that enable her to operate the complicated apparatus. The presence of this outsider in the equation forces trainees to consider the system's simplicity of use and elegance of design at every stage of development.

In another simulation, one designed to train sales managers, 10 workers are hired from a temporary agency for the day. The trainees must interview them, select some as sales staff, train them to sell a product, organize them into efficient departments and coach them to success. The use of strangers adds real-world authenticity to the training experience.

Non-trainee participants are not suitable in every simulation (neither is real-world authenticity, as we've seen). But when they are, they can bring it alive.

8 Develop an appropriate performance assessment model.
Because of a perceived superiority of mathematics-based scoring systems in training, simulation designers often attempt to develop quantitative models for assessing trainee performance. These may be appropriate for quantitative simulations — those dealing with financial or other formulaic disciplines — but for most qualitative simulations they are not.

By "qualitative," I mean simulations that teach human-centered subjects like ethics or teamwork or cultural diversity. Mathematical analogs are usually too limited and inflexible to account for their myriad variables — or too complicated to produce meaningful results. Also, trainees often figure out quantitative models and skew the results.

In the marketing simulation for the pharmaceutical company, we considered using a quantitative model to

score the competing marketing plans. But then we realized that measuring every relevant aspect of the plans numerically would require a list of variables as long — and about as informative — as a telephone book. Instead, we used a panel of actual marketing experts to evaluate the plans and assign each a share of the market. This not only produced a realistic outcome, it offered trainees an opportunity to challenge, and better understand, the results.

9 Alpha test your simulation in low-risk circumstances.
Both alpha and beta testing are critical to the development of even simple simulations, but confusing them can be disastrous. A beta test is a real test — a shakedown — of an anticipated final product, always occurring after the design is at least provisionally set. Alpha testing often happens so early in the design process that it might more properly be termed a design technique.

The purpose of an alpha test is to evaluate the basic assumptions of the simulation, its overall structure and the logic of its progression. You should expect problems to surface and be prepared to reinvent the whole simulation if necessary. Never include anyone in an alpha test who has an investment in the success of the simulation. No matter how forcefully you insist that this is only a preliminary test and that nobody should get excited if he sees problems, anybody with a stake in the outcome will panic the minute something goes wrong. And something *will* go wrong.

Do yourself a favor and stage alpha tests with people who love you.

10 Set your own standards for success.
When you spell out the purpose and goals of your simulation at the beginning of the design process, you are defining standards by which to judge its ultimate success. Don't lose sight of those standards as your project nears completion.

By the time you get to beta testing, you may find your simulation seeming to take on a new and unfamiliar personality. This is often due to the cumulative feedback of trainees who take part in the tests. Trainees often overvalue (or undervalue) the participative aspect of simulations; they are, after all, used to sitting passively through lectures. Or they can become so emotionally involved in the simulation that they exaggerate the result, giving you a false positive assessment of what they've actually learned.

Don't get me wrong. You must listen and learn from trainee reactions, good, bad or indifferent. And you must be prepared to modify the simulation when necessary. But you can't let yourself be seduced by enthusiasm or destroyed by criticisms. The success of the simulation depends upon your ability to maintain objectivity.

As you test and modify, you will watch your simulation come closer and closer to accomplishing its purpose. At some point — if you are like me — you will have a surprising but memorable "Aha!" moment of your own. That's when you'll know it's done.

Notes:

No Time To Train

BY CHRIS LEE AND
RON ZEMKE

Evan James was not a happy camper. He had just pulled the plug on next week's Coaching for Performance class, a program that everyone in the organization had agreed was desperately needed, a program that had been on the corporate training calendar since January, a program that was booked beyond its capacity three weeks ago. Now he was going to have to call the five remaining enrollees and tell them the class was postponed — again. Worse yet, he was going to have to call Paul Petters, the contract trainer scheduled to run the intensive three-day workshop, and try to talk him down on the kill fee.

"The hell of it is," James muttered to himself, "Paul has let me off the hook twice already this year. It's not right. But my budget is in a shambles. If they're not going to release people for these programs, why are they so insistent we have them?"

James is a composite character, but his dilemma is real. Trainers we've spoken to by phone, fax and e-mail tell us that despite expressed support — even enthusiasm — for training, managers are more and more reluctant to release employees for any actual courses. The culprit is time: Training takes time, and time is a resource in short supply right now.

One training consultant, who has experienced cancellations and postponements several times this year, reflects on the multitude of frustrations the situation produces: "I suppose I should just take the money and run, but that's not why I'm in this business. I think what I do makes a difference. After I've spent three to six months with these people designing a program that I think really meets their needs, it's no longer just about money.

Freud is supposed to have said, 'You don't get better unless you pay for the sessions.' He should have said something about actually *going* to the sessions as well. If they don't find ways to find the time, they're never going to get the results they desperately need — and have prepaid me to deliver."

Despite the obvious, sometimes glaring, training needs of their people, how frequently do managers find they simply don't have the time to let what needs doing be done? There is no hard data we know of, but a few weeks ago, our interest piqued by reports of this trend, we posted the following question to two training-related, on-line discussion groups. "Are you having trouble convincing managers to release employees for the time needed to do the training they agree needs to be done?"

Within days, we had return messages from 55 people who told us, in essence, "Heck, yes!" Although many described their diligent efforts to solve the problem, they also added, "But if you hear of anything that's working better, let me know right away." While we discovered no ultimate answer to the problem, we did find some interesting approaches.

In the Beginning

The genesis of the "no time for training" trend is pretty clear-cut. In today's newly sleek, flattened-for-efficiency organization, time has become a precious commodity. To be sure, downsizing has taken its toll. In many companies, employees who kept their jobs now do the work that two or three co-workers used to do.

The current work climate at Mortgage Guaranty Insurance Corp. in Milwaukee is a typical example. "We've gone from 1,240 employees to 1,006 over a three-year period," says Deborah Twadell, vice president of corporate development. At the same time, she notes, "The mortgage industry has gone bananas. We've had big increases in sales each year and have shown a phenomenal increase in the volume processed." That growth coupled with leaner staffing puts increased pressure on field personnel, underwriters, and home-office support people.

It's no wonder that Twadell's training group experienced considerable attrition in course enrollments this year. Regardless of subject matter, she says, classes had to be canceled because not enough people could find time to attend them.

Downsizing isn't the only culprit. Everything you hear about the rate of change — demands for turn-on-a-dime service, the revved-up cycle of product introductions, technological advances — contributes to what Stan Malcolm calls the Mad Hatter Syndrome: "I'm late! I'm late!" (Yes, the line actually belongs to the White Rabbit, but you know what he means.)

Malcolm, now a principal with Performance Vision, a consulting company in Marlborough, CT, was until recently learning technologies advocate at Aetna Life and Casualty Co. in Hartford, CT. Although Aetna has downsized over the past few years, time pressure comes from "more than downsizing," says Malcolm. "It's broadening the responsibilities of a specific job, flattening the organization, and moving from a functional organization to customer-based team approaches. We expect people to perform a broader range of functions. All of that exacerbates the learning issues."

So, in many cases, people need to learn more, yet they have less time available in which to learn it. That creates an interesting conundrum that HRD Hall of Fame member Martin Broadwell has observed. "Companies may not slash the training budget, but they change priorities. They just can't afford the time to pull supervisors off the job for training," says consultant Broadwell, president of the Center for Management Services Inc. in Decatur, GA.

Malcolm suspects some of that may be the result of Machiavellian budgeting games. Managers sometimes pad their training budgets with money earmarked for other purposes, never intending to use those dollars to send people to training.

But in many cases, the old Catch-22

comes into play: I'm too busy doing my job to become competent at doing my job.

A trainer at an international financial-services company hears that tune regularly: "Salespeople say, 'I'm too busy selling to learn how to sell.' If I'm expecting someone to show up at training, and the day before they call and say, 'I can't show up, I'm closing a deal worth $5 million,' what am I going to say?"

He sympathizes with employees who are up to their necks in alligators. "These guys are not blowing smoke; they literally don't have the time. We found that out in time management training: Half the time the reason they have problems managing their time is that they have too much to do. That's just a fact of life at this company. Working less would be a solution, but that's not allowed."

Some postulate that the growing pressure on trainers to provide their wares ever better, faster, cheaper is a natural consequence of the precepts of total quality and reengineering. In organizations struggling to compete in the global economy, everyone and every activity must add value, says Jim Pepitone, author of *Future Training* and principal of Pepitone Berkshire Piaget Inc., a Dallas consulting firm. "It started with total quality," he says. "For the first time, we systematically began to look at things we were doing that were wasteful — things that didn't add value to our products and services."

The more recent focus on process improvement and reengineering raised the ante. Organizations examined all their activities with the attitude, "If it isn't adding value, then let's get rid of it," Pepitone says. "Most companies can't tolerate waste and still compete, because their competitors are doing something about waste themselves."

Why not look at training activity the same way? he asks. "If management finds employees spend X hours in training, they're almost obliged to cut that time when they are being asked to operate as efficiently as possible." Pepitone sees a dual application for process improvement in training: reducing class time and reducing the time required to get new employees trained and on the job.

The latter concern continuously pushes Circle K Corp., the Phoenix-based convenience store giant, to improve its new-employee training.

Circle K hires and trains 32,000 new employees each year, so every hour saved in training time saves an enormous amount of money. "These are the people running the cash registers — the people who are making us money — so the quicker we get them behind the counter waiting on customers, the better," says Tom Roney, director of training and development.

In the convenience store business, high turnover is a fact of life, and for the store operators who do daily battle with staffing shortages, it can be an unpleasant fact. "When you've got people who walk out the door today and say they won't be back, you need someone quickly for an eight-hour shift tomorrow. Otherwise, you have to work it yourself. You want to avoid that," points out Roney.

"Companies may not slash the training budget, but they change priorities. They just can't afford the time to pull supervisors off the job for training."

So Circle K store operators continually harangue Roney's training group for faster, more convenient training. It's almost a "Name That Tune" routine, he laughs. "'I can teach that course in six weeks' .... Time is always the challenge. Operators want people as quickly as they can get them."

The frenetic pace at Circle K is echoed at other companies, if for different reasons. At high-tech companies, for example, rapid-fire product introductions and the need for new knowledge create a constant demand for training *now,* not when the next class is scheduled to run.

"Management's reaction to classroom training has always been lukewarm," says Jim Fuller, manager of performance technology at Hewlett-Packard Co. in Palo Alto, CA. "It never occurs at the right time. And rarely can you have someone disappear for three days. Downsizing has created a situation where most people have more than enough to do to fill their days. They can't be away for three solid days or three weeks. Their time is too valuable."

This kind of pressure has created "a new construct for the training industry," he says. "Learners must learn in real time, in smaller chunks of time, wherever they are. That's the reality in which we're operating." Sometimes that reality dictates delivering training electronically, via a desktop computer that doubles as an electronic performance support device; sometimes it simply means rethinking and restructuring more traditional means of delivering training.

The Swiss Cheese Solution

So if they don't have five hours, take three. Or two. Or one. For some trainers the most effective solution seems to be making the training fit the available time.

But simply condensing courses is not the answer. "For experiential-based soft-skills training, condensed courses can be a disaster," says Joe Willmore, principal of Willmore Consulting Group Inc. in Alexandria, VA. Squeeze a two-day course on meeting management and facilitation skills into two hours, and you've reached the point of diminishing returns, he says. "Knowing what we know about facilitation and adult-learning principles, the training has to be experiential. I don't think you can give 15 minutes of practice to 20 people in two hours, let alone deliver much content."

Compressing training time by cutting the experiential and hands-on learning portions of a course is also a mistake. If you're attempting to get managers to engage in new behavior, they need to practice that behavior before they're going to be comfortable using it on the job. Cut their practice time in the name of efficiency, warns Willmore, and you'll end up with less transfer of skills and less bang for your training buck.

But sometimes the solution to the no-time refrain is simply a matter of how you slice up training time. When Toronto-based consultant N. Stefan Nopper was training manager for Honeywell Canada, he couldn't convince managers to give up employees in one- to three-day blocks, but he could carve out as much as 50 hours a year of training if he was willing to offer it in one- and two-hour chunks.

Though instructors balked at the idea at first — "I could see their point," he adds — the challenge led to some new thinking. "Each two-hour module had to function as an independent, stand-alone session, yet be an integral part of a comprehensive curriculum that met our business goals. A major criterion for selecting exercises, for example, became the time they took to complete."

Nopper's flexibility paid off pedagogically and politically: "My willingness to accommodate the constraints of line management gave me considerable influence. If I absolutely, positively needed three hours or half a day, I got it."

Some companies go so far as to ask employees to train on their own time. The practice runs contrary to the notion that if training is important to job performance, then the company ought to make time for it during working hours. But the tactic sometimes succeeds. Consultant Willmore says it's working for one client, an architecture and design firm that agreed to provide training courses if the employees would attend on unpaid time. He notes, however, that the deal may have been attractive to these employees mainly because most design firms provide no training at all.

"Brown-bag lunches" are another popular approach among professional firms — lawyers, architects, engineers and so on — in which the business focus is on billable hours. "They have the illusion of doing training without losing any productivity by doing it during lunch," Willmore says. Government contractors, he adds, sometimes use a different ploy: the "59-minute seminar." Time segments of less than one hour do not have to be formally reported to the contract watchdogs.

But the novelty of tuna and training is wearing thin in some organizations. "In my company, employees see this as time theft by management — and don't like it," one e-mail respondent observed. "They already have to use their lunch hours for bill paying and other personal matters. And the company wants that time as well? I don't think so."

Another twist on the Swiss cheese approach: asking employees to give up some personal time to match company-paid training time. "TRW asks employees to attend training on their own time," says Willmore. "Usually, a four-hour class will have two hours during work and two hours after the workday has officially ended."

Other possibilities abound — if you remain flexible. Audrey Choden, president of Training By Design, a

Kansas City consulting company, proposed a novel approach when she was asked to provide hazardous-material training for truck drivers. She uses a modularized training design that requires minimum time out of the cab. The truckers come to work half an hour early, read the materials, take a quiz, and spend a few minutes checking their understanding with their supervisors.

Consultant Willmore came up with a plan that allows curators at the National Zoo in Washington, DC, to attend team-building training but remain accessible to zookeepers. The curators attend sessions with beepers and walkie-talkies, which zookeepers can use to summon them in case of emergency. "You can get by doing that with a small group that's commit-

---

The fault, some seem to think, lies not in an absolute lack of time, but in a relative lack of time: Managers don't see training as important enough to make it a real priority.

---

ted to the training," says Willmore. "The curators see value in being there, so it works relatively well. Zookeepers don't interrupt unless a situation is life-threatening or endangers an animal." In fact, he says, these interruptions occasionally have served as real-life examples for team-building activities in the classroom.

Some trainers have cause to combine a multitude of options. Bonita Sivi, managing partner of Thomas Baker Associates, a consulting company in Sorrento, FL, says that she offered a complete management curriculum in two-hour blocks before the workday commenced. Though she locked the door of the seminar room promptly at 7:30 a.m., she scheduled every module twice. She also offered the program on a more tailored basis. "I worked with people one-on-one if that was the only way they could get it," she says.

Even the particular challenge of delivering training to part-timers can be met if you put your mind to it. The onset of peak-time staffing in the

banking industry meant Jay Cross, vice president of marketing at Omega Performance Corp., a San Francisco consulting company, had to come up with a creative alternative for financial-services clients. "It's hard to find a way to send someone who only works a few afternoons a week to a three-day workshop," he says. Omega's response: "manager-driven" training programs that consist mostly of short, video-assisted modules that managers can deliver to employees as needed.

Sell, Sell, Sell

The fault, some think, lies not in an absolute lack of time, but in a relative lack of time: Managers don't see training as important enough to make it a real priority.

"Altruism, commitment to the organization, and concern for staff, while motivating for some managers, is largely insufficient to 'move' a manager into action and commitment," observes Robert Bacal, a Winnipeg, Manitoba-based consultant. "I think trainers need to become more adept at translating the benefits of their programs into managerspeak." In other words, managers need to see real improvements in productivity, quality or whatever measures they use to gauge performance.

Kerri Reid, training specialist at the Federal Judicial Center in Washington, DC, agrees. "My experience has been that if managers understand and are involved in the training, if we provide them a specific role in helping the person put the learning to use on the job, then they are more apt to allow employees to go to the training," she says.

Training will not be a priority for managers until they believe in the benefits, says David Gerard, a consultant in Morgan Hill, CA. "It's important to listen to the reasons why they think there is no time," he counsels. "I present a specific plan to the resisting manager that spells out time commitments for all participants." Flexibility is an important sales tool, he adds. "I will break a two-day seminar into four, four-hour modules spread out over two months if that will help overcome the manager's resistance."

At Mortgage Guaranty Insurance, where alarming attrition rates had forced a number of cancellations in scheduled classes, trainers are listening. They began an organizationwide needs assessment to find out why employees had skipped training sessions, what skills employees need help developing, and how the training department can best meet those needs.

Even before the needs assessment was completed, Twadell's department was getting a feel for its clients' requirements. "We're taking a more consultative approach to training than in the past, and customizing to very specific needs," sums up Twadell. That may mean shorter sessions, programs offered in modules or during off-peak times of the month, on-the-job training, and one-on-one coaching. Already, she says, computer trainers have created user groups that meet over lunch hours and share tips on specific software. Apparently, that idea is succeeding: One group ran out of chairs when more than 50 people showed up.

Meg Stephens, staff development specialist at the University of Maryland in College Park, emphasizes that in-house programs need marketing to attract attendees just as external programs do. She increases enrollment at staff-development workshops by securing a guest subject matter expert with impressive credentials. She also publicizes workshops with separate flyers, in addition to including them on the regular staff-development calendar.

Do Better Training

People who offer advice about selling and marketing the benefits of your training courses generally take for granted that there are, indeed, important benefits to sell. There is another school of thought which contends that if employees or their managers are resisting your programs, it's probably because the training you offer is only marginally relevant to the real demands of their jobs or the business.

You won't have to worry about program attendance if you're in tune with the organization's problems, says R. John Howe, chief of training and development for the Employment Standards Administration department of the U.S. Department of Labor in Washington, DC. "I think the reason folks have this nonattendance problem is that often both training staffs and their client organizations feel that it's the training department's job to figure out what training is needed, and to build and deliver it without intruding unduly on operations."

Yet when training staffs operate this way, Howe suggests, their courses are rarely aligned with the real concerns of the managers who, in fact, run the organization. Such marginal training usually cannot compete with real operating pressures.

Dan Topf, senior training consultant at The Principal Financial Group in Des Moines, IA, maintains that by the time you are confronted with management resistance, the game is over. "If we are asked to prove our worth, it's too late," he says. "Our programs have to be focused on needs managers have helped determine."

If employees or their managers are resisting your programs, it's probably because the training you offer is only marginally related to the real demands of their jobs.

Topf is taking that typical bit of training wisdom one step further, however, by offering an abbreviated Training 101 course to the managers who make the decisions about whether or not to send their employees to courses. This half-day session gives them a grounding in needs analysis, training transfer, and what training can and can't do for their staff. Topf wants to help managers distinguish between problems that training can solve and problems requiring other interventions, such as new equipment, performance feedback or incentives. The objective is to create informed consumers and, in turn, better training for their employees.

Re-Examining Assumptions

Alternatives to traditional training — such as computer-based training, structured on-the-job training, and simple job aids — are often more efficient and effective than corralling employees in a classroom and attempting to instill the required knowledge and skills in a given number of hours. Although no one we spoke to would abolish classroom training altogether, most urge careful consideration before holding a class — any kind of class.

Consultant Pepitone flatly insists that a classroom is not the place to transfer knowledge. Instead, he advocates providing information in advance — prework, in other words — and then getting people together only to ask questions, clarify concerns, and to practice or demonstrate the concepts they've already studied.

Prework and self-directed study are good ways to create a foundation of knowledge before you ask people to invest the time necessary to get together, agrees Connie Steward, senior vice president of Forum Corp., a Boston consulting firm. "Designers of educational experiences more than ever before have to be clear about when it's important to bring groups together, and when it's not," she observes. "Traditionally, we'd bring groups together to listen to an expert. And the expert would tell us the newest ideas." But now that expert's ideas are accessible through on-line systems, phone hookups, video conferences, what have you, so it's no longer necessary to assemble the troops to listen to a lecture.

"The time people spend together in training needs to be perceived as a challenge to a higher level," says Steward. "Time is so precious, every minute has to count."

The idea of prework sounds good, but if employees are so time-pressed they can't squeeze in training, what are the odds they will do homework? "Don't give a homework assignment," advises consultant Choden. Instead ask people to prepare for training by thinking about a real-life problem and bringing it to class. "They'll be more motivated if they see that the prework is relevant to their jobs," she adds.

There are still areas in which the classroom is the best delivery mechanism, concedes HP's Fuller. Individuals learning some kinds of skills — overcoming sales objections, for example — need the safe environment offered by a workshop in which to practice and gain confidence, he says. Likewise, if safety or product quality is a consideration, you don't want employees experimenting or learning on the job. "But to the greatest extent possible, whenever it makes sense for the content, we put [training] on an electronic medium. It dramatically accelerates the learning process."

Witness the electronic solution that Circle K applied last year to its new-employee training problem. Training for new hires once required four days: one day in the classroom and three days of on-the-job instruction at a training store. Now new employees spend one day with a computer-based program and one day training at their assigned store.

Evaluations of the new program found that computer-trained employees rang the cash register more accurately and efficiently, and retained information better. But the real measure of the training's success came through what you might call anecdotal evidence.

When one area had a hiring surge, it didn't have enough computers to put all its new hires through computer-based training. Obligingly, the trainer in the area scheduled the old classroom program to handle the overflow. Only two people showed up.

Queried about the attrition, store operators admitted that when they found out the old program was substituted for the computer-based training, they decided to wait until the computers were freed up to send people to training. "They voted with their feet," crows Circle K's Roney. And he got the message: Don't screw around with a quality product. "The store operators know they're getting higher quality in a shorter period of time."

Other time-saving alternatives to traditional instruction? One favorite is the job aid. When consultant Choden is asked to provide training — and get it done in the shortest time possible — she suggests that training is not the total answer. For example, in one case she substituted a desktop reference guide — a job aid — for regulatory-compliance training that would have covered a lot of dry detail that participants weren't going to memorize anyway. In other words, she replaced a training event with performance support.

She sees suggesting such alternatives as part of her job. "It's a matter of educating the managers who are saying, 'We need this training, but I don't see how we have time to take people off the job.'" Often, Choden says, the managers who hold veto power over training tend to see only two alternatives: classroom instruction or unstructured, on-the-job training. And in all too many cases, those are the only alternatives trainers themselves see.

That narrow vision dooms trainers to frustration, says consultant Malcolm. He explains why: "Eighty to 90 percent of the critical competencies of a job are learned on the job. Yet continually in training organizations, we concentrate only on the 10 to 20 percent of learning that happens in a formal setting.

"Managers hold contradictory beliefs," Malcolm continues. "They wish to believe they could send people to class and [those people] would come back competent. At the same time, they know better. So what's going on? Managers are abrogating their responsibility for coaching and development by sending people away

---

> ## "Managers hold contradictory beliefs: They wish to believe they could send people to class and those people would come back competent. At the same time, they know better."

---

to be fixed, and the training department colludes in fostering that belief. [Trainers] take on the role of fixer — even though they know they can't influence more than 20 percent of the learning. It's a well-intended desire to be helpful, so they promise more than they can deliver."

The net result: A long spiraling path that leads only to frustration for trainers and disillusionment for managers. The solution, says Malcolm, is to close performance gaps by designing — but not providing — 100 percent of the learning.

He suggests trainers pursue two all-encompassing learning strategies. First, help managers create a structure for on-the-job learning, such as giving people assignments that incrementally build competencies and pairing them up with the right partners. At the same time, give learners the tools they need to build skills or knowledge: task checklists, reference material, coaching, troubleshooting advice, and on-line training.

Trainers who want to make a genuine contribution to productivity improvement, Malcolm insists, must get into the business of providing learning without trying to take employees off the job.

Get Out of the Training Business

Of course, what we're talking about here is getting out of the training business and into the performance-support business.

That's a 180-degree turn, says Malcolm. "Performance support is learning that is just in time, just enough, in just the right context — specifically, to do the work." Contrast that with traditional training, in which, he says, learning is often just in case, too early or too late.

The change in orientation is perhaps easiest to see in electronic systems that deliver bite-sized modules of information — computer-based granules of training for the task being performed right now.

This is the mind-set Circle K is applying to training it's developing for assistant store managers. After store operators witnessed the time savings produced by computer-based training for new employees, says Roney, they began to push for similar training for store managers.

Currently, store managers in training get eight to 12 weeks of instruction at a training store with a certified mentor/trainer. They also require training on the job at their own store. "They learn all the skills in one shot, and are out of commission for a week at a time," explains Roney. "The operators were saying, 'Can't you deliver this training in incremental pieces so each store can deliver it to people at their own pace?'"

The training group's response: a computer-based program called Career Ladders. It includes modules that train assistant store managers at various experience levels to perform particular sets of tasks. For example, one module teaches assistant managers how to receive vendors correctly; trainees will spend 15 minutes, during their shift, at their store, working through the module. Then structured on-the-job training will kick in: The store manager goes through a one-page checklist with the trainee. This way, the manager will know precisely what tasks the trainee can be assigned.

The program is still under development, but Roney expects it to be ready within a year. He also expects it to be a hit with Circle K's time- and money-conscious store managers. "They don't want to turn people loose for training. They've got a million reasons why they don't want to send them. They can't afford to have them leave the store, but they can afford 15 minutes in the store."

This approach to training is not only more efficient, it also puts learners in control of their own learning. They learn how to do a thing when they need to know how to do it.

A more "pure" performance-support application can be found in the AMP facilitator, an electronic support system developed at Aetna. "AMP" stands for the Aetna Management Process, a structured step-by-step process the company uses to make business decisions and create business-project plans.

The AMP facilitator acts as an electronic coach for users, leading them through the steps: Define the mission and critical success factors, conduct an environmental scan, identify performance gaps, set objectives and action steps, and produce an implementation plan.

"When the user is finished using the software, they've got a competent business plan," says Malcolm. "And by the way, they've learned about the process." In other words, learning the process is an inevitable (or at least highly likely) result of using the AMP facilitator, but learning is only a byproduct. "Learning is not the point," Malcolm says. "The only point is competent job performance: a competent business plan."

That's the whole objective of performance support: Help at the moment of need. When that help is available — right now, not when a class is scheduled — motivation to learn is intrinsic. Ideally, in organizations where it becomes the preferred way to learn, the no-time-for-training problem will dissolve or at least be considerably diluted.

But it does require a new way of thinking about the training role. It requires a shift from trainer to performance technologist. It's a role that some trainers have embraced, but others fear or shun. Despite decades of talk about the subject, "the issue of performance technology caught training people flat-footed," says HP's Fuller. "Trainers figured they'd have a career seeing to it that they had fat course catalogs and filling seats with behinds. Performance technology requires different skills, and that means a lot of trainers are now scrambling to change."

A Final Thought

In every organization, the battle for time and money is unending. Training — just like information systems, marketing, R&D, and other necessary functions — takes its lumps in resource-allocation fights from time to time.

Just now, however, losing those skirmishes is risky. It's risky for the training organization, yes, of course. But more important, it's risky for the long-term future of the organization. When the times demand that every resource be used to its fullest, it is imperative that the organization's human resources be fully competent and contributing as much as possible.

Training executives can cut corners, they can do more with less, they can make doubly sure that their demands for taking employees away from immediately productive tasks are justified. But there are limits to increasing the efficiency of learning — and limits to the effect of pleading and persuasion. Until senior management gives more than lip service to valuing human resources, the battle will continue to be uphill. And ultimately it will be lost to short-term results and myopic vision.

Notes:

SOCRATIC METHOD

Socratic is More Emphatic

BY PAUL J. MICALI

There is nothing new, modern or revolutionary about the Socratic method. The man who perfected it, Socrates, was a Greek philosopher who lived around 450 B.C. His method consisted of asking a series of well-planned questions, through which the prospect's thinking was guided to the only correct conclusion possible — the ultimate truth. When Socrates did the selling, the prospect did most of the talking. As questioner, it was Socrates' role to evaluate his subject's reaction and determine the next question to fire out. He became so good at this that he rarely missed a sale.

Typically, trainers of our day spend a great deal of time and effort prompting salespeople, for example, to use the Socratic method. Why, then, is it so difficult for trainers to use it themselves? Trainers are far from college professors who can be content with lecturing, lecturing and lecturing some more. Adult learners have habits which have changed since their college days, if indeed they went to college. And the material is quite different, both in content and application. As Jay Beecroft, formerly of 3M, puts it, "Education is a simple process; training is not. Educators give people knowledge. Trainers help people put knowledge to use."

The Power of the Question

In contrast to the lecture style of presentation, the Socratic method promises training that is impactful, that comes across with much more emphasis. And if it has positive results with adult learners, its use also serves to enhance the trainer's style and performance.

The Socratic method forces a trainer to prepare more fully. It is fundamental that you can't ask intelligent questions without first thinking them over carefully. It is also fundamental that you cannot jam too much material into too short a span of time and expect it to be absorbed. In both cases, the trainer is compelled to do a more thorough job — admittedly at some cost in time and effort.

In addition to enhanced planning of material and scheduling, there is the benefit of increased learner participation. By listening carefully, the trainer gets a feel for the intelligence level and overall preparedness of the audience, general morale and attitudes toward training, and attitudes toward superiors and the company.

All of this makes it possible to adjust a presentation not only to fit the special needs of the group but also to correct any negative attitudes. And trainers may well learn as much from the answers they receive as they impart to their audience.

Participation also promotes tremendous rapport between trainer and trainees. For the latter, there is a myriad of benefits to be derived from the Socratic method. The best of trainers cannot keep an audience alert for hours on end single-handedly. The questioning approach avoids boredom since it is fueled by both trainer and learners. If trainees know that questions are the rule, they may arrive better prepared for learning, since there is an incentive to read over material very carefully in advance. In addition, the open forum promotes the feeling that personal views can be expressed and won't be criticized, which is always satisfying. The talkers get to talk. The quiet ones get drawn out. The experience is all the more productive for the enthusiastic participation encouraged in attendees.

When Wrong Is Right

Most trainers will concede the advantages of the Socratic method, but many will also offer a laundry list of disadvantages. The time schedule may not permit its use, they will argue, or the material may be new to attendees. Some trainees may be embarrassed by revealing themselves as novices or unprepared, and others will surely contribute the wrong ideas. And what to do with all those sophisticated visuals if time is to be spent in question and answer interplay?

In their simplest form, these arguments indicate a very real problem, though maybe not the predictable one. The Socratic method is ostensibly simple — conduct a training session by asking questions and handling the responses in such a way that the correct answer is ultimately arrived at. The tricky part is handling the answers properly, especially handling the wrong answers properly.

Those who oppose the Socratic method argue that it doesn't make much sense to entertain a bushel of wrong answers until the right one is finally arrived at, or — at last resort — is given by the trainer. It's a waste of time, they claim, since the wrong answers are of no value anyway. Not so. In learning, it is important to understand the wrong way of doing something along with the right way. In fact, when the wrong way is innocently voiced, it gives the trainer a golden opportunity to explain why it is wrong to the benefit of the entire group.

It's almost like handling objections. Done well, there is much to be gained; done poorly, much to be lost. And it really goes beyond that. The trainer must be able to answer *all* questions — right, wrong or irrelevant. Some answers aren't answers at all. They may represent an attitude, egotism, wise-cracking, or some other personal agenda. The trainer must remain in control, but in a positive manner, not by becoming pompous, irritating, insulting, abrasive or in any way terrifying. He or she must reflect the smoothest of salesmanship, appeal to reason where appropriate, and resort to tact and often humor in sidestepping delicate or difficult interchanges.

The acid test of a trainer's ability to set up and effectively maintain a Socratic dialogue is when a trainee offers a wrong idea. If wrong answers are handled properly, much is to be gained by all in attendance. In fact, wrong answers should never be discouraged, whether by ridiculing in any way the people who come up with them or by isolating them from their peers as somehow less smart or less qualified to be a part of the group. This is intimidating as well as embarrassing to the individual, and ultimately counterproductive for the group.

The fact is that wrong answers are far from harmful to the cause. On the contrary, if trainees hear six wrong answers before the right one is finally nailed down, they (including those who offered incorrect responses) will understand the reasons behind the right one even better. It is naturally important to be judicious regarding how much time is spent on wrong answers. In any training, time is always a significant factor whose value is measured by the trainer.

What can be said regarding results obtained with the Socratic method? By many measures, trainees learn and retain more, though how much more is hard to quantify. In one case, however, the average test score of a group of 40 sales trainees after a two-day Socratic style seminar was 22% higher than the average score of a similar group of 85 who attended the exact same seminar in lecture format.

Notes:

SOFT-SKILLS TRAINING

The Myth of Soft-Skills Training

BY JAMES C. GEORGES

Suppose you wanted to become skillful at something. Anything. Golf, karate, selling refrigerators, negotiating, making presentations, being a "leader" instead of just a manager — whatever. The point is, you want to become truly proficient. Your objective is not just to know something about the thing; you want to be able to *do* the thing, and do it well. Would you:

- a. Read a book?
- b. Watch a video?
- c. Hire a motivational speaker?
- d. Attend a seminar?
- e. Try a few role-plays?
- f. Practice with an expert coach under realistic working conditions until you achieved fluency?

The answer is obvious. Any of the first five choices could provide some useful information *about* the skill, but only the last choice will turn potential talent into demonstrable competence. Why? Because when you *do* something repeatedly — trying to perform up to an explicit standard — your mind and body get the "feel" of doing it proficiently.

And the "feel" of doing it *is* the skill. You can confirm that statement with your whole life's experience. If you don't acquire the feel, you haven't acquired the skill. Further, the feel is acquired only by using the skill to produce a real result: a good golf stroke, a sale, a successful negotiation. Coaching the actual performance shortens the time it takes for an individual to become proficient enough to achieve the desired result repeatedly. Eventually, the new behavior becomes a preferred and self-chosen way of behaving.

So the best way to develop skillfulness is to practice doing the thing you're trying to do, under the expert guidance of someone who knows how. Yet when it comes to interpersonal-skills training in the corporate world — the teaching of so-called "soft skills" such as listening, leadership and teamwork — what's the one choice on the list that is almost never used? You guessed it.

Now guess the real reason behind the endless hand-wringing in the corporate training field about how hard it is to get "learned" skills to transfer from the classroom to the job. Guess why trainers find it so terribly difficult to document any measurable business results arising from the soft-skills courses they conduct. Guess why "proving that training makes a difference" has acquired such prominent status as a Big Burning Issue in the training arena.

Here's why: When it comes to soft skills, companies and the "trainers" they employ almost never do any *training* at all. What they do instead is education. "Soft-skills training" is mostly a myth. The reason it doesn't work is because it doesn't happen.

Training vs. Education

There is a great deal of difference between training and education, though the vast majority of corporate trainers are not aware of it. Educating is not the same as training. For most people, there is no causal relationship between education and performance. There is, indeed, a causal relationship between training and performance.

The reason: Knowledge isn't power. Competence is power. Power is the ability to create a desired effect. And creating desired effects is what we mean by "performance."

To *educate* is to increase intellectual awareness of a subject. To *train* is to make someone proficient at the execution of a given task. Many wonderful things can be said about education, but education doesn't cause competence. Only training does.

Try making a youngster competent at riding a bicycle by sitting her down at the kitchen table and explaining how to ride a bicycle. It won't work. It can't work. Because knowing *about* a skill is not the same as being skillful.

Try taking a one-hour golf lesson from someone who uses typical corporate "training" methods. He'll meet you in a conference room far from the golf course, talk to you about a golf swing for 45 minutes, show you a video for 10 minutes, let you take make-believe swings at an imaginary golf ball for one minute ("Let's role-play!"), then ask you to write an "action plan" describing how you will apply what you've "learned." Absurd? Of course.

Skeptics will protest that some people who receive what I'm calling education in soft-skills areas actually do turn out higher performance as a result; they do, in fact, get better at selling or influencing or working in a team. And this is true — for maybe 10 percent or 15 percent of the trainees. Why? Because those people were *already skillful* before they attended your latest educational offering. If you take anyone who is already competent and add more education, you often will get better performance to some degree.

But what about the other 85 percent or 90 percent? It's no good pretending that the training department's job is simply to deliver some information about skills ("The Five Key Practices of Famous Leaders," "The 10 Fabulous Values of Team Players"), and then it's the field manager's job actually to make employees proficient. If you accept the title of "trainer," your task is to make people competent, not just more aware. Blaming managers because the "skills" you supposedly imparted in your educational event failed to transfer to the job site is a cop-out and a lie.

Real Training for Real People

How does real training work? Begin by abandoning notions of what people ought to know or what sort of attitudes they ought to have or even how people acquire knowledge.

Instead ask, "How does one acquire skillfulness?"

The answer is simple and universal. The most efficient and effective way to acquire skillfulness is the same for everyone: 1) Students are quickly *educated* about the results they are being asked to achieve and the skills they will have to execute in order to obtain those results. 2) They practice, with a coach who can cut down trial-and-error time, until they achieve fluency.

That's it. All of it. Every time. In the hands of a good trainer or coach, Step 1 takes up 5 percent to 10 percent of the allotted time. Step 2 takes up the other 90 percent or 95 percent. Step 1 is pure education. Step 2 is training.

Bluntly, if the student isn't *doing* it, it isn't training. A day spent talking about skills will not make anyone skillful. Nobody gets the "feel" for real execution, done to a specific standard of competence. Toss in a role-play or two and they still don't get skillful. You find out only two things from role-plays, games and most simulations: whether people grasped the main idea well enough to *attempt* the task, and whether they are any good at playing make-believe.

Knowledge isn't power. Competence is power.

Again, if they don't acquire the "feel," they don't acquire the skill. Only training accomplishes that. Training is a lot tougher and can be much more time-consuming than education. Maybe that's why so few "trainers" ever do any of it.

Even readers who agree with these points may say: "Fine, but all of that would have to be done in the field. It can't be done in a classroom. And even if it weren't too expensive and difficult to put that many expert coaches in the field, we don't want our trainees practicing on real customers. So how do we make them proficient before we send them into the real job environment?"

There is a way.

How to Do It

Forget the idea of "classroom." A classroom is a place where education happens. It's a place where people learn *about* work instead of doing work.

To do real training in soft skills, start by taking a tip from advocates of "action learning": Invite people to a meeting room for a genuine working session — into which some coaching will be added.

The purpose of this working session is to evaluate and make decisions about ideas for improving the business: real ideas for real improvements that will make a real difference to the company. Ask participants to bring their own ideas to the meeting. Stipulate that these ideas must meet two criteria. First, the people in the meeting must be capable of implementing them; that is, someone in the room must have the authority to give a real yes or no to the idea. Second, if adopted, the improvement must be both measurable and capable of producing financial consequences for the business within 90 days.

In other words, you don't want ideas such as, "Let's change the cafeteria's vending machines." That might be an improvement, all right, but it's unlikely to produce a measurable ROI within three months.

Ideas that would fit the criteria should sound more like these:

• "Suppose that instead of having a single sales rep call on the ABC Co., we put together a sales team of reps and technical specialists. I believe that this team could get ABC's business within 90 days."

• "I think we could achieve 50 percent faster turnaround on customer orders if we combined credit checking and warehouse dispatch under a single management function. We'd be more competitive, and I believe we'd start getting more orders within 90 days."

• "I think we could reduce breakage and waste on the Illinois plant production line if we changed suppliers. Let's use a local company instead of shipping from Detroit."

Explain to the participants that they are gathered in the room to make decisions about issues like these and to execute the ideas they like — or at least to set the execution wheels in motion. They are not just there to "learn stuff."

Now, give them a quick educational overview of the skills that would most likely help them gain the commitment and support they'll need to implement their ideas (see box page 207). You must also clearly define

what "skillful" means — not just what the skills are. For instance, you are skillful at "showing respect" if you can acknowledge another person's point of view so well that the person begins to feel better — you can *see* more positive emotions emanating from the person — within 20 seconds. You are skillful at "leadership" if you can obtain a following of committed supporters who actually will show up and work on a task force to achieve the goals of Project X.

If the student isn't *doing* it, it isn't training.

Make this introduction as succinct as possible. Then put everyone to work on the task of trying to gain commitment and support from one another. Coach them while they do so. (At the same time, you can teach them how to coach one another.) Make them do it over and over again until at least 85 percent of them have become proficient at the skills and have achieved concrete, desirable results.

An obvious "desirable result" is that a participant gains the needed support and approval for a good idea. A less-obvious but no-less-acceptable result is that the participant becomes persuaded that his idea is a stinker, but accepts this with no hard feelings; that is, the participant and his "adversary" *agree* that the idea is a nonstarter, and emerge with their relationship undamaged or even strengthened.

Measurements

Everything that happens after that brief educational introduction is *training*. Measurably defined skills are developed until fluency is observable in the here and now. Further, the outcomes of these interactions are tangible commitments for actual business initiatives that have measurable financial outcomes — the elusive "Level 4" result that trainers talk about so much but discover so seldom.

And you can stop worrying about "reinforcement." Why? Because we all naturally keep doing what works. We only need the goading or encouragement or reminding of managers when we *can't* produce the results we want.

Doing real training is perfectly feasible, even with large groups of peo-

IT'S ALL ABOUT BUY-IN

In the accompanying article, you are instructed to prepare for a training session by asking participants to bring business-improvement ideas to a meeting. Then you are supposed to open the meeting by describing the "soft" skills likely to be most useful in gaining support and commitment for those ideas.

The alert reader may have paused at that point, sensing a skunk in the rosebush: "You say this approach can be used to teach all kinds of interpersonal skills, from leadership to selling to teamwork. If I've got 10 or 20 people in the room, and I don't know what ideas they're going to pitch, how do I know in advance which skills they're going to need? And as far as that goes, it sounds as if the only thing anybody will be learning in this session is how to gain followers or commitment or 'buy-in' for a proposal. Maybe that is essentially what leadership and sales skills are about, but teamwork?"

Glad you asked.

I would argue that when it comes to doing business with one another or accomplishing work together, there really is only one set of interpersonal-communication skills that is truly significant. This skill set (or "master skill") is the one that enables us to achieve a state of rapport, trust, accord, mutual commitment — the condition known in the business world as "buy-in."

The skills taught (or talked about) under headings such as listening, influencing and negotiating are all elements of the skill set that leads us to buy-in. So are the interpersonal pieces of the skills taught under the labels of problem-solving and decision-making.

In the business world, very few of our attempts at interpersonal communication are intended merely to achieve understanding or agreement on an intellectual level. What we're after, most of the time, is buy-in.

Buy-in is what you and I get when we are in union both intellectually and emotionally in regard to a given course of action. When we reach that state of mutual commitment on some recommendation, we will *act* on it without reservation. In a sales situation, I will gladly buy your product. In a "teamwork" situation, we will put forth our best effort. We will keep our promises. We will strive for "quality" performance.

So, yes, you can call it teamwork, as well as leadership or sales or management or anything you like. It all involves the same skill set for the same intended outcome: buy-in.

And these skills are not mysterious or difficult to measure. You can measure my skillfulness at leadership or selling or problem-solving simply by observing my ability to move another person (or people) toward buy-in. You can *watch this happen*. Whether I'm trying to sell Joe a three-piece suit or enlist his support for my new technology task force, you can watch him move, say, from indifference to hostility to competitiveness to moderate interest to full-fledged commitment.

The skills that move Joe toward buy-in are not only measurable, they are teachable. In bits and pieces, they are taught every day in corporate classrooms. But since the classes take an educational approach rather than a training approach — everyone learns *about* the skills instead of practicing them — nobody really becomes skillful.

If you want to *train* people in interpersonal business skills, have them practice gaining support from one another for real proposals, and coach them while they do. Make them practice and repeat each skill until they can perform fluently — with competence and confidence.

What skills are they practicing? Here are the basic ones. I would go so far as to propose that all "soft skills" are derived from these:

• The ability to open a conversation or interaction in a way that elicits open-mindedness.

• The ability to articulate goals.

• The ability to diagnose another person's needs and problems by listening effectively and asking good questions.

• Demonstrating respect for the other's views.

• Obtaining respect for your own views (advocating).

• Raising the conversation "up" the intellectual and emotional ladder in a way that the other person is willing and able to follow (by resolving conflict, forming solutions that meet the other's needs, negotiating for change and so on).

• Carrying the interaction all the way to "buy-in" (the other person is confident and firmly committed to the proposal; she agrees to *act* on it).

Most people *can* learn to do these things skillfully and successfully, at a level of conscious competence. But it takes real practice — practice that leads to a successful result that the person really desires. Education won't do the job. It requires training.

— *James Georges*

---

ple. This approach — educate briefly, then train at length — is the method of martial arts trainers. It's the method of sports teams. It's the method of coaches in the performing arts. It works. The formula once again:

1. Clearly define the measure of skillfulness required. What does the performance look like when it's done right?

2. Clearly define the measurable outcome desired. What is the intend-

ed *result* of the performance?

3. "Educate" quickly and precisely.

4. Then train, via coached repetition, until the measurable performance level and the desired result are consistently achieved.

This formula almost always achieves measurable success, regardless of the skills you're trying to develop: selling, leadership, teamwork, customer service, problem-solving and so on. Instead of seeing slight improve-

ments in the performance of those 15 percent of trainees who were already capable, you'll send 85 percent out the door with genuine skillfulness instead of mere awareness.

Because the group is producing real initiatives that will make or save money, your company can expect a very healthy return on investment within three months. And nobody will have to ask you again if your training actually makes a difference.

The Systems View of Human Performance

BY GEARY A. RUMMLER
AND ALAN P. BRACHE

Most attempts to improve human performance in organizations are doomed to failure from the start. Training initiatives aimed at getting workers to turn out higher quality products? Doomed. Motivational schemes to boost productivity? Doomed. Programs intended to improve customer service, to cure production problems, to introduce more efficient sales methods? Doomed.

Sorry to be so gloomy. But most of these efforts fail, and they'll go on failing because they proceed from the fundamentally false assumption that people perform in a vacuum. Any time we try to improve an individual's *output* solely by changing the *input* of knowledge or information or skills to that individual, we are making the naive assumption that the person exists in a performance vacuum, isolated from and immune to the rest of the organization. We are ignoring the performance environment. That environment — that "system" — has an enormous impact on the way people do their jobs and on the results the organization achieves.

Take a typical improvement initiative — a request for training. The senior vice president of insurance operations in a large casualty-property insurance company sends a memo to the training director. What the VP wants is "a one-week refresher course for 500 claim representatives on handling claims, with special emphasis on scoping damage." By "scoping damage," the VP means figuring out the nature and extent of the loss a policyholder has suffered, and estimating what it will take to fix it. A claim rep is "scoping damage" when she looks at a half-burned house and says, "The foundation is probably OK, but it will need a new roof."

A typical response to the vice president's request is: "Fine. Now let's see, shall we develop this course ourselves or shop for a packaged program on the market?"

If the training department does respond that way it has fallen victim to the fallacy of the performance vacuum: It's assuming that a training input will automatically lead to a valuable performance output. So what? Well . . . .

• We don't know what, if anything, is broken, so how will we know if we've fixed it? How *can* we know, unless we ask what shortfall in the organization's performance has prompted this request for training?

• Assuming there is some particular shortfall, we don't know its extent. So how can we estimate the value we'd gain by fixing the problem? Maybe investing the same dollars in some other area would give the company a bigger payoff.

• Again, assuming there is some organizational shortfall, we don't know that it's caused by a human performance problem. And if it is, we don't know whose performance is deficient, so how do we know if we're trying to "fix" the right people? Is the claim rep the critical performer here?

• We don't know what, if any, duties the claim reps are failing to perform, so how do we know we should focus on scoping damage?

• If there is a deficiency in that particular activity, we don't know what's causing it. So how do we know that training is the right cure? What about all the other factors that affect the claim reps' performance — and the "scoping damage process" itself?

No, if training is to make a real difference in the organization, we need an alternative to the vacuum view of performance. There is such an alternative view. It springs from two fundamental premises. First, every individual operates within the context of a performance *system*. Second, improvements in individual and organizational performance will happen only if we understand and manage the variables in that system. With those thoughts in mind, let's begin at the beginning.

Performance, Part I

Every person in an organization has a job. The point of the job is to produce various outputs that the organization values for some reason. For instance, a correctly settled claim is an important output for an insurance company.

But every performer exists within a particular human performance system. Will we get the output we desire from a performer? That's determined by the five components of the performance system (see Figure 1).

The performer (1) is required to process a variety of inputs (2), such as a form, a sales lead or a phone call. For each input, there is a desired output (3) — inquiry answered, form processed correctly, etc. For every output produced (and for each action required to produce an output) there is a resultant consequence (4) — some event occurs that affects the performer. This event is interpreted by the performer (often uniquely) as either positive or negative. A basic behavioral law holds that behavior is influenced by its consequences; people ultimately will do things that lead to positive consequences and avoid things that result in negative consequences.

The final element in the system is feedback (5). The performer must receive information about the outputs he or she is producing. Are they satisfactory or deficient in some way?

How do they help or harm the organization as a whole?

As Figure 1 suggests, individual performance will be a function of several factors relating to the components of the performance system:

• *Performance specifications:* Have we adequately specified and communicated the performance we want?

• *Task interference:* Have we removed barriers to effective performance by good job design and by providing any necessary resources?

• *Consequences:* Do the things we do to the performer support the desired output?

• *Feedback:* Does the performer know if his output is on target and, if not, how to get it on target?

• *Knowledge/skill:* Does the performer know how to produce the output we want? And even if she knows the procedure or the formula, does she have the expertise to do it effectively?

• *Individual capacity:* Assuming that the other five factors are adequate, does the performer have the basic physical, mental and emotional capacity to produce the output we're after?

It's critical to understand that consistent performance is a function of all six of these variables, not five out of six. For instance, you can have a group of capable, well-trained workers who know exactly what is expected, face minimal interference and get regular feedback. But if they receive (or perceive) negative consequences when they perform as desired, we will not continue to get the outcomes we want. A classic example is the outstanding worker who, precisely because he is outstanding, keeps getting loaded up with extra work by his supervisor. If the only noticeable consequence of being outstanding is that you get saddled with more burdens than your comparably paid peers, you'll probably stop performing so well.

This "systems" view gives us a useful framework for troubleshooting performance problems. Instead of saying, "Let's train them," we ask, "Where has the performance system broken down? Which components are inadequate? What do we need to 'fix' in order to fix this problem?" The systems view also helps us design new jobs, new responsibilities and new organizations by urging us to ask, "What components do we need to put in place to support the new output we want?"

Performance, Part II

We have now placed the individual in a "loop" of inputs, outputs, consequences and feedback. But the performance environment is not that simple. Each performer most likely is part of a hierarchy of performers, and that hierarchy is part of a function.

For example, a claims representative in our insurance company is part of a hierarchy consisting of a claims supervisor and a claims office manager. This hierarchy is part of the field-claims function.

Each function is expected to produce certain outputs. These are determined by the larger organization, based on its customers' needs. The function's outputs are the results of key business processes to which the function contributes.

For instance, the claims office (field-claims function) must produce a number of outputs, not least of which is "claims settled." This output results primarily from the "claims-handling process." Other business processes that operate within the field-claims function include the "policyholder-inquiry process" and the "claim-filing process." Several jobs might be required to support each process.

The business processes dictate the performance or outputs required of all people in a hierarchy. This is a key point, and not necessarily an intuitive one, so we'll illustrate it.

In our view, the first performer in the hierarchy, the claims rep, exists to work with the claims-handling process to produce that process's desired output: "claims settled." The specific outputs of the claim rep's job are determined by the requirements of the steps in the claims-handling process.

At the next level of performer, the claims supervisor exists to ensure that the claims rep works effectively with the claims process to produce the same desired output: claims settled. The specific outputs required of the claims supervisor are determined by the interaction of the claims reps and the claims process.

And so it continues. At the third level, the claims office manager exists to ensure that the supervisors provide the support that enable the claims reps

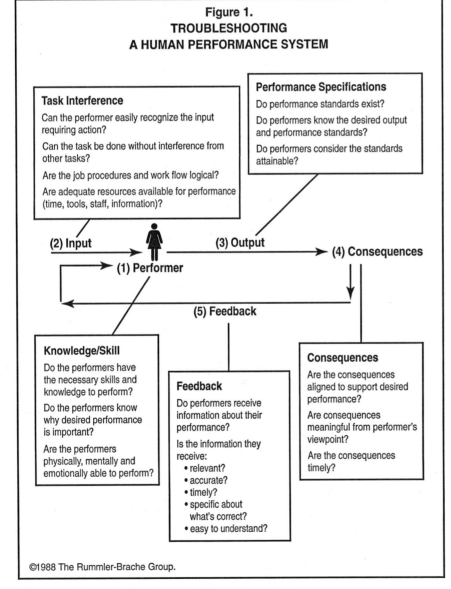

Figure 1.
**TROUBLESHOOTING
A HUMAN PERFORMANCE SYSTEM**

Task Interference

Can the performer easily recognize the input requiring action?

Can the task be done without interference from other tasks?

Are the job procedures and work flow logical?

Are adequate resources available for performance (time, tools, staff, information)?

Performance Specifications

Do performance standards exist?

Do performers know the desired output and performance standards?

Do performers consider the standards attainable?

(2) Input

(1) Performer

(3) Output

(4) Consequences

(5) Feedback

Knowledge/Skill

Do the performers have the necessary skills and knowledge to perform?

Do the performers know why desired performance is important?

Are the performers physically, mentally and emotionally able to perform?

Feedback

Do performers receive information about their performance?

Is the information they receive:
• relevant?
• accurate?
• timely?
• specific about what's correct?
• easy to understand?

Consequences

Are the consequences aligned to support desired performance?

Are consequences meaningful from performer's viewpoint?

Are the consequences timely?

©1988 The Rummler-Brache Group.

and the claims process to be effective. At this level, the manager may be concerned with several hierarchies and a number of major business processes, but the principle is the same: The function manager's core responsibilities are determined by the requirements of the function and the business processes therein.

We have now formed a performance "linkage" for the claims function (see Figure 2). It starts with the requirement for a specific output (claim settled) and links to the requirements of a specific process (claim handling). One step in that process is "loss scoped," which dictates what is required of the claims rep (the first-level performer) and of performers on all higher levels. In other words, our expectations of performers must be linked to the business process that underlies the work they do and to the requirements of that process.

Performance, Part III

Now we come to the broadest view of the performance environment. We've seen that the individual is part of a human performance system and part of a hierarchy that is related to a business process that is part of a function. But each process and every function is part of a larger organizational system. The inputs and outputs of all processes and functions are tied to and determined by other functions and by the needs of the organization as a whole.

Furthermore, the organization itself is part of a larger economic environment. A company can be seen as a processing system (Figure 3) that responds and adapts to factors such as the strength of the marketplace, competition, regulations and technological advances. At a macro level, every business exists in a larger performance-system context.

If we visualize our insurance company as a system (Figure 4), we see that the claims function is tied tightly to the product development and underwriting functions. The settlement of claims (that is, the "payout") is not just a function of the claim-handling process and the way it is executed by the people in the claims office. The payout also reflects the quality of the policy conceived by the product-development function in the first place, and the rate set by the underwriting function for any given policyholder.

In essence, this systems view of

performance breaks down to three levels:

• *The organization level:* The total organization is part of an economic system. It responds to the marketplace, competition, fluctuating resources and so on. At issue is how well the organization is adapting to the demands of this "external system."

• *The process level:* The organization is a giant processing system, converting a range of inputs into products and services for the marketplace. This conversion takes place via a myriad of processes and subprocesses, which must be wired together to form an efficient system. The outputs required of each process are determined by the demands of the marketplace, as inter-

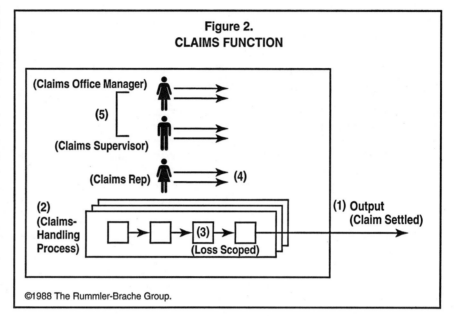

Figure 2.
CLAIMS FUNCTION

©1988 The Rummler-Brache Group.

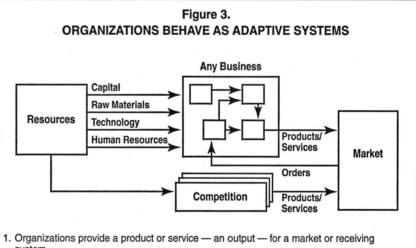

Figure 3.
ORGANIZATIONS BEHAVE AS ADAPTIVE SYSTEMS

1. Organizations provide a product or service — an output — for a market or receiving system.

2. Organizations function in some fundamental way as processing systems, converting inputs (sales orders, technology, capital, human resources) into outputs of value to the market.

3. Organizations are adaptive systems. Either they adapt to the feedback from the market (sales, customer complaints, market trends), or they cease to exist.

4. The functions or departments in the organization either act as subsystems that support the basic organizational process or converting inputs into outputs, or they cease to exist.

5. Organizations exist in a larger environment (or system) consisting of, among other things:
   • competitors, who are competing for both the organization's markets and its resources;
   • the general economy;
   • legislation;
   • government policy;
   • culture.

©1988 The Rummler-Brache Group.

preted by management. At issue on the process level is whether these are the correct outputs for the business to remain competitive, and whether the internal processes are sufficiently effective and efficient.

• *The individual job level:* Each performer's job outputs are determined by the demands of the various processes. Further, each individual is part of a human performance system. At issue is whether the job outputs have been correctly identified as the ones needed to support the process and whether the performance system will support the employee's efforts to achieve those outputs.

Toward Better Performance

The idea of those three distinct yet interdependent levels is useful when we try to analyze and improve performance in an organization.

A project intended to improve the performance of an individual or group must start with the question, "What outputs do we want from the job?" To answer, we have to identify the key processes served by the job and understand the demands placed on those processes by the organization. Because we're aware of the components of the basic human performance system, we are interested not just in training solutions but in the feedback and consequences the performers are getting. We're also interested in the feedback the process itself is getting: What consequences does the organization experience as a result of this process being conducted this way? In short, even in a project focusing on the job level, we must consider the larger performance context.

What about a company-wide quality improvement project? This will necessarily begin at the organization level; we'll have to determine the level of quality demanded by the marketplace. But soon our analysis must move to the processes that are key to producing that quality: product design, production, customer billing, etc. What do those processes require? Finally, we'll have to look at the job level to determine the critical outputs we need from various performers and to design a performance system that will support those outputs. In this case, failure to take the analysis all the way down to the job level probably will give us no appreciable increase in quality.

For a project intended to improve a process (filling customer orders, for instance), we would have to determine the organization's demands upon the process, then specify what we'd require of individual performers and what they would require of us. Again, we'd need to operate on all three levels.

This systems view of performance has important implications for the training function. It suggests some

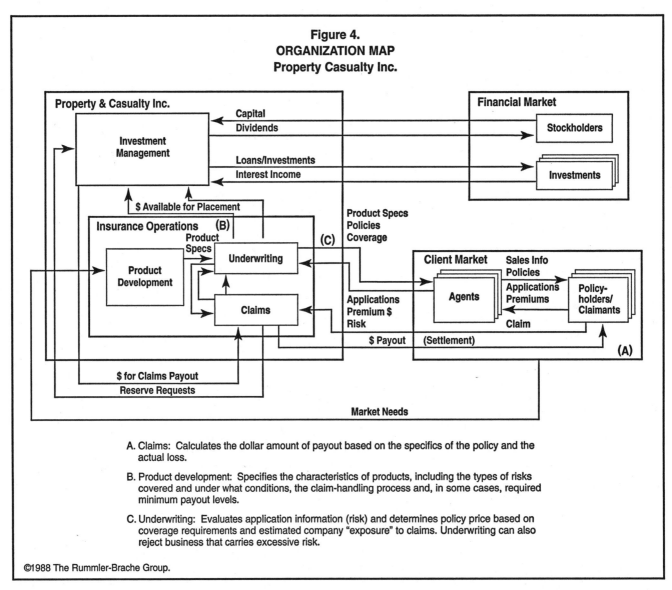

Figure 4.
ORGANIZATION MAP
Property Casualty Inc.

A. Claims: Calculates the dollar amount of payout based on the specifics of the policy and the actual loss.

B. Product development: Specifies the characteristics of products, including the types of risks covered and under what conditions, the claim-handling process and, in some cases, required minimum payout levels.

C. Underwriting: Evaluates application information (risk) and determines policy price based on coverage requirements and estimated company "exposure" to claims. Underwriting can also reject business that carries excessive risk.

©1988 The Rummler-Brache Group.

things about how we ought to determine training needs, and about how the function in general ought to be managed.

Needs

Let's take another crack at the vice president's request for a refresher course on handling claims and scoping damage.

If we believe in the systems view of performance, we are skeptical. Would such a training program make a significant difference? We have no idea. So we ask six questions (Figure 5):

1. *What performance output (of the function or the organization) is subpar? In other words, what makes you think you have a need for training?*

Our claim payouts are too high, and it takes too long to settle claims.

2. *What process affects this function's performance? What process outputs are subpar?*

Claim payouts are affected by the product development, underwriting and claims-handling processes. Settlement time depends on the claims-handling process. Let's focus

on claims handling to begin with.

3. *What process step is breaking down?*

Through observation and interviews with claims reps and their supervisors, we find that "scoping damage" is not a deficient step in the process. However, the first two steps, "claim qualified" and "claim assigned," are often not handled properly. This seriously affects claim payouts and settlement times.

4. *Which performer in the hierarchy affects the critical process step?*

Through observation of claims reps and their supervisors, we learn that qualifying and assigning claims are duties performed by the claims supervisor, not the rep.

5. *What desired output of this key performer is subpar?*

The supervisors are not properly qualifying claims and assigning them to the reps.

6. *What is the cause of the subpar output?*

In most cases, the claims supervisors don't know how to qualify and assign claims properly. And in all

cases, they get no feedback on this aspect of their performance and perceive no negative consequences for poor performance.

According to the systems view, we haven't identified a significant training need until we have answered those six questions — which is to say, until we have examined the performance system. In this case, we did find a real need for training, but "scoping damage" isn't the topic and claims reps aren't the trainees. We also discovered breakdowns in two other components of the performance system — lack of feedback and negative consequences for poor performance — for which training is not the solution.

Managing It

The systems view of performance has two important implications for managing an organization's training function. The first one dawns on you when you realize that the training function is a subsystem in the larger organizational system, and as such must follow all the system laws. Take

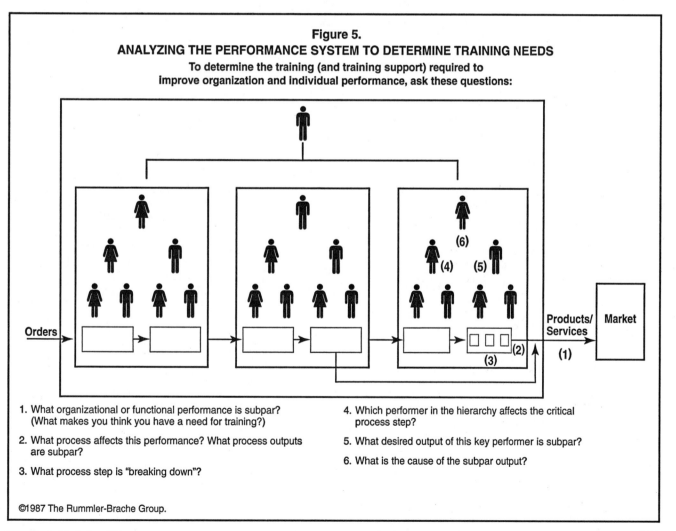

Figure 5.
ANALYZING THE PERFORMANCE SYSTEM TO DETERMINE TRAINING NEEDS
To determine the training (and training support) required to
improve organization and individual performance, ask these questions:

1. What organizational or functional performance is subpar? (What makes you think you have a need for training?)

2. What process affects this performance? What process outputs are subpar?

3. What process step is "breaking down"?

4. Which performer in the hierarchy affects the critical process step?

5. What desired output of this key performer is subpar?

6. What is the cause of the subpar output?

©1987 The Rummler-Brache Group.

another look at Figure 3: The training function exists to meet the needs of its receiving systems or customers (who have to be identified), and it must adapt swiftly to its environment.

The second implication relates to the function's mission. We have described two views of performance, the vacuum view and the systems view. Organizations can choose one or the other. A company that accepts the vacuum view will have a training department that responds to requests for programs (on scoping damage, for instance) by whipping up programs. Regardless of the language it uses in its formal mission statement, we can argue that this training function really sees its mission as "provide skills and knowledge." It will see its outputs, therefore, as "employees trained." The function will be evaluated along feedback loop 1 (Figure 6) in terms of "heads trained per budget dollar." It will get little systematic feedback from its receiving system — the organization's performance environment.

A company that believes in the systems view, on the other hand, will have a training function that responds to requests for training by asking questions. Its mission will be to "improve the organization's performance." Its outputs will be training programs and other performance-improvement initiatives (involving feedback, incentives, job design, etc.). It will be evaluated according to its impact on the organization. It will be able to link its output to the organization's output — that is, to the quality, quantity, value or cost of the company's products and services, and to the efficiency and effectiveness of the performance system.

The choice of missions also will determine the structure of the training function — the processes that drive it. A vacuum-view training function most likely will have three internal processes: course development, course delivery and course evaluation. A systems-view function will require some additional processes, such as: organizational needs analysis (based on the company's strategic, operating and human resource plans); performance analysis; performance improvement initiatives aside from training (for example, design of measurement, feedback and consequence systems).

These processes in turn dictate the kinds of measures required to manage the training function effectively. A function operating according to the systems view will measure its outputs in terms of actual performance improvements noted in individuals, functions and the organization as a whole. It will not be concerned merely with ratings of its training programs.

The processes that drive the training function also determine the kinds of people needed to manage and staff it. A systems-view function requires "performance analysts" and organization development specialists in addition to instructors and instructional designers.

In a nutshell, an organization's view of performance — whether it adheres to the vacuum view or the systems view — will determine the mission of its training function, how it goes about identifying training needs, the operating components of the training function (its units and processes) and how much impact the function will have on the organization's performance.

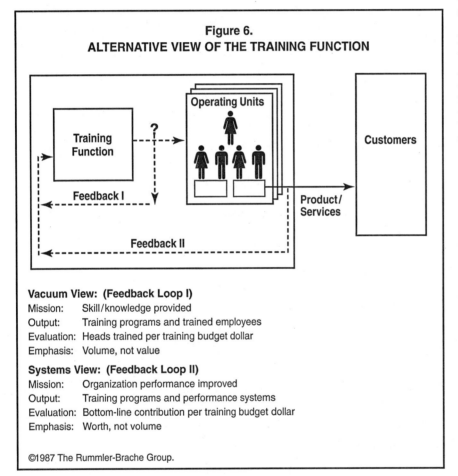

Figure 6.
ALTERNATIVE VIEW OF THE TRAINING FUNCTION

Vacuum View: (Feedback Loop I)
Mission: Skill/knowledge provided
Output: Training programs and trained employees
Evaluation: Heads trained per training budget dollar
Emphasis: Volume, not value

Systems View: (Feedback Loop II)
Mission: Organization performance improved
Output: Training programs and performance systems
Evaluation: Bottom-line contribution per training budget dollar
Emphasis: Worth, not volume

Theory X or Theory Y?

BY BEVERLY GEBER

Theory Y: A form of participatory management. You really do have a say in how things are run. Sure you do. — Business Week

The editors at *Business Week* were having a little fun with the lingo in their cover story "Business Fads — What's In — And Out." Of course, Theory Y is a perfect target because thoroughly modern managers like to talk a good game about how they used to be Theory X but then they saw the light and now they're so Theory Y their spouses and children barely recognize them anymore. Some things just *beg* to be satirized, you know?

The trouble is, *Business Week* got it wrong, confusing the theory with its common extension in practice. The writers were exercising poetic license, no doubt, but it's a mistake lots of people make. After all, as people in this society are wont to ask, what good is a theory if it doesn't have any *practical* application? It's probably the same reason business schools spit out MBAs at supercomputer speed while cobwebs grow in the philosophy department.

But because this is a column on definitions, we're going to give short shrift to the practical applications (Do you really want to read another article telling you that participative management is the best thing that happened to this country since Donny and Marie broke up?) and go straight to the theory of Theory X and Theory Y.

Strictly speaking, Theory X and Theory Y merely represent philosophies, two different ways that managers typically interpret the motivations and character of workers. Although the concepts had been around for awhile — at least since the 1920s, when Elton Mayo tinkered

with worker motivation at Western Electric's Hawthorne Works in Chicago — it wasn't until 1960 that Douglas McGregor defined and named them in his book, *The Human Side of Enterprise* (McGraw-Hill, New York).

McGregor's thinking drew heavily upon the ideas of Abraham Maslow, who published his theory of human motivation in 1954 (*Motivation and Personality*, Harper and Row, New York). Maslow, a clinical psychologist, classified human needs into five categories and asserted there is a definite order (a hierarchy) in which those needs must be satisfied. The order: 1) physiological needs, 2) safety and security, 3) love and belonging, 4) self-esteem, 5) self-actualization.

One assumption generally made when applying Maslow's theory to the modern worker, especially by Theory Y managers, is that physiological, safety and belonging needs already have been met. So the workers are searching for something that will fulfill higher-level needs involving self-esteem or self-actualization. The job is one such source.

Along came McGregor, a professor at the Massachusetts Institute of Technology and former president of Antioch University, to define the self-actualization view a bit more completely and place it within the context of the workplace. He argued that most managers fall into one of two camps, defined by their assumptions about workers, and that those assumptions have a profound effect on their supervisory styles.

Theory X managers (that is, managers holding Theory X assumptions about people) believe that workers are essentially lazy, spend most of their time avoiding work and responsibility, want security above all, have little ambition and need to be threatened with punishment before they'll do

what they're supposed to do. Therefore, managers who see their subordinates through the Theory X prism tend to be crack-the-whip types. McGregor's observations led him to believe that most managers adhered to the school of scientific management; they were Theory X types who severely underestimated the capabilities of their workers and, consequently, their organizations.

Theory X serves as a nice polar opposite (some would say straw man, because it is so extreme) to the theory of the worker McGregor preferred. Theory Y managers, he said, believe that the effort people expend at work is as natural and self-rewarding as play — or rest. They believe that work is not inherently a source of dislike and can instead be a source of satisfaction. If you proceed from this theory, it follows that management control and threats aren't necessary to get people to do their jobs because workers are controlled internally — people will be self-directed toward goals to which they are committed.

What's more, commitment to those goals comes about because self-esteem and self-actualization are gained through a sense of accomplishment. McGregor holds that under Theory Y conditions, people seek responsibility as a means of achieving satisfaction in their work. Moreover, he argues, these motivated people are the rule, not the exception; most would love to use their imagination and ingenuity to serve the organization. Sadly, McGregor concluded, modern industrial life is so deeply imbued with Theory X assumptions, it hinders the individual's intellectual achievement.

If the Theory Y model were instituted company-wide (here it comes, practical application fans), it probably would lead to things like elimination of the time clock, flextime, job enrichment programs and ... yes ... participative management. McGregor's ideas captured a lot of managers' imaginations in the 1960s and 1970s, when the Theory Y bandwagon got rolling. Today, most managers seem to be Theory Y in theory (see *Business Week's* definition again). It has become common wisdom that people produce better in a developmental environment than in a punitive one.

While that may be true, McGregor himself sort of backed away from the trend he inspired. He quickly grew distressed with the interpretation given his theories, objecting to the simplistic "either/or" configuration of Theory X/Theory Y that implied polar opposites with no middle ground.

In *The Manager's Motivation Desk Book* (Ronald Press Publications, New York, 1985) Thomas L. Quick argues, "These two views were not at opposite ends of the spectrum but were two points on a continuum extending through all perspectives of people." McGregor simply observed a management style common at the time and suggested another way — not *the* way — to do things, Quick says.

Quick's view is that the either/or approach to Theory X/Theory Y is just one more example of our tendency to oversimplify things into black and white generalizations. The fact is, some people need and want direction while others chafe under the slightest bit of control. Some people live to work; others work to live.

"In short," concludes Quick, "some people in the work force justify Theory X assumptions about them, just as there are those who make Theory Y assumptions legitimate. And there are many people at various other points along the continuum." Wise are the managers who can recognize the difference and mold their management styles to fit the employees.

THEORY X	THEORY Y
Assumptions about People	**Assumptions about People**
Most people . . . • Dislike work and want as little as possible to do • Are lazy • Dislike responsibility • Resist change • Are indifferent to organizational goals • Are self-seeking • Are primarily motivated by money • Prefer to be directed	**Most people . . .** • Enjoy and want meaningful work • Will work hard to accomplish worthwhile goals • Like responsibility • Will adapt to change • Will become committed to meaningful organizational goals • Are able to seek team goals • Are primarily motivated by challenging work • Prefer self-direction
Supervisory Practices	**Supervisory Practices**
A supervisor should . . . • Plan, organize, direct and control closely the efforts of people • Make most of the important decisions • Punish mistakes • Not get too close to employees • Assume that his or her authority is unquestionable • Push people to keep them motivated	**A supervisor should . . .** • Let employees become involved in planning, organizing and controlling their own efforts • Delegate the authority to make decisions • Focus on resolving problems, not punishing mistakes • Know each employee personally • Rely on earned, not formal, authority • Motivate people by giving challenging assignments

From *Supervisory Management* by D.D. Warrick and Robert A. Zawacki (Harper and Row, 1984). Reprinted by permission.

How to Make Training 'Stick'

BY JACK GORDON

Suppose you teach a group of people to perform some task in a certain way. At the end of the training course you test them and find that they have mastered the subject; they all are able to do the thing — tune an engine, conduct an interview, wait on a customer — exactly the way you taught them. From an instructional standpoint, therefore, your course was a smashing success.

But why did you run the course in the first place? If the training is sponsored by the students' employer, then expanding the students' repertoire of skills or knowledge probably is not intended as an end in itself. Rather, it's a means to the end of improving their performance on the job. The point of the whole exercise is not just that they be able to perform the task correctly, but that they go ahead and do so — and keep on doing so — once they return to work.

If that happens, the learned behavior is said to have "transferred" from the training environment to the job. If it doesn't happen — if students return to work certifiably able to do the job the way you taught them to, but instead they perform in some other way — then the training has not transferred.

That's what "transfer of training" means, as far as corporate trainers are concerned: the impact of instruction on the trainees' subsequent job performance.

In educational theory, the term has a different meaning. It refers to the effect of knowledge or abilities acquired in one area on a person's subsequent ability to acquire knowledge or skills in other areas. For instance, if you first learn geometry, what impact (if any) will that knowledge have on your ability to learn physics? When prior learning is helpful to new learning, you get "positive transfer." When it's a hindrance, you get "negative transfer." Negative transfer is what team-building courses run up against when they preach participative decision making to managers who have been weaned on rugged individualism and taught that a committee is an animal with many heads and no brain.

Transfer in the positive/negative sense obviously can play a role in determining whether trained behavior will transfer to the job. But it is that first definition that concerns us here. The premise that trainees will, in fact, return to work and do the things they were taught to do is the implicit rationale for most corporate training. "How do you ensure that training will transfer?" is a burning issue of long standing. Oceans of ink have been sloshed over the flames — to little effect. The issue goes on burning for a simple reason: A lot of the time, training fails to transfer.

The classic pattern works like this: Employees are doing something in a way you don't want them to (or, you think you have found a better way for them to do something). You pull them off the job and train them to do it the way you do want them to. They return to work. Within an hour, or a week, or a month, they go right back to doing it the way you don't want them to.

Transfer is sometimes discussed as if it were the ultimate measure of training success. Not so. Traditionally, there are four "levels" at which you can evaluate the impact of a training course. At level one, you measure the trainees' reaction to the program: Did they like it? At level two, you test them to see whether they mastered the material or acquired the skills that the course intended to teach. At level three, you measure transfer, checking to see if they are doing things on the job the way they did in class. At level four, you ask, "So what?" That is, in what sense is the organization better off because the trained behavior has transferred?

That last question implies a heretical corollary, rarely acknowledged for obvious reasons: Transfer failure is not necessarily a bad thing. If the training was wrongheaded to begin with, the organization may be lucky if employees don't apply their new skills on the job. Witness the salesperson who was taught to achieve rapport with you by using your name a lot: "Well, Jack, I'll be honest with you, Jack, this isn't going to be a typical, high-pressure buying experience, Jack."

The point is worth making only because practically everything you will ever read about transfer will proceed as if it is axiomatic that if your course graduates do the job the way you taught them to, the organization will be better off. It's left to you to remember that this is really only a working assumption, the validity of which depends largely upon you.

Good Training

In 1985, TRAINING's senior editor Ron Zemke and consultant John Gunkler combed the academic and professional literature on the subject of transfer and reported their findings in an article called "28 Techniques for Transforming Training into Performance." One of those findings was that most of the published advice about ensuring that trained behavior will transfer to the job boils down to a broad admonition: Do good training.

Or, more precisely, be a good performance technologist. Transfer is not really an issue, except in a very broad sense, unless the training program was intended to change somebody's job performance in some definable, observable way. If you're teaching Greek mythology to engineers on the premise that a well-rounded education makes for a better employee, you don't necessarily expect the engineers to start dropping Poseidon's name into conversations back at the shop. The same principle applies to many courses whose goals (increasing employees' self-awareness, for instance) are seen more or less as ends in themselves. And it applies to many "developmental" strategies (send fast-tracker Perkins to Brazil for a few years of international experience), as opposed to "training" courses per se.

What does "Do good training" mean in the performance technology sense? It means, for instance, that the training is aimed at some identifiable discrepancy between the performance you want from people and the performance you're getting. Good training means you made sure before running the course that the performance problem you were trying to correct was worth correcting, and that management genuinely wanted to correct it. Good training means you checked to see that the problem was, indeed, a training problem. That is, the reason people were doing the job "wrong" was because they *didn't know how* to do it right, and not for any of 100 other reasons. Good training means you convinced the trainees during the course that the things you were teaching them to do were valid and worth doing. Good training implies good timing. For instance, you taught them to use the new computers as the new computers were arriving, not nine months before they showed up. Good training means that you involved the trainees' supervisors in the course, at least to the extent that when the trainees return to the job, supervisors will reward or praise them, instead of ignoring or punishing them, when they do things the way they were taught. And so on.

In short, most of the principles and techniques associated with the "systems approach" to performance improvement — from needs analysis to job aids to reward structures — are useful in getting training to transfer.

All of the talk you hear about the need to get top-management support for a training program? And about how crucial it is to get the supervisor to "buy in" before you train the workers? You don't need that enthusiastic backing for training, as such; you need it for transfer.

Similarly, when you hear someone mention "critical mass" in connection with training, the discussion is about transfer. This principle holds that if you train only a few people at a time to do something in a new way, and then send them back to work, the masses of untrained workers will con- vert the few trained ones back to the old way of doing things, rather than vice versa. Trained behavior probably won't transfer, the theory says, unless you train a critical mass of the people doing the job in question.

Hard and Soft

In technical-skills training, transfer is a pretty straightforward issue. It's relatively easy to tell if people are assembling widgets, operating computers or repairing fax machines the way they were taught. Assuming that the preferred widget-assembly method isn't punishing in some overt or covert way and that they bear no grudge against the company, workers probably won't *resist* assembling widgets the way they were taught. When technical skills fail to transfer, the reason why is rarely a huge mystery.

"You have a skill only when you are able to *do* something skillfully."

With "soft" or interpersonal-skills training, it's a different ball game. Time management, decision making, creative thinking, communication skills, leadership, participative management techniques — here is where the arguments rage throughout the training world. Assuming you can even tell for sure that the course graduates *aren't* using their new skills on the job, why did transfer fail to occur?

Because the corporate culture didn't really support a participative management style. Because leadership can't be learned in a classroom in the first place. Because your time-management course was trying to force left-brained behavior patterns onto right-brained people. Because your decision-making course wasn't linked to any real issues of concern to the organization. Because, despite your protestations that you're only offering them some new "behavioral tools," you're really trying to alter their personalities — and personality patterns are extremely resistant to change. Because your "communication skills" program had nothing to do with skills; you just gave the trainees a bunch of information *about* interpersonal communication. Transfer presupposes that some new behavior has, in fact, been acquired. If your course had no behavioral objectives, the trainees didn't learn to *do* anything that they *could* go back and do on the job.

Or, according to one iconoclastic view, your course did have behavioral objectives, you did deem the trainees to have acquired some new "skills," but you were playing word games. They merely learned some steps to follow; they didn't build any genuine skills. "It's not what you do but how well you do it that determines whether you are skilled," argued James C. Georges, president of Par-Training Corp. of Atlanta. "You have a skill only when you are able to do something skillfully."

Most training programs that teach interpersonal skills produce graduates who are able to perform only crude, forced imitations of people who actually use the recommended techniques effectively, Georges claims. ("In the real world, the question is not, 'Did you remember to acknowledge that you took the other person's point of view seriously?' That's the step . . . the question is, 'How *believable* were you while you were acknowledging that you took the other person's point of view seriously?' That's the skill.") Course graduates are told that the clumsiness and artificiality they felt when practicing their new "skills" in class will vanish if they practice enough back on the job. But people don't want to look clumsy and artificial to their bosses, peers or customers. Therefore, they quickly stop practicing. Genuine mastery and confidence must occur during the training course, Georges says, for new behavior to transfer to the job.

The more orthodox view is, of course, that the graduates' bosses simply don't make them practice enough.

Validity and Reliability

BY DALE FEUER

Before I went to graduate school, validity and reliability were just a couple of awkward, academic-sounding words that I never dreamed of using in everyday conversation. By the end of my first year the terms had become common parlance, and I was calculating correlation coefficients in my sleep.

After three gut-wrenching courses in statistics, I understood that it's not just cars and people that are more or less reliable; the term takes on a whole new meaning with respect to test scores and survey data. As for validity, I figured out this much: If your assessment instrument (i.e., ability test, attitude survey, opinion poll, etc.) has any, you're golden.

It's a long, tedious story full of complications and qualifications, and unless you plan to become a statistician, industrial psychologist or some other kind of social-science researcher, you really don't want to hear it. However, when people tell you that their survey is "highly reliable" or that their job screening test is "extremely valid," it's nice to know, basically, what it is they're claiming.

In the most familiar sense, a test or survey is said to be *reliable* if it yields consistent results at two different points in time, assuming there have been no major changes in people or circumstances and no intervening treatments. Scores from an assessment instrument are judged to be *valid* if the instrument accurately measures what it's supposed to measure.

Let's say you take someone's temperature five days in a row and get consecutive Fahrenheit readings of 97°, 98.4°, 98.1°, 99° and 96.5°, when, in fact, the person's body temperature has been a normal 98.6° all along. What you have here is an unreliable measuring instrument, one influenced by *unsystematic* or random error. Since the thermometer is sensitive to some kind of irrelevant factors, it doesn't give a pure measure of body temperature, and the readings are not valid. In this way, a measurement instrument's reliability puts a ceiling on validity; that is, scores or readings from a particular instrument can only be as valid as the instrument is reliable.

What if the thermometer had registered 72° on all five days? (Assume the heat-sensing device is at the wrong end of the stick, so to speak, so that it actually measures room temperature, albeit accurately.) The *constant* error of 26.6° affects validity but not reliability. Because the thermometer gives consistent readings on repeated occasions, it is highly reliable. However, because it doesn't measure what it's supposed to measure — body temperature — its readings are not valid.

In order to get measurements that are reliable *and* valid, you need a thermometer that gives accurate and consistent readings of body temperature, undistorted by any kind of error, random or constant.

As one more example, consider the measurement of time. A watch that is sometimes fast, sometimes slow and sometimes on time (unsystematic error), is neither reliable nor valid, since it is affected by extraneous factors, such as humidity, a faulty battery, arm movement, etc. A watch that is always five minutes fast (constant error) is reliable but not valid. Only a timepiece that consistently gives the right time is both reliable and valid.

Measuring Intangibles

As you move from the realm of physical properties to cognitive ones (attitudes, opinions and psychological characteristics), from thermometers and watches to surveys, tests and job screening procedures, the concepts of reliability and validity get more com-plicated. Yet at the simplest level, the same basic principles apply.

Any test or survey that yields dissimilar results when given on separate occasions to identical or matched groups of people is neither reliable nor valid. Random fluctuations in scores across repeated administrations may be due to any number of variables — time, place, administrator, instructions, etc. In general, reliability tends to increase as the number of test items or survey respondents rises.

Tests and surveys that are subject to constant error are like watches that are consistently five minutes fast — reliable, but not valid. Response bias is one type of constant error that often affects surveys. Response bias occurs when people who feel a particular way about the subject of the survey (e.g., flexible benefits) are more likely to complete the survey than those who feel differently. Ratings of the popularity of flexible-benefit plans will be skewed as long as the response bias exists. Loaded questions and inappropriate rating scales also can introduce constant error.

With tests, both the individual and the instrument can be sources of constant error. In the former case, an individual's test anxiety, a constant but irrelevant source of variation in performance, may consistently lower the person's score on a mechanical aptitude exam by a certain number of points. As for the instrument itself a test intended to measure math skills may actually assess verbal ability if it contains lengthy word problems. Again, validity suffers, while reliability is unaffected.

Half-truths

As threatened, the story gets more involved. For those of you who've already learned more than you ever wanted to know about reliability and validity, this is a good place to get off: But we've really only scratched the surface, and in the interest of warding off letters from indignant statisticians, I'll attempt to expand briefly on the half-truths told so far.

The concept of reliability described above is actually only one kind. Called *test-retest* reliability, it refers to how stable results are over time.

Reliability is always represented mathematically by a correlation coefficient ranging from zero (no correspondence) to one (total correspondence). You can calculate this coefficient of correspondence between *any* two sets of scores or measurements, not just those from a single test given on separate occasions. Scores can be from two similar tests, independently constructed to measure the same thing. Called *parallel forms* reliability, this type indicates the degree of equivalency between two separate forms of a test. Correlating scores from two or more judges or raters yields *inter-rater* reliability and indicates the degree of agreement among different raters.

Yet another kind of reliability is *split-half* reliability. Also known as internal consistency, it is computed by correlating scores from one half of the items on a test with scores from the other half. Jay Hall, president of the Woodlands, TX-based consulting firm Teleometrics International, says that a split-half reliability coefficient tells you "whether or not the items in the first half of an instrument do as good a job of measuring the factor of concern as the items in the last half do — i.e., whether the items used do a pretty uniform job of measurement from start to finish."

Validity is an even more multidimensional concept than reliability. The three most common types of validity include *content, criterion-related* and *construct* validity. Content validity refers to the relevance and scope of the test or survey items. Criterion-related and construct validity deal with the relationship between test scores and other psychologically

meaningful characteristics. Employers sometimes have to prove in court that their applicant-screening tests meet the requirements of all three types of validity.

Briefly, the content validity question asks whether the items on the test or survey adequately sample the entire content domain, be it spatial relations ability, reading comprehension, job satisfaction or whatever. Considerations of content validity, then, have to do with inferences about test construction.

Criterion-related validity involves inferences about test scores. The criterion-related validity of a test has to do with how well test scores correlate with existing or future attitudes or behavior. Organizations that use assessment centers to predict future managerial success are concerned about the criterion-related validity of the assessment procedure.

The third type of validity is the most important, encompassing the other two in its definition. In a nutshell, construct validity is an inference made on the basis of all the information relating to a given construct (i.e., trait, characteristic, aptitude or ability) and to the theory surrounding the construct.

The most common way of inferring the construct validity of a set of scores is to find out how those scores correlate with other measures of an identical or theoretically related construct.

For instance, do people who score highly on your creativity test also score highly on other tests of creativity? If your theory holds that creative people are good problem-solvers and bad organizers, then correlations between measures of creativity and problem-solving should be positive while scores on tests of creativity and organization skills should be negatively correlated. What's more, there should be no correlation, positive or negative, between scores on tests of hypothetically unrelated constructs.

Hall sums it up like this: "An establishment of good construct validity requires both a sound theory base for new instrumentation and an understanding of 'to be expected' relationships between old and new measures."

Validity is a judgment made about a set of scores, based on both rational and empirical inquiry. Reliability, on the other hand, is an intrinsic property of a measurement instrument. Wayne Cascio probably said it as well as anyone in his classic text, *Applied Measurement Concepts for Personnel Decisions:* "Validity is . . . a complex and dynamic function of the sample chosen, the particular situation in which the procedure is used and, above all, the objectives of the user. Validity is *inferred*, not directly measured."

Notes:

A Trainer's Guide To Videoconferencing

BY MICHAEL EMERY
AND MARGARET SCHUBERT

Suppose you're the training manager for a multinational company. The European and Asian offices have complained for years that they have had too little access to corporate training resources. At the same time, however, travel expenses are getting more and more out of hand. Now the company has decided to install a videoconferencing system. Henceforth, people at offices all over the world will be able to communicate "face to face," in real time. It's a big investment, but the organization figures it's the only realistic way to cut travel costs.

At a meeting at your U.S. headquarters, a senior overseas executive turns to you and says: "One of the best applications for videoconferencing is supposed to be 'distance learning.' Now that we've invested in this system, I want every training program you offer here at corporate available to us in Europe. When can you send me a schedule?"

The past few decades have brought many technological "solutions" to the problem of distance learning. Videocassettes, computer-based training, interactive video and other technologies have been offered as viable alternatives to flying people to a single training site from around the country or around the world. All of these media can increase access to training, ensure consistency of instruction and reduce the cost of delivering (though not designing) educational programs. All have certain potentials and certain limitations.

Videoconferencing presents a different kind of challenge because it brings far-flung learners together with a live trainer — and with one another. The technology is still in its new-and-exotic phase, as far as most of us are concerned, but in light of the rapidly decreasing prices of videoconferencing equipment and the increasingly global nature of many businesses, it's bound to become much more common. Many training professionals will need to know how to use it effectively.

The advice that follows is based on our experience as senior trainers with the Faxon Co., headquartered in Westwood, MA. Faxon is a journal-subscription agency that manages periodical subscriptions for academic, corporate and medical libraries. Faxon first linked its American and European offices with a videoconferencing system in 1991.

Getting Started

Videoconferencing systems frequently are "owned" by the networking or telecommunications specialists in the organization. They develop the cost models that justify the purchase of the system, and they manage the installation and maintenance of the equipment. The risk to the organization is that the new system may be seen primarily as a technical challenge and not one of changing the relationships and communication practices among the various remote sites. From the training professional's point of view, the risk is that you may end up being driven by outside cost decisions to change your practices; instead, you should be pursuing a strategy for meeting the distance-learning challenge.

The trainer's initial task, therefore, is to get involved from the beginning in the planning process that justifies the organization's investment in a videoconferencing system.

For instance, most justifications rely on predicted cost savings in travel expenses, particularly training-related travel. The basic assumption is that the programs currently run at a central training facility will be run via videoconferencing, and travel budgets will be cut accordingly.

But what if the organization could be persuaded to focus on the benefits to be gained instead of the money to be saved? Videoconferencing removes barriers to communication by improving both its quantity and its quality. In other words, more training could be done more effectively rather than the same amount of training done more cheaply.

Planning on cost savings as the only justification for videoconferencing is unrealistic when it assumes, for example, that field salespeople will reduce travel to the home office at a rate equal to their use of videoconferencing. It's more likely they will use videoconferencing to augment travel, not to replace it. Whether the main purpose of a trip is for training or anything else, people travel between headquarters and remote locations for a variety of reasons, only some of which can be accomplished by videoconferencing. Trips are used to build individual and group relationships, for instance. And they're often a perquisite that people will resist losing.

The other task the training professional should take on from the beginning is to identify, encourage and support good practice in the use of videoconferencing, whether for meetings, for training or for whatever purpose. This suggests a number of activities:

Advertise videoconferencing: Employees are unlikely to make good use of the new medium if they're unaware of the possibilities and resources associated with it. Information sessions and demonstrations, heavy on the hype, can go a long way toward encouraging people to experiment. Gimmicks work. For example, we called our demonstration area the "Travel Center" and festooned it with trappings borrowed from a local travel agency. During the demo we would pan the camera out the window of our European office for a real-time view of downtown Amsterdam.

Demonstrations also give you an opportunity to ask people about the type of activities they want to conduct via videoconferencing, and to promote workshops and other opportunities to help them learn how to do these things well.

Develop guidelines: Written guidelines for using the system should cover technical procedures for operating the equipment as well as suggestions for using the medium effectively. These will help users decide when it is appropriate to use videoconferencing for a given need and how best to manage and facilitate the interaction. A user's guide can be a stand-alone document or it can form the basis for a training session.

Resources for these guidelines can come from your vendor, outside reading and your own hands-on experience. Schedule some videoconference meetings with your counterparts at remote sites to review the possible uses and experiment with the technology. Some relevant characteristics of the videoconferencing medium include:

- A short delay as the video signal is "compressed" so it can be transmitted over phone lines.
- Moderate to good video quality. This is not (yet) broadcast-quality video, so the nuances of participants' expressions and interactions are easy to miss.
- Distortion of movement. One consequence of video compression is that movement appears somewhat blurred and jerky.

As a result of these characteristics and others, the medium does introduce barriers. Looking at a video screen is more draining for participants and facilitators alike than looking at a live presenter. This suggests, for instance, that you may want to design more breaks and different activities than you would for a standard live training session.

Conduct introductory training sessions: These sessions should follow and expand upon the initial demonstrations. The purpose is to give people a feel for the way an actual videoconference works, to provide them with hands-on experience, and to start introducing prospective users from remote sites to one other. These sessions should be fun as well as educational. Ideally, groups should be small — five or 10 people at each site — so that everyone gets a chance to experience what it feels like to interact with people at remote sites. If you want users to know how to manipulate the equipment, the training session should let them do that as well.

We organized our training program at Faxon into three parts: 1) a demo and discussion, 2) an "offline" section during which, although the equipment was on, each site worked independently to let participants practice basic operations of the equipment, and 3) a conclusion with both sites back "online."

Provide ongoing support: Be prepared to answer questions and provide guidance on an ongoing basis, especially while the company is learning to train and communicate with videoconferencing. This may mean setting up a formal videoconferencing help desk. The goal is to support people in the early going, ensuring that their first experiences with videoconferencing are as successful as possible.

Training

"Everything you do face to face can be done via videoconferencing" has become a familiar refrain among enthusiasts and vendors. The claim is largely true, but as we've already suggested, videoconferencing requires different strategies and practices, particularly when used for training.

To date, the heaviest users of videoconferencing as a training medium have been universities, which broadcast live programs to large groups of students at remote campuses. Certainly these are interactive learning events, but they tend to be mostly lecture.

Videoconferencing doesn't lend itself to conducting a nitty-gritty workshop on, say, coaching skills or team leadership — a workshop in which small groups of people are actually challenged to change their behavior. This sort of thing usually requires close interaction and feedback from the facilitator.

There are answers to this dilemma. In fact, it is possible to end up with a learning event more powerful and effective than if you were forced to travel to the remote site to run the session. Your standard three-day leadership session, for example, can be run once a week over three weeks instead, giving participants a chance to practice new skills between sessions. Introductory meetings can be held ahead of time (before the actual training begins) to let participants get to know each other and to work on any cultural barriers that may exist. Even more important, it's much easier for participants' managers to become involved in the training if the class is taking place at or near the work site instead of in some distant city.

As a general rule, all of the standard good practices for the design and

---

THE BASICS

Videoconferencing is a means of joining two or more distant groups using a combination of audio and video equipment. It allows people in one city or country to communicate live with people in another — or with groups in several other cities. The communication links are established either via satellite or by sending digitally compressed audio and video signals over telephone lines. The latter method is less expensive, and is the one described in the accompanying story.

A typical videoconferencing system includes the following components at each site:

Control panel or "command center": The control panel dictates the visual and audio messages to be sent and received — a lecturer speaking vs. the image of an overhead transparency, for instance. Other controls on the panel operate the movement of the main cameras at both the sending and receiving sites.

Monitor station with main camera: Each site has a video monitor station that includes two color television monitors and the main camera. Generally, one monitor displays the signal being sent to the remote site and the other displays the image being received. It's also possible to send two images to the remote site, one from the main camera and the other from the document camera (see below) or a VCR.

Document camera: The document camera can transmit any kind of image. It looks like an overhead projector and functions similarly. It can display paper documents, overheads, photographs, slides and small three-dimensional objects. It can send images either as "live video," allowing the trainer to manipulate the image in real time, or as a "graphic," which is a still picture.

---

delivery of classroom training apply to videoconferencing. With the additional layer of the medium, however, many of the old rules must be followed more rigorously and a few new ones must be added. The instructional-design process, for example, usually needs to be far more exact. Deciding on the fly to take up a discussion on a flip chart or white board is more difficult if you don't have an appropriate camera preset. Trainers have less flexibility in expanding the number of participants or changing the room setup if everyone is to be included in the picture.

Given these caveats, here are some guidelines for effective training via videoconference:

Designate and prepare a remote site co-trainer (or co-facilitator): If you make only one change to accommodate the medium, this is the one. Your co-trainer can be another instructor at the remote site or, even better, the sponsoring manager. The role of the co-trainer may include:

• Coordinating presession activities such as needs analysis, participant invitations and room setup.

• Introducing participants at the beginning of the session and translating if there is a language barrier.

• Managing the remote-site room. The co-trainer should intervene as necessary to ensure that the local perspective is brought in and all participants get heard. It is difficult for you to "read" the remote room through the video monitor.

• Facilitating breakout sessions and exercises. Managing small groups is almost impossible over the video link.

• Conducting follow-up activities. This could include work or practice groups, distribution of materials, collection of evaluations and so on.

The requirements to prepare co-trainers obviously vary depending on who will be filling the role. At a minimum, co-trainers should be involved in a thorough dry run of the training session so that they understand their roles and activities.

Separate the learning objectives into educational (knowledge) and training (skill-development) components: Educational aspects of the program — lectures and presentations that introduce facts, concepts and background information — lend themselves well to direct adaptation to the videoconference medium. Skill development is often another matter. Practice and breakout sessions for skill acquisition and feedback are best done "offline" and facilitated by the co-trainer. (This also provides a useful break from staring at the video monitor.) If significant behavioral changes are being asked of participants, they'll need an opportunity to challenge the wisdom of these changes. This suggests a discussion that is led locally, with the primary facilitator involved but taking a less-active role.

Develop new or revised outlines and descriptions of existing programs: New constraints and new opportunities suggest that you might want to organize some of your training programs differently. Some possibilities:

• Redesign long workshops into several shorter modules. Why have you traditionally squeezed 24 hours of training into three consecutive days? A lot of it probably had to do with the expenses and logistics of travel. Those logistics no longer apply. Take advantage of the opportunity to travel instantly. Break down that multiday seminar into digestible chunks.

• Organize your sessions to allow a maximum of about one hour of "online" time in each sitting. Videoconferencing is a fatiguing medium for both facilitators and participants, so provide as many breaks and activities as possible. Certainly, it's not unheard of for classrooms full of people to sit riveted for more than an hour before the video image of some famous speaker. But unless you plan to be that enthralling, break it up.

TIPS FOR THE TRAINER . . .

Preparation

• Avoid bright, flashy jewelry or clothing that is heavily patterned. This could cause greater distortion of the video image during movement.

• Arrive at least 15 minutes early.

• Test all equipment you will be using.

• Adjust the monitors, cameras, tables, chairs, etc., for minimum movement during the session, and enter camera presets for both delivering and receiving sites.

• Adjust lights (if necessary and possible). Lighting should be on the front of participants to avoid distracting shadows.

• Touch base with your receiving-site facilitator.

• While people are assembling, focus the main camera on some nondistracting visual and make sure the microphone is on mute. A good idea is to use a flip chart or white board displaying the agenda or a welcoming message. Muting the microphone alleviates confusion caused by miscellaneous noise and conversation being transmitted.

Facilitating the session

• Have all participants introduce themselves, maybe through an icebreaker exercise. Introductions are critical in this environment to help alleviate its inherently less-intimate and less-personal nature.

• If there are large numbers of participants at both delivering and receiving sites, avoid focusing on one group or the other. A common tendency is to present just to the video monitor and not to the participants. Fight it.

• Support your co-facilitator by introducing her, describing the co-trainer's role and thanking her at the conclusion of the meeting.

• Project your voice and speak clearly. If people at the remote site have a different native language, keep yours free of jargon and needlessly complex words. (This also makes a translator's job easier, if you're using one.) All participants need to be able to hear and understand easily.

• Keep physical movement to a minimum. Excessive movement of the facilitators, participants or the camera will cause distortion of the video image.

• Remember the transmission delay and allow extended pauses for others to comment.

• Discourage side conversations that limit discussion and cause distractions.

• Don't shuffle papers or tap objects near the microphone.

• Good luck.

- Allow more time for everything. Because of the extra pauses due to the transmission delay, expect an average session to take about 5 percent to 10 percent longer than it would in a single classroom.
- Design in some opportunities for the co-trainer to take over the spotlight from you and do some genuine facilitating. Contrary to marketing claims, the videoconferencing medium does inhibit participation to a certain degree. Remain conscious of the need to draw out participation and interaction, especially at the remote site.

Dry run, practice, then rehearse some more: Again, the planning for a videoconference training session needs to be rigorous. The flow of visual aids and exercises through the medium needs to be practiced and smooth.

Develop contingency plans: It's a fact of life that when you depend on a

---

USING VISUAL AIDS IN VIDEOCONFERENCING

Given that videoconferencing uses a visual medium, the trainer's choice of visual aids deserves special attention. Videoconferencing allows you all the traditional choices, including transparencies, flip charts and white boards. It also introduces another layer of complexity, however, demanding that you think carefully about the visual aids you use and the way you use them.

Regardless of which type of visual aid you choose, always send hard copy to the receiving sites prior to the program. Fax or mail copies of anything you have prepared ahead of time. Videos, in particular, will be clearer when they have accompanying scripts.

Graphics, such as bar and pie charts, are better than text. Tables and matrices can be difficult to read at receiving sites due to the slight distortion of the video signal. Use handouts and your own verbal description to add "text."

Prepare overheads using the same rules that apply in single-site training: Each visual should be limited to one idea or point; no more than seven lines per transparency; use at least a 36-point type font; and so on.

Here are some advantages and disadvantages of various visual aids in a videoconference.

Overhead Transparencies

Advantages: Receiving audience can maintain control of what it sees (when using main camera). Ensures consistency between image shown to all sites (when using main camera). Easy to photocopy and mail to receiving sites. Can be written on during use.

Disadvantages: Poorly designed transparencies detract from presentation. Image may not be clear to remote-site participants.

Techniques: Establish camera presets before meeting begins. Send hard copy to remote sites prior to meeting. Use pointer (such as a pencil) to identify each point. Keep trainer's physical movement to a minimum.

A good choice when: Delivering audience is large. Remote-site audiences are relatively small. Focus is on participating in meeting, content of visual aid being secondary. Visual is a "working document" (you plan to write on it during the meeting).

"Live Video"
(Using the Document Camera)

Advantages: Image sent to remote sites will be clearer than using overhead transparency. Can be written on during use.

Disadvantages: Remote sites no longer see the image from the main camera, showing participants at the sending site (they see the graphic on one of their monitors, and their own image on the other). More difficult for remote participants to participate in the discussion, since they can hear, but not see, the sending-site participants. Image will not be as clear as using the document camera to send a graphic.

Techniques: Actively facilitate participation from remote sites by allowing pauses and asking questions. When using a pointer or writing on the document, keep physical movement to a minimum to avoid image distortion.

A good choice when: Visual is a working document. Remote participants don't need to view delivering site and document at the same time. Clear view of the document at remote sites is important.

"Still Graphics"
(Using the Document Camera)

Advantages: Image quality is excellent. Remote participants can join in discussion more easily, since they can see the graphic on one monitor and the delivering site on the other monitor. Good for sending clear images during breaks.

Disadvantages: There is a delay of 10-15 seconds between sending the graphic and having it appear to remote-site participants.

Cannot be written on or pointed to during discussion (unless you resend the graphic image).

Techniques: Meeting must be carefully planned to allow proper timing of sending graphic and discussing it.

A good choice when: Meeting is for the purpose of presenting information, as opposed to discussion. Remote sites need to view delivering site and visual at same time. Visual is not a working document. Clear view of document at remote sites is critical. Visual is used in context of a presentation, as opposed to open discussion or training session.

Flip Charts or White Boards

Advantages: Can be used spontaneously. Flip charts can be posted around room. Takes little preparation or experience to use. Remote sites maintain control over images they see.

Disadvantages: Handwritten images may not be as clear or legible. Usually requires more physical movement of trainer, producing distortion. Difficult to send hard copy to remote sites.

Techniques: Use a black pen to ensure legibility. Establish appropriate camera presets before meeting. Verbally check legibility with remote site.

A good choice when: Groups are small and informal. Meeting involves free-flowing discussion. Visuals need to be created during the meeting.

---

technology, you need to be ready for it to fail. The co-trainer should be coached and ready with activities if there is a disruption in the video connection. Usually, any disruption will be temporary.

There is very little you can do in a classroom that can't be done via videoconferencing, provided you adjust to accommodate the demands of the technology. The medium is not as forgiving as ordinary stand-up training. There are enough flaws in the current technology so as to allow little room for flaws in your design, preparation and presentation. But here's the good news: Almost everything you know about how to create a successful learning experience applies directly to videoconferencing. Good training is hard; by comparison, the rest is easy.

Notes:

The Woo-Woo Factor

BY JACK GORDON

As far as anybody around here knows, the term "woo-woo" was first used by Philip Jones, former editor and now editorial director of TRAINING Magazine, as an adjective to describe certain activities that go on in the name of job-related training. Like Victor Frankenstein, Jones promptly lost control of his creature. In mounting horror, he watched it rampage through the editorial offices, causing selected promotional brochures and quotations to be spit-taped to walls and made objects of scorn. Quickly, inexorably, the term snowballed, gaining arrogance and power until it achieved common usage as an adjective, a noun and even a verb to apply to any number of things, including some that had nothing to do with training.

Finally, Jones turned his back on the debacle and retreated in sorrow to his executive office on the fifth floor of the Lakewood Building. He cannot be held responsible for this essay any more than St. Peter can be indicted as the guilty party in the matter of the Spanish Inquisition. He is more to be pitied than blamed for the fact that it has become necessary to turn the monster loose, to go public with it, to force it into more coherent shape, to give it a manifesto. Nevertheless, historical accuracy demands that Jones be fingered as the Father of Woo-Woo.

As for why we now feel compelled to let the thing out of the box, it has to do with a number of societal forces that are combining, we believe, to produce a swelling wave of woo-woo upon which a lot of us will be mind-surfing into the 21st century. In short, America's woo-woo level is going to increase, in the training game and elsewhere. There's probably not a damn thing we can do about it, even if we want to — a prospect we face with some ambivalence. But that part can wait.

First, what do we mean by the woo-woo factor?

On a scale of one to 10, a woo-woo level of one might be awarded to a half-hour training session that teaches people to fill out time cards correctly, using examples of properly filled-out time cards as instructional aids. That's assuming everyone remains fully dressed and that no deep, hidden significance is attributed to the training activity.

A garden-variety management team-building session would register about a four — jumping to a six if it involves climbing trees.

The "getting acquainted" games and exercises trainers sometimes like to use to open their sessions — the ones some participants always love and others always hate — range roughly from threes to eights. The scoring is based on factors including the overall cuteness or preciousness of the exercise, the likelihood that you might run into the same exercise at a baby shower or a Tupperware party, and the specific things trainees are asked to do. "Tell us about your summer vacation" scores lower, for example, than "Look at your partner carefully. Now close your eyes. What green vegetable do you associate with your partner and what do you think that association means?"

A "creativity training" workshop in which adults are given crayons and asked to use them for almost any purpose whatsoever would come in at around a seven.

Here's a 10: You and several other people enter a large room with no tables or chairs, just woven-reed mats on the floor. You are instructed to take off all your clothes, lie down on a mat and put on a stereo headset. The lights dim. Your headset begins to produce the trickling-reverb strains of

a sitar, accompanied by the sounds of waves lapping gently on a beach, seagulls squawking, and something that may or may not be three dolphins trying to recite Dwight D. Eisenhower's first inaugural address. Gradually, you begin to distinguish a human voice rising out of this primeval symphony. Barely audible at first, the voice gains power, authority and a tantalizing familiarity until . . . . Yes, it really does sound just like Lorne Greene. "You are about to embark on an out-of-body experience," the voice intones. "I am the Guardian. I will protect your body while you are gone. When it is time for you to return to your body, you will hear this tone: Beep boop. Beep boop."

If, upon encountering a book, or a magazine article, or a speaker, or a training program, or some segment of a program, you wiggle your eyebrows rapidly and hum the theme music from *The Twilight Zone*, you are implying that the thing has a high woo-woo level. If you want to say so outright, instead of just implying it, imitate a train whistle: "Woo-wooo."

Yes, but what is the woo-woo factor, exactly? TRAINING's senior editor Ron Zemke and I tried and failed to come up with a definitive statement that was not, in itself, pure woo-woo. But we did develop a list of phenomena that become increasingly likely to characterize the training experience as you move up the woo-woo scale. The list's only claim to validity is that two people were able to agree that each item "works" as a characteristic of the woo-woo factor. Its defense is that this exactly duplicates the validation procedure you tend to run into in training programs at the high end of the woo-woo scale.

As the Woo-woo Level Increases:

• Goals or expected outcomes of the training become more subjective. The goal of a program that registers a one on the scale is to produce some clearly demonstrable skill: "Upon completion of course, trainee, presented with a broken toaster, will be able to repair it." The goal of a 10 is for trainees to affirm that the experience was meaningful to them. In Werner Erhard's est training, the point is for trainees to "get it." "Getting it" is like "getting a joke." And it may be years after the actual training experience before a trainee "gets it." The main or only evidence that the trainee has, indeed, gotten it may be that the trainee says so, and tries to convince you to go get it.

An employer footing the bill for employees to attend the program is required to accept its cost-benefit value and the entire issue of learning transfer ("How does what they learned in the class translate into better performance on the job?") increasingly on faith or "gut feel," rather than demanding empirical evidence of the training's results.

• Goals become more personal, focusing less on teaching the trainee to do something specific and more on changing the trainee's overall behavior, attitudes, values or personality.

• Goals tend to become more ambitious. A one training program wants to teach you to operate a forklift. A five wants to transform elements of your corporate culture. A 10 wants to rearrange your view of reality and transfigure your life.

• Trainee "buy in" becomes a more vital issue, not only due to the increasingly subjective nature of goals and evaluation criteria, but because the training has more to sell. By that we mean....

• The basic assumptions from which the training proceeds and upon which its credibility and value hang grow in number and scope — and become progressively open to argument. Trainees either must arrive with philosophical baggage that is compatible with the training or be loaded up with it before the train can leave the station.

• Assuming trainees represent a random sample of people, a wider range of opinion will turn up in their evaluations of the program. Some will love it, others will hate it. Middle-ground evaluations will dwindle. This rule needs the "random sample" qualifier because the same people who love (or hate) one high woo-woo program will tend to love (or hate) another, regardless of content changes. If participation is by choice, therefore, a self-selection principle will tend to pack the audience with woo-woo lovers. Woo-woo is very much a matter of taste.

• There will be more disagreement about whether the thing the program purports to teach *can be taught* to any meaningful degree (charismatic leadership, for example), or about whether the thing exists at all in the form of discrete "behavior" (listening), or about whether the program's method of defining and teaching the thing actu-

ally just eviscerates and debases the concept (creativity). Assuming agreement that the subject can be taught, there also will be more disagreement about whether the program's stated goals can really be achieved in the proposed format ("Teamwork on a white-water rafting expedition will translate into more productive teamwork back on the job"), or whether any results it does achieve will be strictly temporary ("Motivational speeches to sales-people increase sales").

• Advocates of the program (staff trainers or outside vendors) will find it increasingly difficult to sell management on the idea that the program is necessary or worth the money. On the other hand, if the company president attended an outside seminar and

---

The higher the "woo-woo" level, the more certain you can be that words and phrases never paired together in nature will be slammed together by your facilitator.

---

loved it, staff trainers will find it increasingly difficult to squelch the notion that it would be a good idea to send other employees to the course in large numbers.

The Higher the Woo-woo Level:

• The less aware you will be to begin with that you need the training; that is, that the problem the training intends to solve is, indeed, a problem, and that you have been suffering from it. Let's say the problem involves certain behavior or personality traits that the trainer finds displeasing or counterproductive. At around the six level it strikes you that the thing you're supposed to avoid being was never awful until you heard the facilitator describe it. (In fact, you may find the facilitator's personality considerably more awful.) At the 10 level you realize that if, an hour ago, you had met something in a bar that exhibited all of these negative characteristics, you'd have married it.

• The further the program will stray from a basic principle of adult-learning theory which states that adults are most likely to learn and use

things they *need to know* in order to perform specific tasks or to achieve specific goals that they *want to achieve.*

• The more ambiguous the title of the seminar will be, and the less descriptive it will prove of the actual content.

• The more debriefing you get — and the more you need — after various segments of the program. The facilitator's question, "What did we learn from that last experience?" gets trickier to answer. This is because the higher the woo-woo level....

• The less the real point of any activity, comment or exercise resembles its tangible or surface meaning, and the more unlikely you are to guess the real meaning until the facilitator explains it to you. Intermediate level: "What were we learning about ourselves when we allowed our partners to draw on our foreheads with those crayons?" Passe level: "What did you learn about communication by walking around wearing those prism glasses for an hour?" Advanced level: "What do you suppose my associate, Professor Fear, was saying just then when he knocked you to the ground, stole your shoes, spat in your face and called you all those nasty names? And how does it achieve closure with what the dolphins told you?"

• The higher the likelihood that the training will be necessary to prepare you to make the transition to the "New World" or "New Age" of the 21st century; that this new world will be considerably better than the one we have now; and that the reason it will be better will involve the way people relate to one another, not just more advanced technology.

• The more certain you can be that words and phrases never paired in nature will be slammed together by the facilitator ("healing relationships," "creating yourself," "grieving for joy," "implosion of knowledge," "global wellness"), and that new words and phrases will be coined ("transpersonal organizationalism").

• The more likely that the facilitator will be presenting a new "paradigm" and that the word paradigm will be used inaccurately.

As the Woo-woo Level Climbs:

• Paraphernalia proliferates. Training sessions become more likely to include recorded music; an inspirational cassette tape to take away with you for reinforcement; blindfolds; bricks ("How many things can you think of to do with one?"); isolation tanks; hot tubs; crayons; bananas ("Life is like one because..."), etc.

• Programs tend to focus on making the simple complex, rather than vice versa. The point of a one is to make a difficult task easy, manageable and learnable. After about a six, the point often is to find (or create the appearance of) significance and complexity in the seemingly obvious. Sometimes there *is* significance and complexity in the seemingly obvious. But one effect of this characteristic is that it becomes easier to stretch 20 minutes worth of information into a three-day workshop, a bromide into a book, two pedestrian (and often shopworn) insights into a dramatic new "system," and (let's not discount the possibility) a simple essay on weird stuff in the training biz into a Woo-Woo Manifesto. Conversely....

• Any complexity that really is there but that would cast doubt on the value or practicality of the training will tend to be glossed over, ignored or denied.

• It becomes a progressively safe bet that at the end of the three-day workshop, a person named Bubba from Ratcheese, Arkansas will be able to stand up, say, "In other words..." and restate the entire functional content of the program in 25 words or less.

• References in the bibliography or list of suggested readings handed out at session's end are more likely to include names such as Ram Das, Baba, Gupta or Shirley MacLaine. And the chances improve that John Denver will be listed among the course's enthusiastic alumni.

• Regardless of the program's content, the odds get better that the facilitator will state at some point that a major problem in American society is too much left-brained thinking. The basic idea implied by that statement may not have a particularly high woo-woo level, but it is worth bearing in mind that an example of a quintessentially left-brained question is: "If we spend the money to send our employees to this course, what, exactly, will be the bottom-line payoff to our company, and how will we know when and if we have achieved it?" Woo-woo sometimes comes packaged in complex, left-brain-sounding terminology, but generally speaking, left-brained thinking is the enemy of woo-woo.

The training becomes increasingly

"guru-driven" as opposed to content-driven.

• The guru is more likely to be blazing a trail on the "frontier of thought" — which is one reason the guru is forced to abuse the language so grievously by coining phrases like transpersonal organizationalism. English hasn't caught up with the guru yet.

• The odds improve that the guru will possess a year-round suntan and extremely straight, extremely white teeth. The guru's suits and shoes will become progressively more expensive than yours, as well. Large chunks of the guru's system may have been borrowed from another guru who wears a robe, but robed gurus rarely work the business-training market. Subsidi-

---

People in the woo-woo camp tend to take a "holistic" approach to employee development.

---

ary gurus, licensed to deliver high woo-woo programs developed by others, often will remind you of TV weathermen.

• The odds improve that the response you'll get if you question or disagree with anything the guru says will be a veiled insult. The guru wants you to know that she accepts you as a person and doesn't blame you for failing to grasp the full significance of the issue; you probably just need to do some more growing and maturing. Either that, or your objection really has less to do with the content of the program than with some deep-seated personality problem (yours, not hers) which the guru would be happy to discuss with you after the session, but not now.

• The subject matter becomes more a concept and less a procedure. "How do I do it?" becomes progressively less relevant. A corollary principle is that almost any procedure can be woo-wooed into a concept.

• Any specific "how-to" information you do get is likely to be a major letdown compared to the implied import of the concept. If a subject like "networking" is being woo-wooed into cosmic significance, the list of specific networking tips will be handed

out when time has expired on the session and it is too late for you to protest that it reads like the unedited result of a brainstorm among the characters in "Mr. Rogers' Neighborhood": "Take somebody to lunch, speak to strangers on elevators," etc.

• If the guru does talk about a process, it is increasingly likely that the process in fact may be nothing more than the guru talking. Because of this and many of the other factors on this list....

• It becomes progressively difficult to distinguish brilliance from banality; insight from insanity; trends from trivia; genuine conviction from cynical charlatanism; Confucius from Chance the Gardener; night from day; up from down; your arse from your elbow; satire from sincerity; a parody of the old "Kung Fu" television series, with the blind master babbling deliberate nonsense at young "Grasshopper," from an actual episode.

Choosing Sides

Training professionals tend to be divided into two camps on the woo-woo issue.

On the woo-woo side, you find people who argue that the training department or the human resources development (HRD) function should take a highly proactive role in leading the organization forward to achieve its real goals (which may or may not coincide with the goals management and stockholders have in mind), in establishing some "correct" management philosophy or organizational atmosphere, in determining who needs to be trained to do what.

On the anti-woo-woo side, you tend to find people who argue that training is pretty strictly a support function for other staff or line operations — that it is the responsibility of line managers to determine training needs (what their employees need to know), and of trainers to respond to those needs.

People in the woo-woo camp tend to take a "holistic" approach to employee development, an approach that draws its original rationale from the fact that work life and non-work life are interconnected. They then push training forward as a sort of healing force to address broad personal and behavioral issues in a lot of areas where distinctions between "work issues" and "life issues" blur.

Anti-woo-woos talk a lot about sticking to the knitting and about using the training department's resources to tackle bite-sized, performance-related problems in limited areas where training is highly likely to alleviate those problems (as opposed to "impacting" them or whatever). They enjoy drawing strict distinctions between "training problems" and "non-training problems." To the woo-woo type, they appear myopically obsessed with the question of learning transfer — that is, whether and how the stuff trainees learned in the program is being used on the job.

People on the woo-woo side of the fence tend to be optimistic about life, other people, the future and especially the efficacy of training as a solution to problems. Though generally too sensitive to others to say so, they tend to see non-woo-woo types as prosaic, small-minded, unimaginative, wrong-headed and perhaps lacking true direction and meaning in their lives. To the woo-woo type, the non-woo-woo-type is essentially pretty dull, definitely not living up to his full potential, and almost certain to stay that way until a high woo-woo seminar sets him straight. According to the woo-woo type, the reason why the training and development profession often fails to gain the respect of top management is that a lot of top managers fit that description and need to be set straight.

As far as the anti-woo-woo type is concerned, the prime reason the training and development profession gets so little respect from top management is the woo-woo type. Anti-woo-woo people attending HRD conventions beat regular retreats to nearby saloons, where they mutter darkly into their beers about it being no wonder that training budgets are first to feel the knife in hard times, what with all these harebrained activities going on in the name of job-related training.

Megatraining Trends

There's no denying that this little treatise has a distinctly anti-woo-woo flavor about it (a matter of taste), but as to who is "right" and who is "wrong," I, for one, am genuinely not prepared to say. Right and wrong are not terms that can be applied to woo-woo with any final confidence.

I am prepared to say that the prevailing woo-woo level in America runs in cycles, and to propose that we're headed into a high woo-woo cycle. The entire TRAINING editorial staff is behind me on this one, with the ironical exception of Phil Jones, the Father of Woo-Woo, who is betting that the Reagan Era will pin the best to the mat for the next several years, at least.

Whence the majority reasoning? Listen:

"We are living in the time of parenthesis, the time between eras. Those who are willing to handle the ambiguity .... and to anticipate the new era will be a quantum leap ahead of those who hold onto the past .... it is a great and yeasty time, filled with opportunity ... we have extraordinary leverage and influence — individually, professionally and institutionally — if we can only get a clear sense ... of the road ahead. — **John Naisbitt,** Megatrends

You don't have to buy the "New Age" theory — not even Naisbitt's relatively low woo-woo version, let alone the "Aquarian-style" versions — in order to concede the likelihood that the approaching millennium is going to confront us all with some pretty high-voltage woo-woo. As the year 2000 draws near, you can bet large sums that you'll be running into a lot more robed and sandaled characters on street corners yelling things like, "Prepare to meet thy doom!" Mysticism of all sorts will again be a bull market (happens every millennium). And December 31, 1999 will not be an evening when you want your teenage daughter out on the streets celebrating the New Year.

But never mind all that. Let's stick to business. Not since the 1950s has it been so pervasively true that "The business of America is business." In the 1950s, that statement described a low woo-woo, albeit boring, social climate — very much Calvin Coolidge's cup of tea. But exactly what kind of business are we engaged in now?

"In the recent past, the American economy was run by a professional class of faceless managers willing to submerge their personalities in exchange for the safety and rewards of corporate bureaucracy..." [Today] the elite [of American business] strongly believes in leadership, personality and intuition ... A humanistic rhetoric exalting individual initiative, teamwork and creativity pervades the corporate culture not only of Apple Computer but also of General Electric. 'Self-enrichment through self-enhancement' is a pervasive message."* — **Business Week,** "The New Corporate Elite," January 21, 1985.

Then there is the small matter of the high-tech revolution and its impact on the nature of work:

"In terms of a catch-up or retraining ... I think it's going to take more of a 'left turn.' What I mean by a left turn is that as we go forward, the kinds of new skills that will be required will not be just more of the same, acquired at a faster pace, but a heightening of people's skills in analysis, judgment, decision-making, problem-solving — those skills that aren't learned in the traditional way in the traditional classroom. We now have computers ... that can do most of the adding, subtracting, multiplying and dividing types of basic skills. What we need now is people who have the skills computers don't: making sophisticated judgments, intuitive skills, skills to do things that computers will never be able to do." — **Chip Bell,** consultant, TRAINING, October 1983.

If the nation is, indeed, going to reach for Naisbitt's yeasty opportunities, if we intend to place a high value on "personal initiative, teamwork and creativity" (and to reconcile conflicts between at least the first two of those three characteristics), if the skills involved in Bell's "left turn" will indeed be prime currency in tomorrow's business world — and it appears likely — then training increasingly will be both called upon and pushed forward to build those skills. And when it comes to training programs purported to do so, every one of them — intuition, decision-making, problem-solving, judgment, initiative, teamwork, creativity — is wide open to the mischievous workings of the woo-woo factor.

It's going to get very ... interesting.